"Have you not been as an inclosed garden to
me, and I a wall of fire round about you?"
THOMAS SHEPARD, *Eye-Salve.* May 15, 1672

THE WALL
AND THE GARDEN

Selected Massachusetts Election Sermons 1670–1775

edited by A. W. PLUMSTEAD

UNIVERSITY OF MINNESOTA PRESS · MINNEAPOLIS

© COPYRIGHT 1968 BY THE UNIVERSITY OF MINNESOTA. ALL RIGHTS RE-
SERVED. PRINTED IN THE UNITED STATES OF AMERICA. PUBLISHED IN GREAT
BRITAIN, INDIA, AND PAKISTAN BY THE OXFORD UNIVERSITY PRESS, LONDON,
BOMBAY, AND KARACHI, AND IN CANADA BY THE COPP CLARK
PUBLISHING CO. LIMITED, TORONTO

LIBRARY OF CONGRESS CATALOG CARD NUMBER: 68-19742

in memory of
PERRY MILLER

ACKNOWLEDGMENTS

A CANADA COUNCIL summer research grant in 1963 made it possible for me to visit Cambridge to read the Puritans; it was there that the idea for this edition originated. A grant from the Graduate School of the University of Minnesota in the summer of 1965 enabled me to return to complete my reading and selection. Grants from the R. W. Emerson Memorial Association, the University of Minnesota, the Center for Editions of American Authors, and the McKnight Family Literary Fund of Minneapolis made it possible for me to take a year's leave from teaching, 1966-67, to work at Harvard University on a volume in the new edition of Emerson's journals; access to the collections of Puritan materials in and around Boston allowed me to finish research on the sermons which would have been difficult, if not impossible, to complete anywhere else. To these foundations and institutions I am deeply indebted.

Most of the work for this book was done in the Houghton and Widener libraries, and I wish to thank the librarians, especially Miss Carolyn Jakeman and her staff, for their assistance. To those who helped me at the libraries of the Harvard Divinity School, Massachusetts Historical Society, Congregational Library, Boston Public Library, State of Massachusetts Archives, and the Antiquarian Society, I am also grateful.

THE WALL AND THE GARDEN

I will not attempt to acknowledge here my reliance on other scholars; the footnotes suggest my indebtedness. The book is dedicated to one who made colonial New England so exciting for me eight years ago that I had to come from the Canadian prairies to Boston to read, and see for myself. Scholars will argue with Perry Miller in the years to come — as I do here — but he will remain an indispensable and respected authority in the colonial field for which he did so much to create interest.

William H. Gilman, Ruth Mortimer, and J. E. Parsons read portions of the manuscript at various stages and offered helpful suggestions. Errors which remain are mine. Kenneth B. Murdock graciously answered some queries, and David E. Smith and Jacob Blanck offered bibliographical help. I am, alas, one of those with small Latin and less Greek; Suzy Q. Groden provided translations and struggled with the often poorly printed Greek in the pamphlets to get a clear reading. Carol Goodman, Michèle Simon, Judi Andra Harding, and Frances Webb helped with research and typing. Jeanne Sinnen of the University of Minnesota Press has offered guidance at every stage en route to publication. To them all I am much indebted.

I have often chuckled at the various ways a scholar acknowledges his wife in books like this, but now I see how it is. If I were to put down in detail how much Niki Plumstead has contributed at every stage of typescript, research, and collation, the reader either would not believe it, or would wonder why her name is not on the title page where it belongs. Suffice it to say that only I know how appropriate the cliché is here that, without her help, *The Wall and the Garden* would not be in print.

A. W. P.

Osatig, Temagami
September 1967

TABLE OF CONTENTS

THE WALL AND THE GARDEN

"A wilderness is not hedged in nor fenced about; what is in the wilderness hath no defense, but lies open to the injury of those that will break in to bark the trees thereof and root up the same; the wilderness is no inclosure; have I then been so to you? Have I left you without defense, without an hedge of protection?" THOMAS SHEPARD (1635–77), in an election sermon, *Eye-Salve* . . . , preached in Boston, May 15, 1672

"The glorious arm of divine conduct hath fenc'd us with the hedge of government. Oh what a favor is this! to give government, to establish authority, to have a wall of magistracy set and kept about a people; this is a thing of unspeakable concernment; otherwise a people would be left to anarchy and heaps of confusion." JEREMIAH SHEPARD, in an election sermon, *God's Conduct* . . . , preached in Boston, May 25, 1715

AN INTRODUCTORY ESSAY

THERE were moments of superb oratory in early Massachusetts. The charmed listeners to Arthur Dimmesdale's election sermon in *The Scarlet Letter* had their living counterparts in seventeenth- and eighteenth-century Massachusetts. The sermon can be a work of art. A didactic genre, it has aesthetic possibilities and is allied to drama, as the sermons of Chaucer's Pardoner, Melville's Father Mapple, John Donne, and Jeremy Taylor show. American literature has always been strong in oratory. From Cotton Mather to William Ellery Channing, from Emerson and Thoreau to Mark Twain, from Lincoln to John F. Kennedy, Americans in frontier halls, battlefields, pulpits, and political assemblies have held oratory in high esteem. The election sermons are both a source and an achievement in this tradition. These annual, formal addresses to the newly assembled legislatures helped to shape the traditions of the Inaugural, Fourth of July orations, and State of the Union messages.

The nine sermons which follow are arbitrarily limited to the colonial period up to the beginning of the Revolution in 1775 in order to have a manageable area for survey and selection for one volume. They are not "representative" sermons. Of the ninety-eight surviving Massachusetts election sermons printed as pamphlets between 1634 and 1775, many are dull, supratheological, and stereotyped. These nine are in my opinion the best of the ninety-eight sermons judged by two criteria: literary excellence and ideas and points of style relevant to later developments in

3

American literature and history.[1] There are changes in style and theme in the one hundred and five years between the first and last selections, and brief introductions to each sermon will discuss these changes and the individual sermon's relationship to the tradition as a whole. The selections demonstrate the versatility of the colonial sermon as an art form—from apocalypse and myth to political treatise. The election sermon tradition offers a vantage point for seeing both continuity and change in colonial intellectual history. Within the confines of these sermons one can see intoleration giving way to toleration, the church accepting and adjusting to an increasing separation from the state, and emphasis changing from a desire to plan New England as a parallel to Israel, to a more reasoned, eighteenth-century discussion of the nature of government. The liberalizing of the New England mind—the distance traveled from John Winthrop to John Adams—is clear here.

The selections fall into two groups, but not by predetermined plan. They were not chosen to prove a thesis. They were chosen because they have style—that rare and sometimes beautiful way of making old ideas seem clear and fresh, commanding, textured, dramatic. When the fifteen originally selected were winnowed to nine—and only then—a pattern emerged. The first five became chapters in a Puritan epic mythology, a story with a beginning, middle, and end, of a chosen people's errand into a wilderness. The last four, beginning in 1734, are in tone, ideas, and shifts in emphasis representative of the eighteenth-century enlightenment. The two groups show the change from seventeenth-century emphasis on God's providence to eighteenth-century emphasis on man's reason.

[1] To have chosen the nine "best" of ninety-eight sermons is a large, subjective claim. In the introductions to the selected sermons I discuss several other distinctive election sermons. If the reader is interested in pursuing the tradition further than the selections in this volume, I suggest he look first at the following: John Higginson, *The Cause of God* . . . (Cambridge, 1663); John Davenport, *A Sermon* (1670), fac. reprint, *Publications of the Colonial Society of Massachusetts*, X (Boston, 1907), 1–16; Thomas Shepard (1635–77), *Eye-Salve* . . . (Cambridge, 1673); Urian Oakes, *New England Pleaded With* . . . (Cambridge, 1673); Increase Mather, *The Great Blessing of Primitive Counsellors* . . . (Boston, 1693); Samuel Willard, *The Character of a Good Ruler* . . . (Boston, 1694); Cotton Mather, *A Pillar of Gratitude* . . . (Boston, 1700); Samuel Belcher, *An Essay Tending to Promote the Kingdom of Our Lord Jesus Christ* . . . (Boston, 1707); Ebenezer Pemberton, *The Divine Original and Dignity of Government Asserted* . . . (Boston, 1710); Charles Chauncy, *Civil Magistrates Must Be Just* . . . (Boston, 1747); Thomas Frink, *A King Reigning in Righteousness* . . . (Boston, 1758); Andrew Eliot, *A Sermon* . . . (Boston, 1765); Charles Turner, *A Sermon* . . . (Boston, 1773). All subsequent references to sermons are to Massachusetts election sermons unless otherwise noted.

The historian of American literature may find in these sermons rudimentary evidence of the popular theory of tensions in American experience which critics like F. O. Matthiessen, R. W. B. Lewis, and Daniel Hoffman find informing the richest American literature.[2] Considering these sermons as a tradition in which selected spokesmen engage in a search for a common identity, one finds here side by side myth and reason, a passionate love for the archetypal and symbolic along with a clearheaded, pragmatic approach to law and lawmaking. Equally pervasive is a tenuous balance between a spirit of rebellion—from Europe, Catholic and Anglican, and the domination of priest, king, and synod—and a conservatism, a desire to hold fast, to preserve, restrain, and obey.

Three of the selections stand out, perhaps because the historical moment offered a special challenge and called forth an original performance. Cotton Mather preached in 1689 only a few weeks after Sir Edmund Andros, the King's first royally appointed Governor, had been confined in the first Boston revolution; Thomas Prince in 1730 celebrates the centenary of the first landing in Boston harbor; and Samuel Langdon, President of Harvard, preached his emotional sermon of 1775 only six weeks after the firing of the shots, "heard round the world," at Lexington and Concord. Two of the selections come close to the description of Arthur Dimmesdale's sermon; Hawthorne, who had read at least one volume of collected election sermons, describes Dimmesdale's topic as "the relation between the Deity and the communities of mankind, with a special reference to the New England which they were here planting in the wilderness. And . . . whereas the Jewish seers had denounced judgments and ruin on their country, it was his mission to foretell a high and glorious destiny for the newly gathered people of the Lord." [3]

The sermons in this collection will complement colonial studies by bringing the reader closer to the spirit of the times. Much colonial literature, for the middle colonies and the South as well as for New England, is

[2] F. O. Matthiessen, *American Renaissance; Art and Expression in the Age of Emerson and Whitman* (New York, 1941); R. W. B. Lewis, *The American Adam: Innocence, Tragedy, and Tradition in the Nineteenth Century* (Chicago, 1955); Daniel G. Hoffman, *Form and Fable in American Fiction* (New York, 1961).

[3] *The Scarlet Letter*, ed. Larzer Ziff (Indianapolis, 1963), 234. See Marion L. Kesselring, *Hawthorne's Reading 1828–1850* (New York, 1949), 23, 28. The Salem Athenaeum Charge Books show that Hawthorne borrowed a volume of election sermons on September 20, 1828, and returned it a week later. The sermons in the present edition which come closest to Hawthorne's description of Dimmesdale's sermon are Danforth's (1670) and Prince's (1730).

still unavailable outside rare book libraries. Anthologies at their best produce snippets. Colonial scholars have shown us what to look for and how to interpret it.[4] Their work, however, creates a desire to read the primary texts. There are still discoveries to be made. The first seven sermons in this collection have not been reprinted since they appeared as pamphlets in the year they were preached.[5]

I

The custom of opening the annual General Court in May with an election sermon is unique to New England. Sermons were given in Connecticut from 1674 to 1830, in New Hampshire from 1784 to 1831, and in Vermont from 1777 to 1834; but it is to the Colony of Massachusetts Bay that we turn for the selections in this volume, for it was the home of the tradition. Here it began and ended.[6] The first sermon was given in Boston in 1634 and the tradition continued for two hundred and fifty years, until 1884—one of the longest in American political history. (Ralph Waldo Emerson was born on election day, and when he was chaplain of the Massachusetts Senate he heard William Ellery Channing give his "noble" election sermon in 1830; when *The Scarlet Letter* was published in 1850, readers in the Boston area could still hear an election sermon—as a few undoubtedly did.[7])

[4] Election sermons are major sources for the following studies: Alice M. Baldwin, *The New England Clergy and the American Revolution* (Durham, 1928; New York, 1958); Perry Miller, *The New England Mind: From Colony to Province* (Cambridge, 1953); Martha Louise Counts, "The Political Views of the Eighteenth Century New England Clergy as Expressed in Their Election Sermons" (Columbia doc. diss., 1956, published in microfilm only); Lindsay Swift, "The Massachusetts Election Sermons," *Publications of the Colonial Society of Massachusetts,* I (Boston, 1895), 388–451.

[5] Mayhew's sermon was reprinted as a pamphlet in London (1755); Cooke's (1770) and Langdon's (1775) are reprinted in *The Pulpit of the American Revolution . . . ,* ed. John Wingate Thornton (Boston, 1860); Langdon's is also reprinted in *The Patriot Preachers of the American Revolution,* ed. Frank Moore (New York, 1862), and in *Puritan Political Ideas,* ed. Edmund S. Morgan (Indianapolis, 1965). There are "timely quotations" from many of the election sermons of the later eighteenth century in *They Preached Liberty . . . ,* ed. Franklin P. Cole (New York, 1941). Andrew Eliot's election sermon of 1765 is announced for publication in Vol. II of *Pamphlets of the American Revolution,* ed. Bernard Bailyn (Cambridge); the sermon of Williams (1762) and a part of Cotton Mather's (1690) are in *Puritan Political Ideas.*

[6] R. W. G. Vail, *A Check List of New England Election Sermons* (Worcester, 1936).

[7] Ralph L. Rusk, *The Life of Ralph Waldo Emerson* (New York, 1949), 1, and *Letters,* ed. Rusk (New York, 1939), I, 303. (However, Emerson also said in a lecture, "Boston," given in 1861 and 1877: "the American sermons before the days

Election day in Boston early developed into a yearly ritual with as much pomp and ceremony as the Puritans allowed themselves, and it remained the most important annual holiday up to the time of the American Revolution. The first Charter of Massachusetts Bay allowed for the election of eighteen Assistants to counsel the Governor and Deputy-Governor of the Corporation. When the Puritan leaders moved the Charter to New England they tried to establish a theocracy with more self-perpetuation and central control, in taxation for instance, than the Charter allowed. In 1632 the freemen of the young Colony won the principle of sending two delegates from each town into Boston for the General Court on the last Wednesday in Easter term, the date stipulated by the Charter. When these delegates arrived in 1634 they took a good look at the actual print of the Charter and decided they had the right to elect not only the Assistants but the Governor too. John Cotton's sermon to this Court urged restraint of democratic inclinations in the freemen; he endeavored to persuade them that it was their God-given duty not to elect a new slate just to prove their power. (However, the Deputies *did* prove their power; they voted Winthrop out and Dudley in, as Governor.) The sermon is not extant, but contemporary references to it warrant the ironic observation that the election sermon tradition started as a defense of theocracy; by the time of the Revolution it was a ready-made vehicle for defining civil liberty and calling for resistance to George III.[8]

Election sermons were given off and on for the next ten years, in 1637, 1638, 1641, and 1643. Thereafter the words "none preached" in Professor Vail's bibliography of the sermons become exceptions to the rule. The habit had caught hold.

In 1644 the Court issued an order that "the Printer shall have leave to print the election sermon with Mr. [Richard] Mather's consent,"[9] but it appears the Court was not yet willing to pay the bill, and these early sermons would have to be printed at the preacher's or a benefactor's expense. The first sermon to have survived as a separately printed pam-

of Channing I resign to the antiquaries" [manuscript in the Houghton Library]. I am indebted to Professor J. Justus for pointing out this remark.)

[8] For the story of the early politics of the Colony, see Perry Miller, *Orthodoxy in Massachusetts, 1630–1650: A Genetic Study* (Cambridge, 1933; reissued in paperback, Boston, 1959), Chapters 5–8. Winthrop describes Cotton's sermon in *Winthrop's Journal: "History of New England" 1630–1649*, ed. James Kendall Hosmer (New York, 1908), I, 124–125. Cf. Larzer Ziff, *The Career of John Cotton: Puritanism and the American Experience* (Princeton, 1962), 99–100.

[9] Vail, *A Check List*, 13–14.

phlet is John Higginson's of 1663. The pattern of the sermons' reaching print is similar to the early years of their being preached: there are a few gaps spaced by printed sermons and then the practice catches on. Beginning in 1667 the sermons were printed yearly with few exceptions.[10]

Between 1645 and 1691, a minister was invited to preach on election day by the Governor and Magistrates one year, and by the Deputies— i.e., the representatives of each town to the General Court—the next.[11] (This arrangement grew out of a dispute recorded by Winthrop in his *Journal*; in 1645 the Deputies wanted Mr. Norton, and the Governor and Magistrates, Mr. Norris of Salem. Norton got the bid.[12]) Most of the best known preachers of colonial Massachusetts gave at least one sermon— John Cotton, Thomas Shepard, Nathaniel Ward, Richard Mather, Michael Wigglesworth, Solomon Stoddard, Benjamin Colman. Jonathan Edwards, Jonathan Wise (who declined two invitations to preach), and Edward

[10] The earliest extant fragment of an election sermon is the manuscript outline of Thomas Shepard's, probably the notes he took with him into the pulpit, discovered and published in 1870 (*New-England Historical and Genealogical Register . . .*, XXIV, Boston, 1870, 361–366). The earliest election sermon in print is John Norton's of 1661 which was not published until 1664 along with two other sermons in *Three Choice and Profitable Sermons . . .* (Cambridge, 1664). The "Advertisement to the Reader" of Stoughton's election sermon of 1668 says: "The helping forward of so good a work hath occasioned a person of worth . . . to adventure the publishing of what the pious author was well nigh invincibly unwilling should ever have come forth." The first pamphlet to be printed at the government's expense appears to be Cotton Mather's of 1690; the verso of its title page reads: "Voted by the Deputies that the Reverend Mr. Cotton Mather have the thanks of this House returned for the sermon preached at their request on the day of election, and that it be forthwith printed. May 29. 1690."

[11] The terminology of colonial politics can be confusing. In the seventeenth century the Governor's advisers are usually referred to as Assistants or Magistrates (legally they are assistants to the Governor; functionally, they are also magistrates in the courts and may hold other civil positions). As a group they were sometimes called the Council. The representatives of the towns, chosen in a town meeting, are called Deputies. Official meetings of these groups together, usually four times a year in Boston, form the General Court or sometimes simply the "assembly." Late in the century the terms begin gradually to change. The body of Governor's advisers, increased by a new Charter from eighteen to twenty-eight, is now regularly called the Council and a member is often referred to as a Councilor. The new Charter specified a "House of Representatives," and the term Deputy changes to Representative. The House or legislature usually means the old "General Court," but sometimes distinctions are important. Usually the Council identifies itself and votes with the popular body of Representatives to whom it owes its political life; but the Council often contains "prerogative" men, those who uphold the Governor who has to follow unpopular directions from London. Thus, although the House usually means the Council and Representatives together, it can in some contexts mean the (democratic) Representatives only, as distinct from the (more royalist) Council.

[12] *Winthrop's Journal*, II, 226–227.

Taylor are notable exceptions.[13] Several preachers gave two sermons; Increase and Cotton Mather preached four times each. The three Boston ministers singled out by both their contemporaries and historians since as playing a prominent role in the patriot thinking which led to the Revolution—Jonathan Mayhew, Charles Chauncy, and Samuel Cooper —preached election sermons.[14]

The first Charter of Massachusetts Bay was revoked in 1684 and the Governor was no longer elected locally but appointed by the King. There were no sermons preached during the strained years of Governor Andros' regime; the colonists must have wondered if the liberty to elect their leaders was gone forever, and the election sermon with it. The new Charter of 1691 retained the appointment of the Governor by the King but allowed for a body of councilors to the Governor to be elected by a "House of Representatives." The election sermon was revived; born of one political crisis, it outlived a second. The new Charter designated the last Wednesday of May as election day. The preacher was still invited to the "Desk" alternately by the House of Representatives and the Council, but Sewall's *Diary* shows that there were times when the choice became a bit sticky. When Samuel Mann declined his invitation in 1710, this is what happened:

The Governor calls a Council. . . . the choosing another minister is propos'd by the Governor. I thought 'twas not convenient now to go out of town, or at least not far off. I mention'd Mr. Brattle; Mr. Em. Hutchinson [mentioned] Mr. Bridge; Governor said he was a stranger. I think 'twas Col. Lynde mention'd Mr. Angier. I did not think him so square

---

[13] Jonathan Edwards in Northampton and Edward Taylor in Westfield probably lived too far away to be considered. Although John Russell, who preached the election sermon in 1665, lived in Hadley, most of the ministers invited to preach election sermons lived within approximately a forty-mile radius of Boston. Even then, some would need two days of travel to get to the election. The preachers for the years 1670–80 and 1730–40 (these decades chosen at random) were from Roxbury, Boston, Charlestown, Cambridge, Weymouth, Portsmouth, Ipswich, Boston, Rowley, Boston, Concord; Boston, Salem, Framingham, Ipswich, Marblehead, Lancaster, Marblehead, Sudbury, Boston, Salem, Boston.

[14] For John Adams' opinion of Jonathan Mayhew, Charles Chauncy, and Samuel Cooper as important leaders in the movement toward liberty, see *Works* (Boston, 1856), X, 271, 284, 287–288. Samuel Cooper is most often singled out for scorn from among Otis' "Black Regiment" of patriotic ministers in *Peter Oliver's Origin and Progress of the American Rebellion,* ed. Douglass Adair and John A. Schutz (San Marino, 1961), 43–44 and *passim.* Cf. C. H. Van Tyne, "Influence of the Clergy, and of Religious and Sectarian Forces, on the American Revolution," *American Historical Review,* XIX (1913–14), 44–64; Alice Baldwin, *The New England Clergy and the American Revolution,* 91–93, 156–157.

and stable a man and therefore propounded Mr. Wadsworth, and Mr. Pemberton; the Governor said Mr. Pemberton, and all agreed to it.[15]

From the subtle politicking here it appears that the Council had best choose a candidate who had the Governor's approval.

Nathaniel Hawthorne knew his colonial history, and his description of election day in "The New England Holiday" and "The Procession" chapters of *The Scarlet Letter* is accurate for 1650. It is late in May, the opening day of the General Court, and the beginning of the political year. The shops and schools of Boston are closed. The marketplace is "thronged with the craftsmen and other plebeian inhabitants of the town, in considerable numbers," as well as "many rough figures, whose attire of deerskins marked them as belonging to some of the forest settlements, which surrounded the little metropolis of the colony."[16] Some of these "rough figures" would be tourists in Boston for the holiday; some would be Deputies, sent by their towns to Boston to elect the Assistants and take part in the General Court. A formal procession is led by the militia to the meetinghouse, Boston's first church, where the sermon would be preached before the Deputies voted for the Assistants.

Although the basic pattern of military parade, sermon, and election remained the same up to the Revolution, there were changes and variations. After the Charter of 1691 there was of course only one election, for twenty-eight members of the Council, held in the afternoon after the sermon. When the Town House was built in 1658 from the bequest of Robert Keayne, the General Court met in the upper story meeting hall over the merchants' offices on the first floor, and the sermons were given there. The old Town House burned in 1711 and two years later the new State House was finished in time for the General Court in May; it still stands. It is often referred to in contemporary records, in Sewall's *Diary*

[15] *Diary of Samuel Sewall*, 3 vols. (*Collections of the Massachusetts Historical Society*, 5th ser., 5–7, Boston, 1878–82), II, 278. In the sermons the ministers often indicate which group invited them to preach: Appleton (1742) and Lewis (1748) say they were invited by the Council; Rawson (1709), Thayer (1725), and Fisk (1731) acknowledge invitations from the House of Representatives.

[16] *The Scarlet Letter*, 213. Hawthorne would have encountered references to election day and the sermons in several of his sources for New England history (listed in Kesselring's *Reading*), such as Cotton Mather, *Magnalia Christi Americana* . . . , 2 vols. (Hartford, 1820); *Winthrop's Journal*; Daniel Neal, *The History of New England* . . . (London, 1720), II, 613; Caleb H. Snow, *A History of Boston* (Boston, 1828), 54, 283–284. For Hawthorne's knowledge of seventeenth-century Boston, see Charles Ryskamp, "The New England Sources of *The Scarlet Letter*," *American Literature*, XXXI (Nov. 1959), 257–272.

for instance, as the "Court House," and was so described in the *Boston Weekly News Letter* which on December 9, 1747, gave an account of the fire which gutted its interior but left the walls intact. The second floor of the building contained a Council Chamber and a large Hall of Representatives where the Court sat and some election sermons were preached. When the Old South Meeting House was completed in 1730, many of the election sermons were given there. On several occasions of the smallpox, or the Governor's concern over a Boston riot, the General Court moved to the Harvard buildings at Cambridge and at least once, in 1729, to Salem, and in 1764, to Concord.[17] The size of the election sermon audience (assuming that all who attended the opening day of the Court stayed in their seats for the sermon) was about 120 in the mid-seventeenth century (about 90 voting Deputies, an outgoing Council of 18, and perhaps 10–20 ministers) and approximately 150–175 in the eighteenth century (110–120 representatives of the towns, an outgoing Council of 28, and perhaps 20–30 ministers, in town for their annual convention, held simultaneously).[18]

Election day was one of "treats" and feasts as well as sermons and politics. Whether for reasons of pomp, political lobbying, or both, the Governor entertained his Council and the Court at various times of the day—depending, one suspects, on his inclinations, his budget, and his supply. After a Speaker was chosen by the House in the morning, a committee (and in later years the outgoing Council) waited on the Governor at his official residence to present him with the Speaker's name; the Governor sometimes provided "collations" before the ceremonious march to the State House. In 1697, the Court apparently had a

[17] *Journals of the House of Representatives of Massachusetts 1729–1731* (Boston, 1928), VII, 3, 207. *The Diaries of Benjamin Lynde and of Benjamin Lynde, Jr.* (Boston, 1880), 190. In January 1764, a fire destroyed the Library of Harvard College, "the most ruinous loss it ever met with since its foundation. . . . It is conjectured to have begun in a beam under the hearth in the library, where a fire had been kept for the use of the General Court, now residing and sitting here, by reason of the smallpox at Boston" (a broadside, *An Account of the Fire at Harvard-College*, Boston, 1764, reprinted in *The Houghton Library 1942–1967*, Cambridge, 1967, 3).

[18] "Even as late as 1665 only ninety votes were thrown to elect deputies." Lindsay Swift, "The Massachusetts Election Sermons," 445. Although during Governor Shirley's administration (c. 1750) "there were some 160 towns . . . most of which could send two representatives if they desired," only a few "except Boston, Salem, Ipswich, and Newbury ever sent more than one," and frequently a town excused itself from sending any representatives at all. Robert E. Brown concludes that there were on the average 110–120 representatives to the election Court in the eighteenth century; "Representation and Its Restriction," *Middle-Class Democracy and the Revolution in Massachusetts, 1691–1780* (Ithaca, 1955), 61–77.

"treat" at the Town House before the sermon [19] (the preacher that year was John Danforth). The noon meal after the sermon was a gay affair and harangues in the sermons over excesses of drunkenness and the need for shorter pub hours fell on the ears of many a Councilman and Representative whose palate was savoring expectantly the wine to come as soon as the sermon was done. The names of "Wing's," "The Stone House," and "The Green Dragon" taverns dot the cryptic entries of Sewall's *Diary* on election days, and by the 1770's Governor, Council, and Representatives were feted in banquet style at Concert Hall or Faneuil Hall. In 1770, when Cooke preached to the official Court which had been moved to Cambridge because the Governor feared the mob in Boston, Chauncy preached in Boston at the Old Brick Church to the "clergy and a great number of principal gentlemen from this and the neighboring towns." Bostonians were going to have their ceremony and their election sermon maintained in their proper place, Royal Governor or no! On this occasion they must have made the Cantabrigians envious, for their mock ceremony included "music parading the streets" and a roasting on the Common of a whole ox which had been paraded the previous afternoon with ribbons and flowers through the streets of Boston. After the sermon the assembly moved to Faneuil Hall for an "elegant entertainment" which included twenty-two toasts beginning with the King and ending with "our suffering brethren at Cambridge whose hearts are with us while their bodies are unconstitutionally torn from us" —all twenty-two toasts "saluted with loud huzzas and the discharge of guns." [20]

It didn't end there. If the election was over in time, the Governor might entertain at his house in the evening the new Councilors elected in the afternoon. They would then take their oaths and there would be more toasts and treats. On election day in 1692 Sewall records that after the election there was "no treat at the Governor's *but* beer, cider, wine" (italics mine),[21] and in 1686 he notes that at the oath-taking at the Governor's they were "much obstructed and confused by the drums and the vollies" of the soldiers outside who "would not be refrained" even so late in the day.[22] By then they needed refreshments. The day was a long one and

---

[19] *Diary of Samuel Sewall*, I, 453–454.
[20] *Boston and Country Gazette*, June 4, 1770.
[21] *Diary of Samuel Sewall*, I, 360.
[22] *Ibid.*, 136.

pressure to keep the sermons to one hour is understandable. Often the election was not completed until eight or nine in the evening, and if the Governor should introduce a point of contention, as he did in 1705 when he tried to deny the Representatives' right to elect a Speaker, " 'twas past eleven at night before the election was finished." [23]

By 1773 the events of election day as reported in the *Massachusetts and Boston Weekly* for May 27 went like this:

Yesterday being the anniversary of the day appointed by Royal Charter for convening a great and General Court or Assembly of this Province, and for the election of his Majesty's Council, the gentlemen who were returned to serve and represent the several towns, met agreeable to the precepts at the Town-House in Boston at nine o'clock in the morning. A Committee from the honorable Board, authorized and appointed by his Excellency the Governor, administered the oaths required by Act of Parliament, to the members of the House, who after having taken the oath of abjuration and subscribed the declaration, they unanimously chose Mr. Samuel Adams for their Clerk. The House then proceeded to the choice of a Speaker, when the honorable Thomas Cushing, Esq., was unanimously chosen.

At ten o'clock, the honorable his Majesty's Council and a number of the principal gentlemen of the town waited upon his Excellency the Governor at the Province-House, to congratulate him on this anniversary, and having partook of a collation, they went with his Excellency in procession to the Town-House, preceded by the commission-Officers of the Troop of Guards, of the Boston regiment of militia, of the Company of Artillery, and of the Grenadiers, all dressed in their uniforms, escorted by his Excellency's Company of Cadets, who were under arms, commanded by the honorable Colonel Hancock, having an excellent band of music playing on their march. The Governor being in the Council-

[23] *Diary of Samuel Sewall,* II, 131. Cotton Mather (1700), Prince (1730), and Chauncy (1747) refer in their sermons to the "one hour" at their disposal. The title pages of several eighteenth-century election sermons indicate that "several paragraphs which, for want of time were omitted in preaching, are inserted in their proper places and for distinction's sake comprehended in crotchets" (Chauncy, 1747; Mayhew, 1754; Dunbar, 1760). Because the minister could easily enlarge his sermon for the printed version, one should not automatically assume that some of the marathon texts (such as Shepard's, 1672, Oakes', 1673, Barnard's, 1734, and Frink's, 1758) were delivered intact. Still, it is hard to believe that a Puritan of the old school cut down his sermon "for want of time." Undoubtedly there were periodic requests from the House, perhaps at the time of the invitation, to keep the sermons to one hour. Perry Miller quotes the joke from Winthrop's *Good News from New England* (1648): "When 'these persecuted servants of Christ Jesus first set foot on these American shores,' their first concern was to satisfy their long-starved appetites for sermons; realizing that their tongues were at last 'untied from the prelates' injunctions, they preach with all diligence to their auditors, doubling their hours to regain their lost time' " (*Orthodoxy in Massachusetts,* 149).

Chamber, a committee from the honorable House of Representatives waited upon his Excellency to acquaint him with the choice of their Speaker. The Governor sent a message by the Secretary that he was in the chair and ready to receive the Speaker-elect; a committee from the House then went up with the Speaker and presented him for his Excellency's approbation, according to the royal explanatory Charter, and then returned to the House; his Excellency sent a message in writing to the House, approving of the choice. . . .

At eleven o'clock his Excellency the Governor, the members of the honorable his Majesty's Council, and the honorable House of Representatives, went in procession to the Old Brick Meeting-House, according to ancient custom, where a sermon on this occasion was preached by the reverend Mr. Charles Turner of Duxbury, before a very large auditory of senators, ministers, and other respectable persons, from those words in Romans 13. 4: "For he is the minister of God to thee for good."

After divine service, the guns at Castle William and at the batteries in this town were fired; and the procession was to Concert Hall, where an elegant entertainment was provided and a great number of gentlemen of rank dined with his Excellency. After dinner their Majesties' healths, the Royal Family, and other loyal toasts were drank.

In the afternoon the General Court met at the Town-House and proceeded to the choice of Councilors, when the following gentlemen were elected for the year ensuing, viz. . . .

It is all very well for Urian Oakes to say in 1673 that the election sermon was "unsought and undeserved . . . nay thrust upon" him,[24] but such a large, guaranteed audience in the State House on election day provided a challenge and an event of prestige for the preacher. There may have been some sleepless nights for the ministers at the thought of the awesome occasion. It is doubtful if the election sermon could wield as great an influence as that preached by Hawthorne's Father Hooper— even in his black veil—"during Governor Belcher's administration": "he stood before the chief magistrate, the council, and the representatives, and wrought so deep an impression, that the legislative measures of that year were characterized by all the gloom and piety of our earliest ancestral sway."[25] Still, for Cotton Mather election day was "the greatest anniversary solemnity which occurred in the land" and Perry Miller has since called the election sermon "the most important single form of publication concerned with the theory of society."[26]

[24] *New England Pleaded With*, 26.
[25] "The Minister's Black Veil," *Twice-Told Tales, Works* (Boston, 1882), I, 66.
[26] *Magnalia*, I, 331; *The Puritans*, ed. Perry Miller and Thomas H. Johnson (New York, 1938), 792. See also J. W. Thornton, "Introduction," *The Pulpit of the Ameri-*

To preach to the Governor in his regal attire (and after 1690 many of them were Anglicans) was trial enough. For some of the royally appointed Governors the election sermon must have been an almost insufferable bore, tolerated only to keep the provincials contented with their own importance. Ezra Stiles, later president of Yale, was in frequent touch with prominent Massachusetts clergymen; he records in his diary for 1775 that "the kings' governors have long been tired out with election sermons and intended to have put an end to them." [27] In his address to the Anglican but popular Governor William Shirley in 1747, Charles Chauncy manages to say what the Colony expected of him and to praise the Governor at the same time—a fine line to tread.

The opinion we have of your Excellency's integrity and justice forbids the least suspicion of a design in you to invade the civil charter-rights of this people. And tho' you differ in your sentiments from us as to the model of our church state and the external manner of our worship, yet we can securely rely on the generosity of your principles to protect us in the full enjoyment of those ecclesiastical rights we have been so long in possession of . . .[28]

An equally chilling prospect would be the Boston clergy, their numbers swelled by visiting preachers from surrounding towns, concentrated in one awesome section of the hall. The well-established minister like Increase Mather would have an opportunity to demonstrate why he was a prestigious pillar of the commonwealth; but a lesser known man would be on display under searching, learned eyes. Knowing that the printed version would circulate throughout the Colony and that a few copies would find their way to Europe, the preacher was indeed, as Ebenezer Pemberton put it in 1710, under "critical inspection." [29]

II

To preach the election sermon in the seventeenth century was a challenge, however, for more important reasons. Because the audience was both a geographical and political cross-section of Governor, Deputy-

can Revolution, xxvi; C. H. Van Tyne, "Influence of the Clergy, and of Religious and Sectarian Forces, on the American Revolution," 54–55.

[27] *The Literary Diary of Ezra Stiles* . . . , ed. Franklin Bowditch Dexter (New York, 1901), 569.

[28] *Civil Magistrates Must Be Just, Ruling in the Fear of God*, 54.

[29] *The Divine Original and Dignity of Government Asserted*, 4. Statistics suggest that the preachers were invited to give the election sermon after they were well established. Of the 123 sermons preached between 1634 and 1775, only 20 were

Governor, clergy, outgoing Magistrates (who hoped to be re-elected), and voting Deputies, here was the only annual opportunity to speak to the "people" of New England in that special sense of the word as a specific community, with clear lines of identity and cohesion—God's chosen people in New England. The election sermon was destined from the beginning to become an occasion for assessment and prophecy of New England's "errand into the wilderness." Any sermon is important because it "awakens the sparks of light that are in the consciences of men" and "stirs up a principle of grace where it is, and a principle of natural conscience where there is no grace." [30] But the election sermon was more than an address to the individual conscience; it was the center of a ritual in which a community gave thanks and took stock, held at the traditional time of festival, in late May, "when the heads of our tribes are met together in a solemn assembly to give thanks to the God of heaven for the many great and distinguishing privileges, both civil and religious, which we are favored with; and to ask direction and a blessing from on high, upon all the administrations of government in the land . . ." [31]

If the election preachers were to offer thanks for greatness received, they were also to be "watchmen upon Jerusalem's wall, whose proper business is to descry dangers, and give seasonable notice thereof; to observe the sins of the times, and the awful symptoms of God's departure." [32] The colonial preachers had a deep and nervous sense of their role as prophets and "watchmen," and the election sermon was the high point of this responsibility. Perry Miller distinguishes between two mainstreams in Puritanism. There is an "Augustinian Piety," a mystical concern with the inner, psychological status of one's direct relationship with God, a sense of one's tremulous progress in gaining and keeping God's grace. This is the inner battle so remarkably recorded in Cotton Mather's *Diary* and Jonathan Edwards' *Personal Narrative*. But colonial Puritanism was also a concern with the cold facts of building God's city on a hill here and now in the sun and cold of Massachusetts. It was "a program for society,"

given by men in their thirties. The average age was 49; the median, 50. Cotton Mather was the youngest election preacher at 26—the only one to preach while in his twenties—and the eldest was Samuel Cheever who was 73 when he preached in 1712.

[30] Solomon Stoddard, *The Way for a People to Live Long in the Land That God Hath Given Them* . . . (Boston, 1703), 8.

[31] John Webb, *The Government of Christ Considered* . . . (Boston, 1738), 1.

[32] Ebenezer Thayer, *Jerusalem Instructed and Warned* . . . (Boston, 1725), 38.

a rigid system "of law and order, of regulation and control." [33] The election sermon, first in the pulpit and then in print, was the most important occasion to define this civil strain of New England Puritanism; it was an annual trumpet call to review the essential laws which God had put into the Bible for all to see pertaining to how Christians in covenant should govern themselves as God required. It was a special occasion because each year it was a challenge to defend the great paradox of the "New England Way." The Congregational Church of early Massachusetts was based on democratic election of ministers and it cooperated in the election of civil magistrates. But this democratic potential for fresh ideas was restricted by a rigid tradition of ideas. It was a church dedicated to only one view of civil government, the permitted view of God's intentions; "heretics" like Roger Williams, Anne Hutchinson, and the Quakers were banished; law was not susceptible to various interpretations; change was not the way of the world; the church did not accumulate its wisdom from man's traditions nor should it grow like a plant; its nature was immutable; it was like a rock and it was based on commandments etched in stone. It progressed numerically by breaking off pieces of itself to be carried farther into the hinterland and by trying diligently to mold itself more accurately to God's law. It had little conception of evolving (until 1700–1730 at least); the laws of one generation should not be rewritten by the next. The Father of all had spoken once; that was enough. To understand the *raison d'être* of the election sermon tradition in the seventeenth and early eighteenth centuries, turn to Samuel Willard's *Only Sure Way* of 1682 for an apologia of the indispensable necessity of exhortation, definition, and chastisement.

There is perhaps another reason for the election sermon tradition. New England recognized from the beginning that it was being watched by Europe and by other American colonies. The "New England Way" was on trial. Much seventeenth-century Puritan writing—history, sermon, treatise—has an element of propaganda to it. The writers intended their work for a European audience as evidence that the New World experiment was thriving, indeed that it was preparing itself to lead the Protestant world in reform. The election sermon was theoretically an ideal form of

---

[33] "From Edwards to Emerson," *Errand into the Wilderness* (Cambridge, 1956), 191–192 (reprinted in *Interpretations of American Literature,* ed. Charles Feidelson, Jr., and Paul Brodtkorp, Jr., New York, 1959, 114–136). See also the chapter "Hypocrisy," in Miller, *From Colony to Province,* 68–81.

public relations—the first Voice of America—as long as the apostasy theme did not outweigh the evidence that the errand into the wilderness was worthwhile. "We are outcasts indeed, and reproached," says John Norton in his election sermon of 1661, referring to those in England who still looked on the New Englanders as separatists from king and church; "but let us be such outcasts as are caring for the truth, and therefore not to neglect an apology." [34] Norton means "apology" here in the sense of a defense or explanation. One of the motives in the Court's decision to undertake the expense of printing these sermons, and their distribution to every minister in the Colony, was its sense of the sermons' value as an annual apologia. (Samuel Sewall carried election sermons in his pocket in both England and America and gave them out like cigars.[35]) The sermons would show everyone how fortunate the Colony was in its civil liberties, and that it took this liberty seriously. They would also show that the Colony was well educated in political theory and that the New Englanders were earnest in their errand to achieve, at last, a solution to the old dilemma of rendering unto Caesar the things that are Caesar's and unto God the things that are his.

III

It is natural that a few motifs should emerge as the special concern of the election sermons. Of course there is a great range in their length and scope; few are confined to one topic. An occasion which called for an exegesis on the history of Israel, a survey of Biblical ideas on government and the good ruler, a look at the good old days, a catalog of what's wrong with New England, a plea to do better, and a look at what might lie ahead—this hardly lends itself to a narrow scope. Still, in all the extant sermons up to 1775, several related motifs emerge continually.

One of the basic concepts in Puritan thought is the covenant, or meaning of the word "chosen." It is the nature of God to choose or elect both individuals and nations for his kingdom on earth as well as for eternity.

[34] "Sion the Outcast Healed of Her Wounds," *Three Choice and Profitable Sermons,* 14. Cf. Larzer Ziff, *The Career of John Cotton,* 179–180.

[35] *Diary of Samuel Sewall,* III, 7, 348. Governor Belcher so liked Barnard's election sermon that he sent a dozen copies to his son in London and urged him to slip up Queen Caroline's "back stairs into her apartment . . . and present one on your knees yourself. Try this. . . . She'd read it, be pleased, and tell the King" (John Langdon Sibley and Clifford K. Shipton, *Biographical Sketches of Those Who Attended Harvard College,* 13 vols., Cambridge and Boston, 1873–1965, IV, 509).

The election sermon up to about 1730 was a presidential address to the annual convention of God's Chosen People in New England, Inc.—and it was precisely the "incorporated" that mattered. God incorporates a special group and while it is not a closed club, neither is it an open community with a loose sense of identity and fuzzy boundary lines.

The taking down the partition wall between Jews and Gentiles whereby the vine of the church was made to spread its branches over the wall did not take in the whole world into the Lord's vineyard at once; but there is still a distinction to be made between the church and the rest of the world which lies in wickedness; between a religious people by a visible profession and the rest of the world that are perishing for want of vision.[36]

"The churches of Christ in this land," says Peter Clark in 1739, "are founded on a sacred covenant, transacted between God and them, in a more solemn and explicit manner than perhaps in most churches in the world."[37] The clergy seized upon the election sermon from its beginnings to define the boundaries of God's vineyard wherein lived his New England people, and an interesting feature of reading the sermons chronologically is to see the changes in the definition as a unique American community finds itself surrounded by other faiths in the "wilderness" outside, and challenged by the Charter requirement of toleration (after 1691) and the growth of liberal views from within.

The concept of covenant was not only religious and Biblical, however, but a matter of practical politics. God's covenants in the Bible must be extended by man into patents, charters, and compacts, created on paper as legal documents, defended and referred to by courts, enacted by godly men for their own well-being as well as in response to their desire to do things as God would have them. Thus another strong theme in the election sermons is the divine source of government and God's sanction of the study of political science.[38] Government is ordained of God: "that there must be government is not from the bare will of men, but from the most High who ruleth in the kingdoms of men and giveth it to whomsoever he will; he has put his sovereign sanction upon it and made it a fixed ordi-

---

[36] Samuel Danforth, *An Exhortation to All* . . . (Boston, 1714), 33.

[37] *The Ruler's Highest Dignity and the People's Truest Glory* . . . (Boston, 1739), 52.

[38] For discussions of colonial Puritan political theory see Perry Miller, "The Social Covenant," *The New England Mind: The Seventeenth Century* (New York, 1939), 398–431; Miller, "The Puritan State and Puritan Society," *Errand into the Wilderness,* 141–152; Edmund S. Morgan, "Introduction," *Puritan Political Ideas,* xiii–xlvii.

nance of heaven that there be a rule over men; the God of Israel has say'd it and the rock of Israel has spoken it." [39] Without government, Ebenezer Pemberton continues in his fine sermon, "there could be nothing of beauty, proportion, strength, unity, order in societies; liberty and property would be exposed to fatal invasions. The flood-gates of lusts would be open and a deluge of sin and woe would sweep away all that is pleasant and desirable in the world. Men would be like fishes in the sea and as beasts in the wilderness, the greater devour the less." [40] One of the differences between the enclosed garden and the wilderness without is that the wall or hedge of protection separates order from disorder, harmony of parts from confusion of parts, government from anarchy. In his election sermon of 1676, William Hubbard puts it this way:

"Where order prevails, beauty shines forth." It was order that gave beauty to this goodly fabric of the world, which before was but a confused chaos, without form and void. . . . It suited the wisdom of the infinite and omnipotent Creator to make the world of differing parts, which necessarily supposes that there must be differing places for those differing things to be disposed into, which is order. The like is necessary to be observed in the rational and political world where persons of differing endowments and qualifications need a differing station to be disposed into, the keeping of which is both the beauty and strength of such a society. Naturalists tell us that beauty in the body arises from an exact symmetry or proportion of contrary humors equally mixed one with another; so doth an orderly and artificial distribution of diverse materials make a comely building, while homogeneous bodies (as the depths of waters in the sea, and heaps of sand on the shore) run into confused heaps, as bodies uncapable to maintain an order in themselves. [41]

Political science for the Puritan was a required, engaging activity, emblematic and allegorical as well as historical, a study of high calling and importance.

The election sermon tradition began as an apologia for the indispensable cooperation of church and state, and although the eighteenth-century preachers gradually recognized the growing separation between the two, they continued to remind the politicians of their duties to God and to offer the guidance of the church in civil and political affairs. The cohesion of church and state was a concept bearing down on the election sermons

[39] Ebenezer Pemberton, *The Divine Original and Dignity of Government Asserted*, 13.
[40] *Ibid.*, 16.
[41] *The Happiness of a People* . . . (Boston, 1676), 8.

with the authority of centuries, from the Old Testament to Canterbury's control under James and Charles. Orthodoxy in Massachusetts in the seventeenth century was not a new invention. The New England preachers were aware of the religious debates carried on in Europe between 1600 and 1660; Massachusetts was now free to put non-separating Congregationalism into practice—to make what had been theory in England, fact in America. The preachers were not going to miss any opportunity to announce the means of keeping the New England Way pure and functional. This, surely, is where minister and Magistrate saw eye to eye on the need for, and the subject matter of, the election sermon. The clergy would protect the authority of Governor and Magistrate; they in turn would see to it that civil law kept the churches clean, pure, and powerful. It was a masterful scheme until the Charter of 1691, and it was a great memory thereafter. The seventeenth-century preacher of an election sermon was in a unique, central position in the old Town House, surrounded by three audiences, all covenanted together, yet each seeing things in a slightly different light—the Magistrates (oligarchy), the Deputies (democracy), and the ministers (theocracy). It was his job to show them that their different lights might so blend as to produce one radiant white light of Puritanism. There is often a political edge to statements of order, as in this by William Hubbard in 1676:

Let a body politic be never so well proportioned as to its constitution and form of government, and never so well furnished with wise and able men for its conduct and guidance, yet if the several members be not well tuned together by a spirit of love and unity, there will never be any good harmony in their administrations. . . . In the beautiful system of the world, which yet is compounded of sundry elements and those of differing qualities one from the other, yet is there such a necessary and mutual connection between the parts that they are all so firmly knit one to another that it is altogether impossible to make any breach in their union; rather will those several bodies forget the properties of their own nature than there shall be any chasma or vacuum amongst them which would tend to a dissolution of the whole. Thus in the body politic, where it is animated with one entire spirit of love and unity and settled upon lasting and sure foundations of quietness and peace, all the several members must and will conspire together to deny or forbear the exercise of their own proper inclinations, to preserve the union of the whole, that there be no schism in the body, as the apostle speaks.[42]

[42] *Ibid.*, 16. For a discussion of John Cotton's acceptance of theocracy, see Larzer Ziff, *The Career of John Cotton*, 97–98.

Hubbard is telling the Deputies to remember their place. They must elect godly men as Assistants, and then leave them to govern. Factions and "backbitings" are disorderly.

The Representatives' power to elect the Councilmen (and the Governor until 1684) was viewed by the church with both pride and suspicion. If the right men were elected, such democratic power could be the strength of the Colony; but if the wrong men gained office, it could mean the Colony's undoing. That the Governor was appointed by the King and could veto the election of one or all of the elected Councilmen was, after 1684, another potential source of catastrophe. A Governor like Andros could destroy years of achievement in a few harsh strokes. (See the "Introduction" to Cotton Mather's *The Way to Prosperity*, 1689.) Thus it is easy to understand why the subject "The Character of a Good Ruler" (1694) became the most frequent topic in the election sermon tradition, accounting for over half of the printed sermons up to 1775. The electors must be reminded of the kind of man they should vote for and the Governor and candidates for Council must be reminded of the kind of man each should be. The people of Massachusetts have placed "great trust" in their Deputies, says Samuel Belcher in his election sermon of 1707, and they "do presume and expect that in the choice now before you, you will have a special regard" to elect only those who "have subjected themselves to the rule of Christ's kingdom." [43] "Let not private respects sway you in your elections, to be for those that are your friends or favorers," says James Allen in "A Word to the Freemen" in his sermon of 1679; rather, "see how men stand affected to religion and the common good of this people." [44] Peter Thacher in 1711 makes his point with a metaphor: "it is very proper for the sick to choose their own physician; and that is the work of this sick Province this day, to choose provincial healers." [45]

The ideal Councilman to be elected (and the ideal Governor whom, they hoped, the King had appointed) must be wise, godly, just. He must rule for the good of the people.

Men in such a station should moreover approve themselves faithful to the interest of the people whose welfare as Councilors they are bound to endeavor. The prince and the people have not opposite interests; he that

---

[43] *An Essay Tending to Promote the Kingdom of Our Lord Jesus Christ*, 18.
[44] *New England's Choicest Blessing* . . . (Boston, 1679), 7.
[45] *The Alsufficient Physician* . . . (Boston, 1711), 42–43.

promoves the true interest of the one does so of the other also. A great emperor was wont to say, *Non mihi sed populo*; I am set in this high station not for myself but for the nation's sake.[46]

(This concept, lying dormant in the sermons all along, springs up as the guiding principle for resistance to George III in the sermons of 1770 and the following years of crises.) The good ruler must use his power with discretion. An example of this point occurs in Increase Mather's election sermon in 1693. Mather, acutely sensitive to criticism that he had failed as chief delegate to the Courts of James II and William to secure the Colony's old Charter privileges, leaves nothing to surmise about where he stands on the question of the Governor's veto. If there had been anyone else but the beloved "local son" Sir William Phips in the Governor's chair that day, Mather could have been accused of discourtesy approaching treason; as it was, it was all in the family.

And as for yourself excellent Sir, whom God has made the captain over his people in this wilderness, it is a very great power which the divine providence has put into your hands, that you could have a negative on the elections of this day—a power which I confess neither you nor anyone else should have had if any interest that I was capable to make could have prevented it.[47]

A Councilman is a little god, says Ebenezer Pemberton in 1710; God would have him so, with appropriate titles, honors, power, and respect. But he must check any temptation to take advantage of power for luxury and personal gain; he is still a man, and like all men, he will die. Pemberton's discussion of the Magistrates' mutability is one of the high points in prose style in the Massachusetts election sermons.

Their power can't overawe, nor their riches bribe death. Where are all those sons of fame, the mighty, rich, and honorable we read of in story! The kings and princes that filled their houses with gold and silver, and the counsellors of the earth! Are they not gone to sleep in those desolate places they built for themselves! Are not all the bright stars of the morning cover'd with the dark cloud of corruption! Where are those children of pride and oppression, who made the earth to tremble, shook kingdoms, made the world as a wilderness, and destroyed the cities thereof! How are they fallen, their pomp brought down to the grave, and become as weak as the meanest of their vassals! . . . Death causes all titles of honor to burst into air and nothing as empty bubbles. It disarms the great of all their power and they go naked into the other world. After all their pomp

[46] Increase Mather, *The Great Blessing of Primitive Counsellors*, 12.
[47] *Ibid.*, 19.

and parade on the stage of life, they drop into their graves, and nothing of all their glory descends after them. Death wrests the scepter out of the monarch's hand, plucks the crown from off his head, and turns his glory into noisesome putrefaction; and the very forethought of it will stain the pride of all their glory. . . . This prospect will pall the unhallowed appetite of dominion and gain . . .[48]

The better election sermons up through 1730 are New World versions of *The Courtier, The Governour,* and *The Prince.*

The election sermons were not only political treatises on the nature of governor and governed, however; many of them, especially in the seventeenth century, contain qualities of myth and epic. For modern readers (as well as for writers like Hawthorne and Longfellow), these qualities are as interesting as their political ideals. The "desk" in the old Town House or the State House of 1713 served as a theater, as New England's "wooden O" where a priest dramatized—in soliloquy, but sometimes creating the voices of protagonist and antagonist, and in shifting tones and modes, history and prophecy, song and narrative—a great, epic story. Various sections of the audience might for political reasons listen to the sermon with cool detachment; but let the preacher begin to weave the magic spell of New England's "errand into the wilderness," and the blood began to tingle.

It was said earlier that when the final selections were made for this volume, the first five sermons took on new significance as a cohesive unit. Like the movements of a symphony, these sermons orchestrate variations on a central motif which I shall call, after Danforth's cue, the "errand motif." It has two basic themes—the first lyrical, magical; the second, heavy, angry, a rousing call to arms. The first theme tells a story about how and why a simple folk left a very old civilization to begin a new one, and their first accomplishments. Like the travels of Odysseus, Aeneas, and Moses, these travels and settlement in a strange new world were perilous but magnificent. Gone are the miracles or metamorphoses of the Old Testament, but God still controls a world by wondrous providences. In the 1660's, however, this community begins to lose the spirit of the enterprise and can no longer see the magic of a wilderness turned into a garden. Hence the second theme of denouncement, explication of the present apostasy, and a call to return to the original errand. Within these sermons is what Perry Miller calls a "jeremiad," but the jeremiad

[48] *The Divine Original and Dignity of Government Asserted,* 59–60, 63, 65.

is only a part of a larger whole.[49] The denouncement is nothing without first looking back to the ideal days of the original errand. On the anniversary of the beginning of the political year, in the capital city, there was a special opportunity—urgency perhaps—to recall that errand. These five sermons contain early versions of "The American Dream."

IV

If a foreign student should ask where to begin in order to understand the meaning and development of "The American Dream," he could not be better advised than to study the environment of America's Age of Reason. The challenge of showing Europe that a democracy could be planned and executed by rational men surrounded by the confusion of war and disconnected from the British crown was successfully met. The Dream emerges in the writings, especially the letters, of Jefferson, Adams, Franklin, Madison, Paine, Hamilton, Freneau. Gilbert Chinard's excellent chapter "The American Dream" in the *Literary History of the United States* defines the phrase in terms of these men and this era. There is no mention of the Puritans.[50]

More recent studies take the Dream back to Puritan New England with illuminating results.[51] It is here that some of the essentials in the Dream first find expression when a group of displaced Europeans come to America to create their version of a great society and discover some unique features of being American.

The Puritan version of the Dream might be paraphrased as follows. God has offered his chosen people several opportunities to create the

[49] "On annual days of election . . . the General Court regularly listened to a sermon which, under the circumstances, was bound to be more a review of recent afflictions than an exposition of doctrine; . . . they developed, amplified, and standardized a type of sermon for which the rules were as definite as for the ode. . . . for the second generation the dominant literary form, almost the exclusive, is something we may term, for shorthand purposes, a 'jeremiad.' " Professor Miller singles out Higginson's election sermon of 1663, Mitchel's of 1667, Stoughton's of 1668, Danforth's of 1670, Shepard's of 1672, Oakes' of 1673, Hubbard's of 1676, and Increase Mather's of 1677 as the chief examples ("The Jeremiad," *From Colony to Province*, 29–30).

[50] Ed. Robert E. Spiller *et al.* (New York, 1948), 192–215. See also Theodore Hornberger, "The Enlightenment and the American Dream," in *The American Writer and the European Tradition*, ed. Margaret Denny and William H. Gilman (Minneapolis, 1950), 16–27.

[51] Frederic I. Carpenter, *American Literature and the Dream* (New York, 1955); Loren Baritz, *City on a Hill: A History of Ideas and Myths in America* (New York, 1964); Cyclone Covey, *The American Pilgrimage* (New York, 1961).

society he wishes for them. Adam and Eve failed to keep their covenant with God, and lost Paradise. The Israelites also fell away from their covenant with God, given to Moses on Mount Sinai; and after Moses, God sent many prophets, some of them great kings and leaders like Nehemiah and David, to warn, to help, to lead them from their apostasy. The second Adam, Christ, reaffirmed God's covenant with man, and the early little pockets of Christian churches after his death were as close to the ideal communities of God as history had, until 1630, shown. But it would seem impossible to preserve such purity for long; soon the church fell into decay, and entered upon a long sleep in the dark ages of Roman domination. Then the spirit of purification rose up out of its sleep in a baptism of fire; the Protestant revolution began a new chapter in the quest for God's covenanted society, and Cartwright and Ames in England carried the work of Luther and Calvin to theoretical perfection. England reformed, but failed to progress beyond a slightly improved church. At this point, when the energy and learning needed to create the long-awaited society were never more available, geography played its part. America was discovered—"a waste and howling wilderness," free of bishops, untainted (in the Puritans' view) except for Indians.

Known unto God are all his works from the beginning of the world. And he that made this new world knoweth why he made it and what to do with it, though men do not. It is certain Antichrist boasted in his American eureka and conquest when he began to be routed in Europe by the reformation. And who can blame him to provide a new world against he lost his old one. But the Son of God followed him at the heels and took possession of America for himself. And this Province, so far as I know, is the very turf and twig he took possession by, as to the reformation and conversion of the natives and gathering of them into churches.[52]

Where was there ever a place so like unto New Jerusalem as New England hath been? It was once Dr. Twiss his opinion that when New Jerusalem should come down from heaven America would be the seat of it. Truly that such a type and emblem of New Jerusalem should be erected in so dark a corner of the world is matter of deep meditation and admiration.[53]

The New England "city on a hill" was another opportunity to fulfill the

[52] Nicholas Noyes, *New England's Duty and Interest* . . . (Boston, 1698), 75; the pamphlet's "ΕΥΡΗΚΑ" has been changed here to "eureka."

[53] Increase Mather, *A Discourse Concerning the Danger of Apostacy* . . . issued with *A Call from Heaven* (Boston, 1685), 77–78.

challenge of the society which God desired and which man had been bungling since Adam.

This New England Dream was not a simple one, however; it was in part a myth of perfection, and in part a matter of practical politics on the first American frontier, and they soon split. The Dream had historical authority in Old and New Testaments and the imaginative attractions of myth. It looked homeward to the historical example of Israel and the early Christian churches in all their purity. Part of the energy of the Puritan Dream came from a renewal in a pure source, a purification which bypassed fourteen centuries of degenerate time in arriving at the meaningful center. "The first age was the golden age," says Cotton Mather in the "Introduction" to his epic history; "to return unto that, will make a man a protestant, and I may add, a Puritan." [54] Mircea Eliade has defined the impact of myth on a community as its attempt to recapture the integrity and energy of a past heroic act. All time which has flowed out from the great event—whether Prometheus' descent with fire or Moses' descent with the commandments of stone—is profane time, unmeaningful time. [55] The early American Puritans had a lively, daily sense of penetrating to the very center of a meaningful, compelling mythology. Their courts of law, their sermons, their primers and children's stories, their idiom—all re-enacted the days of Moses and the early Christians of the first century. The election sermon was a high point in the year when representatives of the people would gather to renew their spiritual energy by focusing on their errand.

But their Dream not only looked backward; it looked forward. If it was a return to the past, it was also a harbinger. If it worked, and the enclosed garden was created, kept clean and lovely, and its walls enlarged to include more people and more land, then it would be a "specimen" for the rest of the world. [56] The myths of utopias and Hesperides, the Golden Age and Atlantis, would now come true and New England would become a strong light that would reach over to Old England, the Low Countries, perhaps even the whole Latin world, illuminating their darkness and drawing some away.

[54] *Magnalia*, I, 25.
[55] *The Myth of the Eternal Return*, trans. Willard R. Trask (New York, 1954), 34–36.
[56] *Magnalia*, I, 25. See also Loren Baritz' discussion of Winthrop in *City on a Hill*, 3–44.

But behold, ye European churches, there are golden candlesticks (more than twice seven times seven!) in the midst of this outer darkness; unto the upright children of Abraham, here hath arisen light in darkness. And let us humbly speak it, it shall be profitable for you to consider the light which from the midst of this outer darkness is now to be darted over unto the other side of the Atlantic Ocean.[57]

The New England Dream was not only a fulfillment of an old prophecy; it was itself a new prophecy. The Puritans had a Whitmanesque sense of looking into the future, a view of a greater civilization for which they were laying the foundations and the guidelines.

Theoretically there was no tension in this looking two ways at once. "If we consider what cognation there is between history and prophecy, it will not seem strange," says Nicholas Noyes in his election sermon in 1698: "For prophecy is history antedated and history is postdated prophecy; the same thing is told in both. . . . And many things in the Old Testament are first set forth in prophecy and afterward in history; and either of them, yea both of them beneficial to the church." [58] Thus New England's errand into the wilderness was a logical, historical fulfillment of the types of errands and attempts at perfection in the Bible; and this new errand could itself be a type or emblem of what the rest of the world might later accomplish. But the challenge of the Puritan Dream was to perfect that which had never been done before. This is the paradox of America; it looks to the past for nourishment, but it has had from the beginning a "case against the past"—the past has never been good enough; so it must continually progress and eclipse its father's world.[59]

And I seriously affirm I know no way else to advance the name of Christianity to its pristine glory in the world. The flourishing beauty of this heavenly grace was that which did so strangely metamorphose the visage and face of things at first in the world, when was fulfilled that of Isaiah, that the wolf and the lamb should dwell together and the leopard lie down with the kid. It was the verdant luster of this divine grace that turned the rough and barren wilderness of the world into a fruitful Carmel or fragrant Sharon. . . . But alas, when this *terras astræa reliquit*, when this spirit of love began to decay, then did iniquity and unrighteousness break in upon the Christian world like a torrent that carried all before it.[60]

The election sermons, official imprimaturs of the young church-colony,

[57] *Magnalia*, I, 26.
[58] *New England's Duty and Interest*, 43.
[59] See R. W. B. Lewis, "The Case against the Past," *The American Adam*, 13–27.
[60] William Hubbard, *The Happiness of a People*, 61.

insisted that New England must perfect and then hold fast to an enclosed garden as no chosen people had ever been able to do before; there was to be no "decay" here. The Dream was compelling, but too much to ask.

"Rip Van Winkle" has become so deeply imbedded in American folk-lore because it dramatizes a unique American experience. Rip is the first deracinated hero in American fiction. When he falls asleep, he has walked up into the mountains to escape a busy, mercantile society. He wants to get away from it all to the simple, green quietness of the hills. Here he completes the archetype of pastoral by returning in a dream to a more idyllic past, the quaint old Dutch Puritans bowling in the hills (idyllic and quaint, that is, for Irving). He returns home to find himself uprooted; his house is empty and decayed. Everything is strange—the village, the faces, the politics. Life is at a faster pace. He escapes to the past only to find himself now too old for the present. Time is terrifyingly accelerated; the future suddenly becomes the past overnight, and he misses the greatest event in American history.

His story is a little symbolic fable of America. The quest for a pure, ideal, communal life seems forever several steps ahead, and one is left with only the change and the fast pace. The ideals pass by in the night without stopping. Theodore Parker in 1848 saw it this way:

The American soul passes away from its work soon as it is finished. So the soul of each great artist refuses to dwell in his finished work, for that seems little to his dream. Our fathers deemed the Revolution a great work; it was once thought a surprising thing to found that little colony on the shores of New England; but young America looks to other revolutions, and thinks she has many a Plymouth colony in her bosom. If other nations wonder at our achievements, we are a disappointment to ourselves, and wonder we have not done more. *Our national idea out-travels our experience, and all experience.* [Italics mine.] [61]

The Puritans wanted to fulfill the mission that the Israelites and early Christians began; they wanted to capture the elusive purity for which Moses delivered the guidelines; that was their "national idea." The ministers from 1660 to 1730 found that the people were slipping further and further away from these ideals; their "national idea" was out-traveling their experience. The preachers found themselves caught in the conflict between pressing on for a better, purer rendition of the Biblical blueprint,

[61] "The Political Destination of America and the Signs of the Times," an address Parker gave "here and there" in 1848; reprinted in *The American Transcendentalists*, ed. Perry Miller (New York, 1957), 358.

and holding fast to what they had because it might be as much as they were going to get. They called for a synod. By the time of the earliest election sermon reprinted here, perfection means a return unto the good old way of the first generation of New Englanders. Like Rip Van Winkle, New England had grown old much too fast; it changed too much in spite of the controls and in spite of the identity with Israel's pilgrimage. A communal wail arises, the chant of Ichabod: "the glory has departed." Increase Mather is the best example of many clergymen in the pulpits of 1660–1730; they appear early versions of Rip Van Winkle, trying to rub the strangeness from their eyes as if they had suddenly returned to a society which had left them behind and was full of new ways and strange gods.

O generation, see the Word of the Lord! Is there any new way more eligible than that good old way (for the substance of it I mean) which the Lord's people have already tried, and have experimentally found to be the way of blessing from God? Shall we seek and enquire after any new found out way as the Lord speaks of new gods? . . . Upstart gods which our fathers knew not; should some of our fathers that are now asleep in Jesus, and that have with so many prayers and tears, hazards, and labors and watchings and studies night and day to lay a sound and sure and happy foundation of prosperity for this people, arise out of their graves and hear the discourses of some and observe the endeavors of others . . . crying "Rase it, rase it, even to the foundation!" (Psal. 137. 7) by plucking up if they could that hedge that hath been here set to fence our all—would they not even rent their garments and weep over this generation? [62]

There are many ways in which this Puritan Dream of an iron grip on an old, pure formula was a dead end in America. Two later seminal Americans, Jefferson and Emerson, believed that the sons *should* rewrite the laws of the fathers, that change *was* the way of the world. Life was organic, like the growth of a plant, and must not be enclosed by walls, or thought of as immutably decreed in rock. There was no holding fast; there was only growth.

The errand sermons do illustrate, however, a continuous American motif. If Americans have never quite fulfilled their national dreams in fact, in their literature they have made capital of the attempts. "Deracination" means uprooted. When the Puritans left England, they engaged in a

---

[62] Thomas Shepard, *Eye-Salve*, 18; for comparable "Ichabod" passages in election sermons, see especially Benjamin Colman, *David's Dying Charge* . . . (Boston, 1723), 17ff; Ebenezer Thayer, *Jerusalem Instructed and Warned*, 19ff.

longed-for uprooting—sad, but of epic greatness and hope. In America, they became deracinated in a far more serious way. Their Dream was still too compelling to throw over, and the actual achievement of a functional congregationalism and covenant was too solid to deny. But they never quite made the Dream come true. The wall around the enclosed garden showed gaps before it was fully built. Perhaps there never were any "good old days." The errand remained a quest, and became a national theme. If it could not flourish politically, the Dream found life in festival and art.

V

Any generalization about the style of the election sermon must begin with its rigid, logical, highly patterned form.[63] The sermon conformed to the general threefold division of Puritan sermons everywhere in the seventeenth century, a form which grew out of medieval traditions and was taught and perfected in centers of Puritan theological training such as Emmanuel and Christ's colleges, Cambridge, and Harvard.[64]

The sermon begins with a Biblical text followed by an "Explication" which "opens up" the text by a careful scrutiny of the words, including in some cases their derivations and their different meanings in context. The preacher may point out controversies among Biblical scholars over the proper English translation of the Hebrew or Greek, adding his own authority to the reading he is sure is correct. This meticulous examination of the text is often accompanied by a brief narrative of the historical events leading up to the time the words of the text were first spoken, whether

[63] For discussions of preaching and the sermon genre in New England, see Perry Miller, "Rhetoric" and "The Plain Style," *The Seventeenth Century*, 300–362; *The Puritans*, ed. Miller and Johnson, 64–74; Josephine K. Piercy, "The Sermon and Religious Discourse," *Studies in Literary Types in Seventeenth Century America (1607–1710)* (New Haven, 1939), 155–167; Babette M. Levy, *Preaching in the First Half Century of New England History* (Hartford, 1945); Kenneth B. Murdock, "The Puritan Literary Attitude," *Literature and Theology in Colonial New England* (Cambridge, 1949), 31–65; Howard M. Martin, "Puritan Preachers on Preaching: Notes on American Colonial Rhetoric," *Quarterly Journal of Speech*, L (Oct. 1964), 285–292.

[64] Louis B. Wright points out that about two-thirds of the sixty-five ministers who came to New England in the Great Migration were educated at Cambridge, and the majority of these were from "that great nursery of Puritanism, Emmanuel College." *The Colonial Civilization of North America 1607–1763* (London, 1949), 84–85. The most influential textbooks on preaching in seventeenth-century New England were William Perkins, *The Art of Prophecying . . .* , trans. Thomas Tuke (London, 1607); Richard Bernard, *The Faithfull Shepheard . . .* (London, 1607; revised, London, 1621); William Ames, *The Marrow of Sacred Divinity . . .* (London, 1642).

by Samuel, Asa, Nehemiah, or Christ. Cotton Mather's *The Way to Prosperity* is a good example. Quite often this historical review plays a functional role in the sermon's success, for the preacher will emphasize incidents which his audience, trained to think in terms of typology and prophecy, will recognize as having an obvious parallel to their own life in America. The "Application" later in the sermon will come then as no surprise. The astute in the audience will early see what the preacher is driving at, and they will await the "Application" with something of the expectancy of the Greek audience watching a drama, the story of which they knew—they will want to see how the preacher does it, how well he will say what must be said. This pattern of expectancy in the audience would come only with training, but it was probably a real part of the aesthetics of the errand sermons; many in the audience, continuing members of the General Court, might hear several such sermons at election time.

With the philological and historical details explained, the preacher then announces the "Doctrine"—the second part of the sermon. Sometimes the word is set apart in large capitals as a separate heading in the printed texts; more often it is a small heading preceding a paragraph. In the seventeenth century the Doctrine is almost always italicized for emphasis. The heading was announced from the pulpit. Samuel Sewall's manuscript notes that he took during sermons show clearly the divisions "Doct." and "Prop. 2."[65] (In the 1728–31 years, these headings first begin to drop away as formal titles in the printed sermons. The word "Doctrine" may appear in the first sentence of a new paragraph, or be dispensed with entirely.)

In the section labeled "Doctrine," the preacher announces in his own words the lesson or law that he draws from the text. He works from the specific to the general, to the "maxims of wisdom"[66] that lie behind the specific words and context of the Biblical prophet. This general law is then broken down into several "Propositions" (or "Reasons"), each a slight expansion or variation of the central idea. It is here that the preacher

---

[65] Some manuscript notebooks of Sewall's sermon notes are in the collection of the Massachusetts Historical Society. Such note-taking during sermons, often in shorthand, seems to have been a common activity. There are several anonymous manuscript books in the collections of Harvard and the Massachusetts Historical Society, in addition to sermon notes by Cotton Mather and other ministers.

[66] Nathaniel Appleton, *The Great Blessing of Good Rulers . . .* (Boston, 1742), 11.

makes his own contribution; here he is creative. He will show with ingenuity the various and often delicate shades of multiple meanings which open out from the text, once one sees the general law. He works carefully and logically through his propositions so that the audience can trace them easily. In print, the distinctions between propositions often look like hairsplitting in the worst traditions of scholasticism. (See the "Doctrine" of Cotton Mather's *The Way to Prosperity*.) The reader must keep in mind, however, that the sermon was intended for simple farmers as well as educated theologians. The preachers erred on the side of simplicity and repetition according to the old law of rhetoric that a listener must be led carefully and gently around each turn in a logical path, as if he were blind. Still, there are times when the reader of the election sermons gazes with amazement at the naiveté, wordiness, and circular repetition. The "Doctrine" part of a Puritan sermon had a built-in propensity to be plain to the point of foolishness, and some preachers succumbed.

[Prop.] 3. To lead quiet and peaceable lives is to live quietly and peaceably together. When they are at peace among themselves and live quietly together, when families live peaceably and quietly, when there is peace and quietness in towns and churches and in all societies among a people, they may be said to lead quiet and peaceable lives.[67]

Sometimes a "Proposition" will be announced in a general heading, and subsequent paragraphs or groups of paragraphs united under a number will discuss the proposition. In these cases, the opening sentence of the first paragraph is often grammatically incomplete. The Puritans did not as a rule write incomplete sentences for rhetorical effect. Rather, such incomplete sentences are completions of the syntax of the proposition, or main point, made in a heading perhaps two or three paragraphs (or as much as a page or two) earlier. The modern reader must remember to keep a general proposition suspended in his mind while he attaches each unit developing it to its original syntax.

The third section of the sermon is the "Application" of the "Doctrine" and "Propositions" to present-day Massachusetts. It is usually expounded in several "Uses." [68] The Biblical past becomes an analogy to the present, and each is as close to, or equidistant from, the will of God. In the errand sermons, the "Use" is generally the relevancy of the text and its doctrine

[67] Joseph Baxter, *The Duty of a People* . . . (Boston, 1727), 7.
[68] For a discussion of the various "uses" in the application, see Levy, *Preaching in the First Half Century*, 95.

to the apostasy of New England. Sometimes the use can be blunt in its recommendations of curbs for specific abuses. Joseph Sewall in 1724 prevails on the Magistrates to create laws to curtail extensive traveling on Sundays and to shorten pub hours; three years later Joseph Baxter returns to the latter point by asking, "Is there nothing more to be done to keep town-dwellers from sotting away their time at taverns?" [69] Ebenezer Thayer in 1725 asks for magisterial support for higher salaries for ministers so that the profession will not fall into contempt. Requests for laws requiring congregations to honor their contracts with ministers so as not to take advantage of inflation and shifting standards of value, to the ministers' detriment, are often heard in the "Applications" of sermons in the 1720–50 years. Israel Loring, in an otherwise conservative election sermon advocating strict observance of Biblical and civil law, makes a unique request in 1737:

There is one thing more which I would recommend to the serious consideration of this great and General Court; and that is whether there is not a great duty lying upon us respecting the transactions of the year 1692, when not only many persons were taken off by the hand of public justice for the supposed crime of witchcraft, but their estates also ruined and their families impoverished. . . . the question is (if it be not beyond all question) whether a restitution is not due from the public to them, and we are not bound in justice to make it. [70]

Harvard College is also singled out continually as worthy of the Magistrates' special care; it is the "darling of the country," and a "nursery" which supplies the Colony with health-giving milk.

The sermon usually concludes with a direct word to each section of the audience. The Governor is praised, as are his sponsor the King, the House of Orange or Hanover (which through God's mercy has replaced the Stuarts), and the British Constitution (the best in the world). Some tributes to the Governor are dry and stereotyped; he is "damned with faint praise." Others are genuinely warm and well meant, such as John Barnard's in 1746 to William Shirley after the capture of Louisburg. [71]

After the tribute to the Governor, the House of Representatives is reminded of its duty to elect godly men to the Council. Finally, the

[69] Joseph Sewall, *Rulers Must Be Just* . . . (Boston, 1724), 55ff; Joseph Baxter, *The Duty of a People*, 32.

[70] *The Duty of an Apostatizing People* . . . (Boston, 1737), 51–52.

[71] John Barnard, *The Presence of the Great God in the Assembly of Political Rulers* . . . (Boston, 1746), 28.

ministers are acknowledged. (After 1747 they are merely mentioned, because a special sermon is to be preached the following day at their convention.)

That the preachers considered the election sermon a firm tradition is evident from frequent quotations and references to earlier election sermons and the "worthies" who preached them. Sometimes extensive quotations are incorporated, perhaps enlarged from the pulpit version for the pamphlet. Several append a few pages from earlier sermons to fill out a printer's form. Many phrases, such as "errand into the wilderness," "God's controversy with New England," "the noble vine," and "counsellors as at the beginning," recur frequently.

Because the format of the sermon is so rigid and the subject matter limited to several interrelated motifs, there is a sense in which any minister who graduated at the bottom of his class could put together a sermon mechanically and meet the occasion with some success. Some sermons read as if this is just what happened. As time went on, the challenge of saying the same old things vigorously and with meaning became more difficult. Several preachers in the eighteenth century freely admit the problem, such as John Prentice in 1735: "So many of my reverend fathers and brethren have gone before me in this service that there is but little room left to offer anything proper to the present occasion without repetition at least of the same thing. I have therefore omitted many things that I might have mentioned . . ."[72] By 1751, William Welsteed could wish with good reason that "the religious solemnities of this day never degenerate into an empty formality, nor sink away into vain flourish, cold and lifeless harangue upon politics."[73]

With a genre, an occasion, and a tradition contributing pressure for conformity and a highly conventional art form, it is surprising, not that there are as many poor sermons as there are, but that there are as many good ones. The sermons printed here, I submit, surmount the convention of time, place, and clichés with the ring of conviction, with passion as well as control. The familiar ideas find their perfect expression.

In the best errand sermons, the preacher transcends his role as a teacher of law, and becomes an actor. He has many roles to play. He may create different parts and speak them, as do Danforth in 1670 and Prince in 1730. He is a teller of tales, of great moments and epic quests in the

[72] *Pure and Undefiled Religion* . . . (Boston, 1735), 27.
[73] *The Dignity and Duty of the Civil Magistrate* . . . (Boston, 1751), 28.

history of his nation. He is to do for New England what Shakespeare did for his audience—bring the dead pages of history alive, with their shame and their glory, into significance and meaning. He will tell of heroes, Biblical as well as American, and he must recapture for his audience the idealism of the original errand to America—its innocence, its momentousness. The story must be told simply, but with passion, longing, and pathos. He must don the mask of the wise politician, of Samuel or Nehemiah or Asa. He must be like Portia in his understanding of the wise, sweet laws of God; yet he must also be like Bishop Carlisle in his wrath of exhortation and prophecy. It was not an easy task, and only a few did it well.

The biography of a Puritan sermon from conception to delivery appears in John Barnard's *Autobiography*; because it is so clearly spelled out by an able practitioner (his election sermon of 1734 appears in this collection), and because his practice must be representative of many of the ministers (he graduated from Harvard in 1707), it may be beneficial to close this brief review of the sermon's rhetoric by quoting it in full.

Here suffer me to take occasion to show you the manner of my studying my sermons, which I generally pursued when I had time for it, and upon some special occasions I made use of even in my advanced years. Having in a proper manner fixed upon the subject I designed to preach upon, I sought a text of Scripture most naturally including it; then I read such practical discourses as treated upon the subject; I read also such polemical authors on both sides of the question as I had by me, sometimes having ten or a dozen folios and other books lying open around me, and compared them one with another, and endeavored to make their best thoughts my own. After having spent some time (perhaps two or three days) in thus reading and meditating upon my subject, I then applied myself to my Bible, the only standard of truth, and examined how far my authors agreed or disagreed with it. Having settled my mind as to the truth of the doctrine I had under consideration, I then set myself to the closest meditation upon the most plain and natural method I could think of for the handling the subject. Sometimes, not always, I penned the heads of the discourse. Then I took the first head and thought over what appeared to me most proper to confirm and illustrate it, laying it up in my mind; so I went through the several heads; and when I had thus gone over the whole in its several parts, then I went over all in my meditation, generally walking in my study or in my father's garden. When I thought myself ripe for it, I sat down to writing, and being a swift penman, I could finish an hour and a quarter's discourse, with rapid speaking, in about four hours' time. This manner of studying sermons cost me, 'tis true, a great deal of time, perhaps a week or fortnight for a sermon, and sometimes more; but I had this advantage by it, that there was a greater stock laid up in my memory for future use, and I found it easy to deliver my discourses *memoriter*; and by the full and clear view I had of my subject, I could correct the phraseology in my delivery. I kept indeed my notes open, and turned over the leaves as though I had read them, yet rarely casting my eye upon my notes, unless for the chapter and verse of a text which I quoted. When I was settled in the ministry, I found this method too operose, yet when called to special public services, if I had time I practised it, only penning head by head as I meditated on them. Observing also that the aged Mr. Samuel Cheever, with whom I settled, very much failed in his memory (for he was wholly a *memoriter* preacher), I thought I might be reduced to his circumstances if I lived to old age, and therefore betook myself to reading my notes; and I find the advantage of it, since it hath pleased God to spare me to a great old age.[74]

[74] *Collections of the Massachusetts Historical Society*, 3rd ser., V (Boston, 1836), 187–188.

ON EDITING THE TEXT

THE editorial principles for this edition have been formed in a desire to produce a normalized text for the general reader which will also be acceptable and useful to scholars.

Copy Text. Establishing copy text for these sermons has been a relatively easy matter. I have not made an exhaustive search for the manuscripts; a check of places where one might expect to find them resulted in some delightful visits but no texts.[1] Copy text has been, then, the first —and in almost every instance the only—edition, printed as a pamphlet shortly after the sermon's delivery. Aside from printers' errors, the pamphlets should be substantively complete and reliable. The transmission of the text from author to print was a special case for the election sermons; they escaped the devious routes to print which some sermons suffered in the seventeenth century.[2] In the first place, the preacher knew well ahead of time that the sermon would be printed and that he must prepare a copy for the press. In some cases he obviously worked up footnotes and expanded his text for the printed version (on occasion he even says "dear reader"). Second, from author to printing house was a direct route. The day following the sermon's delivery, or within a few days (as

---

[1] Harvard College Library, Massachusetts Historical Society, Congregational Library (Boston), Boston Public Library, State of Massachusetts Archives, American Antiquarian Society.

[2] See Babette M. Levy, *Preaching in the First Half Century of New England History* (Hartford, 1945), 83–85, 141.

the *Journals* of the House of Representatives show), the House ordered a committee of from two to five members to "give the thanks of this Board" to the preacher for his sermon "and desire a copy thereof in order to its being printed" by the current official printer for the Colony.[3]

Printer's copy was either a fair copy made from the preacher's notes or the original draft of the sermon. Even a minister who preached habitually from notes might write out a finished version for delivery on election day, knowing he would have to supply a copy for printing. A footnote was misplaced in the pamphlet of Mayhew's election sermon of 1754, suggesting that material added to the pulpit copy for the printer was written on separate, interleaved sheets, easily misplaced.

Reprintings in the author's lifetime which could carry authorial revision are rare. In the one case of a second printing of a sermon included in this volume, Jonathan Mayhew's of 1754, the texts have been carefully collated for variants. In the case of John Barnard's sermon of 1734 we are fortunate. The copy text is the first edition in the Houghton Library, bound with Barnard's other sermons in an autographed, leather-bound volume—undoubtedly his own collection from his library. Some corrections in pen are taken as the author's and are incorporated silently into the present edition.

Spelling, Capitalization, and Contractions. Spelling has been modernized, but not so as to affect the sounds the words make. Thus "stopt" becomes "stopped," "shewed" becomes "showed," and "dye" becomes "die" (the minister is talking about death, not color). However, "alarum" does not become "alarm," "frighted" is not changed to "frightened," nor "differencies" to "differences."[4] "Christs Herauld" becomes "Christ's herald," but the old possessive structure "Caesar his men" is not changed. Capitalization has been normalized in accordance with *The Chicago Manual of Style.* In the seventeenth and early eighteenth centuries, capi-

---

[3] After preaching his election sermon in 1700, Cotton Mather prayed that it might be published (as six of the eight preached had been, by order of the Court, since he gave his last one, which was published in 1690); "immediately" the House of Representatives asked that it be printed and Mather "gave it unto the bookseller." The next entry in his *Diary* is dated June 4, so presumably the copy was in the printer's hands within five days of election day. *Diary of Cotton Mather*, 2 vols. (*Collections of the Massachusetts Historical Society*, 7th ser., 7–8, Boston, 1911), I, 352.

[4] Much guesswork is still involved. When in doubt about whether normalizing seriously alters colonial pronunciation, I have let the pamphlet spelling stand if I think it will be easily understood by today's general reader; otherwise I have normalized the spelling and put the pamphlet spelling in a textual note.

talization of the first letter of words other than proper names, within sentences, is frequent. Beginning with James Allen's election sermon of 1744, this excessive capitalization is noticeably reduced, and by the time of Mayhew's sermon (1754), capitalization is almost "normal" by modern standards. Contractions such as "Doct." and "Reas." have been expanded, but shortened forms like "call'd," "tho' " (though), and "wro't" (wrought) have been retained. Biblical references which are an integral part of the text and would have been given from the pulpit, but which were printed in the first edition in short form ("as in Jer. 5. 22"), have here been expanded ("as in Jeremiah 5. 22").

Punctuation. Punctuation in the nine selected pamphlets is without exception heavier than modern usage sanctions, especially in those before 1750. The theory of rhetorical punctuation is attractive and at first glance appears sacrosanct. This theory maintains that seventeenth- and eighteenth-century ministers punctuated their sentences not for logic or grammar but for rhetorical cadences and rhythms. The punctuation in the printed version was put in the printer's copy by the author because he observed those pauses in the delivery. After examining other sermon manuscripts (some printed, some not), reading the selected sermons aloud as well as silently, and trying the pragmatic test of submitting both a normalized version and the originally punctuated version to colleagues whose opinions I respect, I abandoned the rhetorical theory and its implications for the editor. Individual ministers varied a good deal in their pointing habits. It appears that some of them left the punctuation up to the printing house and that the printed version represents as much a printer's style as the author's.[5] In at least two *errata* notes at the end of sermons, substantive corrections are pointed out but the "divers mispointings" are left to "the candid reader" to "remit." In the absence of more study and evidence about ministers' and printers' understandings about punctuation, I choose to follow the pragmatic test of punctuating for the sense of the prose according to modern usage. Although written

[5] Generalizations here are dangerous; each author and his printer must be considered individually. Some sermon manuscripts by Cotton Mather which I have examined show careful attention to punctuation—a heavy punctuation compared to modern usage. However, the manuscript of John Barnard's *Elijah's Mantle* (in the Congregational Library, Boston) has very light punctuation; comparison with the printed version shows that the printer introduced many changes in accidentals. A survey of printers' treatment of colonial writing of all sorts—where manuscripts survive—is needed.

originally to be spoken, the sermons will now (unlike drama) only be read.

In only a few instances has punctuation been added. The pamphlets' termination of sentences has normally been followed, with only a few exceptions where a full stop has replaced semicolons or colons in long sentences in which there is a distinct transition in the idea. The pamphlets' paragraphing has been followed without exception. Within Biblical quotations, punctuation follows the Thomas Nelson edition of the King James Bible.

Brackets and Parentheses. For purposes of clarity, authors' brackets have been changed to parentheses and all editorial additions in the text (Biblical references and commentary in authors' footnotes) have been placed in brackets.

Italics and Quotation Marks. Italics were used to set off quotations up through the eighteenth century. (Mayhew's sermon in 1754 prints some quotations in italics and others within quotation marks.) Wherever italicized matter has been identified as a quotation—the bulk of it Biblical— it has been set off in this edition in quotation marks only. Some passages present special problems, however, because italics were also used for paraphrase. Some ministers like Barnard and Mayhew quote carefully; others appear not to see any important difference between an accurate quotation and coming close. It would appear that some ministers "quoted" from memory and getting the gist of the matter was less trouble, and seemed to them as useful as quoting accurately. This problem is complicated by the possibility that some quotations may be from Bible translations earlier than the King James (although it was the most widely used), or that some "quotations" may be the minister's own version of the Greek or Hebrew texts. I have not attempted to trace to earlier Bibles italicized passages that vary from the King James translation, although such a study would be worthwhile to ascertain to what extent other Bibles were used. Where italicized passages followed by Biblical references are reasonably accurate quotations from the King James Bible, I have placed them in quotation marks. However, where the italicized passage is a paraphrase—and in some cases they combine ideas and phrases from different parts of the Bible—I have not put the passage in quotation marks. Thus paraphrases are here distinguished from quotations where they are not so differentiated in the pamphlets. For example, the pamphlet of Danforth's sermon in 1714 has: "ALSO when God ordaineth Praise and Pro-

41

motes His Own Glory, even *by Instruments as unlikely as Babes and Suck-lings,* Psal. 8. 2." The only direct quotation here from Psal. 8. 2 is "Babes and Sucklings"; to set it off by quotation marks would distort Danforth's intention, for he intended *"by Instruments . . . Sucklings"* as either a paraphrase or a quotation. In cases like this the reader has the author's reference and if he wishes to study the amount of direct quotation he may do so. The "Doctrines" are usually italicized in the pamphlets and as the minister obviously wished them to stand out with special emphasis, I have left them in italics.

Biblical References. Biblical references supplied by the author usually precede the quotation in the pamphlet; except where introduced by con-junctions or prepositions making them a grammatical part of the sentence (e.g., "As the prophet says in Jeremiah 25. 31 . . ."), the references here have been placed in parentheses at the end of the quotation in keep-ing with modern, scholarly usage. Wherever a reference is incorrect for the King James Bible, it has been changed to the correct chapter or verse, noted with an asterisk—the symbol for all textual notes in this edition—and the original reference supplied in the textual notes. Wherever a quo-tation or other use exceeds the number of chapters or verses given in the preacher's reference, the additional material used is noted in editor's brackets. Thus (Jer. 5. 22, 23 *) means that although verses 22 and 23 are the correct references, the first edition of the sermon gives a different reference, which may be found in the textual notes; on the other hand (Jer. 5. 22, 23, [26]) means that although the pamphlet refers the reader to verses 22 and 23, verse 26 should also be included. Where an author's reference appears to include more verses than he has used, the reference is reproduced intact without comment. All the authors' references have been checked against the King James Bible. Where Biblical quotations are italicized but no reference is given, the reference is supplied in editor's brackets; thus the reader may see at a glance which references are the authors' (in parentheses) and which the editor's [in brackets]. Such ap-paratus and source-hunting are justifiable because they show the reader without unduly distracting him how extensively the Bible was used, and they offer an opportunity to study a minister's habits of composition. Some, like Cotton Mather, appear to be careless in giving accurate refer-ences; other ministers supply few references. More study is needed. How many of the incorrect references are to different Bibles? Why are some quotations taken from earlier Bibles or translated personally by the minister from the Latin, Greek, or Hebrew, when obviously the King James is most widely used? By giving references to some quotations but not to others, are some ministers covering up their extensive use of the Bible, or do they assume the reader will recognize them anyway? What conventions and understandings between preacher and audience apply here?

Other Emendations. Obvious printers' errors involving only a letter or two have been silently corrected, and corrections in *errata* lists sometimes printed at the end of a pamphlet have been silently adopted. All other substantive additions and changes (with the exception of Barnard's corrections in his own hand which have been adopted silently) carry a textual note symbol * and the pamphlet reading is given in the textual notes. Thus "they gone" becomes "they have gone" * and "he seen" becomes "he saw" *.

Footnotes. In sermons in which there are both author's and editor's footnotes, those by the author are designated by [a], [b], etc., and appear on left-hand pages; editor's footnotes are designated by [1], [2], etc., and appear on right-hand pages. The reader may thus put himself in the position of the seventeenth- or eighteenth-century reader and consult only the authors' notes if he wishes.

Editorial comment added to an author's note is placed in brackets following the note. Where an author's note occurs in the pamphlet at the beginning of a quotation, it has been moved to the end of the quoted matter. Otherwise the placing of the author's note in the text is followed even though many of them interrupt syntactical units and would be considered awkward in modern practice. The bibliographical information in authors' footnotes has not been normalized but reproduced exactly; the reader can see what cryptic bibliography was then acceptable (see for example Prince's notes). Obsolete and curious words are defined from the *NED* only if they do not occur in the one-volume, seventh edition of *Webster's Dictionary* (1965). Latin and Greek passages are translated, except where the minister translates a passage himself in the immediate context. Biblical quotations or paraphrases not italicized and without a reference in the pamphlet are footnoted wherever recognized. Within the notes to each sermon, subsequent references to a book use a short title only. Unless otherwise specified, Cambridge in bibliographical citations refers to Cambridge, Massachusetts.

Preparing the Text. Printer's copy was arrived at as follows: A normalized typescript was prepared from electroprint copies of the pamphlets in the Houghton Library. (Where the electroprints were not clear, they were first checked against the pamphlet and emended.) The first carbon copy of this typescript was then collated against the electroprint copy texts twice, once each by two readers, who then conferred on their readings and transferred changes to the printer's, ribbon copy. Galley proofs were collated twice against the electroprint copy texts, once each by two readers, with the edited carbon copies close by for reference.

I SAMUEL DANFORTH'S SERMON OF 1670

AN INTRODUCTION

I

SAMUEL DANFORTH's *Errand into the Wilderness* is the seventh printed election sermon to have survived between 1634 and 1670.[1] Although the evidence is sketchy because of the paucity of early texts, it appears that by 1670 there were two general topics already established in the tradition. There were sermons on political theory concerned with such ideas as the nature of the good ruler, the meaning of liberty, the Biblical source of political ideas and types of government, and the proper relationships between Governor, Assistants, and Deputies. Jonathan Mitchel's *Nehemiah on the Wall,* 1667, is an example. A heroic Old Testament leader is singled out to exemplify the virtues of a good magistrate. Thomas Shepard's sermon in 1638, the first election sermon to have survived in any

---

[1] Samuel Danforth (1626–74) came to America with his father, Nicholas, from Suffolk, England, in 1634; when his father died four years later he was cared for by Thomas Shepard. Danforth graduated from Harvard in 1643 and remained there as Fellow until his ordination in 1650 as assistant to John Eliot at Roxbury. He was interested in astronomy, and after observing the journey of a comet in 1664, wrote an astronomical description and theological application of it. He published several almanacs, some of them containing poems. He published just one other sermon, in 1674. For biographical sketches of Danforth, see Cotton Mather, *Magnalia Christi Americana* . . . , 2 vols. (Hartford, 1820), II, 48–54; John Langdon Sibley and Clifford K. Shipton, *Biographical Sketches of Those Who Attended Harvard College,* 13 vols. (Cambridge and Boston, 1873–1965), I, 88–92; William B. Sprague, *Annals of the American Pulpit* . . . , 9 vols. (New York, 1857–69), I, 138–140.

form—in this case a manuscript of the skeletal notes for the sermon—calls upon the Deputies to beware of electing a "Bramble governor" whose roots do not penetrate deeply into religion, who offers little protection, who will in his ambition and pride scratch the Colony and hurt it, and who feeds on faction and deceit.[2]

A second general topic is what I have called the errand sermon, contrasting recent apostasy with the intentions and practice of the first settlers. William Stoughton has a succinct phrase for this topic: "New England's day and season of probation."[3] John Higginson's *The Cause of God* in 1663 is an example of this type. Point after point, he lists why Massachusetts was established and wherein it is failing to meet its goals. New England will match old England's Restoration in 1660 by a return to its own good old days. The phrase "errand into the wilderness" first occurs in Mitchel's sermon in 1667; three years later, Danforth knew a good title when he saw it.[4]

Because its title was often quoted in subsequent election sermons and because Perry Miller adopted it in 1956 as the title of a book of essays on colonial Puritanism, Danforth's sermon is already famous by hearsay.[5] It merits publication here, however, even without such advance publicity. It is beautifully written and its imagery spells out the tensions inherent in living in a "wilderness" in the Puritans' special sense of the word. Whether it was included in the volume of election sermons Hawthorne borrowed from the Salem Athenaeum is not determined, but he was astute enough to recognize in the sermons he read that the word "wilderness" was crucial, for he uses the phrase "planting in the wilderness" in describing the topic of Dimmesdale's sermon. The "wilderness" is a basic concept for the New England migration, a key word in their new enterprise. These errand sermons form an early chapter in the history of American pastoral.

[2] "Thomas Shepard's Election Sermon, in 1638," *The New-England Historical and Genealogical Register* . . . , XXIV (1870), 361–366.

[3] *New England's True Interest* . . . (Cambridge, 1670), 19.

[4] Perry Miller attributes the phrase's invention to Samuel Danforth (*Errand into the Wilderness*, Cambridge, 1956, 2), but it appears at the conclusion to Jonathan Mitchel's election sermon preached three years earlier, although not printed until 1671, *Nehemiah on the Wall* . . . (Cambridge, 1671), 28. Mitchel could have added the phrase to the printed version after he heard it from Danforth (it is italicized and in capitals), but it is just as likely that he first used the phrase in 1667.

[5] The phrase "errand into the wilderness" appears in the election sermons of Urian Oakes (1673, 33), Increase Mather (1693, 21), and William Williams (1719, 23); Benjamin Colman also refers to the "errand" (1723, 30).

II

There are two basically different versions of pastoral, whether one is speaking of the finished work of art or of the ideas and attitudes which inform it. Most pervasive in American literature is the wild or primitive pastoral of the Leatherstocking novels, *Huckleberry Finn,* and *The Bear.* Leatherstocking, Huck Finn, and Isaac McCaslin become "good" less from books and school than from the laws of the forest and by following their intuitions. Even so bookish a man as Emerson places books second to nature in his list of teachers for the American Scholar, and in his first book he speaks of "the advantage which the country-life possesses, for a powerful mind, over the artificial and curtailed life of cities." [6]

A second, earlier version of pastoral is the pre-Rousseau tradition of Ovid, Horace, *The Tempest,* and *Lycidas.* It attempts to capture the rejuvenation of withdrawal from a stereotyped, busy, and often corrupt "court" to the simple countryside or garden. However, the members of this community abhor the license of relaxed law. They wish to bring the basic virtues of the civilized world into the countryside with them: order, beauty, harmony (in musical instruments) and knowledge (in books). Shakespeare's Prospero makes it clear wherein he differs from the "natural savage" Caliban. Prospero's magic is the symbolic beauty of knowledge well used. He has the sweet reasonableness of a shepherd in the pastoral tradition; a love of beauty, righteousness, and simplicity. He has control of "natural" passions such as pride and lust; he wishes to train his daughter in the ways of those who respect order, harmony, and education as ends in themselves rather than means to worldly fame. [7]

The Puritans' version of pastoral is in the Christian humanist tradition of Shakespeare and Milton; it is *not* a first stage in the development of the primitive pastoral in America. Leatherstocking and Daniel Boone would have been put in the stocks in Puritan Boston as wild, satanic men, and if they did not mend their ways, probably exiled. "Wilderness" is in the Puritan dictionary a pejorative term. [8] The Dutch sailors who looked on

---

[6] *Nature* (1836) in *The Complete Works* . . . (Boston, 1903–4), I, 31.

[7] For discussions of *The Tempest* as a pastoral see Frank Kermode's "Introduction" to the Arden edition (New York, 1954), xi–lxxxviii, and Leo Marx's chapter "Shakespeare's American Fable" in *The Machine in the Garden: Technology and the Pastoral Ideal in America* (New York, 1964), 34–72.

[8] Alan Heimert, "Puritanism, the Wilderness, and the Frontier," *New England Quarterly,* XXVI (Sept. 1953), 361–382. George H. Williams in his chapter "The Enclosed Garden in the Wilderness of the New World" maintains that the connotations of the "wilderness" which he finds throughout the history of Christian thought

the green beauty of Manhattan island in the seventeenth century may have been "compelled into an aesthetic contemplation," as F. Scott Fitzgerald puts it in his idyllic ending to *The Great Gatsby*,[9] but any joy the Puritans experienced as they viewed the green wilderness for the first time came less from its intrinsic beauty than from thoughts of what they could *do* with it for God—how they could change it and make it into an "enclosed garden" and a "city on a hill." For a Puritan, the "wilderness" is a place of wild beasts and uncontrolled lusts, of disorder and disharmony. It is a place of darkness, the home of Satan, the meeting place for his witches and black priests. It suffers the weather of disorder; floods, drought, and tempests are more common there than the regulated weather of "ordinary providence." The Puritans had their own version of Shakespeare's "tempest music." The wilderness is a wasteland: it is dry, a desert, a place of weeds and of dead bones; here life shrivels and decays. The wilderness is not only a place or terrain, but a human condition; it is a metaphor for man's estrangement from God. Thomas Morton of Merrymount and the Pequod Indians were truly men of the wilderness in every sense of the term; and the banishment of Roger Williams and Anne Hutchinson from Boston to the forest was theologically symbolic.

The Puritans' errand into the wilderness was a new challenge in an old battle. There could be no sanctuary from Satan even in America. The New Jerusalem would come when the Puritans had replaced the wilderness with a series of many gardens; when they had imposed their order, their polity, and their men and women filled with the grace of God, on the whole land. The utopian quality of the American frontier for them lay in its being free of the European restraints to keep them from making of it what they wanted. Their new civilization would have its university, its sermons and lectures for adult education, its platform of laws; but it should also have the peace and harmony of a well-cared-for garden, the simplicity and renewal of pristine, elemental things, the constant diligence

—from the pejorative meanings of death and wasteland, through the neutral meanings of a place of testing and discipline of purgation, to the honorific meanings of a place of refuge and contemplation—are evident in colonial Puritan writing (*Wilderness and Paradise in Christian Thought*, New York, 1962, 98–131). The election sermons in Massachusetts stress the "waste and howling" wilderness of disorder. For the history of nineteenth-century ideas of the West as the attractive place of freedom, economic opportunity, and inherent virtue, see Henry Nash Smith, *Virgin Land: The American West as Symbol and Myth* (Cambridge, 1950), and Leo Marx, *The Machine in the Garden*.

[9] F. Scott Fitzgerald, *The Great Gatsby* (New York, 1953), 182.

of weeding and care. Life in the garden would, to use Thoreau's language, "front only the essential facts of life . . . . drive life into a corner, and reduce it to its lowest terms" of pure, Biblical Christianity.[10]

Errand into the Wilderness is a quiet, controlled, at times lyrical and at times dramatic, Puritan pastoral. The "wilderness" of its title is less the "place" than it is a metaphor for the threat facing New England in 1670. (For its frontier audience, however, every use of the word would remind them of the vast physical frontier surrounding them. Danforth can concentrate on the psychological and metaphysical wilderness; the physical one he can take for granted.)

The errand into the wilderness is a flight away from courtly pomp and an overly sensuous and worldly court.[11] There must be no opulence and gorgeousness of dress and ceremony in New England. John the Baptist, the hero of this sermon (and the antitype of Danforth himself, and the other old worthies now dying off), is dressed rudely and simply like a country shepherd.

A close analysis of the imagery here shows clearly the demarcation between a holy city, with its temple in the garden or vineyard, and the "wilderness" outside. Although the wilderness is first described in the neutral terms of a "woody, retired place," it is later likened to a "desert," and in a Biblical passage to "a land of darkness." The wilderness which greets the first settlers is "waste and howling." The apostasy of New England is described in terms of "lusts," "distempers," "pollution," "uncleanness." When the house of God lies waste, "floods" and "earthquakes" visit the community; the old prophets who used to stand in the gaps in the hedge surrounding the enclosed garden are dying off, letting the evil influences of the wilderness enter. The heresies against the New England Way are associated with "lime pits" and "coal pits" which one would encounter in the terrain of a wilderness. Coal pits suggest, of course, the black pits of hell.

In contrast to this cluster of images, Danforth sets off another group associated with God's vineyard—the wilderness metamorphosed by God into a noble vine. Herein is the "sweet music" of David's harp; here the weeds and thorns are separated from the good seed. (This image would

---

[10] *Walden and Other Writings of Henry David Thoreau*, ed. Brooks Atkinson (New York, 1937), 81–82.
[11] Perry Miller discusses the meanings of "errand" in his essay on Danforth's sermon, *Errand into the Wilderness*, 1–15.

have an impact on those Deputies and Assistants in the audience who were farmers of the stony New England soil.) In the vineyard Christ's people are "serious . . . sober . . . and steadfast." There is "order" in Christ's house; the children are brought up in "awe of government" and taught to restrain their "extravagancies."

Danforth closes his sermon by bringing it full circle to the dramatic form of the dialog in imitation of Christ's method in the text from Matthew 11. Danforth creates the voice of a cynic, a voice from the wilderness. The cynic has lost his way, his sense of errand; he fears that God has withdrawn his protection, but far worse, he despairs that the Lord can be attracted back again to a cleansed garden. The weeds are too high, the adversaries too great, the wall broken beyond repair.

This conclusion is functional to the psychological drama of a modern prophet in the American wilderness. In his concluding dialog Danforth recasts the New Testament situation of the growing skepticism over the prophecy of John the Baptist into the present situation of Massachusetts. In the repartee between Danforth and his cynic, the audience hears the parallel to Christ's attempt to restore the significance of John the Baptist's errand.

A BRIEF
RECOGNITION
OF
NEW-ENGLANDS
ERRAND
INTO THE
Wilderneſs;

Made in the Audience of the General Aſſembly of the
Maſſachuſets Colony, at *Boſton* in *N. E.* on the
11th of the third Moneth, 1670. being the

DAY of ELECTION
THERE.

By *Samuel Danforth*, Paſtor of the Church of
Chriſt in *Roxbury* in *N. E.*

Jer.2.2. *Go, and cry in the ears of Jeruſalem, ſaying, Thus ſaith the Lord, I*
remember thee, the kindneſs of thy youth, the love of thine eſpouſals,
when thou wenteſt after me in the wilderneſs, in a Land that was not
ſown.
3. *Iſrael was Holineſs unto the Lord, and the firſt-fruits of his increaſe—*
5. *Thus ſaith the Lord, what iniquity have your fathers found in me, that*
they are gone far from me, and have walked after vanity, and are be-
come vain ?

CAMBRIDGE:
Printed by *S. G.* and *M. J.* 1 6 7 1.

THE PREFACE

Christian Reader:

"A word spoken in due season," saith Solomon, "how good is it!" (Prov. 15. 23). And again, "A word fitly spoken is like apples of gold in pictures of silver" (Chap. 25. 11). Such were the words of our Lord Jesus, who (accommodating himself to the way of doctrine used by those eastern nations) did by parabolical discourses delight to breathe forth the deep mysteries of divine and heavenly wisdom. And how plain, but pungent, his sermons were, how perspicuous yet unspeakably profound were those oracles which flowed out of his lips of grace, none are ignorant who are not unacquainted with what the holy evangelists do harmoniously relate concerning him. No more excellent pattern than the Lord Jesus for the ministry of the New Testament to imitate; and of all the words of the sacred Scripture (though all are of equal authority, as being of the canon, yet) none seem to have a more eminent immediation of heart-commanding virtue than those which proceeded directly out of the mouth of the Lord himself; whereof this text is one, upon which the following sermon is spent. And how much of the Spirit of our Savior appears therein I need not say, and which perhaps will not, at the first dash, be discerned by the ordinary or cursory reader; "but wisdom is justified of her children" [Matt. 11. 19; Luke 7. 35]. The seasonableness and suitableness of this work which is now in thine hand, unto our present wilderness state, will commend itself unto the judicious Christian, whose heart doth indeed

54

travel with the laboring interest of the kingdom of our Lord Jesus in these ends of the earth—the text carrying with it so much heavenly argumentation, being so profitable for doctrine, for reproof, for correction, for instruction in righteousness, as though intended by our Lord Jesus for such a day as that whereon this sermon was preached (and also before such an auditory). Whoso applauds the former will not disapprove the latter; the reverend author thereof observing therein the saying of that apostolic man of God (and very judicious in his advice to younger ministers about such matters), his most reverend father of blessed memory, Mr. Wilson, viz., that he delighted in such a sermon wherein the preacher kept close unto his text and the proper scope thereof, and wandered not from it by needless excursions and impertinent enlargements.

The loss of first love, first to Christ and so to the subjects and order of his kingdom, being a radical disease too tremendously growing upon so great a part of the body of professors in this land unto a Laodicean lukewarmness in the matters of God, notwithstanding the signal and unparallel experiences of the blessing of God upon this people, a people so often saved by the Lord in the way of Moses' and Aaron's meeting and kissing one another in the Mount of God; and the observation of that declension justly calling for so meet an antidote and faithful caution, as is the ensuing sermon (οὐκ ἐν πειθοῖς ἀνθρωπίνης σοφίας λόγοις, ἀλλ' ἐν ἀποδείξει Πνεύματος καί δυνάμεως[1]) unto such, to review and consider in earnest their errand into this wilderness; and the recovery of their affections to the name of Christ in the chastity, vigor, and fervor thereof, by a thorough reformation of things in the matters of his worship, being a special duty in this hour of temptation, incumbent as on the magistracy in their sphere, so on the ministry in theirs, whereby they may declare themselves loyal to Christ in their generation work, hath no doubt inclined the heart of this servant of his to yield unto the persuasions of divers, that these his meditations might be published and so (through the blessing of God) advance that desired reformation. It is not a loose toleration nor a rigid independent separation, but an holy and brotherly reformation which all should in such an hour be endeavoring. And how perilous a skeptical indifference or a reed-like vacillation much more willful opposition to the doctrine and way of the first fathers and founders of this colony in matters of religion would be—were it only in those two points about the Magis-

---

[1] "Not in the persuasive power of human wisdom, but in the proof of power and of spirit."

trates' coercive power in matters of religion (contrary to that toleration aforesaid), and about communion of churches in synods, etc., described also by them from the Word of God in the platform of discipline (contrary to that independent separation aforesaid) [2]—will be evident to those that understand what these things mean: *scil* 1. *Quod liberi sunt spirituales a jugo potestatis secularis*; and 2. *Quod ecclesia non potest errare*.[3] It is said, I remember, that "Israel served the Lord all the days of Joshua, and all the days of the elders that outlived Joshua, and which had known all the works of the Lord, that he had done for Israel" (Josh. 24. 31). It is much to Israel's advantage in the service of God when the Lord graciously continues those who are acquainted with the first ways of such a people as hath been holiness to the Lord, and with the first works of the Lord in his laying the foundation of that glory which might dwell in their land. And it is recorded as an inlet to Israel's calamitous state, in that place where the Lord had greatly multiplied and blessed them, that "there arose up a new king which knew not Joseph" (Exod. 1. 8). When Joseph or Joshua are unknown or forgotten and the work and way of God in leading his people by the hand of Moses and Aaron in their primitive glory not understood, or not minded by these or those, how fearfully ominous to Israel must it needs be! and how necessitating the affectionate repetition, again and again, of that expostulatory, sad interrogation of our Savior, "But what went ye out into the wilderness to see?" And should there arise such another generation (as is mentioned Judges 2. 11) after our fathers are removed to rest from the warfare of the service of the tabernacle of God in their generation, as should not know the Lord nor regard the works which he hath done for our Israel, what may be expected but that (as the following context shows) "the anger of the Lord should wax hot against Israel, and that he deliver us also into the hand of spoilers," etc. [Judg. 2.

---

[2] Shepard refers here to Chapters 17, "Of the Civil Magistrates' Power in Matters Ecclesiastical," and 16, "Of Synods," in *A Platform of Church Discipline* (Cambridge, 1649); see Williston Walker, *The Creeds and Platforms of Congregationalism* (New York, 1893; Boston, 1960), 233–237. The church does not oppose, but strengthens the magistrate's jurisdiction, says the *Platform*; he in turn should not restrain the churches but help them and seek their advice and support. Magistrates have no power to "compel" their subjects to become church members and they may not "meddle with the work proper to church officers." Magistrates deal only with "acts of the outward man," not with his thoughts; but "if any church one or more shall grow schismatical, . . . or shall walk incorrigibly or obstinately in any corrupt way of their own, contrary to the rule of the Word, in such case the magistrate is to put forth his coercive power as the matter shall require."

[3] "In that holy men are free from the yoke of the secular power; in that the church cannot be mistaken."

14]? Strangers to the first intention of the people of God in their planting in this wilderness, and so to the doctrine of faith and order left in print behind them (more sure and credible than some unwritten traditions thereabout), may prove dangerous instruments to our ruin if the Lord in mercy prevent not.

It was the commendation of Timothy by Paul as also a profitable instruction and encouragement to him when he saith, "But thou hast fully known my doctrine, manner of life, purpose, faith, longsuffering, charity, patience, persecutions, afflictions, which came unto me at Antioch, at Iconium, at Lystra; what persecutions I endured: but out of them all the Lord delivered me" (II Tim. 3. 10, 11). The like may be said of this reverend servant of the Lord, my dear brother in Christ, to whom it hath seemed good παρηκολουθηκότι ἄνωθεν πᾶσιν ἀκριβῶς[4] (according to that word of wisdom which is given to him by that same Holy Spirit from whom proceed those diversities of gifts which he divides to every man severally as he will) to leave this ensuing testimony of his solicitude for the poor woman fled also into this wilderness, unto the consideration of all such as are wise-hearted in Israel. His nearness to, and intimacy with my ever honored father now with God (he being brought up with him as a son with a father), commands from my pen a glad apprehending the opportunity of performing this service of waiting upon it to the press, praying that the Lord would make the words thereof "as goads, and nails fastened by the masters of assemblies," and "given by that one Shepherd" [Eccles. 12. 11], the Lord Jesus, in whom I am

Thine, for the service of thy faith,

Thomas Shepard.

A BRIEF RECOGNITION OF
NEW ENGLAND'S ERRAND INTO THE WILDERNESS.

"What went ye out into the wilderness to see? A reed shaken with the wind?

But what went ye out for to see? A man clothed in soft raiment? Behold, they that wear soft clothing are in kings' houses.

But what went ye out for to see? A prophet? Yea, I say unto you, and more than a prophet" (Matt. 11. 7–9).

These words are our Savior's proem to his illustrious encomium of John the Baptist. John began his ministry not in Jerusalem nor in any

---

[4] "Having investigated carefully all things from the beginning."

famous city of Judea, but in the wilderness, i.e., in a woody, retired, and solitary place, thereby withdrawing himself from the envy and preposterous zeal of such as were addicted to their old traditions and also taking the people aside from the noise and tumult of their secular occasions and businesses, which might have obstructed their ready and cheerful attendance unto his doctrine. The ministry of John at first was entertained by all sorts with singular affection: There "went out to him Jerusalem, and all Judea, and all the region round about Jordan" (Matt. 3. 5); but after awhile the people's fervor abated, and John being kept under restraint divers months, his authority and esteem began to decay and languish (John 5. 35). Wherefore our Savior, taking occasion from John's messengers coming to him, after their departure gives an excellent elogy[5] and commendation of John to the intent that he might ratify and confirm his doctrine and administration and revive his authority and estimation in the hearts and consciences of the people.

This elogy our Savior begins with an elegant dialogism which the rhetorician calleth communication, gravely deliberating with his hearers and seriously enquiring to what purpose they went out into the wilderness and what expectation drew them thither.[6] Wherein we have: 1. The general question and main subject of his inquisition; 2. the particular enquiries; 3. the determination of the question.

The general question is, "What went ye out into the wilderness to see?" He saith not, "Whom went ye out to hear," but "What went ye out to see?" Θεάσασθω. The phrase agrees to shows and stage plays, plainly arguing that many of those who seemed well affected to John and flock'd after him were theatrical hearers, spectators rather than auditors; they went not to "hear," but to "see"; they went to gaze upon a new and strange spectacle.

This general question being propounded, the first particular enquiry is whether they went to see "a reed shaken with the wind?" The expression is metaphorical and proverbial. A reed when the season is calm lifts up

---

[5] *Elogy*: a brief character sketch, usually favorable; a eulogy (*NED*, III, 94).

[6] *Dialogism*: a rhetorical device whereby a subject is discussed in the form of a dialog in which opinions may be imputed and controlled by the writer: "a question is made and forthwith readily answered, as if two were talking together. . . . It stirs up attention and makes the manner manifest with delight. This our Savior used, speaking to the people of John Baptist" (Richard Bernard, *The Faithfull Shepheard*, London, 1607, 67). The "rhetorician" is probably Thomas Wilson, who discusses communication briefly in *The Arte of Rhetorique* . . . (London, 1553; Gainesville, 1962), 210. See also n. 16 below.

itself and stands upright, but no sooner doth the wind blow upon it but it shakes and trembles, bends and bows down, and then gets up again; and again it yields and bows and then lifts up itself again. A notable emblem of light, empty, and inconstant persons who in times of peace and tranquility give a fair and plausible testimony to the truth, but no sooner do the winds of temptation blow upon them and the waves of troubles roll over them but they incline and yield to the prevailing party; but when the tempest is over, they recover themselves and assert the truth again. The meaning then of this first enquiry is, "Went ye out into the wilderness to see a light, vain, and inconstant man, one that could confess and deny and deny and confess the same truth?" This interrogation is to be understood negatively and ironically, q.d., "Surely ye went not into the desert to behold such a ludicrous and ridiculous sight, a man like unto a reed shaken with the wind." Under the negation of the contrary levity our Savior sets forth one of John's excellencies, viz., his eminent constancy in asserting the truth. The winds of various temptations both on the right hand and on the left blew upon him, yet he wavered not in his testimony concerning Christ; "he confessed, and denied not; but confessed" the truth [John 1. 20].

Then the general question is repeated: "But what went ye out for to see?" and a second particular enquiry made—was it to see "a man clothed in soft raiment?" This interrogation hath also the force of a negation, q.d., "Surely ye went not into the wilderness to see a man clothed in silken and costly apparel." The reason of this is added: "Behold, they that wear soft clothing are in kings' houses." Delicate and costly apparel is to be expected in princes' courts and not in wild woods and forests. Under the negation of John's affectation of courtly delicacy our Savior sets forth another of John's excellencies, viz., his singular gravity and sobriety, who wore rough garments, and lived on coarse and mean fare (Matt. 3. 4), which austere kind of life was accommodated to the place and work of his ministry. John preached in the wilderness which was no fit place for silken and soft raiment. His work was to prepare a people for the Lord, by calling them off from worldly pomp and vanities, unto repentance and mourning for sin. His peculiar habit and diet was such as became a penitentiary preacher.

Thirdly, the general question is reiterated: "But what went ye out for to see?" and a third particular enquiry made—was it to see "a prophet"? This interrogation is to be understood affirmatively, q.d., no doubt but it was to see "a prophet." Had not John been a rare and excellent minister of God, you would never have gone out of your cities into the desert to have seen him. Thus our Savior sets forth another of John's admirable excellencies, viz., his prophetical office and function. John was not an ordinary interpreter of the Law, much less a teacher of Jewish traditions, but "a prophet," one who by the extraordinary inspiration of the Holy Ghost, made known the mysteries of salvation (Luke 1. 76, 77).

Lastly, our Savior determines and concludes the question: He whom ye went out to see was "more than a prophet," περισσότερον προφήτου,[7] much more or abundantly more than a prophet. This he confirms by his wonted asseveration, "Yea, I say unto you, and much more than a prophet." How was John much more than a prophet? John was Christ's herald sent immediately before his face to proclaim his coming and kingdom and prepare the people for the reception of him by the baptism of repentance (ver. 10).[8] Hence it follows: "Among all that are born of women there hath not risen a greater prophet than John" (ver. 11). John was greater than any of the prophets that were before him, not in respect of his personal graces and virtues (for who shall persuade us that he excelled Abraham in the grace of faith, who was the father of the faithful, or Moses in meekness, who was the meekest man on earth, or David in faithfulness, who was a man after God's own heart, or Solomon in wisdom, who was the wisest man that ever was or shall be?), but in respect of the manner of his dispensation. All the prophets foretold Christ's coming, his sufferings and glory, but the Baptist was his harbinger and forerunner that bare the sword before him, proclaimed his presence, and made room for him in the hearts of the people. All the prophets saw Christ afar off, but the Baptist saw him present, baptized him, and applied the types to him personally. "Behold the Lamb of God. He saw, and bare record that this is the Son of God" (John 1. 29, 34). "But he that is least in the kingdom of heaven is greater than John" [Matt. 11. 11; Luke 7. 28]. The least prophet in the kingdom of heaven, i.e., the least minister of the Gospel since Christ's ascension, is greater than John; not in respect of the measure of his personal gifts nor in respect of the manner of his calling, but in respect of the object of his ministry, Christ on the throne having finished the

[7] The Greek in the pamphlet is not clear; the phrase from the Greek New Testament, Matt. 11. 9, is reproduced here.

[8] This is the first of several instances where Danforth gives his reference as merely "ver." This should be read as *ibid.*, referring to the chapter last quoted (here, his text, Matthew 11). His short form is retained here.

work of our redemption, and in respect of the degree of the revelation of Christ, which is far more clear and full. John showed Christ in the flesh and pointed to him with his finger, but the ministers of the Gospel declare that he hath done and suffered all things necessary to our salvation and is risen again and set down at the right hand of God.

Doctrine. *Such as have sometime left their pleasant cities and habitations to enjoy the pure worship of God in a wilderness are apt in time to abate and cool in their affection thereunto; but then the Lord calls upon them seriously and thoroughly*[9] *to examine themselves, what it was that drew them into the wilderness, and to consider that it was not the expectation of ludicrous levity nor of courtly pomp and delicacy, but of the free and clear dispensation of the Gospel and kingdom of God.*

This doctrine consists of two distinct branches; let me open them severally.

Branch I. Such as have sometime left their pleasant cities and habitations to enjoy the pure worship of God in a wilderness are apt in time to abate and cool in their affection thereunto. To what purpose did the children of Israel leave their cities and houses in Egypt and go forth into the wilderness? Was it not to "hold a feast to the Lord," and to "sacrifice to the God of their fathers"? That was the only reason which they gave of their motion to Pharaoh (Exod. 5. 1, 3); but how soon did they forget their errand into the wilderness and corrupt themselves in their own inventions? Within a few months after their coming out of Egypt, "they make a calf in Horeb, and worship the molten image, and change their glory into the similitude of an ox that eateth grass" (Psal. 106. 19, 20; Exod. 32. 7, 8). Yea, for the space of forty years in the wilderness, while they pretended to sacrifice to the Lord, they indeed worshipped the stars and the host of heaven and together with the Lord's tabernacle carried about with them the tabernacle of Moloch (Amos 5. 25, 26; Acts 7. 42, 43). And how did they spend their time in the wilderness but in tempting God and in murmuring against their godly and faithful teachers and rulers, Moses and Aaron (Psal. 95. 8)? To what purpose did the children of the captivity upon Cyrus his proclamation, leave their houses which they

[9] The pamphlet has "throughly," but since this word was synonymous in the seventeenth century with *thoroughly* in the meaning of wholly, or completely, and *throughly* is now obsolete, the modern word is substituted here, and silently throughout the edition (see *NED*, IX, 337, 375).

had built and their vineyards and oliveyards which they had planted in the province of Babylon and return to Judea and Jerusalem, which were now become a wilderness? Was it not that they might build the house of God at Jerusalem and set up the temple-worship? But how shamefully did they neglect that great and honorable work for the space of above forty years? They pretended that God's time was not come to build his house because of the rubs and obstructions which they met with, whereas all their difficulties and discouragements hindered not their building of stately houses for themselves (Hag. 1. 2–4). To what purpose did Jerusalem and all Judea and all the region round about Jordan leave their several cities and habitations and flock into the wilderness of Judea? Was it not to see that burning and shining light which God had raised up? To hear his heavenly doctrine and partake of that new sacrament which he administered? O how they were affected with his rare and excellent gifts! with his clear, lively, and powerful ministry! The kingdom of heaven pressed in upon them with a holy violence and the violent, the zealous, and affectionate hearers of the Gospel took it by force (Matt. 11. 12; Luke 16. 16). They leapt over all discouragements and impediments, whether outward, as legal rites and ceremonies, or inward, the sense of their own sin and unworthiness, and pressed into the kingdom of God as men rush into a theater to see a pleasant sight or as soldiers run into a besieged city to take the spoil thereof; but their hot fit is soon over, their affection lasted but for an hour, i.e., a short season (John 5. 35).

Reason 1. Because the affection of many to the ministry of the Gospel and the pure worship of God is built upon temporary and transitory grounds, as the novelty and strangeness of the matter, the rareness and excellency of ministerial gifts, the voice of the people, the countenance of great men, and the hope of worldly advantage. The Jews had lain in ignorance and darkness a long time, being trained up under the superstitious observances of their old traditions which were vain, empty, and unprofitable customs, and the Church wanted the gift of prophecy about four hundred years; and therefore when John the Baptist arose like a bright and burning light shining amongst them with admirable gifts of the Spirit and extraordinary severity and gravity of manners, proclaiming the coming and kingdom of the Messias (which had been oft promised and long expected) and pressing the people to repentance and good works, O how they admire and reverence him, especially when grown popular and countenanced by Herod the Tetrarch. What sweet affections are kindled! what great expectations are raised! what ravishing joy is conceived! hoping (as it's probable) to make use of his authority to cast off the Roman yoke and recover their civil liberties, riches, and honors. But after a little acquaintance with John (for he was a public preacher but a year and half), his doctrine, administrations, and prophetical gifts grew common and stale things and of little esteem with them—especially when they saw their carnal hopes frustrated, the rulers disaffected, and Herod's countenance and carriage toward him changed.

Reason 2. Because prejudices and offenses are apt to arise in the hearts of many against the faithful dispensers of the Gospel. The Pharisees and lawyers came among others to the baptism of John, but when they hear his sharp reprehensions of their viperous opinions and practices, they nauseate his doctrine, repudiate his baptism, calumniate his conversation (Luke 7. 30). Herodias hath an inward grudge and a quarrel against him because he found fault with her incestuous marriage (Mark 6. 19). Yea that very age and generation of the Jews were like to a company of surly, sullen, and froward children whom no music can please; they neither dance after the pipe nor make lamentation after the mourner. They inveigh against John's austerity, saying that he was transported with diabolical fury and was an enemy to human society, and they do as much distaste and abhor Christ's gentleness and familiarity, traducing him as being a sensual and voluptuous person given to intemperance and luxury and a patron and abetter of looseness and profaneness (Matt. 11. 16–19). Thus doth the frowardness and stubbornness of man resist and oppose the wisdom and goodness of God who useth various ways and instruments to compass poor sinners; but they through their folly and perverseness, frustrate, disannul, and abrogate the counsel of God against themselves. The evil spirit that troubled Saul was quieted and allayed by the sweet melody of David's harp; but the mad and outrageous fury that transports men against the truth and the ministry thereof cannot be quieted and allayed by the voice of the charmers, charm they never so wisely.

Branch II. When men abate and cool in their affection to the pure worship of God which they went into the wilderness to enjoy, the Lord calls upon them seriously and thoroughly to examine themselves, what it was that drew them into the wilderness, and to consider that it was not the expectation of ludicrous levity nor of courtly pomp and delicacy, but of the free and clear dispensation of the Gospel and kingdom of God.

Our Savior knowing that the people had lost their first love and singular affection to the revelation of his grace by the ministry of his herald John, he is very intense in examining them, what expectation drew them into the wilderness. He doth not once nor twice but thrice propound that question, "What went ye out into the wilderness to see?" Yea in particular he enquires whether it were to see a man that was like to "a reed shaken with the wind," or whether it were to see "a man clothed like a courtier," or whether it were to see a "prophet," and then determines the question, concluding that it was to see a great and excellent prophet and that had not they seen rare and admirable things in him they would never have gone out into the wilderness unto him.

The reason is because the serious consideration of the inestimable grace and mercy of God in the free and clear dispensation of the Gospel and kingdom of God is a special means to convince men of their folly and perverseness in undervaluing the same, and a sanctified remedy to recover their affections thereunto. The Lord foreseeing the defection of Israel after Moses his death, commands him to write that prophetical song recorded in Deuteronomy 32 as a testimony against them, wherein the chief remedy which he prescribes for the prevention and healing of their apostasy is their calling to remembrance God's great and signal love in manifesting himself to them in the wilderness, in conducting them safely and mercifully, and giving them possession of their promised inheritance (ver. 7–14). And when Israel was apostatized and fallen, the Lord, to convince them of their ingratitude and folly, brings to their remembrance his deliverance of them out of Egypt, his leading them through the wilderness for the space of forty years, and not only giving them possession of their enemies' land but also raising up even of their own sons, prophets, faithful and eminent ministers, and of their young men Nazarites, who being separated from worldly delights and encumbrances were patterns of purity and holiness—all which were great and obliging mercies. Yea the Lord appeals to their own consciences whether these his favors were not real and signal (Amos 2. 10, 11). The prophet Jeremiah, that he might reduce the people from their backslidings, cries in the ears of Jerusalem with earnestness and boldness, declaring unto them that the Lord remembered how well they stood affected towards him when he first chose them to be his people and espoused them to himself; how they followed him in the wilderness and kept close to him in their long and wearisome passage through the uncultured desert; how they were then consecrated to God and set apart for his worship and service, as the first fruits are wont to be sequestered and devoted to God; and thereupon expostulates with them for their forsaking the Lord, and following after their idols (Jer. 2. 2, 3, 5, 6). Surely our Savior's dialogism with his hearers in my text is not a mere rhetorical elegancy to adorn his testimony concerning John, but a clear and strong conviction of their folly in slighting and despising that which they sometime so highly pretended unto, and a wholesome admonition and direction how to recover their primitive affection to his doctrine and administration.

Use I. Of solemn and serious enquiry to us all in this general assembly is * whether we have not in a great measure forgotten our errand into the wilderness. You have solemnly professed before God, angels, and men that the cause of your leaving your country, kindred, and fathers' houses and transporting yourselves with your wives, little ones, and substance over the vast ocean into this waste and howling wilderness, was your liberty to walk in the faith of the Gospel with all good conscience according to the order of the Gospel, and your enjoyment of the pure worship of God according to his institution without human mixtures and impositions. Now let us sadly consider whether our ancient and primitive affections to the Lord Jesus, his glorious Gospel, his pure and spiritual worship, and the order of his house, remain, abide, and continue firm, constant, entire, and inviolate. Our Savior's reiteration of this question, "What went ye out into the wilderness to see?" is no idle repetition but a sad conviction of our dullness and backwardness to this great duty and a clear demonstration of the weight and necessity thereof. It may be a grief to us to be put upon such an inquisition, as it is said of Peter, "Peter was grieved because he said unto him the third time, Lovest thou me?" (John 21. 17); but the Lord knoweth that a strict and rigid examination of our hearts in this point is no more than necessary. Wherefore let us call to remembrance the former days and consider whether "it was not then better with us than it is now" [Hos. 2. 7].

In our first and best times the kingdom of heaven brake in upon us with a holy violence and every man pressed into it. What mighty efficacy and power had the clear and faithful dispensation of the Gospel upon your hearts? How affectionately and zealously did you entertain the kingdom of God? How careful were you, even all sorts, young and old, high and low, to take hold of the opportunities of your spiritual good and edification, ordering your secular affairs (which were wreathed and twisted together with great variety) so as not to interfere with your general calling, but that you might attend upon the Lord without distraction? How diligent and faithful in preparing your hearts for the reception of the Word, "laying apart all filthiness and superfluity of naughtiness," that you might "receive with meekness the ingraffed [10] word, which is able to save your souls" [Jas. 1. 21], "and purging out all malice, guile, hypocrisies, envies, and all evil speakings, and as newborn babes, desiring the sincere milk of the Word, that ye might grow thereby" [I Pet. 2. 1, 2]? How attentive in hearing the everlasting Gospel, "watching daily at the gates of wisdom, and waiting at the posts of her doors, that ye might find eternal life, and obtain favor of the Lord" [Prov. 8. 34, 35]? Gleaning day by day in the field of God's ordinances, even among the sheaves, and gathering up handfuls, which the Lord let fall of purpose for you, and at night going home and beating out what you had gleaned, by meditation, repetition, conference, and therewith feeding yourselves and your families. How painful were you in recollecting, repeating, and discoursing of what you heard, whetting the Word of God upon the hearts of your children, servants, and neighbors? How fervent in prayer to almighty God for his divine blessing upon the seed sown, that it might take root and fructify? O what a reverent esteem had you in those days of Christ's faithful ambassadors that declared unto you the word of reconciliation! "How beautiful" were "the feet of them that preached the Gospel of peace, and brought the glad tidings of salvation!" [Rom. 10. 15]. You "esteemed them highly in love for their work's sake" [I Thess. 5. 13]. Their persons, names, and comforts were precious in your eyes; you counted yourselves blessed in the enjoyment of a pious, learned, and orthodox ministry; and though you ate the bread of adversity and drank the water of affliction, yet you rejoiced in this, that your eyes saw your teachers, they were not removed into corners, and your ears heard a word behind you saying, "This is the way, walk ye in it," when you turned to the right hand and when you turned to the left (Isa. 30. 20, 21). What earnest and ardent desires had you in those days after communion with Christ in the holy sacraments? With desire you desired to partake of the seals of the covenant. You thought your evidences for heaven not sure nor authentic unless the broad seals of the kingdom were annexed. What solicitude was there in those days to "seek the Lord after the right order" [I Chron. 15.

[10] *Ingraffed*: a variant of engrafted, that which is grafted in, implanted, incorporated (*NED*, III, 81). The King James Bible has here "engrafted."

13]? What searching of the holy Scriptures, what collations among your leaders, both in their private meetings and public councils and synods, to find out the order which Christ hath constituted and established in his house? [11] What fervent zeal was there then against sectaries and heretics and all manner of heterodoxies? "You could not bear them that were evil" [Rev. 2. 2] but tried them that pretended to new light and revelations, and found them liars.[12] What pious care was there of sister churches, that those that wanted breasts might be supplied and that those that wanted peace, their dissensions might be healed? What readiness was there in those days to call for the help of neighbor elders and brethren in case of any difference or division that could not be healed at home? What reverence was there then of the sentence of a council as being decisive and issuing the controversy, according to that ancient proverbial saying, "They shall surely ask counsel at Abel: and so they ended the matter" (II Sam. 20. 18)? What holy endeavors were there in those days to propagate religion to your children and posterity, training them up in the nurture and admonition of the Lord, keeping them under the awe of government, restraining their enormities and extravagancies, charging them to know the God of their fathers and serve him with a perfect heart and willing mind, and publicly asserting and maintaining their interest in the Lord and in his holy covenant and zealously opposing those that denied the same?

And then had the churches "rest" throughout the several colonies and were "edified; and walking in the fear of the Lord, and in the comfort of

[11] There were by 1670 three memorable synods in Massachusetts history—in 1637, to deal with Rev. John Wheelwright's charges in the Antinomian and Anne Hutchinson crisis; in 1647–48 when the Westminster Confession of Faith and a Platform of Church Discipline were adopted; and in 1662 when during March, June, and September, a synod adopted among other matters of church discipline the controversial "Half-Way Covenant." Texts of the 1648 *Platform,* and *Propositions Concerning the Subject of Baptism*, the major result of the synod of 1662, are in Walker, *The Creeds and Platforms of Congregationalism*, 194–237, 301–339.

[12] Some of the more famous "heretics" who were tried and banished are Thomas Morton of Merrymount, sent to England from Plymouth in 1628 and again in 1630, finally jailed in Boston in 1643; Roger Williams, banished from Boston by an order of the General Court in October 1635 (who then founded Providence in 1636); Samuel Gorton, banished from Boston in 1637 and again in 1644; John Wheelwright, the minister colleague of John Cotton, banished from Boston in November 1637; Anne Hutchinson, banished in early spring 1638, when she went to Rhode Island. Dr. Robert Child was not banished, but was found guilty of heresy and sedition in 1647 and charged such a large fine of £200 ("equal in purchasing power to fifteen or twenty thousand dollars to-day," writes Professor Morison in 1930), that he "departed from our shores forever" (*Builders of the Bay Colony*, Boston, 1930, 260).

the Holy Ghost, were multiplied" [Acts 9. 31]. O how your faith grew exceedingly! You proceeded from faith to faith, from a less to a greater degree and measure, growing up in him who is our head and receiving abundance of grace and of the gift of righteousness, that you might reign in life by Jesus Christ. O how your love and charity towards each other abounded! O what comfort of love! What bowels and mercies![13] What affectionate care was there one of another! What a holy sympathy in crosses and comforts, weeping with those that wept and rejoicing with those that rejoiced!

But who is there left among you that saw these churches in their first glory and how do you see them now? Are they not in your eyes in comparison thereof as nothing? "How is the gold become dim! how is the most fine gold changed!" [Lam. 4. 1]. Is not the temper, complexion, and countenance of the churches strangely altered? Doth not a careless, remiss, flat, dry, cold, dead frame of spirit grow in upon us secretly, strongly, prodigiously? They that have ordinances are as though they had none; and they that hear the Word as though they heard it not; and they that pray as though they prayed not; and they that receive sacraments as though they received them not; and they that are exercised in the holy things using them by the by as matters of custom and ceremony, so as not to hinder their eager prosecution of other things which their hearts are set upon. Yea and in some particular congregations amongst us is there not instead of a sweet smell, a stink; and instead of a girdle, a rent; and instead of a stomacher,[14] a girding with sackcloth; and burning instead of beauty?[15] Yea "the vineyard is all overgrown with thorns, and nettles

[13] Bowels were considered the seat of the tender and sympathetic emotions; hence the word became synonymous with pity, compassion, heart. It is used in this sense often in the 1611 King James Bible; see for example "bowels of mercies," Col. 3. 12 (*NED*, I, 1031).

[14] *Stomacher*: a kind of waistcoat worn by men (usually, in the sixteenth and seventeenth centuries, of fur or lamb's skin) to protect the chest against the cold. The word also designated a medicated cloth applied to the chest (*NED*, IX, 1006).

[15] The "stink" and "rent" in "some particular congregations" is probably an allusion to the secession of a minority of the First Church congregation over appointment of John Davenport as its minister. After bitterness and subterfuge in Davenport's release from New Haven and his invitation to Boston, a group broke from the First Church and formed the Third or Old South Church at Charlestown on May 12, 1669. Danforth knew of this "rent" at first hand, for Davenport had written a letter to the church at Roxbury to dispel "reports that may be bruited" and to ask for advice. For a brief account of this dispute, see the "Biographical Sketch," *Letters of John Davenport*, ed. Isabel M. Calder (New Haven, 1937), 10–12, and the letters on 280ff. See also Perry Miller, *The New England Mind: From Colony to Province* (Cambridge, 1953), 106–108.

cover the face thereof, and the stone wall thereof is broken down" (Prov. 24. 31). Yea and that which is the most sad and certain sign of calamity approaching: "Iniquity aboundeth, and the love of many waxeth cold" (Matt. 24. 12). Pride, contention, worldliness, covetousness, luxury, drunkenness, and uncleanness break in like a flood upon us and good men grow cold in their love to God and to one another. If a man be cold in his bed let them lay on the more clothes that he may get heat; but we are like to David in his old age: "They covered him with clothes, but he gat no heat" (I Kings 1. 1 *). The Lord heaps mercies, favors, blessings upon us and loads us daily with his benefits, but all his love and bounty cannot heat and warm our hearts and affections. Well the furnace is able to heat and melt the coldest iron; but how oft hath the Lord cast us into the hot furnace of affliction and tribulation and we have been scorched and burnt, yet not melted but hardened thereby (Isa. 63. 17)? How long hath God kept us in the furnace day after day, month after month,* year after year? But all our afflictions, crosses, trials have not been able to keep our hearts in a warm temper.

Now let me freely deliberate with you what may be the causes and grounds of such decays and languishings in our affections to, and estimation of, that which we came into the wilderness to enjoy. Is it because "there is no bread, neither is there any water; and our soul loatheth this light bread" (Num. 21. 5)? "Our soul is dried away: and there is nothing at all, besides this manna, before our eyes" (Num. 11. 6). What, is manna no bread? Is this angelical food light bread which cannot satisfy but starves the soul? Doth our soul loathe the bread of heaven? The Lord be merciful to us; the full soul loatheth the honeycomb (Prov. 27. 7).

What then is the cause of our decays and languishings? Is it because the Spirit of the Lord is straitened and limited in the dispensers of the Gospel and hence our joys and comforts are lessened and shortened? "O thou that art named the house of Jacob, is the spirit of the Lord straitened? Are those his doings? Do not my words do good to him that walketh uprightly?" (Mic. 2. 7). Surely it is not for want of fullness in the Spirit of God that he withholds comforts and blessings from any; neither doth he delight in threatenings and judgments, but his words both promise and perform that which is good and comfortable to them that walk uprightly. The Spirit is able to enlarge itself unto the reviving and cheering of every man's heart; and that should we experience did not our iniquity put a bar. "O ye Corinthians, our mouth is open unto you, our heart is enlarged.

69

Ye are not straitened in us, but ye are straitened in your own bowels"
(II Cor. 6. 11, 12). The Spirit of God dilateth and enlargeth the heart of
the faithful ministry for the good of the people; but many times the people
are straitened in their own bowels and cannot receive such a large portion
as the Lord hath provided for them. What then is the cause of our coolings,
faintings, and languishings? The grand and principal cause is our unbelief.
We believe not the grace and power of God in Christ. Where is that lively
exercise of faith which ought to be in our attendance upon the Lord in his
holy ordinances? Christ came to Nazareth with his heart full of love and
compassion and his hands full of blessings to bestow upon his old acquaintance and neighbors among whom he had been brought up; but
their unbelief restrained his tender mercies and bound his omnipotent
hands, that he could not do any great or illustrious miracle amongst them.
"He could do there no mighty work. . . . And he marvelled because
of their unbelief" (Matt. 13. 58; Mark 6. 5, 6). Unbelief straitens the
grace and power of Christ and hinders the communication of divine favors and special mercies. The Word preached profits not when it is not
mixed with faith in them that hear it (Heb. 4. 2). We may pray earnestly,
but if we ask not in faith, how can we expect to receive anything of the
Lord (Jas. 1. 6, 7)?

But though unbelief be the principal yet it is not the sole cause of our
decays and languishings; inordinate worldly cares, predominant lusts, and
malignant passions and distempers stifle and choke the Word and quench
our affections to the kingdom of God (Luke 8. 14). The manna was
gathered early in the morning; when the sun waxed hot, it melted (Exod.
16. 21). It was a fearful judgment on Dathan and Abiram that the earth
opened its mouth and swallowed them up. How many professors of
religion are swallowed up alive by earthly affections? Such as escape the
lime pit of Pharisaical hypocrisy fall into the coal pit of Sadducean atheism and epicurism. Pharisaism and Sadduceism do almost divide the professing world between them. Some split upon the rock of affected ostenta-
tion of singular piety and holiness and others are drawn into the whirl-
pool and perish in the gulf of sensuality and luxury.

If any question how seasonable such a discourse may be upon such a
day as this, let him consider Haggai 2. 10–14:

In the four and twentieth day of the ninth month, in the second year of
Darius, came the word of the Lord by Haggai the prophet, saying, Thus
saith the Lord of hosts; Ask now the priests concerning the law, saying,

If one bear holy flesh in the skirt of his garment, and with his skirt do touch bread, or pottage, or wine, or oil, or any meat, shall it be holy? And the priests answered and said, No. Then said Haggai, If one that is unclean by a dead body touch any of these, shall it be unclean? And the priests answered and said, It shall be unclean. Then answered Haggai, and said, So is this people, and so is this nation before me, saith the Lord; and so is every work of their hands; and that which they offer there is unclean.

It was an high and great day wherein the prophet spake these words and an holy and honorable work which the people were employed in. For this day they laid the foundation of the Lord's temple (ver. 18). Nevertheless, the Lord saw it necessary this very day to represent and declare unto them the pollution and uncleanness both of their persons and of their holy services, that they might be deeply humbled before God and carry on their present work more holily and purely. What was their uncleanness? Their eager pursuit of their private interests took off their hearts and affections from the affairs of the house of God. It seems they pleased themselves with this, that the altar stood upon its bases and sacrifices were daily offered thereon and the building of the temple was only deferred until a fit opportunity were afforded, free from disturbance and opposition; and having now gained such a season they are ready to build the temple. But the Lord convinceth them out of the Law that their former negligence was not expiated by their daily sacrifices, but the guilt thereof rendered both the nation and this holy and honorable work which they were about vile and unclean in the sight of God. And having thus shown them their spiritual uncleanness, he encourageth them to go on with the work in hand, the building of the temple, promising them from this day to bless them (ver. 19*).

Use II. Of exhortation, to excite and stir us all up to attend and prosecute our errand into the wilderness. To what purpose came we into this place and what expectation drew us hither? Surely not the expectation of ludicrous levity. We came not hither to see "a reed shaken with the wind." Then let not us be reeds—light, empty, vain, hollow-hearted professors, shaken with every wind of temptation—but solid, serious, and sober Christians, constant and steadfast in the profession and practice of the truth, "trees of righteousness, the planting of the Lord, that he may be glorified" [Isa. 61. 3], holding fast the profession of our faith without wavering.

71

"Alas there is such variety and diversity of opinions and judgments that we know not what to believe." [16]

Were there not as various and different opinions touching the person of Christ even in the days of his flesh? Some said that he was John the Baptist, some Elias, others Jeremias, or one of the old prophets. Some said he was a gluttonous man and a wine-bibber, a friend of publicans and sinners; others said he was a Samaritan and had a devil; yet the disciples knew what to believe. "Whom say ye that I am? Thou art Christ, the Son of the living God" (Matt. 16. 15, 16). The various heterodox opinions of the people serve as a foil or tinctured leaf to set off the luster and beauty of the orthodox and apostolical faith. This is truly commendable, when in such variety and diversity of apprehensions you are not biased by any sinister respects, but discern, embrace, and profess the truth as it is in Christ Jesus.

But to what purpose came we into the wilderness and what expectation drew us hither? Not the expectation of courtly pomp and delicacy. We came not hither to see men clothed like courtiers. The affectation of courtly pomp and gallantry is very unsuitable in a wilderness. Gorgeous attire is comely in princes' courts if it exceed not the limits of Christian sobriety; but excess in kings' houses escapes not divine vengeance. "I will punish the princes, and the kings' children, and all such as are clothed with strange apparel" (Zeph. 1. 8). The pride and haughtiness of the ladies of Zion in their superfluous ornaments and stately gestures brought wrath upon themselves, upon their husbands, and upon their children, yea and upon the whole land (Isa. 3. 16–26). How much more intolerable and abominable is excess of this kind in a wilderness, where we are so far removed from the riches and honors of princes' courts? [17]

[16] At this point Danforth begins his own "dialogism" or "communication" by creating the persona of a cynic who interjects questions and defeatist opinions for the remainder of the sermon so that the minister can answer them. The cynic's words are italicized in the printed pamphlet. By inflecting his voice in the pulpit for the cynic's part Danforth could easily dramatize the dialog for his audience.

[17] In his election sermon of 1673, Urian Oakes also condemns the "garish attire, in affected trimmings and adornings" of those dressing "beyond what their state and condition will allow," and exceeding "their rank and degree (whereas one end of apparel is to distinguish and put a difference between persons according to their places and conditions)" (*New-England Pleaded With* . . . , Cambridge, 1673, 34). The manifesto of the "Reforming Synod" of 1679 also included in its list of "evils that have provoked the Lord," in the second category, "pride in respect to apparel." Again the complaint is twofold: "the poorer sort of people" are dressing beyond their "estates," and "many, not of the meaner sort, have offended God by strange apparel, not becoming serious Christians."

To what purpose then came we into the wilderness and what expectation drew us hither? Was it not the expectation of the pure and faithful dispensation of the Gospel and kingdom of God? The times were such that we could not enjoy it in our own land, and therefore having obtained liberty and a gracious patent from our Sovereign, we left our country, kindred, and fathers' houses, and came into these wild woods and deserts where the Lord hath planted us and made us "dwell in a place of our own, that we might move no more, and that the children of wickedness might not afflict us any more" (II Sam. 7. 10). What is it that distinguisheth New England from other colonies and plantations in America? Not our transportation over the Atlantic Ocean, but the ministry of God's faithful prophets and the fruition of his holy ordinances. Did not the Lord bring "the Philistines from Caphtor, and the Assyrians from Kir" as well as "Israel from the land of Egypt" (Amos 9. 7)? But "by a prophet the Lord brought Israel out of Egypt, and by a prophet was he preserved" (Hos. 12. 13). What, is the price and esteem of God's prophets and their faithful dispensations now fallen in our hearts?

The hardships, difficulties, and sufferings which you have exposed yourselves unto that you might dwell in the house of the Lord and leave your little ones under the shadow of the wings of the God of Israel, have not been few nor small. And shall we now withdraw ourselves and our little ones from under those healing wings and lose that full reward which the Lord hath in his heart and hand to bestow upon us? Did we not with Mary choose this for our part, "to sit at Christ's feet, and hear his word" [Luke 10. 39]? And do we now repent of our choice and prefer the honors, pleasures, and profits of the world before it? "You did run well; who doth hinder you that you should not obey the truth?" (Gal. 5. 7).

Hath the Lord been wanting to us or failed our expectation? "O my people, what have I done unto thee? and wherein have I wearied thee? testify against me" (Mic. 6. 3). "What iniquity have your fathers found in me, that they are gone far from me? O generation, see ye the word of the Lord. Have I been a wilderness unto Israel? a land of darkness?" (Jer. 2. 5, and ver. 31). May not the Lord say unto us, as Pharaoh did to Hadad: "What hast thou lacked with me, that, behold, thou seekest to go to thine own country?" (I Kings 11. 22). Nay, "what could have been done more" than what the Lord hath done for us (Isa. 5. 4)?

How sadly hath the Lord testified against us because of our loss of our first love and our remissness and negligence in his work? Why hath the

Lord smitten us with blasting and mildew now seven years together, super-adding sometimes severe drought, sometimes great tempests, floods, and sweeping rains that leave no food behind them? Is it not because the Lord's house lyeth waste, temple-work in our hearts, families, churches is shamefully neglected? What should I make mention of signs in the heavens and in the earth—blazing stars, earthquakes, dreadful thunders and lightnings, fearful burnings?[18] What meaneth the heat of his great anger in calling home so many of his ambassadors? In plucking such burning and shining lights out of the candlesticks; the principal stakes out of our hedges; the cornerstones out of our walls? In removing such faithful shepherds from their flocks and breaking down our defensed cities, iron pillars, and brazen walls? Seemeth it a small thing unto us that so many of God's prophets (whose ministry we came into the wilderness to enjoy) are taken from us in so short a time?[19] Is it not a sign that God is making a way for his wrath when he removes his chosen out of the gap? Doth he not threaten us with a famine of the Word, the scattering of the flock, the breaking of the candlesticks, and the turning of the songs of the temple into howlings?

It is high time for us to "remember whence we are fallen, and repent, and do our first works" [Rev. 2. 5]. Wherefore let us "lift up the hands

[18] References to unusual weather and astronomical phenomena are conventional in providential histories and sermons, but in this case Danforth was more than casually interested in such calamities as he mentions here. He kept records and wrote four almanacs printed in Cambridge, 1646–49, in which he documents earthquakes, tempests, droughts, and meteors. See for example his *An Astronomical Description of the Late Comet* (1665), an excerpt from which appears in *American Thought and Writing*, ed. Russel B. Nye and Norman S. Grabo, 2 vols. (Boston, 1965), I, 423–427. The summer of 1669 was unusually hard on grain according to Rev. Simon Bradstreet's *Journal*: "Blastings of all sorts of grain. Greater scarcity having not been known for many years" (*New-England Historical and Genealogical Register . . . ,* VIII, Boston, 1854, 327).

[19] Three famous ministers of the first generation of colonists had died within the past two years. Jonathan Mitchel (who preached the election sermon at Boston in 1667) had died in 1668, and Richard Mather, the father of Increase, in 1669. The third, John Davenport, had just come from Connecticut to take the most distinguished pulpit in Boston at the First Church after John Wilson's death in 1667; he died a few months later, in March 1670, only two months before Danforth preached this sermon. Three sons who had followed their famous fathers as ministers had died recently: Samuel Shepard, son of the beloved Thomas of Cambridge, and John Eliot, son of the Indian missionary, both in 1668; Eleazar Mather, son of Richard, died in 1669, the same year as his father. The cutting down in their prime of a new generation of Shepards, Eliots, and Mathers must have seemed ominous. Still, lament over the apparently extra-heavy recent loss of ministers is conventional in the errand sermons and other treatises on "God's controversy with New England" in the 1660–1720 years.

that hang down, and strengthen the feeble knees; And make straight paths for our feet, lest that which is lame be turned out of the way; but let it rather be healed" (Heb. 12. 12, 13). Labor we to redress our faintings and swervings and address ourselves to the work of the Lord. Let us arise and build and the Lord will be with us and from this day will he bless us.

"Alas, we are feeble and impotent; our hands are withered and our strength dried up."

Remember the man that had a withered hand; Christ saith unto him, "Stretch forth thy hand. And he stretched it forth; and it was restored whole, like as the other" (Matt. 12. 13). How could he stretch forth his hand when it was withered, the blood and spirits dried up and the nerves and sinews shrunk up? The almighty power of Christ accompanying his command enabled the man to stretch forth his withered hand and in stretching it forth, restored it whole like as the other. Where the sovereignty of Christ's command takes place in the conscience there is effectual grace accompanying it to the healing of our spiritual feebleness and impotency and the enabling of us to perform the duty incumbent on us. Though we have no might, no strength, yet at Christ's command, make an essay. Where the word of a king is, there is power.

"But alas, our bruise is incurable and our wound grievous; there is none to repair the breach, there is no healing medicine."

The Lord Jesus, the great Physician of Israel, hath undertaken the cure. "I will restore health unto thee, and I will heal thee of thy wounds, saith the Lord" (Jer. 30. 17). No case is to be accounted desperate or incurable which Christ takes in hand. If he undertake to heal Jairus his daughter he will have her death esteemed but a sleep, in reference to his power. "She is not dead, but sleepeth" (Matt. 9. 24). When Christ came to Lazarus his grave and bade them take away the stone, "Martha saith, Lord, by this time he stinketh: for he hath been dead four days." But Christ answereth, "Said I not unto thee, that, if thou wouldest believe, thou shouldest see the glory of God?" (John 11. [39], 40). Let us give glory to God by believing his Word and we shall have real and experimental manifestations of his glory for our good and comfort.

"But alas, our hearts are sadly prejudiced against the means and instruments by which we might expect that Christ should cure and heal us."

Were not the hearts of John's disciples leavened with carnal emulation and prejudices against Christ himself? They would not own him to be the Messias nor believe their Master's testimony concerning him insomuch that the Lord saw it necessary that John should decrease and be abased that Christ might encrease and be exalted; and therefore suffered Herod to shut up John in prison and keep him in durance about twelve months and at length to cut off his head, that so these fondlings might be weaned from their nurse. And when John was dead, his disciples resort to Jesus, acquaint him with the calamity that befell them, and were perfectly reconciled to him, passing into his school and becoming his disciples (Matt. 14. 12).

"But alas, the times are difficult and perilous; the wind is stormy and the sea tempestuous; the vessel heaves and sets and tumbles up and down in the rough and boisterous waters and is in danger to be swallowed up."

Well, remember that "the Lord sitteth upon the flood; yea, the Lord sitteth King forever" (Psal. 29. 10). "His way is in the sea, and his path in the great waters, and his footsteps are not known" (Psal. 77. 19). "He stilleth the noise of the seas, the noise of their waves, and the tumult of the people" (Psal. 65. 7). He saith to the raging sea, "Peace, be still. And the wind ceaseth, and there is a great calm" (Mark 4. 39). Yea he can enable his people to tread and walk upon the waters. To sail and swim in the waters is an easy matter, but to walk upon the waters as upon a pavement is an act of wonder. Peter at Christ's call "came down out of the ship, and walked on the water, to go to Jesus" (Matt. 14. 29), and as long as his faith held, it upheld him from sinking; when his faith failed his body sunk, but he "cried to the Lord, and he stretched forth his hand, and caught him, and said unto him, O thou of little faith, wherefore didst thou doubt?"

"But what shall we do for bread? The encrease of the field and the labor of the husbandman fails."

Hear Christ's answer to his disciples when they were troubled because there was but one loaf in the ship: "O ye of little faith, why reason ye, because you have no bread? perceive ye not yet, neither understand? have ye your heart yet hardened? having eyes, see ye not? and having ears, hear ye not? and do ye not remember?" (Mark 8. 17, 18; Matt. 16. 8, 9). Those which have had large and plentiful experience of the grace and power of Christ in providing for their outward sustenance and relieving of their necessities when ordinary and usual means have failed, are worthy to be severely reprehended if afterward they grow anxiously careful and solicitous because of the defect of outward supplies. In the whole evangelical history I find not that ever the Lord Jesus did so sharply rebuke his disciples for anything as for that fit and pang of worldly care and solicitude about bread. Attend we our errand upon which Christ sent us into the wilderness and he will provide bread for us. "Seek ye first the kingdom of God, and his righteousness; and all these things shall be added unto you" (Matt. 6. 33).

"But we have many adversaries and they have their subtle machinations and contrivances, and how soon we may be surprised we know not."

Our diligent attention to the ministry of the Gospel is a special means to check and restrain the rage and fury of adversaries. The people's assiduity in attendance upon Christ's ministry was the great obstacle that hindered the execution of the bloody counsels of the Pharisees. "He taught daily in the temple. But the chief priests and the scribes and the chief of the people sought to destroy him, And could not find what they might do: for all the people were very attentive to hear him" (Luke 19. 47, 48). If the people cleave to the Lord, to his prophets, and to his ordinances, it will strike such a fear into the hearts of enemies that they will be at their wits' ends and not know what to do. However, in this way we have the promise of divine protection and preservation. "Because thou hast kept the word of my patience, I also will keep thee from the hour of temptation, which shall come upon all the world, to try them that dwell upon the earth" (Rev. 3. 10). Let us with Mary choose this for our portion, "to sit at Christ's feet, and hear his word"; and whosoever complain against us, the Lord Jesus will plead for us as he did for her and say: "They have chosen that good part, which shall not be taken away from them" (Luke 10. 42). Amen.

FINIS.

II SAMUEL WILLARD'S SERMON OF 1682

AN INTRODUCTION

SAMUEL DANFORTH'S *Errand into the Wilderness* may have started something. There followed a ten-year period of errand sermons with heavy emphasis on the apostasy theme. Thomas Shepard's *Eye-Salve* in 1672 and Urian Oakes' *New England Pleaded With,* 1673, are the most labored and elaborate errand sermons until Thomas Prince's performance in 1730. (Prince's, however, is a better sermon, stylistically.) Taken together, the sermons of Danforth, Shepard, and Oakes represent the apogee of the errand type. The apostasy of New England would not again get such a concentrated going over. These three sermons must have made a great impression. Shepard's sermon covers fifty-one pages of tightly printed octavo; Oakes' sermon runs to the top of page 64 of a slightly larger, tightly printed octavo and would have required about three hours to preach, if all that is printed was given in the pulpit. Samuel Torrey followed with a lesser performance (in bulk at least) on the errand and apostasy themes in 1674, and Increase Mather added another *Discourse Concerning the Danger of Apostacy* in 1677.

By 1682, trade and material prosperity were growing in the young Colony. It would appear to the layman that God was favoring his newly chosen band. Yet at festival-election time, the Boston holiday was being blackened by the sermons of Shepard, Oakes, Torrey, and Mather, undermining prosperity by insisting that New England was neglecting its real errand and losing God's favor. There were complaints that the New England prophets were too glum.[1]

There were good reasons, then, why Samuel Willard in his election sermon in 1682 felt a need to defend the role of Jeremiah.[2] *The Only Sure Way* is included in this volume because it is a serious attempt to justify the Jeremiad theme especially as it was concentrated in the 1670–80 years. It is an apologia on behalf of all the New England Jeremiahs.

Willard sets out to remind the representatives of the people of Massachusetts that the real heroes of their errand are the very prophets they would condemn. The sermon has a twofold message. On the one hand, it clearly enunciates the structure of an Old Testament, theocratic society. The minister-prophets are special people. They guard from the watchtower (and the metaphor of their place high on the ramparts is suggestive of their higher social and political status as well as higher, or more difficult, responsibility). They are awake while the people sleep. In another metaphor, they stand in the gaps of the hedge surrounding the garden, fighting off the wild beasts which would like to enter from the wilderness. Emphasis here is less on a priesthood of all believers than on a hierarchy at the top of which are those prophets whose fundamental business is to pray, read, scan society, hear God's voice, report, and warn.

[1] Thomas Shepard (1635–77) speaks of "the averseness that there is in so many against faithful, plain, zealous, and thorough condemning the sins of the times we live in" (*Eye-Salve* . . . , Cambridge, 1673, 33). See also Urian Oakes, *New England Pleaded With* . . . (Cambridge, 1673), 35, 39–40.

[2] Samuel Willard was born in Concord on January 31, 1640. He entered Harvard in 1655, and took two degrees. He was minister at Groton from 1663 until its destruction by Indians in 1678. He then joined Thomas Thacher at the Old South Church in Boston. Willard was an outspoken opponent of the court during the witchcraft trials in New England. After becoming Vice-President of Harvard in 1700, he carried on the dual role of minister at the Old South and college administrator until just before his death, September 12, 1707. Willard did not require a public confession upon admission to the church, and he baptized persons refused by other churches. He baptized Benjamin Franklin on the day of his birth, January 14, 1706. Willard published many sermons in his lifetime, but his major work is the posthumous *A Complete Body of Divinity* . . . (Boston, 1726), two hundred and fifty expository lectures on the Assembly's Shorter Catechism delivered monthly over a period of nineteen years, the first folio on theology published in America. For biographical sketches, see John Langdon Sibley and Clifford K. Shipton, *Biographical Sketches of Those Who Attended Harvard College*, 13 vols. (Cambridge and Boston, 1873–1965), II, 13–36; William B. Sprague, *Annals of the American Pulpit* . . . , 9 vols. (New York, 1857–69), I, 164–167; *DAB*, XX, 237–238; Samuel Eliot Morison, *Harvard College in the Seventeenth Century* (Cambridge, 1936), II, 538–540. The Johnson Reprint Corporation's Series in American Studies, ed. Joseph J. Kwiat, intends to reprint Willard's *A Complete Body of Divinity* with an introduction by Edward M. Griffin.

On the other hand, there is an implicit lament in Willard's words. He wishes to enhance the prophet's role by arousing sympathy. If the minister-prophets have power, they also have the burden of their responsibility. Willard admits to the heartache of being a prophet, to the pain of knowing when to warn. When does the prophet hear a legitimate call from God, and when does his zeal stem merely from his own pride? The unpopularity of being a prophet is tiring, an "insupportable" role were it not for "God's assistance." In a rare moment of personal confession in the election sermons, Willard admits that the private conversation among ministers in New England is sometimes woeful: "I myself have heard some of them expressing what combats, what wrestlings they have had in their own minds, how loath to speak, how fearful about their message, how well they could have been content to enjoy the goodwill of the people, and how greatly unwilling they were to be an occasion of adding to the guilt of those that had already run too deep on account with God." Perhaps Hawthorne had such a passage in mind when he created "The Minister's Black Veil." Father Mapple in *Moby-Dick* also attests to the agony of standing forth "his own inexorable self" against "the boisterous mob." "And now how gladly would I come down from this mast-head and sit on the hatches there where you sit, and listen as you listen, while some one of you reads *me* that other and more awful lesson which Jonah teaches to *me*, as a pilot of the living God."[3] In this sermon, Willard, like Hawthorne's Hooper and Melville's Mapple, takes his listener into the mind of the prophet: his convictions, his premises, and his fears.

As for the theology of the apologia, Willard wishes his audience to understand that the prophet-minister has at least three difficult challenges to meet. First, he must make both the people's sins and the inevitability of God's punishment clear and precise *without* bringing on despair. He must defend a God of wrath and also remind his people that they can still avert God's withdrawal as their Patron, and can draw forth his mercy, love, and protection again. Second, he must make it clear that *God* does not go back on his word or protection; it is the people who fail the terms of the covenant. God's covenant cannot be taken for granted; he both may and does withdraw his support without being inconsistent in terms of the covenant. Willard's apologia for the prophet's role rests on the basic premise of a just God. Though often unpopular, a prophet is really just

[3] *Moby-Dick,* ed. Harrison Hayford and Hershel Parker (New York, 1967), 50, 51.

because his God is just. God desires his "ambassadors" to publish his wishes for all men to hear (as in election sermons).

Finally, the people must realize that the presence of such energetic prophets is in fact their greatest blessing. Willard intends his sermon to end optimistically. There would be something wrong if there were no prophets in New England; when quiet smiles come from the pulpits, then will it be time to complain. Massachusetts can be healthy as long as she has doctors to listen to.

In his sermon in 1670, Danforth laid out the reasons for the exodus to New England, the first sweet days of life in the new land, and the latter days of falling away. He established the metaphors of the garden, the wilderness, and the wall, and he peopled this garden with its special heroes. Twelve years later, Willard takes one detail from Danforth's fresco and examines it closely. The leading characters in the New England epic are the ministers (as Cotton Mather would emphasize in his *Magnalia* twenty years later). The new world will be only as great as they can help God to make it; they are its culture heroes, its demigods, and, fresh from the "Reforming Synod" of 1679, the custodians of the original errand.

The only sure way to prevent threatned
CALAMITY : As it was delivered
in a SERMON, Preached at
the COURT of ELECION,
May, 24. 1 6 8 2.

Jer. 26. 12, 13.

Then spake Jeremiah *unto all the Princes, and t⁰
all the People, saying, The Lord sent me to pro-
phesie against this House, against this City, all
the words that ye have heard.*

Verf. 1 3. *Therefore now amend your wayes and your
doings, and obey the voice of the Lord your God,
and the Lord will repent him of the evil that he
hath pronounced against you.*

Uch is the unhappy entertainment that
plain-dealing and open-hearted reproofs do meet with in the World, that
when they are moft needed, they can
be leaft born : The fouler the fto-
mack, the more naufeous is the Phyfick : when
the malady is come to a dangerous Crifis, and

every

"THEN spake Jeremiah unto all the princes, and to all the people, saying, The Lord sent me to prophesy against this house, against this city, all the words that ye have heard" (Jer. 26. 12, 13).

"Therefore now amend your ways and your doings, and obey the voice of the Lord your God; and the Lord will repent him of the evil that he hath pronounced against you" (ver. 13).

Such is the unhappy entertainment that plain-dealing and open-hearted reproofs do meet with in the world, that when they are most needed, they can be least borne. The fouler the stomach, the more nauseous is the physic; when the malady is come to a dangerous crisis and every symptom bodes a sad and sudden change, men are better pleased with a cheating quack that dissembleth the disease and engageth all shall be well, than with an honest and faithful physician who tells them the distemper is malignant, the issue dubious and without the application of some speedy and extraordinary means, desperate. He that will undertake to lay open the true state of degenerous people by ripping up their sins, displaying their impenitencies, and applying the threatenings of divine displeasure, shall expose himself to the hatred and injurious usage of those for whom he doth this kindness—apostasy being a spiritual frenzy, and herein expressing an affinity with madmen in being enraged at none so much as those that in love seek their cure. The truth of this our prophet here experienced, who, being sent by God on an unthankful errand (for when men love the distemper, they do by consequence despise the remedy and hate him that brings it; and I therefore call it unthankful, not from its own nature, for what can be a more obliging courtesy than to give men timely notice of eminent dangers, and counsel how to avoid them? but from the disposition of those who were to receive it, whom custom in sin had wedded to a complacency in it, whose pride and presumption had made them impatient of all threatenings, and in whom deep-rooted impenitence had obstructed the reception of every advice calling them to reformation) —being thus sent, he faithfully and clearly opens their state, shows them their hazards, directs to such duties as the present circumstances required, promiseth them a good issue if they were so followed, but denounceth ruin if they were neglected. And now (as if he had been guilty of treason and had joined hands in some dangerous conspiracy), the priests, prophets, and people, in a transport of fury, lay violent hands on him in the very temple, and nothing can satisfy their hellish rage but the prophet's life. The princes (who, though possibly they had but little if anything more of religion than the rest, yet pretending to more civility) interpose in this fray and call the matter to a legal hearing, which (by the overruling providence of God) determineth in his delivery out of their hands.

The principal things observable in this transaction are the people's accusation and Jeremiah's apology. The former is briefly touched in verse 11, in which, while they pretend to accuse, they undertake to judge, and with a full cry pronounce him a man of death. "This man is worthy to die"; or "the judgment of death is for this man," as the Hebrew text reads it. Which lest they should seem to have spoken of prejudice, they article against him for sedition. "For he hath spoken against this city"; nor need witnesses be sought, for they themselves had "heard it with their ears." We see what different interpretations the words and actions of men lie open unto; how change of times changeth men's opinions of things; how dangerous it is for men to speak the truth in apostatizing times. Micah the Morasthite delivered a more fearful, because a more positive prophecy, in the days of Hezekiah: "Zion shall be plowed as a field, and Jerusalem shall become heaps, and the mountain of the house as the high places of the forest" (Mic. 3. 12); and yet was not branded for a turbulent person nor prosecuted as a ringleader of sedition, but received as a prophet of the Lord, and his prediction improved to repentance, which averted eminent desolation. Jeremiah so threatens calamity as withal to promise mercy in case of sound repentance; and he is an offender, prophesieth against the city, and no less than his blood can serve to expiate his crime. How happy a thing is it to preach to a pious generation who, because they hate their sins, love their reprovers? How unhappy to come to a people wedded to their wicked ways, who count those their enemies who are so to their lust? As for the prophet's apology, I need for the present occasion to take notice only of the just defense which he makes both of himself and his prophecy, which is contained in the text. The persons before whom he makes it are the princes and all the people, under whom we may list the priests and prophets, unless we look on these as his accusers, and the other as those to whom he appeals as judges.

The vindication itself consists of two parts.

1. A clearing up of the authority by which he had spoken. "Their Lord (Jehovah) sent me to prophesy." Divine authority gives a supersedeas[1] to human laws. They may make it capital to speak against their ways and doings, but if God authorize his servants to it, it is no crime in them but a duty to cry aloud and not to spare.

The prophet's commission compriseth the full of their accusation. He might have prophesied against other nations without their offenses, but that he doth it against this city—this is the provocation. He therefore asserts his particular charge, "to prophesy against this house and this city"; Grotius indeed lenifies[2] the expression, and would have the words read "to this house and to this city," noting that the prophecy was for them and not against them. And indeed convincing and awakening preaching would be so if a people had wisdom and grace rightly to improve it. But suppose it against them, yet if God be against a people and would have them to know it, should the prophet obey man or God? Especially if he exceeds not the bounds of his commission, which Jeremiah here further asserts, for the Lord sent him to "speak all the words which they had heard"; he had not added one of his own head. And must the herald be impeached for proclaiming the King's edicts?

2. The end of his prophecy, viz., if it might be to prevent their ruin, which he therefore delivers in way of exhortation: "Therefore now amend your ways and your doings," etc. I name that exhortation as a branch of his defense because he doth therein explicate what he had before delivered

[1] The phrase *to give a supersedeas to* was current in the seventeenth century, meaning to stop, stay, or check (*NED*, IX, 192).

[2] *Lenify*: to soften, assuage; to mitigate a sentence or style (*NED*, VI, 199).

in the prophecy itself (ver. 3), and also insinuates that his errand and business was not to triumph over them, but compassionately to endeavor the prevention of all the evil denounced. It is, q.d., "Wherein have I offended? I have only studied your peace and safety; only advised to means of delivery and establishment, and is this a crime? Must I die for this?" He therefore gives them a safe direction and backs it with a persuasive encouragement.

The direction is to repentance and reformation, and designs the rectifying both of heart and life, projects and practices. "Amend," the word is, "make good," noting they had been bad, which called for amendment or reformation. "Your ways and doings"; Calvin reads it, "your ways and studies." [3] The word signifies a thing done by study, plotting, design, and deliberation. "And obey the voice of the Lord your God." The word is "hear" and is the frequent Scripture expression of obedience. By the voice of God is * intended the will of God delivered in his Word, intimating that he brought no new commands to them but only studied to reduce them to the obedience of God's law, of which they professed themselves the subjects (if they would studiously consider and compare themselves by it, they might easily know their present course to be judged and condemned).

The encouragement is full and clears the prophet from the imputation of any studied mischief, inasmuch as he gives them to understand that if his counsel be embraced and faithfully put in execution, all the threatenings of wrath and ruin shall cease, as having attained their appointed end.

Hence, he brings in God as clothed with human affection, ready to sympathize with the miseries of a penitent people and reverse the sentence passed against them. "The Lord shall repent," etc. The word firstly signifies to be grieved and sorry for one, and then to repent of anything we have said or done against them, and finally to change one's mind, or alter one's purpose. But is God capable of perturbation? Can the infinitely blessed Being suffer any disturbance or grief? Or can the immutable and everlasting will of God be changed? No, but an unchangeable decree may ordain changeable providences, and an immutable God may vary his works according to the changes of the subject, and all this agreeably to

---

[3] Calvin's Latin translation of verse 13 in his commentary on Jeremiah reads: "*Et nunc bonificate (bonas facite) vias vestras, et studia vestra, et obtemperate voci Jehovae Dei vestri, et poenitebit Jehovam omnis mali quod pronunciavit contra vos*" (*Magni Theologi, Praelectiones in Librum Prophetiarum Jeremiae, et Lamentationes,* Amsterdam, 1657, 313).

invariable counsel. And there may be such effects wrought which, to the conception of men, proceed from a different principle. God had pronounced a sentence of desolation against Judah and Jerusalem, but if they repent, the sentence shall not take effect but cease.

Hence the Septuagint[4] translates it he shall cease, or desist, which gives the true intent of the phrase, though not the grammatical construction of the word.

There are two conclusions, proper from the words and pertinent to the present occasion, offer themselves to our meditation, viz.:

Doctrine I. *When God commissioneth his ministers to denounce awful threatenings against an apostatizing generation, they must deliver, and these ought to apply them.*

It is to the one a warrant for justification and to the other a warning for serious consideration. It is true, it is not everyone's place and work. He had need be able to say, "The Lord sent me," that will undertake to pronounce a sentence full of woes upon a whole people; yea and thoroughly to ponder every word that he may be sure he shall have God himself to patronize him. But if God do indeed say, "Go and prophesy and speak all these words in their hearing,"[5] it would be rebellion in them to keep silence and will be pernicious for that people who receive them not.

The way indeed wherein the prophets of old received intimation of the will of God, viz., by visions, dreams, immediate revelations, etc., as it was extraordinary, so it is now shut up. But yet there remains a more sure word of prophecy and no less infallible evidence of God's mind in general and our call in particular.

For,

1. Christ's ministers are set as watchmen under a solemn and strict charge to look out and espy all approaching dangers and give timely warning of them (Ezek. 3. 17, 18). They must give the alarum though it be at midnight when it is like to be most surprising, and men are loath to be bereaved of their beloved sleep. Men naturally love security and like not to be disturbed. But what shall those watchmen do? Christ hath placed them on the watchtower and put a trumpet in their hands, charging them upon pain of death to sound when occasion calls for it.

2. The spiritual presence of Christ with his faithful messengers abides

[4] *Septuagint*: the pre-Christian Greek Old Testament.
[5] Cf. Jer. 26. 2.

perpetually engaged to stand by them and afford them all the necessary assistance which their calling and duty doth require. Were it not for this, their charge were insupportable, their burden intolerable; for "who is sufficient for these things?" [II Cor. 2. 16]. But he hath given his word for it: "Lo, I am with you to the end of the world" (Matt. 28. ult.).

3. The Word of God is a sure rule by which to discover the true and proper state of any people so far forth as to afford sufficient light and direction for their warning, if we compare them thereby. It is true, the sovereignty of his secret will is not there stinted, nor can we from thence certainly determine what God will undoubtedly do with these or those. Neither did God always discover this to his prophets of old, nor yet did they so understand him. Jonah upon this very suspicion waived his errand: "Was not this my saying in my country? Therefore I fled unto Tarshish: for I knew thou art a gracious God," etc. (Jonah * 4. 2). But yet the Word of God evidently declares when it is that a people comes within the compass of the threatening, when they are cast in common law. God's revealed will is one and perpetual; if men break covenant with God and falsify their engagements to him, if they bring themselves under the threatenings of the Word, there is a sentence out against them, and those that are God's watchmen may espy it. If then they declare against such ways and proclaim that there is wrath gone forth and calamities before us, even at the door and daily to be expected, they herein say not a word more than what they have God's warrant and command for.

4. God sometimes gives his servants a particular, special opportunity to declare his mind against a sinful generation. Thus he did unto Jeremiah at this time, when the people were gathered out of all their cities to one of the great feasts at Jerusalem and there was a general concourse of them to the Temple. And when it is thus, to omit the improving a price in our hands is to play the fool egregiously. The wise man tells us there is a season to every purpose, and sometimes this season comes once and no more, the neglect whereof proves irreparable and leaves a woeful sting upon the conscience.[6]

5. There are also sometimes deep and powerful impressions upon the minds of God's messengers which by an irresistible impulse constrain them to bear open and public witness against the sins of the times and places which they live in. I am far from pleading for or justifying anything that

[6] Cf. Eccles. 3. 1, 17; 9. 2.

looks like enthusiasm,[7] or thinking that men should make a secret impetus upon their spirits the rule and plea of their words and actions. But if men who are called by God to declare his counsels, advantaged by his providence to proclaim his pleasure, directed by his Word to speak nothing but what is agreeing thereunto, are pressed in their spirits to a zealous witness bearing against these and those prevailing sins, and solemnly to denounce the judgments of God against them if men repent not, I believe there is much of God in it, and it carries a great evidence along with it that God is about to do some speedy, strange work there if he be not prevented— when we are in such a frame as our prophet was: "His word was in my heart as a burning fire shut up in my bones, and I was weary with forbearing, and could not stay" (Jer. 20. 9)—or as Elihu, "I am full of matter, the spirit within constraineth me" (Job 32. 18).

And when it is thus, it concerns such a people to apply these things to themselves. It becomes them not now to take exceptions and grow into a rage, but to lay them to heart. These things are of God, and not in vain. They alarum a people to prepare to meet their God; and if by repentance they are not rendered healing to them, they will prove killing words; the sword of his mouth will hew them in pieces. "I have hewed them by my prophets; and slain them by the words of my mouth" (Hos. 6. 5). God is not wont to let such words perish and come to nought; yea though he may defer to accomplish, yet he will not disannul them. They may be deferred awhile, but they lie in reserve against the due time.

Doctrine II. *Universal and thorough repentance and reformation is an only and sure way to escape the threatened judgments of God.*

Universal—both referring to the subject, viz., all orders of men from the highest to the lowest (Jeremiah directs his advice to the princes, priests, prophets, and people), and in respect of the term from which; all sin, every false way; and thorough—not in pretense only, or in part. Not like that of Jehu's, who took away Baal out of Israel but retained Jeroboam's sin; nor only like that of some good kings of Judah of whom it is said, they did that which was right, but still the high places were left standing and the people sacrificed at them; but like Hezekiah's and Josiah's, who sought to remove every offense. And there must be both repentance and

---

[7] *Enthusiasm* is used here in its Renaissance, theological meaning of supernatural inspiration (originally, possessed by a god), prophetic or poetic frenzy, private revelation (*NED*, III, 215). The Quakers and Anabaptists were infamous to the Puritans for their enthusiasm.

reformation—a work that reacheth to both heart and life, both inward and outward man. Of what efficacy this is will appear if we shall consider:

1. That this is the privilege of a people in visible covenant with God, that there is no threatening denounced against them but with a gracious reserve and room to reverse it in case of repentance. God sometimes indeed seems to speak positively, but then, to lenify such absolute threatenings and render them equivalent to hypothetical, he speaks after the manner of men, of repenting. God imitates his own law, for in making of war he first proffers peace and presents men with terms of compliance. When he takes up arms, he would be glad if there were some to hold his hands. When he saith, "I will do thus," yet then he wisheth "Israel to prepare to meet him" (Amos 4. 12). If a people of God suffer at his hands, it shall be through their own willfulness. God can threaten and never execute and yet be God unchangeable, always provided his people do truly repent and amend their ways and doings.

2. God therefore sends his ambassadors to plead with his people about their sins and publish his judgments, that they may have motive and opportunity to repent. Divine threatenings are expostulatory and awakening; they are to convince men of their sin and to put them in awe; they are to see if words will do, that blows may be spared. After threatenings therefore God hearkens: "I hearkened and heard, but they spake not aright" (Jer. 8. 6). God might else strike as well as menace; yea it were as easy, nay and as merciful for him so to do, were it not that he had rather men should live than die.

Hence therefore, the proclamations of war which God makes against a revolting people are to be annumerated to his long suffering.

3. This only can put a stop to the wrath of God from proceeding; for as the promise is full to the penitent, so the threatening is as positive and as much without reserves to those that are impenitent. When a people say, either with their tongues or with their practices, there is no hope, but they will follow after their own courses, God also saith there is no hope, but he will pour out his fury upon them. So that when God hath a purpose of mercy to a rebellious people and is resolved to exalt his grace upon them, and also makes known these purposes in those discoveries which we call absolute promises, he doth it so as not to cross this rule of his covenant with people, and therefore engageth not only to give deliverance from his judgments, but also to do it in such a way as withal to give them the condition, "I have seen his ways, and I will heal him," etc. (Isa. 57. 18). If

therefore repentance be (under and after much forbearance) neglected, it is both a reason why and sign that the decree, when it hath gone out its full time, shall certainly bring forth.

4. God expresseth himself better pleased at the repentance of his people and thereby extinguishing of the fire of his anger, than if it had burnt up and consumed them. He therefore gives oath that he delights not in their death, professeth that he rejoiceth in their returning—like a tender father who is glad if any means will reclaim his refractory and disobedient son whom he loveth and for whose good he longs.

Hence, "Oh that my people had been obedient unto me, and Israel had walked in my ways!" (Psal. 81. 13 *). And we may truly apply that of Solomon unto Jesus Christ as the antitype:[8] "My son, if thine heart be wise, my heart shall rejoice, even mine" (Prov. 23. 15). He reckons himself to have gained a greater conquest when he hath won the hearts of his people to fear and serve him, than when he hath broken his enemies as potters' shreds with the scepter of his power.

Use. That I may render these truths practicable and accommodate them to the use and benefit of this people, give me leave to deal in all plainness and integrity. As I would not give flattering words lest God should destroy me, so neither would I designedly provoke or move any to anger, except it be at his sins. I shall therefore endeavor to speak words of truth and soberness, and yet choose rather to offend man than provoke the most High.

There are two uses I have to suggest unto which I shall reduce those few words which I have to speak—the one by way of conviction, the other of exhortation.

I. For conviction. Let us solemnly consider and rightly weigh whether or no those words which have been spoken against this place and people on such occasions as this, were not such words as God commanded those that delivered them to come and speak. I must confess when I seriously look upon this people in their constitution civil and ecclesiastical, molded in the one under wholesome laws, in the other under strict and sacred covenants; when I consider that the management of these is under the

---

[8] *Antitype*: that which is shadowed forth or represented by a type, or symbol (*NED*, I, 376). The word here refers to Christ. This spelling is not to be confused with *antetype* (less commonly used than the shorter word, *type*), which means, on the other hand, a preceding type or earlier example. Important seventeenth-century works on typology are Benjamin Keach, *Tropologia . . .* (London, 1681–82), and Samuel Mather, *The Figures or Types of the Old Testament . . .* (Dublin, 1683).

hands of a pious and prudent magistracy, a godly and learned ministry; when I think how many there are whose hearts are upright with God, and do not wickedly depart from his covenant; when I mind that by the very confession of unprejudiced strangers here is more of sobriety and honest conversation than almost in any place they have occasion to be conversant in [9]—it seems hard to believe that God who is full of mercy and pity, who knows this frame of ours and minds that we are but dust, should declare against us, though many infirmities should appear in the midst of us, and could be willing to think that all the warnings and menaces which have been uttered by these or those were nothing else but the mistakes of an irregular (though well minded) zeal, or the dumps and night visions of some melancholic spirits (and thus indeed were the prophets of old censured). But when I thoroughly weigh all circumstances in an equal balance, I dare not but conclude that the Lord hath sent them to speak all these words. What they have spoken is for the most part upon record and commended to us in print—wherein we are impeached for degeneracy, threatened with the judgments of God if we amend not, and thence solemnly advised and invited to repent. If they understood the mind of God, then are we far from being safe and secure from eminent dangers. I know they have been condemned by some, contemned by many more, scarcely believed by any, if we are to take the evidence of men's faith by their works. But if we shall ponder such things as these, they may leave conviction behind them.

1. They were the Lord's faithful watchmen who gave this alarum. Not men that came upon their own heads, but were set up by the will of God to descry and give notice of his mind to his people. And these are such as God is wont to make known his counsels to: "Surely the Lord will do nothing, but he revealeth his secrets to his servants the prophets" (Amos

[9] "Profane swearing, drunkenness, and beggars, are but rare in the compass of this Patent . . ." (Thomas Lechford, *Plain Dealing* . . . , London, 1642, 29); ". . . one may live there from year to year, and not see a drunkard, hear an oath, or meet a beggar" ([anon.], *New England's First Fruits*, London, 1643; reprinted in *The Old South Leaflets*, Boston, n.d., III, 11); "I thank God I have lived in a colony of many thousand English almost these twelve years, am held a very sociable man; yet I may considerately say, I never heard but one oath sworn, nor never saw one man drunk, nor ever heard of three women adulteresses in all this time, that I can call to mind" (Nathaniel Ward, *The Simple Cobler of Aggawam in America*, London, 1647, 61); ". . . in seven years among thousands there dwelling, I never saw any drunk, nor heard an oath, nor any begging, nor sabbath broken . . ." (Hugh Peters, *The Case of Mr. Hugh Peters, Impartially Communicated* . . . , London, 1660, 3). By the time of Thomas Prince's election sermon in 1730 (see pp. 209–210 below), this propaganda has become folklore.

3. 7). They were such as truly feared God and would not dare to prophesy lies in the name of the Lord.

2. They were such as loved and labored for the peace and prosperity of this people; who could truly (with the prophet) appeal to him who knows the heart, that they desire not that woeful day; friends, and not enemies to our Zion, who loved and stood up for the way of these churches, who prayed for the peace of our Jerusalem, who mourned in secret for the sins of the land and to their ability strongly endeavored to stop the course of them, and to prevent the eruptions of God's wrath, who preached the displeasure of God with pity and compassion, entreating and encouraging to repentance.

3. They delivered not these messages without many heavy pangs and throes upon their own spirits. This role was bitter to them and with a great deal of reluctancy and unwillingness did they declare themselves. I myself have heard some of them expressing what combats, what wrestlings they have had in their own minds, how loath to speak, how fearful about their message, how well they could have been content to enjoy the goodwill of the people, and how greatly unwilling they were to be an occasion of adding to the guilt of those that had already run too deep on account with God; and could they have so satisfied their own consciences, and been clear of blood, would have altogether held their peace—yea sometimes had said as the prophet, "I will not make mention of him, nor speak any more in his name" (Jer.* 20. 9).

4. There hath been great harmony and concurrence in these testimonies. It hath not been the voice only of one or two, but such things have been told us from year to year. And though God may put a lying spirit into four hundred false prophets, yet he is not wont so to deceive his own servants. If they all are misled, what shall we do, or where shall we seek for the word of the Lord, or would not that itself be a clear evidence of God's great displeasure against his people, if it be indeed arrived at this, that "there is no prophet: nor anyone that can tell how long" [Psal. 74. 9]?

5. God himself hath sealed the truth of their warnings with many awful providences, the language whereof, had there been no interpreter, hath spoken his anger with clearest demonstration. The rod hath spoken as well as the word; and every rod hath come after such solemn words of warning as have been too generally entertained in the quality of tales and falsehoods. And if God hath in part accomplished the predictions of his servant, may we not rationally and religiously judge that the remainder shall have

their time of accomplishment too, except we shall attend to the due means of prevention?

6. The grounds and reasons of these threatenings are found in the midst of us. They have not only declared the anger of an holy and jealous God, but also drawn up our indictment and entered God's plea against us, and fully answered all our reasons of appeal. They have shown Judah their transgressions and the house of Jacob their sins; yea such sins as according to the Word of God (that rule of procedure between him and his people) are found to be incentives of divine displeasure, such as raise up God's jealousy and kindle his anger against those that are so found guilty of them. Nor yet have they done this of their own mere surmise.

But, 7. We have, at least verbally, acknowledged a judgment in many, yea the most—if not all—which they have charged us withal. Witness the proposed grounds for many days of fasting, issued out from those who stand as the representatives of this people. Witness the confessions and acknowledgments which have been on such days made unto God. And that which will stand up for a full clearing of this truth against us, witness the records of the last synod, in which we shall find the full and free consent of the elders and messengers of these churches, acknowledging that the hand of God is out against this people awful in tokens of wrath; and giving him the glory by confessing that there are these and those sins not only fallen into through infirmity, but so prevalent in the midst of us as to acquit not only a just but a merciful God too, in all his severities against us.[10] And shall we not yet believe? Or shall we say to Jeremiah, "The Lord sent thee not, but Baruch stirreth thee up"?[11] Shall we say, "We

[10] Although local fasts could be determined by individual churches, the General Court ordered fasts observed throughout the Colony in December 1675 and on May 9, 1676, November 21, 1678, and the second Thursday in July 1679. Willard must have made his point to this Court of 1682, for they ordered a fast to be observed on June 22 (*Records of the Governor and Company of Massachusetts Bay*, ed. Nathaniel B. Shurtleff, Boston, 1853–54, V, 69, 131, 196, 221, 371). See William De-Loss Love, Jr., *The Fast and Thanksgiving Days of New England* (Boston, 1895), 204–238. The "Reforming Synod" of 1679 drew up ten categories of "these and those sins": a decay in Godliness; pride; heresy; swearing, and sleeping during sermons; Sabbath-breaking; decay of family discipline; angry passions and unnecessary legal contentions; sex and alcohol ("the jeremiads record a thriving promiscuity," says Professor Miller); lack of truth; worldliness and materialism. See Williston Walker, *The Creeds and Platforms of Congregationalism* (New York, 1893; Boston, 1960), 409–440; the catalog is conveniently summarized in Perry Miller, *The New England Mind: From Colony to Province* (Cambridge, 1953), 34–36.

[11] See Jer. 43. 1–3. Baruch was Jeremiah's loyal secretary and was censured along with the prophet by the Judean leaders.

have such a magistracy, such a ministry, such churches, and therefore what need we to fear?" When did Micah say, Zion "shall be ploughed as a field"? Was it not in the days of good Hezekiah? When did God say, "I will remove Judah out of my sight"? Or when did Zephaniah deliver his terrible prophecies, but in the days of godly Josiah? All I shall here add is thus much: If God's faithful messengers are to be believed when speaking from God himself; if the Word of God is * to be credited which they have delivered to us; if the concurrence of so many (divers of whom are now with God) be of any weight; if providence may be thought to speak anything and the rod have a voice in it; if to be self-judged and condemned be of any efficacy—then there is an handwriting of God given out against us; and therefore let it be.

II. For exhortation. Be we persuaded to make it our serious endeavor by an universal and thorough repentance, to seek a way to escape the after effects of God's displeasure. Let us obey the voice of the Lord our God; let us amend and God will repent.

I might urge many things strongly argumentative to press the great necessity of this duty; let it suffice to give some brief hints.

1. Remember your profession to the world. How oft have you given it out that your design and main business here is to promote the service of Christ and maintain the interest of the Gospel, which is then only upheld when a people stick close to the law and to the testimony, walking by the holy rules of Scripture, in conformity to the revealed will of God in his Word, and can only be your glory among the nations, and will be so if you thus do; otherwise your very profession will be your shame.

2. Remember your covenants and solemn engagements to be the Lord's. How you have called God to witness, and bound yourselves in an oath and a curse to serve God, and him only. How you have avouched him to be your Lord and Lawgiver and renounced the guidance of your own wills and lusts. And if you lie under breach of covenant, and can so content yourselves, and not return again to the Lord, how can you escape from bringing yourselves under the dreadful guilt of taking his name in vain. To the vindication whereof, his holiness stands firmly engaged.

3. Forget not your own confession. How oft have ye made large and full declarations against yourselves? Such hath been the evident and notorious declination of the power of Godliness and manifest growth of iniquity, that we have been constrained to confess it; God hath extorted it out of our mouths. And know this, that sins confessed and not repented

of will be an heavy indictment against a people professing themselves the servants of God, when out of their mouths they shall be judged, and many stripes shall be inflicted on such as knew the Lord's will and did it not.

4. Think how many calls you have had to repentance. The mercies of God to our fathers and continued to ourselves, by these God expostulates: "What iniquity did your fathers find in me, that ye are gone so far away?" (Jer. 2. 5), and, "Have I been a wilderness to Israel? a land of darkness?" (ver. 31). The judgments of God which have been upon the land, these are doctrinal: "When thy judgments are in the earth, the inhabitants of the world shall learn righteousness" (Isa. 26. 9). The patience of God wherein he hath given you a space to repent, this is not forgotten: "I gave her a space to repent; and she repented not" (Rev. 2. 21). The continual cry of the ministry by powerful convictions, severe comminations, gracious promises followed with earnest and unwearied entreaties, God keeps a register of these: "The Lord hath sent unto you all his prophets, rising up early, and sending them. They said, Turn again everyone from his evil way," etc. (Jer. 25. 4, 5).

5. God hath thoughts of good for you if you will repent. He hath not forgotten the love of your fathers who followed him into a wilderness, a land that was not sown. He hath a respect for the faithful in the land. Though the ax be up and ready to fall, yet he sees a few clusters and will say spare it, for there is a blessing in it. And I cannot but be persuaded that God hath good things yet in reserve for New England; but he expects your reformation and that you acknowledge and turn from your sins. And yet I am afraid there is more to do and some severe trials to befall us in order to this. For God will do for his people in ways suitable to his own ends, and such which shall recommend him to be a God glorious in holiness.

6. Know it, there yet wants such a repentance as God requires; and that notwithstanding all that he hath said or done. Though he hath convinced us, counseled us, warned, threatened, smitten, renewed his judgments with breach upon breach, altered his course, tried us in one fire and after in another, the old scent yet remains. This may be the burden of the song and make up the period of every plea: "Yet have ye not returned to me, saith the Lord" [Amos 4. 6, 8, 9, 10, 11].

7. Our present condition and exigencies call for speedy repentance. It will be our wisdom and can alone be our safety. Men are against us and

that which is most awful to consider is, God seems to be against us too. Providences look to an eye of reason as if they were conspiring to bring a further day of trouble upon us. On all the glory whereon there was sometimes a defense, there now appears to be a blast. We are brought low in our outward affairs and low in spiritual things, and some sudden and doleful change looks as if it were at the door. But if we may recover God's gracious presence and re-engage his protection, all shall be well. Yet if not now done, a few days may sum up and cancel our felicity, and we be left to sigh out our Ichabod.[12]

I shall not need to be prolix in the directive part of this use, since divers that have gone before me have largely unfolded our particular estate, and prescribed rules for our recovery, both informed us what there is of sin prevailing, and wherein we may so testify our repentance as to obtain a repeal of that sentence which hath been passed against us. Yet if I could help to drive home any of these nails I should think it labor not in vain. I need but say, if you will believe the messengers of Christ—nay if you will but believe yourselves and your own confessions—there is work enough cut out for your reformation. Do but amend cordially what you have acknowledged to be amiss and I dare affirm that God will accept it. I shall not so far trespass on the time and other occasions as to urge every particular. It may suffice to hint at some things which seem especially to call for our speedy and extraordinary endeavors, and these do more immediately concern:

1. The body of this people considered as invested with liberties, and engaged as one man for the upholding of them in ways according to God. Let me tell you that "for the division of Reuben there are great searchings * of heart" [Judg. 5. 16].[13] These jealousies and suspicions one to another, those minings and counterminings that are among you, those aspersions and defamations which you cast one upon another and upon your best friends, those endeavors to strengthen a party and countermand your

[12] *Ichabod* means "inglorious," or in the words of I Sam. 4. 21, "the glory is departed." The word became a catch-phrase in colonial Puritanism, 1670–1720, for the declension of New England in its analogy to Israel and the striving for a promised land. In 1702 Increase Mather preached and published two sermons on this theme entitled *Ichabod*; the second, lyric and emotional, deserves to be reprinted. Washington Irving uses the name humorously in his satiric portrait of Ichabod Crane, who takes Mather's *Witchcraft* with him into the hinterlands of the Hudson valley from which he departs "ingloriously" to be sure; cf. Whittier's poem "Ichabod."

[13] The name of Reuben, eldest son of Jacob by his first wife Leah, became attached to one of the twelve tribes of Israel which early lost its foremost position.

brethren, are provoking to God and like to prove ruinating to yourselves. It is not a sin only, but a judgment too, and that which tends to issue in misery. "Their heart is divided; now shall they be found guilty" (Hos. 10. 2). "If ye bite and devour one another, take heed that ye be not consumed one of another" (Gal. 5. 15). Your security is in being one for God; your safety is only in unity. There are enough abroad who watch for your halting, you need not yourselves lay open one another's infirmities. And one would think it might sufficiently awaken you to think how little God's work goes forward, or his glory strenuously promoted, whiles men spend their little zeal in oppositions and invectives one against another, as if herein lay the life of religion. This picks out the cement and crumbleth away the mortar which is the strength of the building, and when gone, with what ease may it be made to fall? To remedy this, put on charity. When God's people agree in the end, though for a while they may not judge alike of the means to it in some critical points and circumstance, it is far from a Christian spirit so to abound in our own sense as to proclaim or declare such enemies to the cause of God that speak not in every punctilio with us. Men of the largest charity here are the best friends to this cause. It is God's will and wisdom that his people should in many things beat out their way by debates. But men that may not be thwarted in their own private sentiments are dangerous coals, fitted to kindle a destroying fire among us.

2. These churches as tied up in the strictest bonds of covenant to be the Lord's; whose great receding from, and manifold notorious breaches of this covenant of God, do strongly call for, and vehemently urge, solemn and serious renewals of it before him. Essays towards this, I confess, have been made by several churches.[14] But what damps and demurs are cast on the work by the many that hold back is matter of lamentation. And truly the reason rendered by many makes it still the more lamentable, viz., lest it should increase the guilt of the churches through neglect of performance. If indeed it be come to that, that we are resolved to mend nothing, then covenants of reformation will prove dangerous things. But may we not upon the same * plea raze out our old covenant, cast off our religion, resolve to be under no engagement to God at all, and say to him, "We are lords; and will come no more unto thee" [Jer. 2. 31]? All I will here urge is this:

[14] For a brief account of the transformation of "a particular and individual recitation" of covenant renewal to "a communal chant," beginning in a few congregations and finally subscribed to by the General Court and the "Reforming Synod" of 1679–80, see *From Colony to Province*, 116ff.

If these churches are not prepared to renew their covenant with God, they are not prepared for mercy. If the way of our anastasy be more dangerous than our state of apostasy, our danger is tremendous.[15] If all confess that spiritual slumber, lukewarmness, earthly-mindedness, slighting of ordinances, undervaluing of the messengers of Christ, carnal compliance with the world, and many the like evils are crept into and prevail much over our churches, and the covenant people of God are not capable of a resolute, strenuous, and voluntary engagement to the rooting of these out, our wound is next to incurable.

3. To the representative body of this government assembled in General Court, on whom it lies as an indispensable duty to endeavor the maintenance of God's glory, and to put forth utmost care for the securing of the interest of the true religion, and extirpation of that which is false. The prevalency of corrupt doctrines and impudent boldness of many in prosecution of them calls for your vigilant and resolute industry in the suppression thereof.[16] I am not ignorant to how much calumny I expose myself in mentioning this point, but it is in God's cause, which I may not decline for fear of reproach. I have often heard (though I must needs confess, not without some secret regrets) the encomiastic titles put upon this government, as if it were singularly a theocracy and carried in it a glorious specimen of the kingly government of Christ. But I fear if this government decline, or think it not their concern vigorously to extend their power in upholding the duties of the first table and secure them from the invasion of perverse men, these will be found no more than a few empty hyperboles. I confess your legislative power is limited and must take its measure from your Charter; nor do I advise to exceed that which God's providence hath invested you withal. I believe it shall never be charged as a sin upon you that you did (with grief of heart) bear with those things which you could not regularly confront. But if men upon pretense of conscience (and who will not pretend it, if they may find it a shelter against justice?)—if thus I say they may be suffered (though it be in your hand to oppose them) without any restraint to run to and fro, disseminate their erroneous prin-

---

[15] This sentence is an echo of James Fitch, *The First Principles of the Doctrine of Christ* (Boston, 1679), 1: "None can learn it [i.e., doctrine of religion] by the book of nature, for there are some lessons in religion which are not to be found in the book of creation, (namely) man's apostasy and anastasy, how man at first did fall, and how he is recovered by Christ . . ."

[16] Contrast Willard's request here with the appeals for toleration made by Barnard and Mayhew in their election sermons; see pp. 264–266 and 304 below.

ciples, make breaches in churches, undermine and seduce silly souls, set up their posts by God's posts, enjoy as free and public liberty to carry on their own ways as those churches of Christ whom you profess to countenance and defend—and that by a total silence and a full connivance—if thus you can tolerate the dishonor of Christ, let me boldly say I believe he will soon and signally testify his dislike of it.

4. To the honored Magistrates and all such as have an executive power in their hands. It is an observation of one that nothing is more dangerous and disgraceful than to suffer laws to lie by unprofitable, for want of execution. The best laws, if only promulgated and not pursued, will not promote a reformation. Some indeed are of the mind that it is good to have laws as a testimony of your dislike of such and such practices though never prosecuted against the breakers of them. But besides that the violating of one law with impunity will naturally embolden to a like violation of others under the same presumption, such laws will indeed be a witness, not for, but against a people, that they thought, and were in conscience persuaded it was their duty, but had not courage or zeal enough to put it in execution. There are many sins, some very crying: profane and scandalous Sabbath-breaking, beastly drunkenness, desperate cursing and swearing, woeful and miserable idleness. There are good and wholesome laws against those sins; let there be such a check and restraint laid upon them that our streets may not be witness of them. If these do prevail, God hath said that the land shall mourn for them. Great industry and zeal is needful here when sin is grown impudent; the exerting of it will be your honor, and by doing these things you shall verify the title God hath dignified you withal, that you are shields of the earth.

5. To the reverend elders, the messengers of Christ, that you be faithful to God, to this people, and to your own souls, in particular much to study and preach the sins of the times and places you live in. God hath placed us as watchmen to descry danger and give due warning of approaching evil. Let us be faithful in our places, vigilant in our work, much in contemplation, seeking to find out the mind of God, and not afraid with boldness to declare it though the times may seem hardly to resent us. We have an account to give for souls, and God will demand of us what is become of those who were committed to our charge. Above all let us take care to do as we say and be ensamples to the flocks. It may be by this means you shall not only save yourselves but also those that hear you. Beware of being idol-shepherds; they are evil times we live in; men love to be let alone and

encouraged in sin, but let us have no fellowship with their works of darkness, but rather reprove them. In all your dealings with men be plain and faithful. Some may for that say with Ahab, "Art thou he that troubleth Israel?" [I Kings 18. 17]. But be not angry but compassionate and mourn in secret for them. Let us study to be men of knowledge, fixed in principles, holy in conversation; in a word, let us do all we can (more than we do) if it be possible, to save a generation from the wrath of God and impending calamities. Let us be still more plain, more particular, more serious in this great work.

To hasten towards a conclusion, I shall strike but one blow more on these nails, to fasten them, and so recommend all unto him who is the great Master of the assemblies. It is an opinion which some seem strongly to be built upon, and it renders them strangely presumptuous, viz., that the foundations of this people are unmovable; that our civil constitutions and church covenants have so engaged the presence of God with us that we lie out of the reach of foreign mischief. Thus the Athenians once chained down the image of Minerva, their tutelary goddess, to her station, and so thought they had secured themselves from all dangers of being subjugated by any enemy or oppressed with any evil. And to think to oblige the true God with verbal covenants, and formal profession, is no other than to make him an idol. Yet thus the cry of many speaks in the language of those Jews: "The temple of the Lord, are these" (Jer. 7. 4), forgetting how many ways they have disobliged, and giving God just reason to be ashamed to own or acknowledge them. How fond such thoughts as these are, the ruinous heaps of many renowned places, which once enjoyed as much of God's presence with them as any in the world, do stand for monumental witnesses. The more of God hath sometimes been among you, the greater is your sin and the speedier may be your calamity, if growing weary of his government you abuse all your liberties to desperate licentiousness. There is nothing so dear or precious unto God or sticks so close and near unto him but if it once comes to interfere with his glory (which is his beloved end and he will upon no pretense part withal), he can remove it far enough from him. See Jeremiah 22. 24, 25. You have here the only remedy to recover a sick and dying people; this will, nothing else will affect it. True repentance and thorough reformation never come in vain, though when judgment was gathered into a thick cloud and ready, yea beginning to drop down in a storm of fury, but it hath blown it over. This God proffered Judah here when they were almost ripe for ruin; and this God once again this day proffers to you. Oh, be not proud and stiff-necked! Be not obstinate and rebellious! Why will you die? Obey the voice of the Lord, do what he bids, do what your consciences say you ought to do, do what you have before God confessed yourselves guilty for because you have neglected to do it. Do what all reason and equity requires, and for the omission whereof you have no just ground or pretense; do this and live. "Be willing and obedient, and you shall eat the fruit of the land" [Isa. 1. 19]. Be grieved for sin and apostasy and it will grieve God to put you to grief. But if all that is said from time to time be disregarded; if these counsels prove as water spilt upon a rock; and though you can lend an ear to hear these words with patience, yet will not do them, but can slightly cast them out of your minds and throw them behind your backs; they will stand on record against you and become a farther aggravation of your guilt. And in that day when all those things shall come to pass of which you have been so frequently and solemnly warned, and the Lord shall suffer none of the words of his servants to fall to the ground—then shall you know there have been prophets among you.

FINIS.

III COTTON MATHER'S SERMON OF 1689

AN INTRODUCTION

THE events which led up to Cotton Mather's sermon, *The Way to Prosperity,* preached in Boston on Thursday, May 23, 1689, to "as much of New England . . . as can be reached by the voice of one address," were the most disturbing of any in the brief history of the Colony. Because some knowledge of the revolution in Boston on April 18 is important to an understanding of the sermon, let us briefly review the circumstances.

I

In October 1684, the Charter of the Massachusetts Bay Company was canceled after a contest carried on for several years at Westminster. On May 14, 1686, Edward Randolph, "the arch-enemy of New England . . . whose memory is still held in detestation as the destroyer of our liberties!" arrived in Boston with the official notice.[1] Ceremonies were soon held to

[1] Nathaniel Hawthorne, "Edward Randolph's Portrait," *Works* (Cambridge, 1882), I, 297. Randolph also appears in "The Gray Champion" as "our arch-enemy, that 'blasted wretch,' as Cotton Mather calls him" (*ibid.,* 25). The historical details here are based on the following sources: *The Andros Tracts* . . . , 3 vols. (Boston, 1868); *The Mather Papers* (*Collections of the Massachusetts Historical Society,* 4th ser., VIII, Boston, 1868); Barrett Wendell, *Cotton Mather: The Puritan Priest* (New York, 1891; reissued with Introduction by Alan Heimert, New York, 1963); Cotton Mather, *Diary of Cotton Mather,* ed. Worthington C. Ford, 2 vols. (*Collections of the Massachusetts Historical Society,* 7th ser., VII–VIII, Boston, 1911–12); Ralph P. and Louise Boas, *Cotton Mather, Keeper of the Puritan Conscience* (New York, 1928); Thomas Hutchinson, *The History of the Colony and Province of Massachusetts-Bay,* ed. L. S. Mayo (Cambridge, 1936), I.

replace the government, which had until then been elected locally. Sir Edmund Andros, the first royal Governor of Massachusetts appointed directly by the King, was commissioned June 3 and arrived in Boston Sunday, December 19, 1686. He was already a suspicious character. Locally it was believed that when Andros was Governor of New York Territory, 1675–76, he connived to supply the Indians at Albany with arms and ammunition to harass Massachusetts. Bostonians were soon to become convinced that their earlier suspicions were correct.

From his arrival until the uprising against him, there was continual hostility between the new Governor and the Puritans. They were incensed at his requirement that the Old South Meeting House should be made available for Anglican services. Town assemblies were limited to one a year. With the loss of the Charter went the privilege of self-taxation, and now taxes were levied directly by the Governor without consultation with, or representation by, the people. Legal matters were tried before juries which appeared to be packed with Anglicans and newcomers from England or New York. The Puritans' desire to maintain their privileges under the old Charter was met with insults and subtle accusations of treason. It also appeared that Andros was up to his old tricks, and under cover of protecting the frontier against attack was quietly urging the Indians on. Finally, there was the land—their cherished garden. Andros discounted individual deeds of property title based on the old Charter and purchase from the Indians; new, more authentic patents must now be purchased from the crown.

What people that had the spirits of Englishmen could endure this? That when they had at vast charges of their own conquered a wilderness, and been in possession of their estates forty, nay sixty years, that now a parcel of strangers, some of them indigent enough, must come and inherit all that the people now in New England and their fathers before them had labored for! Let the whole nation judge whether these men were not driving on a French design, and had not fairly erected a French government.[2]

It was decided late in the fall of 1687 to appoint an emissary to London to negotiate for the restoration of the old Charter or, failing that, to lobby for as much perseverance of the New England Way as the King would allow. Increase Mather was the logical choice. He could leave his son Cotton, recently ordained, in charge of the Old North Church. The fol-

[2] John Palmer, "The Revolution in New England Justified . . . ," *Andros Tracts*, I, 87.

lowing April he managed to board a ship despite the authorities' attempts at delay, and by May 30 he was having his first interview with James. In November Samuel Sewall sailed for London to join him. The Puritans were going to neglect no effort to effect their designs.

In November William of Orange landed in England, and while Sewall was still on the ocean King James fled from London, December 23. In New England Andros was busy with Indian disturbances in Maine, but he arrived back in Boston in time to receive a warning from the King that William was planning an attack. He issued a proclamation on January 10 which described a sinister "invasion from Holland" by "foreigners" who would challenge the good King and jeopardize the safety of all true Englishmen. New England might be invaded by these foreign influences and all loyal subjects were urged to watch for the "approach of any fleet" and to be diligent in weeding out subversive talk or tracts; the wily invaders were attacking under the false pretenses of "maintaining the Protestant religion, or asserting the liberties and properties of his Majesty's people."[3] The Puritans silently rejoiced. They hoped and prayed for William's success. In "The Gray Champion," Hawthorne dramatizes this secret hope as the Puritans wait for further word from England.

The news came on April 4, 1689, when a young Englishman, John Winslow, brought to Boston a copy of William's declarations of succession to the throne, and "news also of his happy proceedings in England with his entrance there . . ." Andros arrested him for distributing treasonable material. It appears Winslow did not take the declarations with him to the Governor's house to which he was escorted by the sheriff, "being afraid to let him have them, because he would not let the people know any news."[4] Two weeks later, the "Declaration of the Gentlemen, Merchants, and Inhabitants of Boston" ended its catalog of grievances with notice that "the almighty God hath been pleased to prosper the noble undertaking of the Prince of Orange."[5] Winslow's copy must have found its way into the right Puritan hands, perhaps those of Cotton Mather himself.

What further plans were quietly in the making by the old, deposed government—men like Bradstreet, Saltonstal, Hathorne—in the two

---

[3] *Andros Tracts*, I, 75–76.

[4] Winslow's own account in Palmer, *Andros Tracts*, I, 78.

[5] *Andros Tracts*, I, 18. Thomas Hutchinson attributes the work to Cotton Mather on the basis of "style and language" (*History*, I, 323), and Mather's bibliographer, Thomas James Holmes, agrees; *Cotton Mather: A Bibliography of His Works* (Cambridge, 1940), I, 229–234.

weeks between Winslow's news and the uprising, it is difficult to determine. Cotton Mather's diary for the year is missing, and the era's most reliable recorder of colonial events in high places, Samuel Sewall, was in England. There are several hints from men on both royal and Puritan sides that there was much ado behind closed doors.[6] According to Samuel Mather, "the principal gentlemen in Boston" met at Cotton Mather's home and agreed to extinguish any local insurrection; "if the country people to the northward by any violent motions pushed on the matter so far as to make a revolution unavoidable," however, local authorities would have to step forward and maintain order. So "a Declaration was prepared accordingly."[7]

On April 18, about "eight of the clock in the morning" (according to an eyewitness, Nathanael Byfield), reports traveled quickly through the town that both the North and South ends were "all in arms."[8] The Captain of the royal frigate, the *Rose*, was seized, and drums began to beat. The "Declaration" was read at noon from the balcony of the Town House, a declaration of independence which stands between the Mayflower Compact and the Declaration of 1776 as a testament of Americans' continuous desire to govern themselves. By nightfall, almost fifty of the Governor's key men, as well as Andros himself, were in custody.

The Puritans next set about to prepare for an election as they had been doing every May (except for the last three) for over fifty years. Representatives of several towns met in Boston on May 10 to declare their wish that the old Governor, the Deputy-Governor, and the Assistants "chosen and sworn in May, 1686" should now take up their positions again. However, since there were present "only sixty-six persons as the representatives of forty-three towns and villages within the said Colony," and the decisions were of such weight, it was decided to call for a larger convention to include towns not now represented.[9]

At this later Convention on May 22, there were differing opinions. Cotton Mather feared that official recognition of the old regime would undermine his father's efforts in England. No decisions were reached. On

[6] See Palmer, *Andros Tracts*, I, 27–28; W. H. Whitmore, "Memoir of Sir Edmund Andros," *Andros Tracts*, I, xxx–xxxi; Boas and Boas, *Cotton Mather*, 83.

[7] Samuel Mather, *Life of Cotton Mather* (Boston, 1729), 43; quoted in *Diary of Cotton Mather*, I, 138–139, n. 1.

[8] "An Account of the Late Revolution in New England . . . ," *Andros Tracts*, I, 3–4.

[9] "Answer of the Council to the Declaration of the Representatives of Massachusetts," *Collections of the Massachusetts Historical Society*, 4th ser., VIII (1868), 708.

the following day, a regular Lecture day, the Convention assembled in the Old North Church.[10] For the clergy it was a dramatic moment, for the Colony had been without election sermons for three years and this present sermon was given in a context where normally clear lines of loyalty and treason were fuzzy. The twenty-six-year-old preacher faced the greatest preaching challenge in his as yet short career.

II

The central political issue was whether or not to ratify the previously elected government of 1686. The theological issue was whether the wall around the enclosed garden had now cracked, like Usher's house, with a fissure that would bring it tumbling down. (Mather uses the wall metaphor in the sermon.) Had the recent events shown that New England's protecting God was gone? That the father was in England and the son preached *this* sermon was symbolic (Cotton Mather knew it and gets all the drama he can from the situation). As some of the old men looked at the young boy they must have wondered if he represented a new generation which would move further away from the ideals of the original errand. But if the new King's treatment of Massachusetts was still in doubt, surely they could count on the son of a Mather who had both in his names and in his education a solid grounding in the good old way.

Young Cotton was not long in letting it be known where he stood. Although he had written the "Declaration of the . . . Inhabitants of Boston" only a few weeks earlier, and so was in an excellent position to speak of the Colony's political grievances, he chooses to put first things first in the sermon, and addresses himself to the theological rather than the political questions. A return to the old government is of little account unless accompanied by a return to the old faith. The Andros regime, the revolution, and the present dilemmas are for Mather only the externals of a deeper problem. It would be a mistake to surmise that in addressing this Convention Mather took the easy way out and ignored the immediate political issue. What still mattered in 1689 was the theory behind the event, the vision which gives events meaning, the providence which informs the daily news. It was easy to lay the Colony's griefs on Andros, or James II, or three thousand miles of Atlantic Ocean, but Mather turns to

---

[10] The election sermon would normally be given in the Town House, but since Mather refers in the sermon to being "in the house of God this day," I assume he was preaching in his own church.

what are for him the real causes of their agonies under Andros—the continuing apostasy of New England. The Andros affair was God's severest warning yet. The sermon is one of wrath, of vigorous condemnation in the mode of a Jewish prophet, one of whom, Asa, gives Mather his theme and identity. Mather dons the mantle of a modern Asa who cries out to a bewildered Massachusetts. But the sermon is not pessimistic; its basic premise is that all is not lost. An angry God is waiting to be pacified.

In the "Doctrine," Mather reviews the argument which is a favorite of his father's, that God does not necessarily remain with a chosen people just because he has chosen them. Unlike the individual, private relationship between God and an elected Puritan—who receives his grace forever—God may and often does remove his favor from a covenanted people when their behavior justifies it. When and for how long God extends his favor and protection rests with the people.

The two-part division between "Doctrine" and "Use" is even more marked here than Mather might wish. In the "Doctrine," the dry scholasticism of his Harvard training is still painfully evident. The first part of the sermon gives a taste of hundreds of pages of election sermons (except that Mather is more saucily erudite and pedantic in his learned references to Lyra, Bochart, Jerome, Owen, Foxe than most ministers). Such a "Doctrine" is of interest to the theologian, but as a literary performance, it is dull. The tone is neutral, with none of the lyric passages of Danforth's *Errand*. With the "Application" however, the rhetoric becomes rhapsodic, the tone changes to wrath, pleading, and chagrin. The dry announcer of doctrine becomes an actor who takes on different parts—of Asa, of the old men of the first New England generation, and of the innocent child who cries "Peace." Mather comes alive; the errand motif brings out all the sensuous fire of this still young, strange man.

Regardless of who preached it, the election sermon of 1689 would have to be a strong contender for inclusion in this volume because of the occasion. Given the situation, what would the preacher say? Because it followed a revolution, it makes a nice point of comparison with the 1775 sermon. But Mather's sermon also proves important because it adds an authority to the errand motif. Amidst the uncertainty of the Colony's political destiny, he chooses to preach an errand sermon. This middle chapter in the fivefold sequence of errand sermons in this volume shows that the motif was deeply ingrained and that the prophets believed in its power even in political emergencies.

The Way to Proſperity.

A
SERMON

Preached to the *HONOURABLE*

CONVENTION

Of the

GOVERNOUR, *Council*, and *Repreſentatives*
of the *Maſſachuſet*-Colony in *New-England* ;
on May 23. 1689.

By *COTTON MATHER.*

Jer. 23. 28.
*He that hath My Word, Let him ſpeak
ſpeak My Word faithfully.*

BOSTON.
Printed by *Richard Pierce.* for *Benjamin
Harris.* Anno Domini MDCXC.

A prophecy in the divine Herbert's "Church Militant."

> *Religion* stands on tip-toe in our land,
> Ready to pass to the *American strand.*
> When height of malice and prodigious lusts,
> Impudent sinning, witchcrafts and distrusts,
> (The marks of future bane) shall *fill our cup*
> Unto the brim, and make our measure up;
>
> .   .   .   .
>
> Then shall religion to *America* flee;
> They have their times of *Gospel,* even as we.
>
> .   .   .   .
>
> Yet as the *church* shall thither *westward* fly,
> So *sin* shall trace and dog her instantly.[1]

THE PREFACE.[2]

The occasion which first produced the following sermon cannot be expressed in better terms than those which were used by the worthy gentlemen that were the conservators of our peace, in their humble address to

[1] George Herbert, "The Church Militant"; see *The Works of George Herbert*, ed. F. E. Hutchinson (Oxford, 1941), 197. The text in Mather's sermon differs from that in Hutchinson's edition in accidentals only; the punctuation and italics in Mather's version are followed here.

[2] "The Preface was written after Dec. 19, 1689, for it mentions the intention to join the sermon with 'another discourse,' *The Wonderful Works of God Com-*

their Majesties, bearing date May 20th, 1689—wherein among other things they say:

Your three several princely declarations encouraging the English nation to cast off the yoke of a tyrannical and arbitrary power which at that time they were held under, have occurred unto the view and consideration of the people in this country, being themselves under alike (if not worse) evil and unhappy circumstances with their brethren in England—first by being unrighteously deprived of their charter-government and privileges without any hearing or trial and under utter impossibilities of having notice of any writ served upon them; and then followed with the exercise of an illegal and arbitrary power over them which had almost ruined a late flourishing country and was become very grievous and intolerable; besides the growing miseries and daily fears of a total subversion by enemies at home and invasion by foreign force. The people thereby excited to imitate so noble and heroic an example, being strongly and unanimously spirited to intend their own safeguard and defense, resolved to seize upon and secure some of the principal persons concerned and most active in the ill management of the illegal and arbitrary government set over them by commission. Accordingly upon the eighteenth day of April last past, arose as one man, seized upon Sir E. Andros the late Governor and other of the evil instruments, and have secured them for what justice order from your Majesties shall direct.[3]

Thus that address.

Upon the late revolutions thus described ensued various debates about the further steps that were needful to be taken for the service of their Majesties and this afflicted country, which debates quickly issued in the return of our government into the hands of our ancient Magistrates, who with the representatives or Deputies of the several towns in the Colony made another address unto their Majesties, bearing date June 6, 1689— in which address there were these words:

Finding an absolute necessity of civil government, the people generally manifested their desires and importunity once and again that the Gov-

memorated*, preached on that day, and with which *The Way to Prosperity* was published" (Thomas Holmes, *Cotton Mather: A Bibliography of His Works*, Cambridge, 1940, III, 1204). The sermon was also bound as a separate pamphlet either from the same sheets or in a second printing from the standing type, for the printing accidentals (including a misnumbered final page) are uniform.

[3] The "framing and writing" of this "address," and the one of June 6 quoted from below, are ascribed by Thomas Holmes to Cotton Mather, based on "the testimony of his son Samuel in the *Life* of his father (pp. 42–43)" and internal evidence of style. The addresses "were sent to Sir Henry Ashurst and were by him presented on August 7, 1689, to the King (William III) at Hampton Court." They were printed as *Two Addresses from the Governour, Council, and Convention of the*

ernor, Deputy-Governor, and Assistants chosen and sworn in May, 1686, according to Charter and Court as then formed, would assume the government.

The said Governor, Deputy-Governor, and Assistants then resident in the Colony did consent to accept the present care and government of this people according to the rules of the Charter, for the preservation of the peace and common safety and the putting forth further acts of authority upon emergencies, until by direction from England there should be an orderly settlement which we hope will restore us to the full exercise thereof, as formerly—notwithstanding we have for some time been most unrighteously and injuriously deprived of it.

That royal Charter being the sole inducement and encouragement unto our fathers and predecessors to come over into this wilderness and to plant the same at their own cost and charge.

In answer to this address, his Majesty in a most gracious letter bearing date the 12th of August, 1689, unto the government here, uses these expressions:

Whereas you give us to understand that you have taken upon you the present care of the government until you should receive our order therein, we do hereby authorize and empower you to continue in our name your care in the administration thereof and preservation of the peace, until we shall have taken such resolutions and given such directions for the more orderly settlement of the said government as shall most conduce to our service and the security and satisfaction of our subjects within that our Colony.

It was in the time of our greatest heats and straits and at a time appointed for a general assembly of this great Colony that the ensuing sermon was expected from me. Through the grace of God the sermon then was not altogether unacceptable to some who desired the publication of it. But I gave not my full consent unto their desire until now they had an opportunity (with their renewed importunity) to join it with another discourse which they have obtained from me;[4] and tho' the little differences which

---

Massachusets Colony . . . (London, 1689), "most probably by Ashurst, to be of further use, with the design to aid the agents of Massachusetts (himself, Increase Mather, Thomas Oakes, and Elisha Cooke) in obtaining the second charter" (*Cotton Mather: A Bibliography*, III, 1139–41).

[4] By 1689 it was a firm practice to print election sermons, and even though *The Way to Prosperity* is not technically a regular election sermon—i.e., it is a sermon preached before an assembly which might make an illegal decision to reinstate the Governor and Council previously elected—still it is difficult to imagine a Mather not taking immediate advantage of a ready-made opportunity to publish. Mather probably hesitated to print his sermon in May until William's attitudes toward the revolution, the Colony, and the colonists' petitions in London became known. By

were among us when the sermon was preached are now so well composed, yet I flatter myself with an opinion that the things here insisted on will not, should not, be judg'd unseasonable.

I confess it is a very bold thing for one every way so mean as myself to address the whole country in such a manner as here I do; but *si crimen erit, crimen amoris erit*;[5] and if the general dispositions of the year will not excuse a breach of order in me, I have but one thing more to offer by way of satisfaction for it: There was once a people in the world with whom it was a custom that when men would conciliate the favor of the ruler, they were to present his own son before him as a sight which would speak more than any advocate. Instead thereof, that I may not want the favor of my country, how blameable soever they may count my freedom with them, I shall only present them with my own father whose cheerful encounter with an hazardous voyage unto a strange land and with innumerable difficulties and temptations there, for no other cause than that he might speak for them, has at least merited a pardon for me with whom he has for near two years now left both his church and family [6]—if I have transgressed by taking a liberty of speaking to them at the same time the things which may promote our enjoyment of the divine Presence with us. Now may salvation be nigh unto us and glory dwell in our land!

COTTON MATHER.

It is the Word of the eternal God in II Chronicles 15. 2: "Hear ye me, Asa, and all Judah and Benjamin; The Lord is with you, while you are with him."

It is a remarkable occasion which has brought these words to be the subject of our present meditations, but it was much more a remarkable occasion which these words were first uttered upon. We find them in the sacred Book of Chronicles, which Chronicles are not the civil records in other parts of the Bible referr'd unto, but an inspired history of things that concerned the line of Christ and the church of God for five hundred more than three thousand years. It seems as an epitome of the whole (for

1710, Mather could say of his *Bonifacius*: "For no man living has demanded it of me; 'tis not published, 'to gratify the importunity of friends,' as your authors use to trifle" (ed. David Levin, Cambridge, 1966, 13–14).

[5] "If it be a crime, it is one of love" (Propertius, *Elegies*, II, 30 (b), 24).

[6] For Increase Mather's mission to England to lobby for a new charter, from his disguised flight from Boston in early April 1688, until his return in 1692, see Kenneth Murdock, *Increase Mather* (Cambridge, 1925), 187–286.

so 'tis in Jerome's language) to be written as late as the last of all the books in the Old Testament, and the Hebrew Bibles give it a place accordingly. The Greeks choose to entitle it "The Book of things (elsewhere) passed by," because as Lyra notes, according to the rule of our Savior, "It gathers fragments that nothing may be lost";[7] and if there were nothing else but the story which affords our text unto us to justify that appellation, it were enough; 'tis a story passed by in the Book of Kings but worthy to be "had in everlasting remembrance" [Psal. 112. 6].

The ready pen of Ezra (for him we conjecture to be the scribe of the Holy Spirit here, notwithstanding those few clauses which may be judged to be added by another hand after his decease—I say the pen of Ezra) is here informing us that the people of God had newly been invaded by a vast army of Cushites; but we are yet at a loss who these Cushites were. Far more scholars in the world than there were soldiers in that army have hitherto been content with our translation which renders them Ethiopians here. But that learned Frenchman Bochart, by whose happy industry more than any man's the treasures in the bowels of the Scriptures have been delv'd into, has with irrefragable demonstration prov'd that not Ethiopians but Arabians are the Cushites mentioned in the Oracles of God.[8] These Arabians, tho' they have not been called Saracens (as has been thought) from their word *sarak,* that signifies to steal, yet for their furacious inclinations they well deserved such an etymology—they were a wild sort of men that liv'd much upon the rapine and ruin of their neighbors; and particularly, a million of them now designed Jerusalem for a prey. The blessed God gave his people a notable victory over these invaders and they were now returning from Gerar (a place between thirty and forty miles off) unto Jerusalem. The Holy Spirit of God excited and inclined a prophet whose name was Azariah to entertain them with a faithful and

---

[7] "The name 'Chronicles' comes from St. Jerome, who in reckoning Chronicles as the seventh book of the Hagiographa . . . writes, '*Septimus "Dabre Iamin" id est, "Verba Dierum" quod significantius "Chronicon" totius historiae divinae possumus appellare; qui liber apud nos "Paralipomenon" primus et secundus inscribitur.*' [The seventh is that '*Dabre Iamin,*' which 'Words of the Days' we can call more significantly, *Chronicles* of the whole of divine history; this book is by us entitled the first and second '*Paralipomenon*' (*Prologus in 'Libros Regum,*' ed. Vallarsi, ix. 458).]" *The Book of Chronicles,* ed. William Emery Barnes (Cambridge, Eng., 1899; trans. here by Barnes). Nicolaus de Lyra (1270–1349) comments on the beginning of "*Paralipomenon,*" the old title for "Chronicles": "*Colligire fragmenta ne pereant . . .*" (*Biblia Latina . . .* , Nuremberg, 1493, I).
[8] Samuel Bochart (1599–1667) published his *Phaleg* and *Chanaan* in 1646 and 1651 respectively; they were published together as *Geographica Sacra.* His *Opera Omnia* were published at Leyden in 1675.

solid sermon hereupon; and in my text you have the sum and substance of it.

We may observe first the preface of it, and that is very awful and earnest: "Hear ye me, Asa, and all Judah and Benjamin." As he was probably none of the greatest, so 'tis like he was none of the oldest men; for it seems by the eighth verse that his father was yet alive and present at this time. Yet being to speak in the name of the great and eternal God, he expects, he demands the attention of the whole army to him.

Secondly, the design of it; and that is to declare both the rise and use of their late prosperity. "The Lord is with you, while you are with him"; or as the vulgar Latin has it, "Inasmuch as you have been with him." What follows is but an explication and amplification of this. He saw they were taken up with various businesses and contrivances; they had their enemies under hatches and their minds were full of thoughts and cares, what to do next. But he calls them off to acknowledge the presence of God as the cause of their coming off so well in their late action, and above all things to obtain and secure the presence of God, that they might come off as well in their future enterprises.

I am therefore to call for your attention unto this faithful saying.

Doctrine. That *the God of heaven will be with a people while they are with him.*

'Tis by the ensuing propositions that the explication of this truth shall be endeavored.

Proposition I: It is the interest and should be the desire of every people to have the God of heaven with them. But we are to enquire, What is implied in that presence of God which we are to be solicitous about?

For answer to this there is a threefold presence of God mentioned in the Scripture of truth.

First, God is naturally present with all creatures. He is an immense Being and no creature can be without him. The apostle thus argued in the court at Athens, in Acts 17. 27: "God is not far from every one of us." No, he is near us all, he is with us all. And Paul could have had the Gentiles themselves confessing it; for besides what their Seneca did own, one of their own poets had said, *"Jovis omnia plena."* [9] It is the speech of our God in Jeremiah 23. 24: "Do not I fill heaven and earth? saith the Lord." Yea, that he does. The Jews call God by the name of *Makom* or of place,

[9] "All things are filled with God" (Virgil, Eclogue 3, 1. 60).

because all things are in him; this is his name in the Book of Esther if I mistake it not. Whether we may count it proper and physical to speak of an imaginary, infinite space beyond the utmost selvage of the world, replenished with our God alone, yet we are sure that the heaven of heavens gives no limits unto his Being, and the ancients were not mistaken when they said, "*Deus ipse sibi, et mundus et locus et omnia.*" [10] We cannot so well say that God is in the world as we may say the whole world is in God; and we may say with the Psalmist in Psalms 139. 7: "Whither shall I flee from thy presence?"

Secondly, God is gloriously present with the inhabitants of the third heaven. The heaven of heavens hath in it most intimate and marvelous manifestations of God. It is the place of which we may say, as 'tis said of that state in Revelation 21. 23: "The glory of God doth lighten it." There the blessed ones have God with them so that they always behold his face and they are satisfied with his likeness forever. When we come to heaven, then as in I Thessalonians 4. 17: "We shall ever be with the Lord." So the Lord will be with us forever. Heaven is the throne of the most High; he is there as a prince in his throne; the great King is in a manner very ineffable residing there. To be there is called in II Corinthians 5. 8,* a being "present with the Lord." Hence unto the heaven and not unto a Bible are we directed to make our corporal applications in our prayers or our oaths before the Lord.

But thirdly, God is graciously present with his people by being favorable unto them. And this gracious presence of God is that which a people ought to be concerned for. It lies in the engagement of divine providence for the welfare of such a people. God is with us when God is for us.

To particularize: First, God is with a people by directing of them. When Israel was to pass thro' the wilderness, they had that encouragement in Exodus 22. 15: [11] The presence of God going with them. What was that? Why, they had a cloudy, fiery pillar miraculously leading of them every step of the way. There was a wonderful pillar which was a cloud by day and a fire by night—the lower part of which rested on the tabernacle while

[10] "God himself, in himself, the world, space, and all things."

[11] Both chapter and verse references here are wrong for the King James Bible. Mather may mean Exod. 13. 21 or Neh. 9. 12. Mather's sermon has more incorrect references to the King James Bible than any other sermon in this volume, if we consider ratio of errors to length of sermon. Some could be attributed to poor typesetting; or Mather may have been using earlier Bibles which vary in their texts. Errors other than Biblical references (see the textual notes) suggest either a poorly written manuscript, poor typesetting, or both.

the upper part was to be seen by the whole congregation—the motions of this being managed by the ministry of angels. Now God was with them and he led them forth by the right way. A people are often brought into a wilderness of difficulties and emergencies, but if God be with them he guides them to a good issue of them all. The presence of God appears in his directing and inclining of a people to such actions as may be for his honor and their safety and such methods as may extricate them out of all distresses. When God is with a people he shapes their counsels for them and he disposes them to the things that should be done. He supplies them with apprehensions beyond the reach and verge of their own wisdom and he lays before them invitations and provocations which as it were push them into "the way wherein they should go" [Psal. 143. 8]. When the Jews were upon a reassumption of the desirable things which the Babylonians had deprived 'em of, they took a right way to disappoint all that were desirous to interrupt them in it. We find in Nehemiah 4. 15 * that while those exercises continued, they waited in a posture agreeable thereunto; and when the danger was over, "then they returned every one to his work." How came this to pass? 'Twas because God was with them.

Secondly, God is with a people by protecting of them. 'Twas the promise of God unto his people in Isaiah 43. 2: "When thou passest thro' the waters, I will be with thee; and thro' the rivers, they shall not overflow thee." On which text blessed Bilney, after his condemnation, so sweetly paraphrased that his friends caused the whole sentence to be fairly written on their tables.[12] A people may be ready to be swallow'd up by a stormy, gaping ocean of troubles, but if God be with them they shall escape clear of all. The presence of God is a defense, a refuge to the people that are partakers of it. It was said unto David in II Samuel 7. 9: "I was with thee, and have cut off all thine enemies out of thy sight." When God is with a people he distracts and confounds their enemies and he troubles those who trouble them. A people who have God with them are too strong for all the malice and power of their enemies; no adversary, no desolation shall make such a people miserable; they are the Jacob unto whom in Genesis 28. 15: "Behold, I am with thee, and I will keep thee, saith the Lord."

Thirdly, God is with a people by his assisting and succeeding of them.

---

[12] John Foxe, "Thomas Bilney, and Thomas Arthur, Who Abjured at Norwich," *The Acts and Monuments of John Foxe,* ed. Rev. Stephen Reed Cattley, IV (London, 1837), 653.

When Joshua had a vast undertaking in hand, it was said unto him in Chapter 1. 9: "Be of good courage: for the Lord thy God is with thee whithersoever thou goest"; q.d., God will assist thee and succeed thee in thy undertakings. The presence of God will carry a people comfortably through all that they take in hand. If they have Canaanites to subdue, if they have enjoyments to obtain or preserve, the presence of God will prosper them in doing all. It was said unto Solomon in I Chronicles 22. 11: "My son, the Lord be with thee; and prosper thou, and build the house of the Lord thy God." Thus if the Lord be with a people, they shall prosper in all their affairs; in every expedition they shall come off with satisfaction and they shall not miscarry in any of their applications. This is the presence of the Lord.

Proposition II: The presence of God with a people in his outward providence has a diverse foundation and continuance from his presence with his people in the covenant of grace. As 'tis well observed by the great Owen in a discourse unto the parliament, these two are to be carefully distinguished.[13] We must not reflect on the stability of the new covenant for what variety and sovereignty we may see in providential dispensations toward this and that people in the world. This matter seems determined by David in II Samuel 23. 5: "Tho' my house be not so with God; yet he has made with me an everlasting covenant, ordered in all things, and sure." David had promises for the prosperity of his house; he had also the sure mercies of the covenant made over to him in the promises of God. These promises had now a different establishment; the sure mercies of the covenant were unto him more absolute and immutable, but the prosperity of his house we find under another law and subject unto a dreadful alteration.

To bring these things into the case before us: God has in the covenant of grace promised that he will be with his people. This we read in Hebrews 13. 5: "He hath said, I will never leave thee, nor forsake thee." The all-sufficient God, who is he that answers our necessities, let them be what they will; the unchangeable God, who is he still, whatever he was to the saints of old—this God hath said (and how much better is this *autos eireken* than the best *ipse dixit* in the world![14] He hath said it, and this)

---

[13] John Owen, *The Advantage of the Kingdom of Christ* . . . (Oxford, 1651), see esp. 5–6, 18ff.

[14] How much better is it that "God hath spoken" (the Biblical Greek phrase) than "he himself has said" (e.g., in a decree of a Roman emperor or high official).

with multipli'd negatives in the original heaped one upon another: "I will not, I will not leave thee, I will not, I will not, I will not forsake thee." Well, but God is not with a people in his outward providence just after the manner therein observed.

This twofold presence of God: First, it has a diverse foundation. When we look on the covenant of grace, there the sins of one are expiated by the sufferings of another; and so God comes to be with his people for whom the atonement is thus procured. Thus 'tis said in II Corinthians 5. 21:* Christ was "made sin (or a sin offering) for us; that we might become the righteousness of God in him." Now come to outward providence and there you see other measures taken. Here God is with a people according to those terms in Ezekiel 18. 20: "The soul that sinneth, it shall die; one shall not bear the iniquity of another."

Again it hath a diverse continuance. When we look on the covenant of grace, there God hath bound himself to be with his people forever; yea to see that they shall therefore forever be with him. He there says as in Jeremiah 32. 40: "I will not turn away from them, to do them good; but I will put my fear in their hearts, that they shall not depart from me." Now come to outward providence and there you see 'tis otherwise. God is with a people for a while; and upon their misbehaviors and provocations he changes the tenor of his dispensations to them. 'Tis with them as it was with that family in I Samuel 2. 30: "I said indeed that thy house should walk before me forever: but now the Lord says, that be far from me."

The sense of these things will prepare your thoughts for one conclusion more, which is Proposition III: A people must be with God or God will not be with them. And here also, to prevent mistakes, let that one text be always carried in our minds: "Being merciful, thou forsookest them not" (Neh. 9. 19 *); there is mercy in the whole of this matter. Let it be noted that tho' this condition seems to be imposed upon us, yet it is grace, pure grace, rich grace that helps us when we are helped unto the performance of it. When a people have so been with God as that he has been with them, they are to shout "Grace, grace!" concerning all. It is also to be noted that this benefit does not depend upon that condition as an effect upon the real and proper cause of it. When a people has been with God, this does not merit and so procure that God should be with them; but that is barely the antecedent unto which this is the consequent.

Having premised this I must now affirm: "God is with you, while you are with him." We need only reflect on the people of Israel for an instance of it. That whole history which almost fills the Bible proclaims nothing more than this; it loudly declares that while a people are with God, God will be with them; but that he will be very terrible in his providential dispensations towards such a people as do forsake him.

But what is it for a people to be with God? In short, our being with God implies the whole of our obedience to him. Our duty to God must be attended, that we may have the presence of God. The whole of this duty is comprised in that expression of our being "with the Lord." Particularly the Hebrew particle *gnim* in our text admits of three significations; it signifies "with" and "for" and "like" (which last signification I make the more free withal because a little philology will acquaint us with many examples of it. For instance, when David saith in Psalms 120. 5: "I dwell in (*gnim*, Hebrew) the tents of Kedar," a very great interpreter translates it so: "I dwell as the tents of Kedar," [15] i.e., like the inhabitants of the stony sunburnt Arabia, whom indeed I don't remember David ever was among). Accordingly, a people have three things incumbent on them if they would enjoy the presence of God.

First, a people should be with God by communion "with" him. This 'tis to be with him. There are certain means of communion between God and us and these we must be continually approaching to him in. We are with God while we are at prayer before him; hence in our context here it immediately follows: "If you seek the Lord, he will be found of you." While we do seek him, we are with him. The Psalmist was a man much in prayer and therefore he could say as in Psalms 73. 23: "I am continually with thee." A people much in prayer may say the same: "We are continually with the Lord." A people that will pray upon all occasions, a people that will pray over all businesses, a people that will retire into the mount for prayer (and fasting too) at every turn—that people is with the Lord. And the whole worship of God must be diligently, graciously, faithfully frequented by a people that would be with him. We are with God when we are at his house. A people should support and esteem and use all the ordinances of God among them. The church of God hath his very special presence in it; the name of the church is that in Ezekiel 48. 35: *Jehovah*

---

[15] In the gloss to his own version of Psalm 120 Mather identifies this interpreter as "Glassius" (*Psalterium Americanum* . . . , Boston, 1718, 349). See Solomon Glassius (1593–1656), *Philologia Sacra* . . . (Leipzig, 1705), 1020. The first edition was published in Jena in 1623.

shammah, "The Lord is there." We should all be there too and there give those encouragements which are due to the institutions of God. So shall we be with the Lord.

Secondly, a people should be with God by activity "for" him. To be for God is to be with God. It was once the summons given in Exodus 32. 26: "Who is on the Lord's side? And all the sons of Levi gathered themselves"; they were with God in doing so. 'Tis a summons given to the world in every generation: "Who is on the Lord's side?" They that obey the summons are with the Lord. A people full of contrivances for the interest of God are with him. A people should set themselves to advance the glory of God; they should own his truths and his ways and endeavor to draw all about them into the acknowledgment of the same. A people should propound the glory of God as their chief end and the main scope of all that they do; and they should think much of no cost, no pains, nor (tho' as a martyr once expressed himself, "tho' every hair on their heads were a life") should a thousand lives be dear unto them in the promoting of it. Then are they with the Lord; they are so when God can say of them as in Isaiah 43. 10: "Ye are my witnesses, saith the Lord, and my servant."

Thirdly, a people should be with God by behavior "like" him. To be like God is to be with God. They that are with him do not walk contrary to him. God and we should be one. A people should have the same designs, the same desires which the written edicts of heaven declare to be in the blessed God; and not only so, but the same virtues too. Is God holy? Thus a people should not bear with them that are evil. Is God righteous? Thus a people should abhor all injustice and oppression. Is God merciful? Thus a people should be disposed unto all fair acts of pity and kindness. Then they will be with the Lord; and O that this people were so with him!

This is the use to be now made of what has been delivered. Let us all now be with God, that God may be with us. I suppose whatever else we differ in, we generally concur in that wish: "The Lord our God be with us, as he was with our fathers: let him not leave us, nor forsake us" (I Kings 8. 57*). O that we might all as much concur in an endeavorous resolution to be with God as our fathers were with him; not to leave him nor forsake him. There is as much of New England in this great congregation as can well be reach'd by the voice of one address; 'tis indeed the best part of New England that is at least represented in this assembly. As the great council at Jerusalem sat near the temple, thus the whole convention of the Massachusetts is here come into the house of God this day; wherefore I take the boldness to say, "Hear ye me, Asa, and all Judah and Benjamin." The chief sinner and least preacher among all your sons now takes a liberty to mind you that God will be with you while you are with him. Now that we may be all of us inspired with a zeal for this great thing this day, let us consider first how desirable, how necessary a thing it is that we should have God with us. Truly this is the *unum necessarium*[16] of New England!

Nothing is more desirable for us than the presence of our God. The Jews have a fable of their manna that whatever any man had a mind to taste, he presently found in the manna a savor and a relish of it. It is very true of this blessed presence; all manner of blessings are enwrapped in it. There is a multitude of blessings which we are desirous of, but they are all contained in this comprehensive thing; it will give every honest man all that he wants. This will extricate us out of all our labyrinths; this will set all things to rights among us; this will wonderfully carry on all the salvations which have been begun for us by the God of our salvations. If Christ, if God be aboard, our little vessel will not sink in the gaping, roaring, formidable waves now tossing of it. Well did the apostle say in Romans 8. 31: "If God be for us, who can be against us?" Thus if God be with us, we have all for us. One God will weigh down more than ten worlds. If we have the presence of that God who made and moves the universe by a word; if we have the presence of that God who can command and create our deliverances—O most happy we! We may then join in such triumphant acclamations as that in Psalms 118. 6: "The Lord is on my side; I will not fear: what can man do unto me?" We may then defy even the gates of hell itself, for *cur metuat hominem homo in sinu Dei positus?*[17] And tho' abroad at this day "the earth is removing, and the waters roar and are troubled, and the mountains are shaking," splitting, tumbling "with the swelling thereof" [Psal. 46. 2, 3]; tho' the great and the terrible God be at this day coming out of his place to make all Europe a stage of blood and fire and make the nations everywhere drink deep of the cup that shall make them giddy with all manner of confusion and astonishment—yet we shall be "helped right early," for "God is in the midst of us" [Psal. 46. 5].

Add to this: nothing is more necessary for us than the presence of God. We are undone, thrice and four times undone, if we have it not. Methinks

[16] "The basic, or first necessity."
[17] "Why should a man who is set in the bosom of God fear a man?"

I hear the almighty God with a voice more awful than that of the loudest thunder saying over us as in Hosea 9. 12: "Woe to them when I depart from them." And woe to us indeed; we are in a most woeful estate if it come to that! How can we endure the mention of it without our most importunate deprecations: "O our God, leave us not!" We can have a prospect of nothing but horrible disorders, agonies, and vexations if we lose the presence of our Lord. We lie open to no less than a fearful dissipation and more than all our late oppressors would rejoice to see brought upon us. We have lately been complaining of burdens that were grievous to us, but I may warn you of our danger to feel one burden more which will infinitely exceed them all; 'tis that in Jeremiah 23. 33: "What burden? I will even forsake you, saith the Lord." Behold a burden that will sink us into a bottomless abyss of calamities! The presence of God, this is no less than the very soul of New England; we are dead and gone if that withdraw. When Israel was nimbly enough possessing themselves of the promised land which God had given them such a charter for, they perished in the attempt; for in Deuteronomy 1. 42, "The Lord said, Go not up; for I am not among you." Alas, if we don't in the first place look to this, that God be among us, we cannot avoid all manner of disappointments, desolations.

Let us consider secondly what uncomfortable symptoms we have had of God's not being with us. It seems as if God had fulfilled that sad word on this poor land in Deuteronomy 31. 17: "I will forsake them, and many evils shall befall them; so that they will say in that day, Are not these evils come upon us, because God is not among us?" There is a vast number of calamities which have given us lamentable cause to fear that God has forsaken us. Why have we suffered such a blast both on our trade and on our corn that the husbandman complains: "I looked for much and lo, it came to little!" And the mariner complains: "I went out full and came home empty!" 'Tis because our God is not among us. Why have we had fire after fire, laying our treasures in ashes? What means the heat of this anger, that Boston, the most noble and vital bowel of the territory, hath with a twice-repeated conflagration suffered such a loss of that which in the body politic answers to blood in the body natural?[18] 'Tis because our

---

[18] "Nov. 27, 1676, 'A fire broke out in Boston about 5 in the morning at one Wakefield's house by the Red Lion, by a candle carelessly set, which so prevailed that it burnt down about 45 dwelling houses, the north meeting-house, and several warehouses . . .' *Idem.* [Interleav'd Almanac.] 'Aug. 8, 1679, about midnight a terrible fire began at one Gross's house, the sign of the three mariners, near the dock in

God is not among us. Why have we had war after war made upon us by a foolish nation? Why have the worst of the heathen had renewed advantages to disturb our peace? And why have so many of our brethren and neighbors been made a prey to the most savage murderers in the world? [19] It is because our God is not among us. Give me leave to say, as in Judges 6. 12: "If the Lord be with us, why then is all this befallen us?" But we may find humiliation enough to convince us of this deplorable thing, from what we have endured upon the loss of our government. She of old said unto our Lord Jesus in John 11. 21: "Lord, if thou hadst been here, my brother had not died." So if the Lord had been here, 'tis possible we had not died. If the Lord had been with us, would he have made our wall so feeble that (as they said of Jerusalem) the "going up of a poor fox upon it should break it down" [Neh. 4. 3]? If the Lord had been with us, had all the wild creatures that passed by this vineyard found such opportunities to be plucking at it? No, our God would have kept us as "a vineyard of red wine" and lest any should have hurt us, "he (the Lord) would have kept it night and day" [Isa. 27. 2, 3]. If the Lord had been with us, had you ever thought you had seen cause to declare, as you have lately and justly done, that a company of abject strangers had made a mere booty

Boston. All the warehouses and a great number of dwelling houses, with vessels then in the dock, were consumed. It continued till near noon the next day; the most woeful desolation that Boston ever saw; eighty-odd dwelling houses and seventy-odd warehouses, with several vessels and their lading consumed to ashes. The whole loss computed to be two hundred thousand pounds.' *Idem*" (Thomas Hutchinson, *History*, I, 295–296).

[19] Since the close of King Philip's War in 1676, in which "one-tenth of the adult males of Massachusetts were killed or captured by the Indians, and two-thirds of her towns and villages suffered directly from . . . raids" (Charles H. Lincoln, "Introduction," *Narratives of the Indian Wars 1675–1699*, New York, 1913, 4), Indian harassment of the frontier continued intense and often bloody, including recent attacks in Maine and Connecticut. See Cotton Mather, *An History of Remarkable Occurrences in the Long War Which New-England Hath Had with the Indian Savages . . . 1688–1699* (Boston, 1699), incorporated into the *Magnalia Christi Americana . . .* , 2 vols. (Hartford, 1820), II, 582–594; Thomas Hutchinson, *History*, I, 309–310, 314–315. King Philip's War produced "at least eight" pamphlets and tracts printed in London, 1675–77 (Lincoln, 22). In addition, there were at least four Boston items which made breathtaking reading in their descriptions of Indian atrocities: William Hubbard, *A Narrative of the Troubles with the Indians . . .* (Boston, 1677); Increase Mather, *A Relation of the Troubles Which Have Happened in New-England . . .* (Boston, 1677); Mrs. Mary Rowlandson's narrative of the attack on Lancaster, *The Soveraignty and Goodness of God* (Cambridge, 1682), which went into a second edition the same year, as well as a London reprint; finally, Increase Mather included in the second chapter of *An Essay for the Recording of Illustrious Providences* (Boston, 1684) deliverances from Indians and "the relation of a captive," Quentin Stockwell (39–57).

of us? Had we ever felt the sore grievances of an illegal and arbitrary government? No. The God of heaven was not with that oppress'd people to whom he said in Isaiah 1. 7: "Your country is desolate: your land, strangers devour it."

What shall I say? It was an appeal made in Joel 1. 2: "Hear this, ye old men. Hath this been in your days?" Even so, I may say to the old men within the hearing of it: My fathers, you remember how we were when God was with us; pray, was it so in your days as it has been in ours? Were you visited with plague after plague in a long series of heavy judgments as we your poor children are? Surely, they will tell us, God is not with us as he was with them.

In all these matters our case may at least have some correspondence with that in Luke 24.* 28, [29]: "He made as though he would have gone; but they constrained him, saying, Abide with us!"

Let us consider thirdly: If we are not with God we shall be guilty of an apostasy, and that under very shameful, very direful aggravations too.

We shall be apostates, and O let us not be so lest our God say, "My soul can have no pleasure in them" [Heb. 10. 38]. But if we are so, we shall be of all apostates the most inexcusable. Let us consider what fathers we have had; they were with God. I may say of 'em as in Hosea 9. 8: They were with my God; and they are gone to be so forever. What an unaccountable thing will it be for us to have that character which we have been so much cautioned against: "There arose another generation which knew not the Lord" [Judg. 2. 10]. What? Shall the grandchildren of Moses turn idolaters and shall the children of Samuel become the children of Belial? Shall we forget the hope of our fathers or forsake our fathers' Friend? The very graves of those blessed men, every post, every stone upon their graves is a witness against us if we do. With dismal accents methinks their very ghosts will groan unto us, "Alas, is our posterity come to this!" Nay Abraham would be ignorant of us and Israel would not acknowledge us if we should be so degenerate as to lose the presence of the Lord.

Let us also consider what warnings we have had. It may be said unto us as in Jeremiah 25. 4: "The Lord hath sent unto you all his servants the prophets." This country has been blessed with a most faithful ministry by which I suppose every assembly in this territory has been called upon to be with God and to keep with him. Especially the sermons which our elections have put the ambassadors of God upon preaching and printing of—these have been so many loud warnings unto us that we leave him not. In them we have been faithfully warned that our true interest is not to lie unto God. We have been warned that the latter end of our misbehaviors will be destruction from the Lord. We have been warned that "we must repent, and do our first works; or have the candlestick of the Lord Jesus removed from us" [Rev. 2. 5]. In a word, we have been warned from heaven that if we forsake our God he will cast us off forever. O miserable we, if we do it after all.

These considerations will not have their due force unless they expire in a threefold request which I must now lay before you; and I may justly assert concerning the things contained therein, they are not vain things, they are our life. Wherefore, "Hear ye me, Asa, and all Judah and Benjamin"; hear ye these things, all ye people of the Massachusetts!

First, let us return to the Lord. We must come to him if we would be with him. We have marvelously backslidden from our God but he calls after us, "Return ye backsliding children and I will heal your backslidings." O that we may all as one man reply what is in Jeremiah 3. 22: "Behold, we come unto thee; for thou art the Lord our God!" If we ask that question in Malachi 3.* 7: "Wherein shall we return?" methinks t'were an harder question, "Wherein should we not?" But behold, we have had a great voice out of the temple in answer thereunto. We have had the elders and messengers of our churches, convened in a synod, solemnly informing of us "wherein we shall return." [20] God forbid the advice of that synod should only serve to convict us and condemn us in the day when he shall take vengeance on us for our contemning of it. That were dreadful indeed! But in compliance with it, let every man seriously now enquire of himself, What have I done? Mark what I say: That man who does not suspect himself of having a share in the sins which have driven away from us the presence of our God—that man, I may safely affirm it, is one of the principal troublers of this Israel; I do without any scruple say it: Thou art the man. Let us all then examine ourselves and set upon the reforming of our own hearts and lives and the renewing of our covenants with the Lord.

Indeed both the objects in which, and the authors from whom, we have

[20] For the "Reforming Synod" of 1679, largely instigated by Cotton's father, Increase, see p. 97 above.

endured our calamities, those are enough to indigitate [21] what sins they are that have exposed us thereunto. Let me in two or three instances use a plain dealing with you, agreeable to my station here this day.

What have been the objects in which we have been afflicted? Our fruits have been blasted—and were they not abused in the excesses of sensuality? Our lands have been threat'ned—and were not they the idols for the sake of which we have offended God and almost renounced all that was holy and just and good? The most happy and easy government in the world was changed with us into what has by the most impartial men been confessed to have become intolerable. Why, did not men despise the best of governments and procure other things to be set over them, because they endeavored to make logs of what they before enjoyed? [22] To pass on—were we not in the late unreasonable extortions of the law invited to consider whether our needless multiplications of litigious, contentious lawsuits formerly amongst us were not a scandal thus chastised? Were we not in the late unsufferable injuries, abuses, and exactions of them that under the pretense of the excise carried on very outrageous villainies, put upon considering whether the multitude or quality of drinking houses in the midst of us had not once been a stumbling block of our iniquity?

Again, what have been the authors from whom we have been afflicted? Our molestations have risen very much from Indian hands. And alas, have we not very much injured the Indians? I do not mean by taking from them their land—for it was hardly possible they should be more fairly dealt withal than they have been in that particular—but by teaching of them our vice. We that should have learn'd them to pray have learn'd them to sin. Endeavors for their conversion have by many people been blown upon, but there have been wicked English who have taught them to drink, yea and to curse and swear—things which they knew not the meaning of till they came to school unto such white pagans as some that wear the Christian livery among ourselves. And have not we also followed the Indians? The Indians are infamous, especially for three scandalous qualities: They are lazy drones and love idleness exceedingly! They are also most impudent liars and will invent reports and stories at a strange

[21] *Indigitate*: to call, proclaim, declare, invoke; to point out as with a finger (*NED*, V, 214).
[22] An allusion to Aesop's fable of the free but vain frogs who desired a king and got a log. See R. Dodsley, *Select Fables of Aesop and Other Fabulists*, new edn. (London, 1809), 5–6.

and monstrous rate; and they are out of measure indulgent unto their children—there is no family government among them. But O how much do our people Indianize in every one of those abominable things! We must repent of these our miscarriages or else our God will take up that resolution concerning us: "I will even forsake them, saith the Lord" [Jer. 23. 33].

Secondly, let not sin be with us and God will be so. 'Tis the purpose of our God in Joshua 7. 12: "I will not be with you, except ye destroy the accursed thing from among you." Let us then "destroy" that "accursed thing."

Especially let us take heed of the sins which at this time we have a peculiar disposition to. It was complain'd in Hosea 7. 1: "When I would have healed Israel, the iniquity of Ephraim was discovered." It has been thus, but God will not be with us if it still be thus among ourselves. Our good God, the Lord our Healer, is now healing of us. O let us not now be impatient patients, lest that our blessed Physician deal hardly and roughly with us. *Impatiens aegrotus crudelem facit medicum.*[23] Let us now no more discover revengefulness against them that have deserved ill of us. Let the law and not the sword measure out their due unto them. No more discover an unthankfulness unto them that have deserved well of us. Requite them not with censure and hatred for their unwearied pains to preserve our peace. No more discover a contempt of the ministers who set themselves faithfully to declare the whole counsel of God and to "lift up their voice like a trumpet, in showing us our sins" [Isa. 58. 1]. They are all agreed (I hope) as one man to live and die studying of your welfare; but if they are unjustly ill-treated with you, the great God whose messengers they are will take notice of it and say, "Ye have despised me!"

And O let us no more discover such a spirit of lying as we have made ourselves worthy to be reproved for. We find mention of an evil spirit that said in I Kings 22. 22: "I will go forth, and I will be a lying spirit in the mouth of all the prophets." Doubtless * the same devil has been suing for a license to go forth and be a lying spirit in the mouth of near all the people here. I would to God this devil were in a shorter chain! I beseech you let not this land have that character, a country full of lies.

But of all our errors there is none of such dangerous and threatening consequence as the contention which we are too prone to break forth into.

[23] "An impatient patient makes the doctor cruel."

We are too much a contentious, and that will soon render us a wretched and a ruin'd people. A divided and quarrelsome people do even say to the Almighty, "Depart from us"; for he is the God of peace. But O what is our meaning then to make a full submission and entire resignation of ourselves to the tyranny of our own passions, as we have too much done while we have been debating about the measures of another submission and resignation in our various resolutions! * I have read of a people with whom it was a law that in a fray where swords were drawn, if a child did but cry "Peace!" they must end the quarrel or else he died that strook the first blow after peace was named. He that considers the feverish paroxysms which this land is now raging in through mere misunderstandings about the means leading to the end wherein we are generally agreed, and how ready we are to treat one another with fiery animosities, had need cry "Peace, peace!" with a very speedy importunity. For my own part, I confess myself but a child and among the meanest, the smallest of your children too;[24] but yet I am old enough to cry "Peace!" and in the name of God I do it. Peace! my dear countrymen; let there be peace in all our studies, peace in all our actions, and peace notwithstanding all our differences. We cannot avoid having our different sentiments, but Peace! I say. O let not our dissents put us upon hatred and outrage and every evil work. It has not a little surprised me to read in a Greek author who wrote fifteen hundred years ago that in the times long preceding his, there was a tradition among them that Europe and Asia and Africa were islands encompassed by the ocean, without and beyond which was another as big as they—in which other world were mighty and long-liv'd people inhabiting of great cities, the two greatest whereof were called, one of them the fighting city, the other of them the godly city.[25] Behold very ancient footsteps of the knowledge which the Old World had of our America some thousands of years ago. But I pray, which of them American cities must New England become incorporate into? Truly if we are a fighting or a disagreeing people, we shall not be a pious one. We have hitherto professed ourselves a country of Puritans; I beseech you then let us have

[24] At twenty-six, Cotton Mather was by far the youngest minister to give an election sermon between 1634 and 1775.

[25] Mather's immediate source remains unidentified, but the ancient idea of a great island, Atlantis, as big as Africa and Asia put together, and lying beyond the known sea, goes back at least to Plato's *Timaeus* and *Critias*; the myth of Atlantis as an early civilization figures in the geographical writings of Strabo and the historical writings of Diodorus.

the wisdom to be first pure, then peaceable. Every man should count himself liable to follies and mistakes and misprisions not a few. Are you so or are you not? If you are not, what do you here in this lower world where you can find no more of your own attainments? If you are so, then be patient and peaceable towards those who see not with your eyes! Let us all condescend one unto another and let no man be in a foaming rage if every sheaf do not bow to his.* There is one ingenious way to unite this people if it were so heeded as it ought to be. I remember an inquisitive person of old, that he might know which was the best sect among all the philosophers, he asked one and another and everyone still preferr'd the sect which he was of himself. But he then asked them successively, "Which do you reckon the next best?" and they all agreed that next to their own Plato's was the best—upon which he chose that as indeed the best of all. Thus we all have our several schemes of things and every man counts his own to be the best; but I would say to every man, Suppose your scheme laid aside, what would you count the next best? Doubtless we should be of one mind as to that. And if we could act by the common measures of Christianity we should soon be united in it. O that we could receive the Word of the Lord Jesus in II Corinthians 13. 11: "Brethren, live in peace; and the God of love and peace shall be with you."

Thirdly, let every man do his part and his best in this matter, that God may be with us.

Behold a work provided for all sorts of men. Pardon me that I first offer it unto you that are or may be our superiors. It was said in Hosea 11. 12: "Judah ruleth with God." When rulers are with God, O happy government! Unto you, much honored, I would humbly address this petition, that your first work may be to think on some considerable expedient by which the presence of God may be secured unto us. A little consultation may soon produce what all New England may bless you for. Yea, 'tis very much in your power to do what may have a tendency to perpetuate the presence of God unto the succeeding generations. I cannot forbear uttering the wish of the great Chytraeus in this honorable audience: *Utinam potentes rerum domini majorem ecclesiae et scholarum curam susciperent!* [26] May a godly and a learned ministry be everywhere encouraged and no plantations allowed to live without a good minister in

---

[26] "Would that powerful men might take on a greater responsibility for the church and schools." David Chytraeus (1531–1600), theologian and professor at the University of Rostock, published many works on theology and history.

them. May the college[27] be maintained, and that river the wholesome streams whereof have made glad the city of God and blessed us with a privilege above the other outgoings of our nation, be kept running, with issues beyond those from the seminaries of Canada or Mexico. May schools be countenanced and all good ways to nourish them and support them in every town be put in execution. You shall then probably leave the presence of God as a blessed legacy with such as may come after you. I know not whether we do or can at this day labor under an iller symptom than the too general want of education in the rising generation, which if not prevented will gradually but speedily dispose us to that sort of Criolian degeneracy observed to deprave the children of the most noble and worthy Europeans when transplanted into America. The youth of this country are very sharp and early ripe in their capacities, above most in the world; and were the benefits of a religious and ingenuous education bestowed upon them they would soon prove an admirable people; and as we know that England afforded the first discoverers of America in these latter ages, whatever the Spaniards may pretend unto the contrary—for it may be proved that both Britons and Saxons did inhabit here at least three or four hundred years before Columbus was born into the world, which the annals themselves of those times do plainly enough declare—so our little New England may soon produce them that shall be commanders of the greatest glories that America can pretend unto. But if our youth be permitted to run wild in our woods, we shall soon be forsaken by that God whom our fathers followed hither when it was a land not sown; and Christianity, which like the sun hath moved still westward unto these "goings down of the sun," will return to the Old World again, leaving here not a New Jerusalem as Doctor Twiss hoped, but a Gog and Magog as Master Mede feared, for the last of the latter days.[28] Now may the God of heaven bless the wisdom and goodness of your endeavors for the continuance of his

[27] Harvard.

[28] Twiss wrote Joseph Mede in March 1635, asking him to comment on the idea that, in view of "the opinion of many grave divines concerning the Gospel's fleeting westward," America might be "the place of New Jerusalem." Mede replied that he thought the Devil, tired and impatient "of the sound of the Gospel and Cross of Christ in every part of this old world," had chosen America for a "seed over which he might reign securely . . ." (*The Works of . . . Joseph Mede . . .* , 3rd edn., London, 1672, 799–800). Increase Mather refers to this exchange of letters in an earlier election sermon, *A Discourse Concerning the Danger of Apostacy* in *A Call from Heaven* (Boston, 1685), 77.

presence with those that may rise up in your stead when you shall be gone to be forever with the Lord. Allow me to say unto the fathers of this country what was said unto the judges of old: "Deal courageously, and the Lord shall be with the good" [II Chron. 19. 11].

And as for us that are and shall be inferiors, let us also do what we can that our God may be still among us. We ought all of us humbly to lay before our worthy rulers that encouragement in Ezra 10. 4: "Arise; for this matter belongs to thee: we also will be with thee: be of good courage, and do it." Let there be a public spirit in us all for the good of the whole—the rarity and mortality whereof among us, New England bewails among the greatest of its calamities. Especially let us pray hard that God would not leave the land. It was a public spirit which was in that famous Prince of Orange who was the first Captain-General of the united Provinces an hundred years ago and the ancestor of that illustrious person whose glorious design and service we have lately with so much unanimity declared for, that when he was basely murthered by the pistol of a Papist, his dying and only words were, "O my God, take pity of my soul and of this poor people."[29] When he had but one breath to draw in the world his poor people had half of it! O let this poor people have no less than half our cares, half our prayers. Let no man say, "I am a sorry creature; of what account can my prayers be?" For you that can do little else but pray can yet be the instruments of saving this poor people by the presence of the Lord. We find in Amos 7. 2, [3], that a poor herdsman and huckster kept the great God from leaving of the land. A poor husbandman, yea a poor woman, by lively prayers may do incredibly much towards the keeping of our God yet among us.

And if God be with us, then his rod and staff, his mighty crook which horribly breaks the bones of all that it falls upon, will crush and wound all that shall go to make this wilderness "a valley of the shadow of death" unto us, and beat away all that may essay to do us any harm. So shall we be led and fed among the sheep of our God; he will restore us and his "goodness and mercy shall follow us all our days" [Psal. 23. 4, 6].[30]

[29] William I, of the Netherlands, was murdered at his home in Delft by Balthazar Gérard in 1584: "In the letters of the states-general to Ghent and to Queen Elizabeth the words are given, 'Mon Dieu, ayez pitié de mon âme! Mon Dieu, ayez pitié de ce pauvre peuple!' " (Ruth Putnam, *William the Silent, Prince of Orange*, New York, 1895, II, 413n).

[30] In both issues of the sermon, there follows a "Mantissa," paginated separately

from 1 to 5, to "fill the remaining pages of this sheet." The Mantissa gives three instances of "memorable providences" to illustrate the folly of rejecting and despising the Gospel—all involving the Indians. The first two tell of the slaughter of the Narragansetts and the death of King Philip, and the third tells of an Indian slaughter of "300" English "at least" in Virginia shortly after they had tried to force out three Puritan ministers who had gone there at the request of some who desired "the means of eternal salvation."

IV SAMUEL DANFORTH'S
SERMON OF 1714

AN INTRODUCTION

I

THE last decade of the seventeenth century belonged to the Mathers; Cotton gave three election sermons, and his father two. The first three sermons of the decade are political, with emphasis on the good ruler. The model in Cotton Mather's *Serviceable Man* in 1690 is Nehemiah. Mather lashes out at the Quakers and asks that the serviceable ruler set up a committee to encourage more missionary work with the Indians. In 1693, his father speaks of "the great blessing of primitive counsellors," and Samuel Willard follows in 1694 with a survey of Renaissance-Puritan ideas on "the character of a good ruler."

The next three printed sermons, by Samuel Torrey, Cotton Mather, and Nicholas Noyes, are of the errand type. Torrey eases the charge of apostasy by arguing that God is always ready and eager to save a backsliding people; when they think they are in greatest danger they may in fact be most secure. The phrase "God's controversy with New England," a favorite one in these sermons, appears along with specific grievances a year later in Cotton Mather's *Things for a Distressed People to Think Upon*. In 1699 Increase Mather blends the two types of errand and political theory sermons; the "surest way" to honor God is to elect good Magistrates and remember the errand still to be achieved. Again a typical rhetorical pattern emerges: the first part of the sermon is dry, cold, pedantic; in the application the tone changes to lyric wail and fiery exhortation.

Cotton Mather's sermon in 1700 comes close to the description of Dimmesdale's sermon in *The Scarlet Letter,* but it is less a prophecy of the future than a survey of what already exists. It is unique because it relegates the apostasy theme to a few brief sentences. The sermon is a *tour de force* on the Puritan Great Society. Mather takes a holiday from the role of a Jeremiah who must concentrate on what is wrong with New England, and indulges in an enormous boast, a classic statement of New England's ingrown sense of its magnificence.

The matchless favors of God unto New England are now to be set before you in a short catalog of them; I say a short one, for who can in a piece of an hour compose a full one, or one that shall not fall short in many instances? Beholding so much of New England from every quarter, under such characters here come together, I shall take this opportunity to be-speak your hearty praises to the almighty God for so dealing with New England as not with any nation.[1]

Indeed New England is not heaven; that we are sure of! But for my part, I do not ask to remove out of New England except for a removal into heaven.[2]

The climate, the college, the government with its theocratic and democratic principles, the wise and good English King, the absence of Socinians, Arminians, and Catholics from the Colony, the magnitude of communities full of godly people—God has indeed favored Massachusetts. "My New England has one thing that will weigh down more than forty of the best things that other countries can brag of; that is, religion, religion, religion!"[3] "Imposters have but seldom got in and set up among us; and when they have done so, they have made but a short blaze, and gone out in a snuff . . ."[4] Fresh from completing the *Magnalia* with its epic survey of achievements, he may have sensed that the beginning of the century was an appropriate time to steer the election sermon in new directions.[5] Perhaps Jeremiah should give way to a psalmist of joy. Perhaps the people were losing sight of how much they had in fact achieved at the hands of God, and harangues on what should be, and what used to be, should be tempered with a reminder of what is.

---

[1] Cotton Mather, *A Pillar of Gratitude* . . . (Boston, 1700), 6.

[2] *Ibid.,* 11.

[3] *Ibid.,* 13–14.

[4] *Ibid.,* 27.

[5] Mather sent the manuscript of the *Magnalia* to London in June 1700; it appeared in 1702. *Diary of Cotton Mather,* ed. Worthington C. Ford, 2 vols. (*Collections of*

The Protestant religion hath not been set up scarce in any nation but it has made them, even in temporals, within a very little while twice as rich and as great as they were before; and one somewhat curious in his calculations has demonstrated that the abolishing of Popery in the English nation is worth at least eight millions of pounds sterling yearly profit unto it.[6]

There is no point in reviewing the years between 1700 and 1713 sermon by sermon. There was little change from the political and errand sermons already discussed—with one exception. If Cotton Mather did have a motive in 1700 of easing the apostasy theme, it went unnoticed, for after a series of sermons on the good ruler between 1701 and 1706, John Norton returns to the errand type in 1708.

The one exception is Ebenezer Pemberton's election sermon, *The Divine Original and Dignity of Government Asserted . . .* (Boston, 1710). The sermon is based on the 82nd Psalm, "I have said, ye are gods . . . but ye shall die like men." Pemberton carefully lays out the dual nature of rulers; they are necessary to an ordered government, so designated by God, and should justly command the respect of the people. But they too will die. They must both hold a sense of the dignity of their position, and not lose sight of their humanity or their humility.

The tone is controlled, quiet, dignified. The sermon has the high seriousness of Milton; it quotes from Pascal, Socrates, Homer, Plutarch, Le Compte, and Plato. Pemberton is more detailed, precise, and restrained than his predecessors. It's a matter of tone. The flamboyance and urgency of the prophet are gone. Pemberton's rhetoric is closer to the eighteenth-century ideal of reason and common sense. His God is not holding men over pits of fire, throwing manna in their way, or waiting to be called back by a degenerate people. Pemberton's is a God of wisdom and reason. Man must discover his laws and act in harmony with them.

. . . he always exercises his supreme authority according to the rules of the most consummate wisdom, spotless righteousness, unblemish'd integrity, and diffusive goodness. He governs not by unaccountable will or inconstant humor, which are imperfections his nature can't suffer, but by stable measures, as may best suit the nature and circumstances of his subjects and the noble end of his government.

Hence rulers of all orders ought to conform to and regulate themselves in all their administrations by this divine standard. Their govern-

the *Massachusetts Historical Society,* 7th ser., VII–VIII, Boston, 1911–12), I, 352–353.

[6] *A Pillar of Gratitude,* 19.

ment should be a transcript and visible image of the divine rule. And the more exactly they conform to this measure, the nearer they approach in their rule over men to the divine pattern, the brighter will be the characters of divine glory reflected on them. . . . He fully understands the nature and powers of all creatures, all things in their several relations and dependencies, the fitness of means to propounded ends, and hence acts all things according to the rules of the most consummate wisdom, and has in all ages so turned the wheels of providence as might suit the end of government.[7]

Stable measures, patterns, models, rules, imitation—for the first time in the election sermons we begin to hear the vocabulary of the eighteenth century. Benjamin Franklin (four years old in 1710) would write an influential *Autobiography* demonstrating the truth of these words of Pemberton's:

There must be skill in the general maxims of government and prudence in a pertinent application of these to emergent cases, that by an orderly conduct the great affairs and designs of a state be carry'd on to an happy conclusion. There is to this requisite a penetrating sagacity to foresee public dangers, and a seasonable precaution to guard against them; and for this end rulers should be men of deep thought, good experience, and of great presence of mind, that they may not be shoved beyond their reason by any unexpected emergencies, but that they may maintain their temper unshocked and well lay'd designs unbroken, whatever may assault them.[8]

Pemberton is ultimately, however, a spokesman for a God of providence as well as law. At the conclusion he focuses on the soul of man bound for eternity. The sermon stands on the watershed between the ages of Cotton Mather and Benjamin Franklin.[9]

II

The election sermon of 1714 was preached by Samuel Danforth, son of the minister who preached *Errand into the Wilderness* in 1670.[10] Its

---

[7] *The Divine Original,* 28–29, 30.

[8] *Ibid.,* 35–36.

[9] Perhaps the reader is wondering why Pemberton's sermon is not included in this volume. In the planning stages it was included, then rejected for two reasons. The sermon is very long and toward the end repetitive. The final third is anticlimactic and drags. Also, Barnard's sermon of 1734 is a better example of the quiet, precise, and reasoned style of some of the eighteenth-century sermons. Barnard, however, quotes from Pemberton; he recognized the pathfinder in the tone and emphasis he wanted.

[10] Samuel Danforth, born in Roxbury on December 18, 1666, graduated from Har-

distinction is twofold: it is surely the finest example of an expanded metaphor in an election sermon up to the time of the Revolution, demonstrating the Puritans' capacity for ingenious analogies and emblems, and its discussion of God's presence with his chosen people emphasizes a dimension of the covenant theory which modern criticism tends to overlook.

In his first book, *Nature,* in 1836 (and without knowing it he was speaking for Hawthorne, Melville, Thoreau, and Whitman), Emerson says that matter is a symbol of spirit. Jonathan Edwards and Samuel Danforth would understand this view. Typology, allegory, emblem—such tools were in constant use by a good Puritan writer; he knew he had to be a seer if he wanted to write well. The unseen is as important as the seen; the suggested as the stated. The Puritan saw the Bible as art as well as law; he recognized the metaphorical sap of the Great Book and he tried to make it flow.

In 1670, the elder Danforth outlined the Puritans' errand into the wilderness. Samuel Willard in 1682 focused on the role of God's ambassadors, the heroes of the errand inside the wall. Here, in 1714, Danforth the younger takes another detail from his father's fresco and examines it closely. The wall of fire separates a wilderness from a garden. Why a garden? What are the implications of this medieval and Renaissance symbol of the macrocosm for the New England errand? Danforth carries the pastoral theme of his father's sermon to its ultimate implications.

The covenanted, chosen people are vines in a vineyard, sucking up the life-giving energies from their Christ-roots, and tenderly cared for by the God-gardener who waters and prunes the garden, cuts out the weeds, and keeps the wall enclosing it in good repair lest the beasts of the wilderness break through and ravage it. As Danforth pushes the metaphor further, the abstractions of the theology become more meaningful and sensuous. There are times here when the reader feels the aesthetic pleasure of reading metaphysical poetry; the conceit is successful on both levels of logic

vard in 1683 and was ordained minister at Taunton on September 21, 1687. He continued in the ministry there forty years until his death on November 14, 1727. Danforth was interested in law, the art of medicine ("he may in fact be called the principal, if not the only, physician and lawyer" of Taunton), and the Indians (John Langdon Sibley and Clifford K. Shipton, *Biographical Sketches of Those Who Attended Harvard College,* 13 vols., Cambridge and Boston, 1873–1965, III, 244). He prepared an Indian dictionary in manuscript, apparently formed from John Eliot's Indian Bible. He published several other sermons. For a biographical sketch of Danforth, see *Sibley's Harvard Graduates,* III, 243–249.

and emotion or "felt thought"—even though out of context the conceits seem forced and theoretically ridiculous. Like Christ's church, the vine is visible, but like the Pentecost of Grace, it contains within an invisible energy. The pain of suppressing man's natural inclination to sin is like the pain of an incision, when a base stock is grafted onto a noble (Christlike) vine. When a great harvest is to be gathered, the husbandman must find many helpers. So with the New England garden; the many worthy ministers of New England have been sent by God to harvest his crop. The images of the garden, the enclosing wall, the vines and temples within, and God as gardener, form a myth which translates the abstractions of Christian theology into a little play, or make-believe toyland. It exists in that neutral territory somewhere between reality and fairyland (as Hawthorne describes a romance); it carries from the here-and-now of Boston, Massachusetts, 1714, a communal knowledge about turning a wilderness into crop-bearing fields, and harvesting; it brings from the Bible certain basic tenets of God's relationship to man, and it blends them in a fiction suspended in the imagination. Although the Puritans distrusted the imagination, it does not follow that they had none.

There is a second significance to this sermon. Although it explores the metaphor of a garden, it is also concerned with the most important element of that garden—God's abiding presence. This presence is not seen directly but surmised from events. Of all the aspects in the errand motif—the departure from England, the voyage, the wilderness, the garden, the wall, the ministerial watchmen, the first generation—the most important ingredient which gives all these others meaning and value is the continuing presence of God's special endorsement and protection. From primitive times to the present day, religious festivals in the spring have celebrated a return to life from its source in a god. Communities reserve for their greatest fear and horror the speculation that their life-giving and protecting gods have departed to leave them to their own resources. Then is chaos come again. Add to this communal instinct the Puritans' emphasis on man's fall and on a chosen society—that without God's grace man is nothing and can accomplish nothing, but God chooses certain communities as his own and enters into covenant with them—and the need for assurance every spring becomes all the more important.

Perry Miller has emphasized that colonial Puritans regarded God's covenant with them as a legal contract. Each party is bound to keep his end of the bargain. God is not arbitrary or capricious; responsibility for remaining his chosen people lies as much with the men and women of Boston or Marblehead as it does with God. This, in Miller's phrase, is their "federal theology." [11]

That such a syndrome of ideas was widespread from 1630 to approximately 1730 is incontrovertible; but it is not the whole story. The election sermons provide abundant evidence of the bargain to be kept by men of right reason, but there is also an undercurrent of magic, mystery, of wooing a mysterious God who is capriciously angry, proud, and demanding in spite of his bargain. Danforth's sermon is a good example. He is less the lawyer than the priest, his oration less a legal exposition than an incantation to drive off the evil spirits and woo back the good. There is magic here. When God touches his favored people, infants and the young on their deathbeds have special messages. Consider the imagery. God's return to his people is accompanied with pangs like labor pains; Christ's adopting his people is like a marriage. To win back their God, the people of Massachusetts must "mourn," "cry mightily," and fall "prostrate." Danforth is talking about a cosmic love affair.[12] A marriage is a legal covenant, but the spirit behind the contract is irrational—the upset stomach and sleepless nights of the courtship, the terror and the ecstasy of affection. God here is not a lawyer waiting for his client's answer; he's a jealous lover off in a pout. The proof of his return and presence is the most magical of all—remarkable providences. The "pomegranate buds forth," the land quickens in its luster, "the worst sort of sinners are changed into saints suddenly and surprisingly." Such metamorphoses are not measurable in a legal contract, but in a poet's vision or a lover's rejoicing.

[11] Miller's early discussions of the federal covenant in "The Marrow of Puritan Divinity" (1935; reprinted in *Errand into the Wilderness*, Cambridge, 1956, 48–98), and the chapters "The Social Covenant" and "The Church Covenant," *The New England Mind: The Seventeenth Century* (New York, 1939), 398–462, are elaborate and detailed; for a brief summary of the covenant theory, see his "Declension in a Bible Commonwealth," *Proceedings of the American Antiquarian Society*, LI (Worcester, 1942), 37–94, especially 42–47.

[12] "The Song of Solomon (Canticle of Canticles) fits well into the bridal conception of the relationship of God and Israel, betrothed in the wilderness (3:6; 8:5) and likened to a garden enclosed (4:12). . . . Even in the Old Testament God was thought of as the Bridegroom of a people who were coming up into history out of the anonymity of the wilderness of the peoples (Canticles 8:5)" (George H. Williams, *Wilderness and Paradise in Christian Thought*, New York, 1962, 16).

AN EXHORTATION

To All :

To use Utmost Endeavours to obtain A Visit of the

𝕲𝖔𝖉 𝖔𝖋 𝕳𝖔𝖘𝖙𝖘,

FOR THE

Preservation of **Religion**, and the CHURCH, upon Earth.

In a SERMON Preached before His Excellency theGOVERNOUR,theHonourable COUNCIL and Representatives of the Province of the *Maſ-ſachuſetts-Bay* in N. E. on *May* 26. 1714. being the Anniverſary Day of the ELECTION of COUNCELLORS of the ſaid Province.

By SAMUEL DANFORTH,
Paſtor of the Church in *Tanton.*

Iſaiah lxiii. 15. *Look down from Heaven, and behold from the Habitation of thy Holineß,& of thy Glory :—*

BOSTON: Printed by *B. Green :* Sold by *Samuel Gerriſh,* at his Shop on the North ſide of the Town-Houſe. 1714.

"RETURN, we beseech thee, O God of hosts: look down from heaven, and behold, and visit this vine" (Psal. 80. 14).

The state of the church of Israel when this Psalm was penned was very calamitous (as appears from the matter of the Psalm itself), both with respect unto sins and judgments. And the whole Psalm is a prayer in the name and behalf of the church unto God for deliverance. In the verse before us we may consider:

I. The description of the church prayed for by that metaphor of a vine, to explain which we may observe:

1. That Jesus Christ himself as Mediator, God-Man, and as Head of the church is the true Vine (John 15. 1). Christ compares himself to a vine according to his usual custom of taking similitudes from things common and obvious; such were vines in Judea (Deut. 8. 8) planted by the sides of their houses (Psal. 128. 3), probably of that house where Christ was when he spake those words. Christ is the principal Vine for whose sake the church of Israel was compared to a vine or vineyard, because out of that church the Messiah was to come who is the true Vine. Christ is that Vine, as God-Man, Mediator, to whom the Father hath given this prerogative to have life in himself (John 5. 26).

And to be a quickening Spirit unto those implanted into him and who are given to him to be his members (I Cor. 15. 45). Christ is therefore likened to that which is the chief part of a vine, namely the root and stock,

151

whenas his members are but like the branches. Christ as he is Man is of the same nature with the branches; as he is God he supplies the branches with spiritual life and grace. The human nature of Christ is as the conduit through which the gifts of the Holy Spirit flow unto his people. As Mediator he both merited grace for men and infuses grace into men, and more truly and perfectly nourishes believers unto eternal life than a vine doth its branches—as an Head of influence unto them. Christ is then the true and proper Vine, others but secondarily so and depending on Christ and deriving all their spiritual life from him, and obtaining all they have for his sake. And that they are vines in any sense is because God the Father, to glorify his Son, hath given them to him in an everlasting covenant, to be brought unto union and communion with him.

Many phrases in this Psalm may be referred to Christ: He is God's Joseph (ver. 1) [1] to whom belongs the right of primogeniture, to be the first-born of every creature; he is the Man of God's right hand (ver. 17), God's Benjamin who is exalted to sit at God's right hand, and if this glorious Benjamin were not there we should not be admitted to see God's face; he it is whom God the Father hath made strong for himself (ver. 15, 17 *), who did stand and feed in the strength of the Lord and in the majesty of the name of the Lord his God (Mic. 5. 4). And as Christ intended to make his church conformable to himself, so in some respect he would be like to his church; therefore he would be the Branch, the Vine, the Fruit of the earth, and would be brought out of Egypt (ver. 8; Matt. 2. 15). So that God's dispensations to his church were typical of the Messiah in many things; therefore also the same title of a vine comprehends both Christ and his church, as the name of Christ is also given to his mystical body, the church (I Cor. 12. 12).

Now God the Father hath engaged himself to be the Husbandman when Christ condescends to be the Vine; the Father will and doth always manifest his gracious presence with Christ as Head of the church, to assist and help him and strengthen him; and out of respect and love to the Lord Jesus Christ it is that the Father takes any notice in a way of pity, compassion, and grace, of any men or societies of men upon earth.

2. The invisible church of the elect are likened to a vine or vineyard— they are the branches ingrafted into Christ. It is an intellectual, mystical vineyard—the mystical paradise of God, partly in heaven and partly on earth. As God planted an earthly paradise in the garden of Eden which

did excel all the rest of the earth, so since the ruin of mankind by Adam's apostasy God will have a remnant among fallen mankind in every age and generation to be his vineyard, garden, orchard (or Eden, Eccles. 2. 5), depending on and united unto Christ the second Adam. For God in his infinite wisdom so ordered the things of the first creation that they might be natural types of what he would do in the new creation of all things by Christ.

The church is God's vineyard which his own right hand hath planted (ver. 8, 15). It is a garden inclosed (Cant. 4. 12),[2] planted, and formed for himself to show forth his praise (Isa. 43. 21), set apart for his own peculiar use, service, and delight. The church owns no other master but Christ, reserves all her fruit for him, and keeps faithful to him. Those planted into this vineyard, tho' by nature they are wild plants and of the wild olive, yet are made noble vines and a right seed by effectual calling and their implantation into Christ. The creating power of God's right hand is put forth in infusing grace into them; man's nature brings not forth the fruits of the Spirit without the skill and husbandry of him that made it— we are therefore called "God's husbandry" (I Cor. 3. 9). The seeds of the fruits of righteousness must be sown in us by God's Spirit and grow in us by his blessing, so that as Israel were not the natives of Canaan but God fetched his vine from afar off, even from Egypt, so grace is not the natural growth of our corrupt hearts but is transplanted into us from a further place, even from heaven. And although the first planting of virtue and piety in men be not without some bitterness (our inoculation into Christ is not without incision), yet the growth of it is pleasant and the fruit sweet and wholesome, even as the fruit of the vine, refreshing the heart of God and man. Variety of precious graces and virtues are implanted in them which are all useful and make them fruitful in good works; and as the fruit of the vine was used in sacrifices, so the good fruits of believers are a sweet-smelling sacrifice unto God. They are made sensible that they are weak and worthless creatures in and of themselves (as a vine is not timber fit for service, Ezekiel 15. 1, 2, fit for nothing but to be cast into the fire unless it bear fruit). Yet being vines planted into Christ himself, the fattest soil, and under-propped by the grace and Spirit of Christ strengthening and supporting of them, and the excrescencies of

---

[1] Whenever Danforth gives the source as "ver." he is referring to Psalm 80 from which he takes the text of his sermon. This short form is retained.

[2] "Canticles" is another title for "Song of Solomon."

corruption being continually lopped off by their careful vinedresser (John 15. 2), and being watered every moment from heaven by the fresh influences of the Spirit (Isa. 27. 2, 3)—they become plants of renown among whom Christ loves to walk; and he delights himself with the observation of the flourishing of this his vineyard (Cant. 6. 11).

This church of the elect is the true Israel of God (ver. 1), his peculiar people on earth, his Joseph, God's first-born among the children of men, to whom all church privileges belong as their birthright for their saving good. They are Christ's flock (ver. 1); God's Benjamin—and like Benjamin, full of changes, sometimes a Benoni, a son of sorrow, and afterwards of joy—the son of God's right hand, whom he loves as dearly as a man doth his right hand or the apple of his eye, whom God is always ready to lead and govern by his right hand and to whom he swears by his right hand that he will be their Preserver (Isa. 62. 8). Israel are often called collectively God's son (as Hos. 11. 1) and his first-born, as if the whole multitude of them were one person (Exod. 4. 22, 23), as here they are compared to one vine.

3. The visible church of God on earth is God's vine. And God's transactions with the church Visible do outwardly resemble the spiritual and invisible dealings of God with the church of the elect, and thereunto are afforded outward means and privileges for the saving good of God's elect among them.

This visible church was built upon Christ the Messiah, that first promise in Genesis 3. 15 being the foundation of the church and of the whole worship of God therein. Christ hath seen his seed in all ages past and shall still see his seed in all ages to come. The great work of God in all ages is to be planting vineyards or churches where there are none and to preserve those churches which he hath already on earth, and to restore them where they are under decays. Tho' Christ's church on earth be a weak and feeble people, yet he makes them strong for himself, defending them against the gates of hell, keeping an hedge of protection about them and guarding them by armies of angels, and so caring for them that the whole world may discern that his special care and gracious providence is concerned for their good more than for the rest of mankind.

And the dispensations of God towards Israel in transplanting them out of Egypt into Canaan and erecting a church-state and ordinances among them (which the former part of the Psalm doth mention) are in some kind of similitude acted over again in New Testament times in all ages of the church, and will still be again acted over while the world continues.

4. Particular churches are the ministerial vineyards of Christ for the exercise of divine worship, ordinances, and discipline, like so many particular inclosures under the inspection of particular keepers, which make up and constitute the visible catholic garden of the church. And each particular professor of religion (whether sound or unsound) is a branch in Christ visibly (John 15). And each Christian hath a vineyard (namely his own soul) to keep and look after (Cant. 1. 6).

II. In our text is supposed that the present state of God's vineyard then in the world was very distressed and calamitous. They were fed with the bread and drink of tears, and that in great measure (ver. 5). Afflictions and sorrows were their constant diet, so that they could not refrain from mixing tears with their food; tho' they had scarcity of bread, yet had trientals,[3] treble measures of tears. *Shalish* notes a cup four times as big as the usual cups they drink in, so that they drank tears in flagons rather than in cups.

They were made a strife to their neighbors (ver. 6). Their enemies strove among themselves which should make a spoil and a prey of them and those who once were neighborly and kind to them now took occasion to quarrel with them, and they had now almost as many enemies as they had neighbors. Israel, out of carnal policy, joined with their neighbors in false worship and refusing to be reformed by the repeated warnings sent them from God by his prophets; therefore (because their ways pleased not the Lord), God made their friends turn to be their enemies (Deut. 28. 47, 48, etc.).

Again, their enemies laughed among themselves (ver. 6), made sport of, and delighted themselves in the calamities of Israel. So the people of the earth make merry when the two witnesses are slain (Rev. 11. 10); Sampson was called for to make sport for the Philistines (Judg. 16. 25); Israel were justly made a derision and hissing among the nations after they forsook God (Psal. 44. 13, 14 and 79. 4).

Again, the hedge of divine protection was removed and all that passed by took liberty to pluck at them (ver. 12). This came to pass as an accomplishment of the divine comminations against them (Deut. 31. 17; Isa. 5. 5). Impure and savage nations, fierce and furious enemies like

---

[3] *Triental*: a third part (e.g., of length or weight); also a Roman drinking vessel containing one-third of a *sextarius*, i.e., about one-third of a pint (*NED*, X, 352).

wild boars and beasts, endeavored to root up this vine and extirpate the true religion.

Thus God's vine was cast as 'twere into the fire (ver. 16), cut down, and become like the burning bush which Moses saw, all in a flame, likely to perish utterly without a miracle of mercy prevented its ruin and total overthrow (ver. 16). They perish at the rebuke of thy countenance. And God seemed to be angry with the very prayers of his people (ver. 4). Tho' they sought deliverance with strong cries and tears, yet obtained it not; but God in anger delivered them up into the hands of their enemies (Psal. 39. 11).[4] One frown of God's face was (like the scorching wind we had this last year[a]) sufficient to blast, wither, and dry up the tender plants of his vineyard. They hoped that their prayers would have ascended like incense and been as a sweet-smelling savor unto God. But the smoke of God's anger against them discovered that fair, flattering words would not pacify a provoked God.

III. In our text is set forth the resolution of the true Israelites, the remnant of sincere believers yet left in this vineyard of the church, not to give over crying to God for relief and help, but to persist in penitential prayers to him even to the last gasp, resolving to go nowhere else for help, and being satisfied and fully convinced that one look, one smile, one visit from heaven would suffice to recover the vine from its apostasies and calamities.

The Doctrine therefore under which the text may be explained is this: *That sincere believers will persevere in their applications to the Lord God of hosts (notwithstanding all repulses given to their former addresses) for a gracious visit from heaven to be made unto his vine upon earth, as the only and the sufficient relief against impending ruin by sins and judgments.*

The plants in this vineyard of the church are reasonable creatures; and in God's visible vineyard on earth in times of greatest degeneracy there will in all ages be left a remnant who belong to the election of grace, who being effectually called and savingly united to Christ the Head and Root of the vine (for the Root of this vine is in heaven tho' the branches, while in a militant state, are on earth). These are true penitents who are mourners in Zion for the iniquities thereof, God's remembrancers who stand in the gap to keep off desolating judgments by their prayers and pleadings with God. They will give God no rest day or night but will plead with him

[a] Aug. 20, 1713.

156

for mercy as long as they have a tongue and breath to speak; and if their breath fails, yet will even then give a look by faith towards his holy temple in heaven. And God knows the meaning of their broken sentences when they are almost out of breath; he knows the sense of their looks and of their stretched-forth hands; and tho' he delay long, yet graciously suffers himself to be overcome at last, and *quasi*,[5] commanded by their prayers, seeing they will not let him alone, he yields to their importunity, yea he assists them by his Spirit in pouring forth their fervent prayers and is so delighted with the work of his own hands in their hearts that he suffers them, as it were, to govern the whole world by their prayers, seeing their petitions are agreeable to and coincident with his glorious ends and designs which he proposes to himself in upholding and governing all things.

I. Let us consider the object to whom their prayers are directed: the Lord God of hosts, God the Father, Son, and Holy Spirit, who hath supreme power, who hath all creatures to militate under him, and can easily vanquish the force of enemies. He sits Chief over the angelical cherubims (ver. 1) and hath his peculiar residence in heaven (ver. 14), on whom the church might depend for salvations when all earthly helps failed them.

The church of the Jews placed all their hopes in the Messiah (when their case was most deplorable), that at his coming he would restore all things. And as God the Father who sent Christ is called "the Lord of hosts" (Zech. 2. 8), so also is Christ himself who was sent by his Father. He sits between the cherubims, noting that his throne is in the third heavens surrounded with angels; yea the angels themselves partly constitute his throne on which he sits.

Thus in our prayers unto God for his vineyard on earth, our faith ought to be acted distinctly on God the Father, the Husbandman, Vine-dresser, and Owner of the vineyard; on the Lord Jesus Christ, the Root and Head of influence to his church; and on the Holy Spirit, by whom the Father and Son do work peculiarly for the good of the church.

II. The matter or substance of their petitions.

1. "Return." God's promise to dwell in the midst of Israel was on condition that they kept his precepts (Lev. 26). When they neglected this their duty they were liable to be forsaken of God (Jer. 7). Upon their

---

[4] Danforth's reference here is incorrect for the King James Bible. He may have had in mind II Kings 21. 14, or Judg. 2. 14; or the reference may be to another Bible.
[5] "As if" or "as it were."

apostasies, God withdrew from them, turned away from them, hid himself from them, carried himself as if he took no notice of their afflictions, took no care of them, and had no compassionate regard to them.

The church then prays here for the tokens and evidences of God's returning unto them in a way of pity, favor, and mercy. It's called God's coming to save them (ver. 2). Unless God did after a sort come from heaven to save them by his efficacious presence on earth, they could not expect to be delivered out of the depth of apostasy and calamity which they were fallen into.

2. "Look down from heaven, and behold this vine." Hitherto God seemed to be so angry with them that it seemed as if he would not design to look on them nor would give them a good look, and would not look after them as if he cared not what would become of them.

The thing prayed for then is a gracious look of divine providence and look of pity and commiseration, as in Isaiah 63. 15: "Look down from heaven, and behold from the habitation of thy holiness and of thy glory: where is thy zeal and thy strength, the sounding of thy bowels and of thy mercy towards me? are they restrained?" God is said to look down from heaven when he pities their case who are extremely afflicted beyond all measure, and gives them such remarkable help that none can doubt but that their deliverance comes from heaven: "For he hath looked down from the heighth of his sanctuary; from the heaven did the Lord behold the earth; To hear the groaning of the prisoners; to loose those that are appointed to death" (Psal. 102. 19, [20]).

So great is the insolency and cruelty of the enemies of the church that believers know if they could but prevail with the God of heaven to turn his eyes towards them and look upon their distressed case, he could not refrain from helping and pitying them when no eye is left on earth to pity them; and they know that one look from heaven is sufficient to turn their enemies into confusion. When God once said that he had seen the oppression of Israel, then deliverance was not far off (Exod. 3. 7, 9).

3. "Visit this vine." I shall chiefly improve the time remaining in explaining what is meant by the divine visit or visitation here prayed for. And it may perhaps be pleasant as well as profitable to those who have learned the Hebrew grammar to hear the word פָּקַד explained, which they have often repeated.

1. Observe that the word פָּקַד commonly notes the "acting of a superior towards an inferior." When inferiors visit their superiors (as

children do visit their parents), it is to comfort them with their company or to receive counsel or reproofs from them, to obtain direction in their difficult cases from their aged experience, and to obtain from them supplies of their wants (and thus men are said to visit God when in trouble, Isa. 26. 16), and to pay their duty and reverence to their superiors. But superiors visit their inferiors in a way of pity and care—so the apostles visited the churches and the shepherds visit their flocks, to provide for them and to redress what is amiss (Jer. 23. 2). Now the visit here prayed for is requested of him who is called the "Shepherd of Israel" (ver. 1), the great Owner of the vineyard who in and by his covenant with them had undertaken the office of a shepherd, to feed, lead, and govern them and to rectify and reform what was amiss among them.

2. The word פָּקַד is commonly used to note the "acting of God towards his people for their good."

Indeed sometimes a day of divine visitation signifies a day of calamity and destruction which comes upon the wicked and impenitent (Isa. 26. 14; Hos. 9. 7). As there is a common visitation of all men by a common death (Num. 16. 29), so there are more special and signal days of visitation by strange and unusual deaths and by desolating judgments (Isa. 10. 3; Jer. 5. 9, 29).

But in our text is meant a merciful visit for the restoration and recovery of the church from sins and judgments. Thus God is said to have visited Hannah when she bare three sons (I Sam. 2. 21), and to visit the earth when he waters and enriches it (Psal. 65. 9). The visit prayed for is that of a father afforded to his children, which is with pity and compassion, with care and faithfulness, as well as with power to help them. Such a visit Joseph promised that God would give to Israel: "God will surely visit you, and bring you out of this land unto the land which he sware to Abraham, to Isaac, and to Jacob" (Gen. 50. 24, 25); "I have surely visited you, and seen what is done to you" (Exod. 3. 16); "When they had heard the Lord had visited the children of Israel, and that he had looked on their affliction, then they bowed their heads and worshipped" (Exod. 4. 31).

3. A divine visit oftentimes signifies a remarkable and sometimes a miraculous appearance of God in bestowing mercies on his people or in delivering them out of trouble. A divine visitation is real and efficacious, an actual accomplishment of mercy for them—and not a bare preparation for action. The ordinary, common visitation of God doth preserve

men's life and spirit (Job 10. 12). But there are more special and peculiar visits of God afforded to his people by the more than ordinary emanations of the power, wisdom, grace, and Spirit of God, when their case, as to men, means, and ordinary helps, seems desperate.

4. This phrase of visiting is especially used to express the gracious actings of God towards his church in and by Christ who is God incarnate. When God sent his Son into the world to take upon him the nature of man, then God is said to have visited his people (Luke 1. 68): "Through the tender mercy of our God; the dayspring from on high hath visited us" (Luke 1.* 78). What a wonderful visit was this! that he who was God should visit the nature of man and advance it into union with the divine nature!

Again, the time of Christ's bodily presence and abode on earth is peculiarly called a day of visitation: Because thou knewest not "the time of thy visitation" (Luke 19. 44); a great prophet is risen up among us and "God hath visited his people" (Luke 7. 16).

5. That which the church hoped would be the happy effect of such a gracious visit from heaven may be collected from several requests made in this Psalm, as:

1. In general, they hoped for all manner of salvations by such a visit of the God of heaven (ver. 2, 3). Visit us, O Lord, and we shall be saved; then our sorrow will be turned into joy (ver. 7, 19).

2. More particularly, such a visit would "turn them again" (ver. 3), i.e., bring a happy turn upon them; it would cause a return of their former prosperous state unto them; they should thereby be recovered from their fainting fits, who were now at death's door.

Or thus, such a divine visit will turn us again to our God by unfeigned repentance and recover us from our apostasies. "Visit us, O Lord, and then we shall be turned unto thee from our sins" (Jer. 31. 18; Lam. 5. 21).

3. Such a divine visit will "quicken us" (ver. 18) and recover us from that death which hath been upon our piety and prosperity; it will make our dry bones to come to life again; it will revive God's work, the work of religion, among us. So shall we call upon thy name and worship thee according to thy will, in spirit and truth. "So shall we not go back from thee" (ver. 18), but a stop will be put to our apostasy from God. The Messiah when he visits us will restore all things, put all things into order again, will subdue our iniquities and reform our evil ways.

6. Let us consider some of those glorious operations of God in an un-

common way of mercy, which may bear the name of such a remarkable visit of God from heaven afforded to his vine on earth.

1. When the God of hosts works by the hosts of heaven, the holy angels, for the good of his vine, that is a remarkable visit. Thus after Rabshakeh's railing and blasphemy, the church's enemies were found all dead corpses, being destroyed by an angel. Also when by the holy angels God stirs up good motions in the hearts of men and spirits them to engage in and perform some work for God. An angel assisted Darius in wielding his new-gotten empire (Dan. 11. 1); angels assisted in raising up and afterwards razing to the ground those mighty empires of Persia and Grecia (Dan. 10. 13, 20, 21)—all which changes on the empires were ultimately for the sake and benefit of the church of God. For God can readily part even with an earthly kingdom and give it for his church's good, so dear and precious is his vine unto him; and God hath invisible state ministers (even the holy angels) to bring about the fates of kingdoms and empires.

2. When suitable means and instruments are unexpectedly raised up and afforded for the restoring religion, peace, and order to the church of God on earth. God remarkably visited Israel in raising up Moses to be their instrumental savior and in preparing him for civil government by a learned education; also in raising up Joseph to be a father and shepherd unto Israel in Egypt. So he raised up judges in Israel to deliver them, who were filled with the Spirit in a more than ordinary measure. David, Solomon, Asa, Jehoshaphat, Hezekiah, Nehemiah, Ezra, Zerubbabel were raised up to promote temple-work and to set forward the work of reformation with all their might. In New Testament times the apostles were in an extraordinary manner acted by the Holy Spirit and made willing and able to undertake that great work of gospelizing the world which was then overspread with paganism and idolatry. In such instruments God's people see the face of God shining mercifully upon them.

Also when God ordaineth praise and promotes his own glory, even by instruments as unlikely as babes and sucklings (Psal. 8. 2), and by things accounted foolish by carnal men, and things weak and base, and by things which are not, doth confound the wise and the mighty and doth bring to nought things which are (I Cor. 1. 25–29); and by men of a modest and meek spirit carries on his work successfully so that they are not daunted and discouraged from their duty by the browbeatings of imperious spirits, which shows that they are acted and assisted by a Spirit beyond their own and that God is with them of a truth.

In such a day of divine visitation God is wont to communicate ministerial gifts in an eminent manner on Gospel ministers, in increasing the
number of preachers and increasing their abilities, and increasing their
forwardness and diligence in their work. When God gives the word, great
is the army of them that publish it (Psal. 68. 11). An army of laborers
are sent forth into God's vineyard when he hath a great harvest to gather
in. In such a day his Spirit is not merely given but poured forth in the gifts
of it most plentifully on such as are to carry on his work (Acts 2. 16, 17,
18). And they have a spirit of forwardness to double their diligence in the
work of Christ's kingdom in such a day and season and to act with more
than usual presence, courage, and vivacity, their hearts being lift up in
the ways of the Lord. They are pressed forwards and go bound in the
spirit about God's work; they set forth with full sail, having the fresh
gales of the wind of God's Holy Spirit to carry them along through most
arduous affairs to promote the glory of God and the good of his vineyard;
and sometimes even youths or young men are so strengthened with might
in the inner man as that they faint not in the work of God—even in great
and almost apostolical enterprises and services for God, as in planting
of religion where it was not before.

III. When God gives his vine such a visit from heaven, he is wont to
give great success to the labors of his servants whom he calls and appoints
to labor in his vineyard.

1. At such a time God is wont to make a people willing to be reformed
by the efficacy of his Spirit on their hearts. They are made to be of a
teachable spirit and desirous to know and be instructed wherein they have
offended God and provoked him to withdraw from them and what it is
that God would have them to do, that they may obtain the returns of his
presence unto them again; now *pars est sanitatis, velle sanari.*[6] The work
of reformation will go on with delight when the people are generally
willing to be healed and to turn from the error of their ways, being convinced of the necessity of it to prevent the total ruin of this vine. It was a
visit of God to the hearts of the people which made them readily to fall in
with the leaders and rulers in proceeding to a public reformation in the
days of Josiah, Hezekiah, and Nehemiah, so that they would excite the
rulers to set about this good work and strengthen their hearts and hands
therein, saying, "Arise; this matter belongeth unto thee: be strong and do
it" [Ezra 10. 4]. Whereupon:

162

2. All ranks and orders of men that fear God are made to unite in promoting the welfare of this vine when God thus visits them from above. It's a remarkable work of God to unite the hearts of good men in determining what ought to be done for the promoting of religion, the reforming of vice and encouraging virtue, and in practicing what they have agreed upon for the good of the Lord's vineyard—that as they see eye to eye, so they draw all one way—and readily to bury all lesser jars and animosities rather than the glory of God and the work of Christ should be obstructed or neglected.

And in such a time men of an inferior rank have been signally animated to give good advice and seasonable reproofs unto others, so far as became their stations. Yea in such a day of visitation, even infants have had such impressions on their hearts as to cry out Hosanna to the son of David, and young persons on their deathbeds have been extraordinarily assisted to give most wholesome and profitable warnings and advice to their companions for their awakening to repentance.

3. In order hereunto God hath been wont to give his people remarkable warnings to awaken them out of their security, to stir them up to prepare to meet the Lord—as by many sudden deaths, removal of aged Christians, amazing fires, pinching scarcities, epidemical sicknesses, perplexing turns in human affairs. And when God is about to revive his work in a particular place or among the body of a people, he doth sanctify those warnings and cause the hearts of men to be deeply affected with the dispensations of his providence and to consider that there is no shelter for them against the calamities impending, but only in God, and no expectation to be safe and secure in the evil day but by making friends with heaven and maintaining a good correspondence with that friend we have in the court of heaven, our blessed Lord Jesus Christ.

4. This success of the laborers in God's vineyard consists in the upholding of religion where it is set up and in planting and propagating of it to other places. It is the good hand of God working for his people which provides pastors after his own heart for his church successively from age to age, so that when fathers in the ministry have left the world, yet the churches of Christ on earth have not been left destitute of qualified persons to feed them with the bread of life and to lead and guide them according to the rules of the Gospel.

⁶ "It is a part of health to wish to be healthy."

Again, it is a gracious visit from heaven that causes this vine to propagate, so that as people are multiplied, churches also should be multiplied and more ministerial vineyards and gardens enclosed for our Lord Jesus to take delight in and to walk in the midst of.

That remarkable breathing of the Spirit in the day of a merciful visit by the God of heaven, which quickens and revives grace in the hearts of old disciples, doth commonly gain home some others unto Christ which were not converted before—as that sermon which much affects an old Christian is likely to be a means of converting sinners unto God. And the increase of the church by new converts doth tend to freshen and quicken grace in old disciples. When the vineyard flourishes and the tender grape appears and the pomegranate buds forth (Cant. 7. 12, 13), which is a proof of Christ's special presence with his people, reviving his work among them, then the affections and delights of gracious souls are abundantly enlarged and drawn forth after Christ so that they want words to express how dearly they love the Lord Christ.

And the propagation of religion to plantations formerly ungospelized is preparatorily attended with the revival and fresh springing up of religion in places where it was before. The church (like a mother) hath many throws and pangs in order to the bringing forth more children to her husband Christ; namely the renewed exercise of humiliation and repentance and pleading and wrestling with God by faith in prayer for the converting and gospelizing of other places. And the fresh breathings and pourings out of God's Spirit on his people who make up his vineyard on earth is a prognostic that Christ hath a marriage day at hand wherein he will espouse some other people to himself, even such as knew him not and that call'd not on his name; and that his church, like a flourishing vine, shall spread forth its branches over the wall and extend itself to those who before were not within the pale of the church.

Oh! what luculent evidences of a visit from heaven are given forth in planting the Gospel in places where it never was before settled, so that all must confess, verily God hath wrought this and not man!—when the worst sort of sinners are changed into saints suddenly and surprisingly and of opposers become promoters of religion. Was it not strange that Israel coming out of Egypt should be willing to lay themselves under bond and covenant-engagements to keep and obey all God's commandments before they knew in particular what God would enjoin them?

And altho' in this age we expect not apostles to be raised up, acted by an infallible spirit, yet it is easy to grant that unto remarkable success granted to men in the use of ordinary means, there is often required a greater concurrence of God's communicative power than in those that are extraordinary. The weakness of instruments tends to set forth the greatness of the power of God put forth by them.

IV. When the Lord God of hosts looks down from heaven and visits his vine on earth, he doth remarkably remove, divert, and overcome the opposition made to his work. The gates of hell are always engaged in opposition to the Gospel kingdom (Matt. 16. 18). The Gospel could never make entrance on the kingdom of Satan did not God remove and divert the powerful oppositions made to it. The erecting of a church-state among Israel was like the creation of a new world, the making a new heaven and a new earth (Isa. 51. 15, 16). And this was a day of visitation to them. Hence it's said, "Today if you will hear his voice," etc. (Heb. 3. 7). Sometimes remarkable rebukes are given by frights and terrors of conscience to restrain those Labans [7] who would stop God's Jacobs in their purposes to build altars to the Lord and set up his worship. There is sometimes a day of judicial visitation wherein the chaff, briars, thorns, and weeds, the sticks and stones which offend the vines and hinder their growth are picked up and thrown out of this orchard and garden of the Lord. Those who are obstinately bent to oppose God's work, God hath a day wherein to remove them, and by terrible things in righteousness doth sometimes answer the prayers of his people for the flourishing of his vine on earth (Psal. 65. 2). Also God doth restrain the wrath, bound and limit the malice of his enemies, and disappoint their crafty projects whereby they endeavor to circumvent, prevent, and obstruct all good designs. The wisdom of God herein is in these latter ages especially exerted rather than his power. And the astonishing hardness of heart judicially inflicted on some at such a time is also a sign that it is a day and season of a divine visitation. When there be instances of some that are provoked, enraged, tormented by that word which converts others (Rev. 11. 10), who are cut to the heart to see the Gospel flourish and the kingdom of Christ prevail, and who do grow worse under all divine cultivations, that sentence is passed upon them: "He that is unjust and filthy, let him be so still" (Rev. 22. 11). The peremptory opposition which such

[7] Laban tricked his kinsman Jacob into marriage with his eldest daughter Leah after promising him Rachel in exchange for seven years' labor, and over twenty years "changed [Jacob's] wages ten times" (see Gen., Chaps. 28–31).

make to the ways and truths of God is a proof that their consciences are scorched with it.

V. In such a day of divine visitation of the vineyard, God is wont to prune and lop off the exuberancies and excrescencies of the good vines which hinder their growth and fruitfulness. God sanctifies those afflictions to them which he exercises his vineyard with, to humble them and to cause grace to take the deeper root downwards in their hearts, that they may bring forth more and better fruits upwards. Some forward humorsome saints, after God hath taken them in hand and pruned and purged them by afflictions, do become very humble, patient, meek, and holy Christians; others almost ruined by a worldly spirit, after divine purgations become of a public spirit and forward to do service for God. The contentious are made peaceable, yea become peacemakers, and the selfish made generous and the slow and dull and sluggish Christian quickened and made forward and ready to every good work. At such a time when there is a revival of religion by gaining new converts unto Christ, aged Christians are wont to experience a new and second conversion in their souls wherein the whole work of repentance and faith is repeated and exercised over again in them.

VI. Such a visit from heaven for the reviving and reforming of God's vine on earth is attended with remarkable preservations, deliverances, and outward prosperity. The fence and hedges about the vineyard are anew repaired. The church (yea the world) always fares the better, even in outward respects, when religion revives and when this vine doth flourish. Never any plantation or nations fared the worse for having God's vineyard planted among them.

VII. When the Lord of hosts doth in mercy give his vineyard on earth a visit, he doth not tarry with them merely for a night as a traveler and a wayfaring man, but makes his abode with them. He grants them days, yea years of his gracious visitation and presence with them (Hos. 9. 7; Jer. 11. 23). He doth not merely come once to look upon his vine but often returns to set things in order that it may flourish. He gives forth repeated effusions of his Spirit and renewed manifestations of God in his glory when he is resolved to build up Zion and to have his work carried on to effect. God will not suffer his tender plants to be nipped in the bud, tho' Satan endeavor it by his power and stratagems.

VIII. When he who is called the desire of all nations doth come and visit his vine and cause it to spread and propagate, there are usually great

166

concussions, convulsions, and shakings among the nations. God then shakes the heaven and the earth, the sea and the dry land; and proportionably in a lesser degree the planting and propagating of religion in any dark corner of a land is not without convulsions among them ordinarily.

But it is time to proceed to some application. Let us all be exhorted to endeavor by prayer and all other proper means to obtain such a visit from the Lord God of hosts unto his vine which his own right hand hath planted in this land. Let us consider:

I. That nothing short of such a divine visitation can recover the church from apostasies and calamities. All the power of men and angels cannot turn a degenerate plant into a noble vine, nor recover a degenerate church, nor revive dying religion. The use of other means of God's appointment will avail nothing 'till God himself do come down from heaven by his gracious, efficacious presence to work with us, by us, in us, and for us. Indeed God accepts of the goodwill and desires of his people and of their weak endeavors to do what they can for the promoting his kingdom and interest on earth; and we have reason to be ashamed of our slothfulness and backwardness to do what we might do in our several capacities to promote virtue and holiness (for who knows but that God would as it were step down from heaven to work with us and by us if we did strenuously engage in his work?). But the virtue and power of man is weakness itself, yea nothing; it is God who brings all to pass which is done for the good of his vine; Paul may plant and Apollo may water, but God alone gives the increase (Acts 3. 12). When Israel by their sins had ripened themselves for ruin, the judgments of God came upon them, even in those times wherein they had godly rulers and good kings and extraordinary prophets who used utmost endeavors to reform them and so to prevent impending judgments from being executed upon them. Vain then is the help of man to save us from sins and judgments. If God forsake a people they are undone and their case becomes as desperate as if they were already cut down and cast into the fire (ver. 16). When a people are entered into a way of apostasy and backsliding from God, tho' at first their motion be slow and gradual, yet at length they (like the possessed swine) run downhill violently and grow worse and worse in a little time: *facilis descensus averni.*[8] What a multitude fell away to idolatry in Rehoboam's time? How many did Mahomet seduce in a little time? Sometimes the

---

[8] "Easy is the descent to the underworld" (Virgil, *Aeneid*, VI, 126).

apostasy (which is a sort of conspiracy against religion) prevails to such a heighth as to carry all before it. In such a time iniquity abounds and none dare or care to oppose it, and none but God can stop men in their career of sin and turn them back from their evil courses, their hearts being fully set in them to do evil—none but God can turn them about and cause them to set their faces to seek the Lord God of their fathers.

II. It is the absence and withdrawing of God from his vineyard that is the reason why all things are out of order therein. When the master and owner of a garden is long absent, fences and hedges soon decay and the garden and orchard yields little fruit for want of digging, pruning, weeding, and other good husbandry which the master's eye and presence would from time to time carefully bestow upon it. The sins of God's visible people provoke him to hide himself from them, yea to forsake his vineyard; we first forsake God by our sins before the Lord forsake us; and when we lose the gracious presence of God, we soon lose both our piety and prosperity. How soon will ill weeds spring up and grow apace in the vineyard and have remarkable success in promoting an apostasy from God; and all attempts for reformation are unsuccessful when God is departed from Israel. The means of grace are evanid[9] when the Spirit of God is withdrawn. "Ye cannot prosper, because ye have forsaken the Lord, he hath forsaken you" (II Chron. 24. 20). After Israel forsook the Lord he deprived them of skillful pilots to direct them, of pious priests to intercede for them; the destroying angel arrested them and delivered them up to the fowls of the air and beasts of the field; and the land of Canaan which God gave their forefathers was delivered up to the most wicked of the heathen—first to the Romans, then to the Saracens, and at last to the barbarous Turks; and because they rejected Christ, the Light of the world, are judicially given up to grope in the very sunshine of the Gospel, like blind men that can't see a beaten path.

III. Consider that the return of the Lord God of hosts in a way of mercy to look down from heaven and visit his vine in and by the Son of his right hand is sufficient to recover his people from the lowest depths of apostasy from God and from the worst of miseries and calamities. God can do everything; with him all things are possible; nothing is too hard for God. One look and visit of this great Physician heals the worst and most incurable maladies. He can open the blind eyes, mollify the hardest hearts, and heal the most grievous backslidings of his people. He may at all times say, "*Veni, vidi, vici.*"[10] When the Lord is pleased to pour out of his Spirit abundantly upon a people and rain down righteousness upon them; when he waters it from above with the fresh influences of his Spirit, then the vine shall revive and spring up as the grass. When God comes to us from heaven and brings much of heaven with him to his people on earth, then they shall be saved (ver. 3, 7, 19). Where Christ comes, salvation comes —so he said to Zaccheus, "This day is salvation come to thy house" [Luke 19. 9]. The Lord never comes empty-handed; wherever he sets up his throne his train fills the temple; he brings a train of mercies with him for soul and body. "There I will meet with thee and bless thee." God's meeting with his people never goes alone without bestowing blessings upon them.

IV. Consider after what manner we should pray for such a divine visit.

1. We should pray humbly and penitently. We should be deeply sensible of our unworthiness that the Lord of hosts should give us so much as one good look, or that he should come under our roofs; and that it is infinite condescension in the high and lofty One to come and dress our wounds and bind them up for us, seeing our sins deserve that the Lord should cast us off forever. We should mourn for our sins whereby we have provoked the eyes of his glory to turn away from us and have provoked him to stop his ears against our cries and to hide his face from us and to frown upon us with the rebukes of his countenance. However, we should humbly spread before him our lamentable state, our decays in grace and fruitfulness, that the vineyard goes to decay and is almost dead; and we should spread before him our miseries and distresses, that we are undone without his helping omnipotent hand be put forth for the revival of religion. We should prostrate ourselves at the feet of divine mercy, resolving if we perish that it shall be in the posture of penitent supplicants at the throne of grace for the returns of God's mercy to us. Who knows but that the merciful God who heard the groanings of Israel (Exod. 2.* 24) and had respect to them will also be moved to compassionate our case?

2. Our prayers should be conjoined with holy purposes and endeavors

---

[9] *Evanid*: vanishing away, fleeting, of short duration, transient (*NED*, III, 330).

[10] "I came, I saw, I conquered," Julius Caesar's famous announcement of his victory at Zela, 47 B.C., in Suetonius, "The Life of Julius Caesar," *The History of the Twelve Caesars* (the Latin words are retained in the English translation, London, 1677, 25); and in Plutarch's "Julius Caesar" in his *Lives*.

to reform our evil ways by the help of God. Would we have the great God come and visit our hearts and our houses and our churches, we should then prepare for his coming by cleansing our hearts, houses, and societies from all that is filthy and ungrateful to him, from all filthiness of flesh and spirit; put all things in order if we intend that the King of glory should come in and walk and dwell among us. Let us find out what the sins are which keep God at a distance from us, which separate between our God and us and provoke him so much that he will not give us a good look. We should cease from doing evil and learn to do well, that so the Lord without diminution of the glory of his holiness may return unto us in mercy. Those who continue obstinate sinners and hate to be reformed, instead of praying in a right manner to the Lord to return to us, do practically say to the Almighty, "Depart out of our coasts" [Matt. 8. 34; Mark 5. 17]. How dare any but the truly contrite put up this prayer in our text, that God would look from heaven and behold them and their behaviors? Those who are going on in a course of sin care not that a God of infinite holiness should behold and observe their wickedness.

3. Our prayers for a divine visit should be fervent and importunate. Wrestle with God in prayer; take no denial at his hand. Oh! let us cry mightily to heaven for one good look more, the smiles of his countenance upon us, and that he would return to us and leave a blessing behind him. Plead with God, "Lord, hast thou no mercy in store for this generation? Hast thou utterly cast off and abhorred them? Art thou resolved not to bestow of thy Spirit upon them?" etc. But how shall we plead in prayer for such a visit?

1. Plead we for the sovereign grace of God to be exerted towards us, that which is undeserved by us and for which we can make no recompense. Let us plead thus: "O Lord, will it not glorify thy sovereign grace and mercy to revive thy work among such a degenerate people, to remove the iniquity of our land in one day?" (Zech. 3. 9). Will not that be a glorious day's work indeed? Will not the Lord gain as much glory to his great name by pardoning our sins, giving us repentance, and by pruning and purging his vineyard, as he can gain to his justice by giving us up to our own hearts' lusts, thereby to ripen ourselves for ruin?

2. Let us plead for a divine visit in the name and for the sake of the Son of man, the Son of God's right hand, who is the Root and Head of the vine, yea most properly he is the Vine itself. Let us exercise faith in our Lord Messiah, our great friend in the court of heaven, to intercede with God

for us that such a gracious visit from heaven may be afforded unto us on earth. The reason why Christ did no mighty works in some places during his bodily presence on earth was because of their unbelief who dwelt in those places. Let us strive against unbelief and labor for a lively exercise of faith on the promises of the covenant and on Christ in the promises; for God hath engaged to return again to his people when they return to him and seek him with their whole hearts. So in Proverbs 1. 23: "Turn ye at my reproof: and then behold (beyond your deserts and beyond your hopes and to your admiration), I will pour out my spirit upon you." Let us plead that promise made by God the Father unto Christ, "that he shall see his seed" or have a visible vine upon earth in all ages, notwithstanding all the power and policy of hell whereby it is opposed. Let us plead the interest which the Lord Christ hath in the church on earth and the glory that redounds to Christ the Mediator by the preserving, propagating, and flourishing of his vineyard on earth. It is the only garden, orchard (or Eden) which Christ hath on earth, wherein he takes delight to walk and recreate himself.

3. Let us plead with God that it is the "vineyard which his own right hand hath planted" (ver. 8, 15). It is such a work wherein the glorious power of God's own right hand appears in every age to plant religion where it was not and to preserve it where it hath been planted and to revive it where it is decay'd and languishing. Let us then plead with God that he would not forsake the work of his own hands; that that work (which above all other works he appropriates to himself to be his own work) may appear to his servants; that work which he is pleased to call his glory may appear to the children of his servants; that work of establishing religion among us, which is the beauty and comeliness of the Lord our God put upon us, may flourish more and more as an evidence of a divine visit granted unto us (Psal. 90. 16, 17). Let us plead with God and put him in remembrance of this, that it is the great end and design of divine providence in disposing of kingdoms and in all the turns and fates that attend them, to promote the good of his vine upon earth; and were it not for God's vineyard upon earth, what would the whole world be but an hell upon earth. Where religion flourishes, all other good interests prosper; but as religion decays, so a people may conclude that things will go ill with them. This vineyard of the Lord on earth he hath an eye and regard to in all other of his works and as it were lays aside all other works that he may mind the good of his vine; yea he dispenses blessings and

curses to men according to that regard or disregard which they have to his vineyard on earth: "I will bless them that bless thee, and curse him that curseth thee" (Gen. 12. 3). Let us then plead with God thus:

Lord, thou knowest how few there be in the world that fear thy name, that profess religion, that bring honor to God their Creator, to Christ their Redeemer; thou hast reserved to thyself but a little spot of ground on earth to be thy garden inclosed; and all the rest of the world are suffered to go on in their own ways to thy dishonor; and wilt thou not stand by those that stand for thee? Wilt thou not honor them that honor thee? Shall Satan prevail and leave Christ no garden spot on earth to walk in? For thy name's sake, let it not be so!

V. Consider some motives to excite us in our prayers to God for such a gracious visit. We have the command of God given forth to us to put up this petition daily, "Thy kingdom come," unto which command we should manifest our ready obedience. We have the example of the church in our text set before us for our imitation, to pray for the Lord's vineyard the church, when under greatest distresses and degeneracies. We have the promises and prophecies of the Scripture wherein mercy is stored up for the people of God; we have the predictions of the future glory of the church and some pledges of it beforehand. In the days of Christ the true Solomon, "the righteous shall flourish; there shall be abundance of peace. He shall have dominion from sea to sea, and from the river to the ends of the earth" (Psal. 72. 6–8). The taking down the partition wall between Jews and Gentiles whereby the vine of the church was made to spread its branches over the wall did not take in the whole world into the Lord's vineyard at once; but there is still a distinction to be made between the church and the rest of the world which lies in wickedness; between a religious people by a visible profession and the rest of the world that are perishing for want of vision. Therefore God's dealings with some particular nations and people may yet in times to come resemble his dispensations towards Israel, in taking them to be a select people to himself, in forming them to be a people peculiarly for himself to show forth his praise, by erecting his visible kingdom in all the privileges, ordinances, and worship thereof among them. Let us then be moved to pray in faith and with hope and expectations of the glorious things which are spoken of concerning Zion the city of our God.

Another motive may be turned into an expostulation with our own souls. Are we willing that God's mystical paradise, his garden of pleasure upon earth, should be quite defaced, razed, and extinguish'd? Are aged Christians willing that religion should die with themselves? No, sure we dare not harbor such cruelty in our hearts! Let us then cry mightily to God for the preservation of his vineyard, that religion may be propagated to the succeeding generation by new descents of the Lord God of hosts from heaven, by new and plentiful effusions of his Spirit on all flesh! We can't find in our hearts to be willing that religion should take its flight from our land or that the vineyard of Christ here should be under a divine dereliction! Let us then cry fervently to God to revive his work among us in the midst of the years, that it may not be charged on us that we by our luke-warmness and slothfulness and other sins contributed to the ruin of these churches and drove away the gracious presence of God from this his vineyard.

Let me add another motive, namely that we might enjoy more of heaven upon earth were it not our own faults. We might have more visits from the Lord God of hosts and the Man of his right hand, did we fervently pray for them; for Christ hath promised to give his Holy Spirit to those that ask it of him. What God has wrought by some glimpses of his gracious aspect from heaven in some persons, families, and plantations for the reviving of religion, demonstrates what he could and would do more generally and abundantly when there is a general application in a right manner made to him for this mercy. May we not esteem it a good omen that the God of hosts will lengthen out the day of his gracious visitation unto us (unless by our apostasies persisted in we refuse his company) even in this century also, seeing he hath so ordered in his providence that this new and famous house should be erected wherein we now assemble in the metropolis of our Province for that best of uses, the celebration of divine worship; and that this house should with such expedition and success be completely finished in a day of many and great distresses upon us whereby occasion has been given to many to show their love to God and his house by their liberal donations towards this building—withal exercising their faith and hope that God will still build up his mystical house and vineyard in this land, and that in this house we shall enjoy much of heaven upon earth, the manifestations of God to our souls, and those delights appropriated to his mystical paradise.[11]

---

[11] The State House, built on the site of the old Town House destroyed by the fire of 1711, was completed in the spring of 1713. Danforth's was the second election sermon in the new building.

VI. And lastly, consider who they are that should more especially concern themselves for the obtaining such a visit from heaven to be made to his vineyard upon earth, and more particularly to the vine which the Lord of hosts by his own right hand (working by remarkable providences) hath planted in this wilderness. Now all sorts of men are ranked into rulers and subjects and something might pertinently be spoken from this subject to them all.

As to those in chief rank among us in the state and in the church, my innate modesty forbids me to say much; yet I shall not wholly pretermit the usual custom of saying something with suitable brevity.

And in the first place, my speech may be directed to his Excellency our Governor in Chief who hath been betrusted with the care of the Lord's vineyard in this land for many years past.[12]

Excellent Sir, we acknowledge the great mercy and kindness of our God who hath moved the heart of the Queen's most excellent Majesty to impower and improve your Excellency to lead, guide, and govern us; and that the Lord hath preserved your life hitherto and your abilities of doing eminent and remarkable services for his vineyard in defending it against the boars and wild beasts of heathen adversaries and our other neighboring enemies during the late long war;[13] and in managing the civil affairs of this Province so as that the vineyard of the Lord of hosts therein hath enjoyed tranquillity hitherto; and in giving forth proclamations and exhortations to your people here from time to time to excite and encourage them to set about the work of reformation; and in countenancing and encouraging the propagation of religion, the planting it in the dark corners of our land, and the upholding of it where it was planted. We heartily render our thanks to your Excellency for these favors and believe your Excellency doth esteem it your glory and a sufficient reward of itself that the Lord of hosts is pleased to accept of such your desires and endeavors to promote the flourishing of his vineyard in this land; and that on these accounts all the churches of this Province salute you and pray for your prosperity. God grant we may have always such a Governor who like Moses is daily lifting up his hands and heart to God in the heavens for the prosperity of these churches; for the fervent prayers of rulers keep off dismal strokes from a people.

Nextly, to the honorable members of her Majesty's Council and of the House of Representatives: I would only add that as you have hitherto, so we trust you will still hold on and continue in your pious endeavors to promote the flourishing of religion in this land, the suppression of vice, the encouragement of virtue, the regulating of disorders, the composing of differencies that arise; that you may be able to say that all that could be done by men in your stations, according to the best of your abilities, for the good of this vine, you have endeavored to be found in the performance thereof. May the Lord God of hosts accept of your endeavors and give them success through his blessing upon them!

Thirdly, to my reverend fathers and brethren in the ministry: I take leave in all humility to say that when the Lord of hosts intends a remarkable visit to his vine on earth, he is wont to raise up ministers and fill those that are the standing ministry in his churches in a more than common measure with his Holy Spirit, so that they are carried forth with more than usual courage, forwardness, diligence, and activity in their station for the restoring and preserving religion in their several charges. They have at such a time peculiar impressions from above, both as to the subjects they are to handle and as to the manner of treating of them; their faculties and abilities are quickened and enlivened, their ministerial gifts and graces enlarged, their good affections and zeal encreased, and their watchfulness over their flocks to promote their spiritual good more abundant than before; and a spirit of prayer is in such a day of visitation poured out upon the ministry in a high degree, and the bent of their souls is to promote religion, to convert and edify souls, and they are made resolute in this work, to pursue and prosecute it, notwithstanding all the oppositions and discouragements that attend them therein. And they are forward and ready to reform whatever is amiss in themselves, that they may become patterns to the flocks of Christ, exemplary in good works, and as shining lights in a dark world. Blessed be God who hath supplied his churches with such a ministry hitherto; and let us all cry to heaven that such a ministry may be continued unto these churches successively and that God will be pleased to accompany their labors with his blessing.

Fourthly, to aged Christians: Give me leave to say you are the peculiar friends and ancient acquaintance of the God of heaven, who are yet left

---

[12] Joseph Dudley (1647–1720), son of Thomas Dudley who was sometimes Governor during Winthrop's administration, served as temporary Governor of Massachusetts until the arrival of Sir Edmund Andros in 1686. After several years in England at the turn of the century, Dudley returned to Massachusetts as Governor in 1702, a post he held until 1715 when he was replaced by Shute.

[13] The "War of the Spanish Succession" fought in Europe and America from 1702 until the Treaty of Utrecht in 1713 was known in America as "Queen Anne's War."

on earth. Oh! therefore improve your interest in God to prevail with him to look down and come down and visit this his vine!

Fifthly, to the churches of New England who have been and are yet the vineyard of the Lord of hosts, who enjoy the privileges of his visible kingdom, the tokens of his presence, the ordinances of his house, and in that respect have from the first founding of our churches and first planting of this vineyard enjoy'd a day of divine, gracious visitation. And altho' we have experienced great decays and declensions, the loss of our first love, and the withdrawings of God's Spirit, so that the churches sometimes complain of their barrenness, that few are converted and newborn to Christ and the work of Christ is sometimes under sensible and visible languishments, yet we have reason to bless God who gives some revivals of his work, sometimes in one church and sometimes in another; and from thence should be encouraged to plead with God for a more general effusion of his Spirit upon all his churches, that all parts of his vineyard may flourish—even the dark corners of our vineyard—that they may have wisdom to know the day of their visitation and to accept of the Gospel offered to them and bid welcome to our Lord Jesus Christ who offers to come and dwell among them, lest they should provoke God to visit them in judgment and fury.

Lastly, to impenitent sinners and hypocrites: Let me say, What will you do in the day of visitation? For when God gives his vineyard a visit in love, in order to its fruitfulness, oh! what danger are they in who are as dry and withered branches, they are as thorns and briars in the vineyard, that hinder the flourishing of religion in the places where they live? They may justly expect to be plucked up by the roots, cut down, and cast into the fire, unless speedy repentance and reformation prevent it.

Having thus after my weak manner given you the explication of the text with some application, as by divine leave and help, let us all as one repeat it in way of supplication: "Return, we beseech thee, O God of hosts: look down from heaven, and behold, and visit this vine."

FINIS.

V THOMAS PRINCE'S SERMON OF 1730

AN INTRODUCTION

THE year 1730 was the centennial of the landing of the *Arbella* bringing Governor John Winthrop and the first settlers to Boston harbor. The occasion called for a special tribute. The logical choice of preacher would have been Cotton Mather, foremost historian of New England and patriarch of one of the great families of the first hundred years. But Mather, who loved auspicious occasions, did not live quite long enough; he died in 1728. The choice fell to Thomas Prince, Harvard graduate of 1707, preacher, collector of New England manuscripts and books, European traveler, amateur scientist and historian known to be at work on another history of New England, "said to be the most learned man of his time, excepting Dr. Cotton Mather."[1] It was a wise decision.

Prince's election sermon, *The People of New England,* comes as close to epic as the sermon genre will allow. It is the most detailed of the errand

[1] Samuel Lorenzo Knapp, *American Cultural History 1607–1829,* ed. Richard Beale Davis and Ben Harris McClary (Gainesville, 1961), 77. Thomas Prince was born on May 15, 1687, son of Samuel Prince of Sandwich, Mass., and grandson of Governor Thomas Hinckley of Plymouth Colony. After graduating from Harvard in 1707 he traveled to London and spent the next seven years in England. Returning to Boston, he became the colleague of Joseph Sewall at the Old South Church. Prince published many sermons, some editions of historical tracts, and notes on earthquakes and other phenomena of nature; he was interested in science and medicine, logic, philosophy, and mathematics. He prepared the chronological table for Daniel Neal's second edition of his *History of New England,* and with his son Tom published America's first religious periodical, *Christian History.* His most important work is the *Chronological History of New England, in the Form of Annals* (1736).

179

sermons, the climax to a conventional type that by 1730 had a history of about seventy years. It is the most complete statement of the Puritan version of the American Dream in the election sermons and perhaps, with the exception of the "Introduction" to the *Magnalia,* in all Puritan colonial writing. By condensing both Hebrew and New England history into a few dramatic sequences, Prince creates a work with the American sense of epic destiny to appear later in *The Vision of Columbus, The Rising Glory of America, The Ages, Passage to India,* and *The Bridge.* He uses history to ask the question "What is an American Puritan?" He uses history to pare the errand motif to its essentials, to see again the utopian opportunities which the New World can afford.

In his parallel between the Israelites' and the New Englanders' exodus into the wilderness, Prince makes an interesting tactical move. The Biblical exodus was accompanied by miracles such as the parting of the Red Sea and the pillar of fire by night. The latter-day exodus to New England might appear tame, perhaps forced in its analogy. Prince wants to meet objections from two different groups at once—the literalists who would harp on the absence of miracle from the New England exodus, and the unbelievers who don't see the analogy at all. He manages to convey the wonder of New England's survival of hardships and setbacks. The New England errand was, if one will stop to think of it, also miraculous. But if it is still less miraculous than the Egyptian deliverance, if no one New England event compares, for instance, with the parting of the Red Sea or the pillar of fire, it does not follow that the New England exodus was not therefore the planned and protected deliverance of God. In arguing his point, Prince engages in some shrewd logic. Instead of insisting on the miraculous quality of the New England errand, he asks his audience to suppose that the Israelite exodus had *not* been miraculous. If God had told the enslaved Israelites that he would deliver them in a more natural way (Prince creates the persona of God announcing an alternative plan to the Israelites, without miracles), both the Israelites and mankind since would think no less of God or the exodus for its being less spectacular. Prince wants to catch the ear of those cynical of miracles as well as those

The Prince Collection of his carefully annotated books and manuscripts is in the Boston Public Library. For biographical sketches of Prince, see William B. Sprague, *Annals of the American Pulpit . . . ,* 9 vols. (New York, 1857–69), I, 304–307; *DAB,* XV, 232–233; John Langdon Sibley and Clifford K. Shipton, *Biographical Sketches of Those Who Attended Harvard College,* 13 vols. (Cambridge and Boston, 1873–1965), V, 341–368.

looking for new miracles. The errand into the wilderness is God's special doing, any way one wants to look at it.

Surely many of the Representatives in 1730 could see that this original errand was farther away than ever, to the point where it was now a sweet story of scarred hopes outworn. The ideal of an enclosed garden for a special people with such partisan heroes (from 1630 to 1660) as Winthrop, Cotton, and Hooker hardly applied any longer to a Boston which contained growing numbers of Anglicans, Quakers, and Baptists, as well as immigrants of non-Puritan stock.[2] A dream can be a consciously held goal which one strives for, such as a dream of racial equality; or it can be an unconscious reverie which visits one in the night but has only superficial or tangential meanings for daytime reality. When Danforth preached *Errand into the Wilderness* in 1670, he intended to revive the ideals of the original errand as a conscious goal. In 1730, Prince must have sensed that he was a cultural historian and no longer a seriously regarded prophet. The old errand motif, still compelling, was but an explanation of what might have been. With the passage of time between the event in history and the memory of it, mythic art becomes increasingly possible. Perhaps the Puritans had to wait until 1730 to see the errand as beautifully as Prince does here.

D. H. Lawrence has made a famous comment about the Leatherstocking tales and a basic American myth. He contrasts the chronological life of their hero with the chronology of Cooper's composition of the books, and notes that after killing his hero in the third novel Cooper resurrects him and in the last novel written, *The Deerslayer,* takes him back to his initiation into manhood—the earliest event in the hero's life: "The Leatherstocking novels . . . go backwards, from old age to golden youth. That is the true myth of America. She starts old, old, wrinkled and

---

[2] On pressure from the Quakers and Baptists for toleration and exemption from church taxes in Massachusetts, see Susan Martha Reed, "The Quakers and Their Allies," *Church and State in Massachusetts, 1691–1740* (Urbana, 1914), 86–147. By 1730 there were at least six Anglican churches in the Colony: in Bristol, Newbury, Marblehead, Braintree, and two in Boston, King's Chapel and Christ Church. An Anglican church was built in Scituate in 1732. They too influenced the passing of more liberal laws (*ibid.*, 148–189). Cf. Robert E. Brown, *Middle-Class Democracy and the Revolution in Massachusetts, 1691–1780* (Ithaca, 1955), 105–110. Perry Miller argues that the most important changes from the ideals of the early settlers came not from pressures from other faiths, but from economic prosperity. The ideas of men like Cotton, Winthrop, and Willard on a "just price" and limited profits "fell to the ground" after 1670; "Declension in a Bible Commonwealth," *Proceedings of the American Antiquarian Society,* LI (Worcester, 1942), 37–94, especially 83–94.

writhing in an old skin. And there is a gradual sloughing of the old skin, towards a new youth. It is the myth of America." [3] Like Cooper, Prince in 1730 revives a corpse; his sermon is to the earlier errand sermons as *The Deerslayer* is to Cooper's earlier novels—the purest and freshest. To read through the election sermons, especially those in the heyday of the errand type in the 1670's, to see the type gradually becoming an empty skin of clichés in the eighteenth century, and then to come to Prince's passionate sermon here, is to feel that he too (and he knew the earlier sermons) was writing backwards. What Lawrence might have said is that the sloughing of the old skin to find a new youth is the myth in American literature. While America continues to age, many of her myths protect the innocence of youth. In this sense, Prince created in 1730 a work with far more significance for later readers than he intended or could then conceive.

[3] *Studies in Classic American Literature* (New York, 1951), 64.

The People *of* New-England *Put in mind of the* Righteous Acts *of the* LORD *to* Them *and their* Fathers, *and Reasoned with concerning them.*

A

SERMON

Delivered at *Cambridge*

Before the

Great and General Assembly

Of the Province of the

MASSACHUSETTS

May 27th M D C C X X X.

Being the Anniversary for the *Election* of His Majesty's Council for the Province.

By Thomas Prince, *M. A.*

And one of the Pastors of the South Church in Boston

Psal. cv 5, 6. *Remember his marvellous Works that HE has done, his Wonders, and the Judgments of his mouth; O ye Seed of* Abraham *his Servant, ye Children of* Jacob *his Chosen!*

BOSTON in New-England:

Printed by *B. Green,* Printer to His Honour the Lieut. Governour & Council, for *D. Henchman* in Cornhil. 1 7 3 0.

A Sermon at the General Election.

"A ND Samuel said unto the people, It is the Lord that advanced Moses and Aaron, and that brought up your fathers out of the land of Egypt. Now therefore stand still, that I may reason with you before the Lord of all the righteous acts of the Lord, which he did to you and to your fathers" (I Sam. 12.* 6, 7).

That we may form a clear prospect of the occasion and propriety of this address of Samuel, we must imagine we see the tribes of Israel assembled now before him at Gilgal to behold this illustrious person laying down the chief part of his civil power and resigning it to another whom the God of heaven had so highly honored as to raise him up from among his brethren and set him over that distinguished people.

And it is indeed astonishing to see with what a noble, unaffected, and inimitable majesty this most extraordinary judge and prophet makes the public resignation, with what a just concern for the security of his own unblemish'd character and with what a flaming zeal for the continued honor of God, the maintenance of his pure religion, the welfare of his people, and the prosperity of the succeeding governor.

Read this admirable chapter and keep in view the great occasion, the superior person speaking, the vast and attentive audience, the chief ruler now before him, the things deliver'd, and the air and manner of the whole

184

transaction—and you will see in all such a plain, venerable, and sublime grandeur as I know of nothing among the mere sons of men has been ever like it, unless it were in Moses, and none but one apparently inspir'd and filled with the divine Spirit can pretend to imitate.

Having first receiv'd their universal approbation of his entire conduct, he cannot leave his beloved people without the most public, plain, and solemn admonitions and advices that they may prove a wise and happy people under the influence of their new governor.

Resigning therefore now the chief seat of civil power, but retaining the superior office and authority of a public prophet, he becomes a divine preacher to the listening congregation and begins his sermon with the awakening introduction in the words before us. Of which I now propose by the divine help to treat under these three general heads:

I. To consider the words as applicable to that special people to whom they were at first directed.

II. Raise some general observations from them. And then,

III. And lastly, apply the words and those observations to this particular people in our own land.

I. To consider the text as applicable to that special people to whom it was at first directed.

"And Samuel said unto the people"—i.e., to the whole assembly then and there convened, not only comprehensive of the common people, but also in a special manner the heads and representatives of the several tribes and towns of Israel.

In the first verse of the chapter they are said to be "all Israel"; in the last of the foregoing to be "all the men of Israel"; and by the 8th verse it seems they were at least "three hundred thousand."

But we may by no means imagine that this was a mere confused multitude without any comely order or distinction. For they had an excellent frame of government established over their several tribes and families whereby their tribes and families were both kept in order and preserv'd entire from their original.

It wou'd be a very instructive entertainment to trace it out in all its branches and alterations as they are successively represented in the sacred records. But the time wou'd fail me and I may only observe that before ever they came out of Egypt, they had their elders in their several tribes who were men of chief renown and esteem among them for their singular abilities and public virtues, who by reason of these had a public influence over them and to whose especial conduct they resign'd their public affairs and interests.

For thus says God to Moses at his first appearance, in the burning bush, "Go, and gather the elders [a] of Israel together," etc. (Exod. 3. 16, 18). In the following chapter we read that "Moses and Aaron went and gathered together all the elders of the children of Israel" (ver. 29) and these very elders are called the "people" in the following verses, which seems to intimate that either there were a considerable number of them and 'tis likely all their rulers both of the higher and lower orders, or they represented the community, or that a great company of others out of every tribe attended and assembled with them; on which account the whole convention is styl'd the "people."

Of these elders we also read upon their coming into the "wilderness" in the 12th, 17th, and 18th chapters. And then under their sovereign ruler Moses there were chosen out of every tribe the most known among them for ability, wisdom, understanding, religion, truth, and the hatred of covetousness, to preside over them and the several "thousands, hundreds, fifties, and tens," i.e., not of persons but of households in them (Exod. 18. 13, etc.).[b] And in Chapter 19. 7, we read again of Moses calling for the "elders" of the people and these are also styl'd the "people" in the two following verses.[c]

In Exodus 24 and Numbers 11, we read of "seventy" men selected out of the abovesaid elders, who with Moses and Aaron seem to be form'd into a supreme court of judicature over all the tribes—not destructive of the other orders but superior only to them. And in Deuteronomy 19, 21, 22, 25 and Joshua 20, there are several laws requiring "elders" in "every city." Agreeably to this we read in Gideon's days of the princes and elders of Succoth, a city in the tribe of Gad (Gen. 33. 17; Josh. 13.* 27; and

[a] The Septuagint here calls them the senate of Israel; and the learned Ainsworth observes they were not only men of age but also teachers and rulers among the people, as there were among other nations (Gen. L. 7; Numb. xxii 4, 7. Josh. ix. 11).

[b] Compared with Deut. I. 9, - - - 18.

[c] Of these see likewise, in Lev. iv. & ix. Numb. xvi. Deut. v, xxvii, xxix, xxxi. Josh. vii, viii, xxiii, xxiv. Judg. ii, xxi. and I Sam. iv. And by the general tenor of their history they seem to be not merely rulers over the people but their representatives also; or rather representatives in a double quality; i.e., they both represented the privileges and mind of the people, who chose them, to their sovereign ruler, and the mind and power of the sovereign ruler, who approv'd them, to the people. They seem to be wise and grave mediators between the will and power of the one and the privileges and inclinations of the other; and their business was to observe, advise, and temper both and balance them together.

I Kings 7. 46), even "seventy-seven" men (Judg. 8. 6–16); in Jeptha's days of the "elders of Gilead" (Judg. 11. 5–11); in the days of Boaz of "ten" of the elders of Bethlehem (Ruth 4. 2–11); and in Samuel's days of the "elders of Jabesh," in the chapter before our text, verse the third.

In I Samuel 8. 4, we read of "all the elders of Israel gathering themselves together" to him and in the following verses these are likewise styl'd the "people." By these elders may be therefore meant not only all the members of the supreme court of the seventy but also all others in place of power throughout their tribes and cities. And in that great convention they may be styl'd the people because they seem to come as their chosen representatives and 'tis likely that a numerous company of others assembled with them.

To such another great and general assembly comprehending all Israel in a regular epitome together with a vast confluence of people of the civil, ecclesiastical, and military orders, does this great prophet now direct his inspired oration.

And in the text are these two things:

1. A preliminary observation made as the general ground of his designed argument.

2. A general inference he derives from thence to excite their close attention to his treatment of it.

1. A preliminary observation made as the general ground of his designed argument. "It is the Lord that advanced Moses and Aaron, and that brought up your fathers out of the land of Egypt."

Behold how this wise and great master of assemblies first leads them back to the fountainhead of their present state and happiness, that they may take a lively and short review of the divine appearance for their forefathers in raising up such superior persons as Moses and Aaron as their distinguish'd heads and leaders, and by these renowned men conducting them out of the land of their oppressions and thro' all the difficult and hideous scenes of their progress thro' the wilderness to their desired country.

And in this review we in the first place see the soaring piety this divine preacher wou'd infuse into his listening hearers. For he first raises up their minds to heaven and begins with this: "It is the Lord that advanced" those extraordinary leaders "Moses and Aaron, and that brought up your fathers out of the land of Egypt."

By their fathers is most plainly meant, not the immediate fathers of

187

the generation then subsisting in Samuel's days, but those more ancient fathers who came out of Egypt about 400[d] years before and were first in forming their civil and ecclesiastical state. They were the near descendants of Jacob, Isaac, and Abraham, who had a little before renounc'd the idolatry of the nations round about them, reform'd their families, embrac'd the pure worship of God, and were accepted into covenant with him.

Egypt, a very fruitful land and where all sorts of arts and sciences both for use and ornament were flourishing in those early ages, was the place of their nativity and education, and there they had both houses, flocks, and pastures of their own propriety. But they were of a particular religion purely reveal'd from God and free from all those human inventions and superstitious customs which were then the establish'd and reigning way of worship in that ancient kingdom. And those pious fathers adhering closely to their inspired religion, refusing mixtures with their neighbors, preserving a visible distinction from them, and growing numerous and powerful, they became obnoxious to the Egyptian jealousy.

Thro' the reigns of some of their former sovereigns they were very kindly entertained and indulged. But upon the rising of a new King over Egypt who had no favor for them, he tho't to deal wisely with them and as the martyr Stephen expresses it, "He evilly entreated our fathers" (Acts 7. 19). Yea Moses, a public eyewitness, tells us that the King and his courtiers "set over them taskmasters to afflict them with their burthens";[1] and these cruel officers "made the children of Israel serve with" so much "rigor" that "they made their lives bitter with hard bondage" (Exod. 1. 7–14).

However, as they sigh'd and cried, their cry came up to heaven, and God heard their groaning and remembered his covenant and had respect unto them, as in the latter end of the following chapter.

Now therefore he advances Moses and Aaron to espouse their cause and head their tribes and lead them out of this inhospitable land to distant regions of ease and liberty.

If I were to display the characters of these illustrious persons I should not know when to end. And yet I cannot forbear observing they were two most lovely brethren, the sons of Amram, the son of Kohath, the son of

---

[d] 426. according to the accurate Mr. TALLENTS. [See Plate II in Francis Tallents and Gilguson Sealford, *A View of Universal History* . . . (London, 1685).]

[e] ἀστεῖος τῷ θεῷ ["beautiful like (or acceptable to) a god"].

Levi; of vastly different educations but remarkably raised up by heaven, inspir'd and strengthened in a happy union to lead the people out of Egypt and become the several heads—Moses of the civil and Aaron of the ecclesiastical orders—under God in Israel.

As for Moses, he was exceeding fair and beautiful when born (Acts 7. 20). The original[e] seems to intimate as if a divine beauty appear'd upon him. But his parents being afraid to keep him in their own house thro' the cruel inquisition of the times laid him in an ark of rushes among the flags on the river Nilus where Pharaoh's daughter, finding him, had compassion on him, took him up, and nourish'd him as her own son. By this means he came to be learned in all the wisdom of Egypt. He liv'd in the royal family for forty years and then from a principle of faith and piety he renounc'd it, refusing to be called the son of Pharaoh's daughter, rather choosing to suffer affliction with the people of God than to enjoy the pleasures of sin for a season, esteeming the reproach of Christ greater riches than the treasures in Egypt; for he had respect to the recompense of the reward. Forty years more he lived as a stranger-shepherd in the land of Midian. And then the Lord appeared to him in a flaming bush, yet unconsumed, and called him to take the care of his afflicted people and lead them out of Egypt.

He was the meekest man upon the face of the earth and on this account most eminently fitted to bear the burthen of so difficult and great a people. He was made a god to Pharaoh by a divine appearance that attended him in all his transactions with that haughty Monarch. He was mighty both in word and deed. And he became King in Jeshurun when the heads of the people and the tribes of Israel were gathered together. And then with what wonderful patience did he for forty years bear their ungrateful murmurings and strivings! with what an astonishing greatness of soul, that all their provocations cou'd never but once roil him into an indecent expression! How often did he stand in the breach to turn away the wrath of God, that he might not destroy them! How nobly refuse the offer of having his own posterity made a greater nation, rather than they should perish and the name of the God of Israel be dishonored in their utter ruin! How he pray'd that God wou'd rather blot him out of his book than not forgive their provoking sins; and how earnest, pressing, and persevering in his intercessions for them!

[1] "Burdens."

In short, of all the prophets that arose in Israel, there was none like him whom the Lord knew face to face and spake to him as a man speaks to his friend. And behold—what surprising honors the God of heaven was pleas'd to do him above every other mere man that ever liv'd on the earth! While all the tribes are trembling round about Mount Sinai, Moses goes up into the glowing fire and speaks with God and bears it for forty days and forty nights together, while the divine brightness wro't such transforming and astonishing impressions on him as to make his face to shine with so great a luster that when he came down the mountain, Aaron and all the children of Israel were afraid to draw near him, and he was forc'd to veil it that they might be able to endure his presence. When he goes into the tabernacle in the sight of all the people, the pillar of fire descends down to the door in honor of him; when he comes out, it rises up in the midst of the firmament to signify it has * nothing now to do but enlighten and awe the congregation and observe the reverence they paid him. And when some of the chief among them spake against him, the Lord came down in the pillar of the cloud and stood in the door of the tabernacle and called them and said,

Hear now my words: If there be a prophet among you, I the Lord will make myself known to him in a vision, and will speak to him in a dream. My servant Moses is not so, who is faithful in all mine house. With him will I speak mouth to mouth, even apparently, and not in dark speeches; and the similitude of the Lord shall he behold: wherefore then were ye not afraid to speak against my servant Moses? (Num. 12. 6–8).

And the anger of the Lord was kindled against them.

And as for Aaron—he was the elder brother of Moses, commended of God for the grace of his lips and honored with this distinguishing title: the saint of the Lord. He made him the spokesman and prophet of Moses,

ᶠ Arab.

ᵍ Sept. Syr. Chal. Vulg. & Mont. in Bib. Polyg. &c. [The Septuagint (Greek), Syriac, Chaldaic (Targum Onkelos), Vulgate (Latin) and the Hebrew text by Benedictus Arias called Montanus (1527–1598) in the Polyglot Bible *Biblia Sacra Polyglota* . . . ed. Brian Walton (London, 1657).]

ʰ Vid. Mercer. Buxt. Castle. Leigh & Pol. Synops. [Prince's references appear to be to Jean Mercier (?), d. 1570, *Commentarii Locupletiss* . . . (Geneva, 1583); either Johannes Buxtorf (1564–1629), *Biblia Hebraica* . . . (1618), or his son, Johannes Buxtorf (1599–1664), *Lexicon Chaldaicum et Syriacum* (1622) and *Tractatus de Punctorum Origine* . . . (1648); Edward Leigh (1602–71), *Critica Sacra in Two Parts* . . . *Containing Observations on All the Radices or Primitive Hebrew Words of the Old Testament* . . . 3rd edn. (London, 1650); Matthew Poole (1624–79), *Synopsis Criticorum*, 5 vols. (1669–76). Castle is unidentified.]

both to the people and to Pharaoh. The God of heaven also spake immediately to him and sent him to meet and unite with Moses; and he went and met him in the mount of God and kissed him and they rejoiced in meeting and uniting for the redemption of Israel. He first spake the words of the Lord to the elders of the tribes and did the signs in the sight of the people. He went in with Moses to Pharaoh with the rod of God in his hand and he said to the King, "Thus saith the Lord God of Israel, Let my people go" [Exod. 5. 1]. He cast down the rod before him and it became a serpent which swallowed up the rods of the magicians; he stretched it out upon the waters and they were turned into blood; he stretched it out again and the frogs came up and covered the land; he smote the dust of the earth and it was turn'd into swarms of lice round about, and the magicians own'd it to be the power of the Almighty.

With Moses he combin'd in leading Israel out of Egypt, in receiving the revelations of the mind of God, and in delivering them to the congregation. And when he came to Sinai he was by the divine appointment raised to the head of the priesthood; he was chosen out of all men living to offer sacrifice and incense to the God of heaven and he had the singular honor of the priestly office conferred upon his offspring as long as the seed of Israel should continue a nation.

These are that Moses and Aaron which the Lord advanced in the days of their fathers to lead them out of Egypt and found their state, to establish their sacred relation to God, to give them their excellent constitutions and laws and make them so renowned in the world.

The word "advanced" signifies both provided, created,[f] made,[g] prepared, instructed, trained and raised up, improv'd, adorned, furnish'd, fitted, constituted, preferred, and promoted to power and dignity. It is comprehensive of all these senses and so 'tis rendered by learned men.[h] And the general meaning is: it is the Lord that made them in such a special season when his people wanted them; that gave them their several excellent natural powers, that brought them forth, that rais'd them up; that every way accomplished them for the superior works and stations he design'd them for; endow'd them with such admirable gifts and graces; inspir'd them with such a public zeal and spirit, courage, wisdom, meekness, faith, and patience. In fine, that call'd them out and sent them, made them such illustrious persons, magnified them in the eyes of all that saw them, prosper'd them in their great undertakings, and made them so renowned, admired, and reverenc'd among all the nations round about them.

And as it was the Lord that thus advanced Moses and Aaron, it is he that also brought up the fathers of the tribes of Israel out of Egypt.

This is often indeed ascrib'd in Scripture to those two eminent human leaders and even this in the verse immediately following our text, because the God of heaven was pleas'd to honor them as agents under him and to put upon them some of his own transcendent excellence. But Moses and Aaron were only distinguished instruments, made, accomplish'd, and employed by this sovereign Agent; and to him does the pious preacher therefore justly carry up the minds of the people and render him the glory of that whole transaction.

And here we must observe that the bringing them out of Egypt implies the doing it thro' mighty obstructions and the surmounting every difficulty. The Egyptians were then an independent, great, and powerful nation and utterly averse to let the people go. The children of Israel were small and feeble in comparison with them, and their spirits broke and sunk with severity, labor, and slavish usage in the land of their affliction. Nor was their coming out of Egypt any other than the beginning of their deliverance. For they had a sea to pass; a great and terrible wilderness to go thro'; a waste and howling desert wherein were fiery serpents, scorpions, drought, and scarcity both of bread and water (Deut. 8. 15, and 32. 10); and they had also to beat their way thro' many mighty nations to the possession of their designed land.

In short, their case was so perplexed, helpless, and desperate, that none cou'd see how they could be delivered; the utmost wit and power of men were insufficient and none but God cou'd begin and carry on the mighty work and bring it to perfection. To Moses he therefore first appears and says, "I have surely seen the affliction of my people in Egypt, and have heard their cry by reason of their taskmasters; for I know their sorrows; And I am come down to deliver them out of the hand of the Egyptians, and to bring them out of that land unto a good land and a large, to a land flowing with milk and honey" (Exod. 3. 7, 8. So ver. 15–17, and Chap. 6. 4–8).

It wou'd take up too much of the present hour to mention the particulars of this surprising history. It wou'd lead us into a vast field of wonders, into a perpetual train of miracles for above forty years together. I shall therefore only now give it in this brief abridgement.

The Lord did great things for this people of his in Egypt, wondrous works in the land of Ham, and terrible things at the Red Sea. Besides the three several judgments we mentioned before, he went on to pour out seven others yet heavier than those till he forced the Egyptians to let Israel go. He sent innumerable swarms of insects among them which corrupted the air and vexed the people. He destroyed their cattle with plagues and tormented the inhabitants with very sore diseases. He thunder'd, lightned, and rain'd down hailstones mingled with fire, which ran * along upon the ground and consumed their substance. He sent infinite numbers of locusts which clouded the heavens and devoured the fruits of the earth. He wrapped them up in chains of thick darkness, that they could not stir from their places. He sent evil angels among them and smote all the firstborn of their land.

But he brought forth his people with joy and his chosen with gladness. In the daytime he led them with a cloud and all the night with a light of fire. He rebuk'd and divided the Red Sea and led them thro' the depths as thro' the wilderness. He brought them to Mount Sinai and showed them his glory. He spake aloud to them out of the midst of the burning flame and there he gave them his law and confirmed his covenant. He rained flesh among them as dust and feathered fowls as the sand of the sea. He commanded the clouds from above and poured down manna every night for forty years. He opened the rocks in the dry desert and the waters gushed out; the streams ran * down and overflowed like rivers. He set up his beautiful pavilion among them and dwelt in a cloud of glory between the cherubims. He marched before them in his pillar of light which in the daytime appeared as a cloud, in the night as a body of fire, that covered their camp and cast a terror round about. He smote great nations and slew mighty kings and gave their lands for an heritage, even an heritage to Israel his people.[2]

Thus we see how the Lord had bro't up their fathers out of Egypt as well as advanced Moses and Aaron to lead them, which was the preliminary observation made by the sacred orator as the general ground of his designed argument.

We proceed to consider: 2. The general inference he derives from thence to excite their close attention to his treatment of it; "Now therefore, stand still, that I may reason with you before the Lord, of all the righteous acts of the Lord which he did to you and to your fathers."

Herein with a divine authority he therefore now demands their most

[2] "The Lord did . . . Israel his people" is a paraphrase of Psal. 78. 12–54.

reverent and devout attention to the solemn argumentation he was, in the holy presence and name of God, a-going to make with them upon all his righteous acts both to them and their fathers.

To those more ancient and signal works of God which concern'd the raising up of those admirable leaders and the bringing up their fathers out of Egypt, the pious preacher here adds the other acts of the Lord to that distinguished people as worthy likewise of their most serious remembrance and consideration: both the works of God to them, which their own eyes had seen, and to their fathers, which they had read or heard of, from their first becoming a separate people to that very day. He comprehends them all and he points them out to the review of all in the universal term, and for their better observation and improvement he calls them "righteous acts" or "righteous things" or "dealings," as the word (for 'tis but one) may be rendered.

It is by some indeed translated "mercies"; by others, "benefits"; by others, "judgments," but other ancient and modern versions render it by "righteousnesses" or "righteous acts" or "things." [1] And the word indeed includes them all, as might easily be proved from other Scriptures and as sufficiently appears by the preacher's instances he proceeds to mention; for he goes on to recollect both signal acts of judgment and of mercy to that peculiar people.

The word in Scripture is by no means restrained to works of judgment, but in general signifies works of righteousness and is comprehensive both of judgments and mercies to a covenant people, as the tribes of Israel in a special manner were. For when the righteous God either chastens or visibly shows favor to such a people, he is in both those kinds of dispensations righteous: he is just and faithful to fulfill his word and all his dealings with them are in a just conformity to his peculiar covenant relation and engagements to them.

By these righteous acts of God are therefore meant both chastisements and mercies and especially those of a public nature or signal observation. And the prophet here wou'd signify that the Lord in all his dealings with them had shown himself a righteous and faithful God, both in bestowing greater mercies on them than others and in dispensing more severe corrections when they publicly sinn'd against him.

[1] Vid. Bib. Polyg. Pol. Synops. Eng. Marg. &c. [Probably the marginal notes in the Walton Polyglot Bible of n. g above, Poole's *Synopsis* of n. h above, and the King James Bible.]

What these righteous acts in particular were, I may not stay to mention. I may only observe in general, they were on the one hand very sore afflictions for their forgetting the God of their fathers, and on the other, wonderful salvations upon their humbling themselves before him and crying for mercy.

To the pious commemoration of these does the inspired preacher invite this obliged people. For as he had doubtless observed with sorrow, how soon they forgot the works of the Lord when they had been singing his praises for his appearances for them in their times of extremity; he wou'd have them know that those wonderful works both to them and their fathers were not merely to serve a single or transient occasion but were also designed for future benefit. And as they were now partaking in the influence of them, it became them therefore to rise up in their minds to the original works themselves and to that adorable wisdom and goodness which had in them a gracious view to their present both temporal and spiritual advantage, and began the train which brought them to their present felicity.

Nor was it merely the grateful remembrance of these that the inspired preacher had in his eye, but a pious and suitable improvement of it. He would now reason with them of all these righteous acts of the Lord both to them and their fathers; i.e., he would plainly show this people the divine ends and motives in these works of God, with the distinguishing and great obligations they were thereby laid under to adore and obey him more than others. He wou'd faithfully show them how unsuitable and sinful their behaviors had been, with their present eminent and growing guilt and danger, and he wou'd earnestly argue with them of their future duty, wisdom, and interest thence arising.

And all this he wou'd do before the Lord in a lively apprehension of his presence, citing them to his awful tribunal which he represents them as standing now before with his holy eye looking on them, and therefore he requires them with great authority to stand still, be silent, and give him their most reverent and religious attention.

And thus have we considered the words as applicable to that particular people to whom they were at first directed.

We proceed in the II. place to raise some general observations from them which are as so many practical and momentous lessons they very clearly teach and strongly urge upon us.

And they are plainly such as these: 1. *When there at any time arise,*

either in the civil or ecclesiastical order, men of eminent wisdom, good-
ness, power, and usefulness among a people of God, we must consider it
is the Lord their God that made, accomplished, and raised them up, and
this in special favor to that particular people.

2. *That when such a people are in a remarkable manner brought out*
of the hands of those that vexed them to a place or state of ease and liberty,
the gracious conduct of the Lord their God is herein to be religiously ob-
served and acknowledged by them.

3. *It behooves such a people so treated of God to remember all his*
signal operations, both of judgment and of mercy, both to them and their
fathers, to view them as acts of faithfulness and righteousness to them and
consider the special and great obligations arising from them.

4. *And lastly, it becomes their public teachers to remind them therefore*
of all these things and from thence to reason with them before the Lord
about their answerable carriage towards him.

All these articles are so many fair deductions most naturally rising
from the text, or rather so many doctrines clearly represented in it. They
are the general grounds themselves upon which the inspired orator goes
in his pathetic applications to that ancient and highly favored people.
They were the very reasons of his public addresses to them on that great
occasion. They are as well obliging upon every other people of God whom
he has treated with signal favors, chastisements, and mercies, as well as
those; and they are therefore written for our admonition upon whom the
ends of the world are come.

All the difference we can imagine between their obligations and the
obligations of others can only rise from this: that the works of the Lord
for them were of a miraculous nature; they were the visible operations of
God beside the course of natural causes, whereas his righteous acts for
others are done in a more veiled way by his invisible tho' real influence
on material and intellectual agents, according to the course of nature,
which is nothing else but his usual manner of acting and ruling the world.

But if we search these things exactly, we may clearly see that the obligations in both these cases are either the same or at least nearly equal.

---

[1] I take this Account from the Map in the Apparatus of the POLYGLOT BIBLE; where
the way is measured as running between the ranges of mountains, and amounts to
seventy horary miles, which is the same as leagues with us; and Moses tells us there
were but eleven days journey from Horeb to Kadesh-Barnea which lay on the southern border of Canaan (Deut. I. 2). [See p. 55 of Vol. 1 of the Walton Polyglot Bible.]

For let us here consider that the great God might if he pleas'd not only have rais'd up Moses and Aaron, but also brought up his people out of Egypt, led them thro' the neighboring countries, given them the victory over their enemies, and put them in the possession of Canaan, by his operations in the course of nature as well as by a continual train of miracles.

There was no necessity in the nature of things that any of those wonders should be wro't in Egypt in order to make the Egyptians willing to let the people go. He might have raised such an hatred in the Egyptians towards them as that Pharaoh might rather in displeasure have banish'd or commanded them to get out of the kingdom. No necessity they shou'd go thro' the sea or that the mighty waters should be divided for them; there was another and a near passage by land and they even took a circular march to go to the sea. No necessity they should travel thro' the terrible wilderness; they might have gone a much shorter and easier way in beaten roads by the sides of towns and cities, from whence they might have had supplies of bread and water. No necessity of their journeying forty years in the desert; it was but about two hundred ᶦ miles from the Red Sea to the southern border of Canaan. No necessity of a pillar of fire to guide them; Moses was a great mathematician, historian, and geographer, and the situations* of the countries about them were perfectly known. No necessity of dividing the waters of Jordan; they went a great way about to get to the river. In fine, no necessity of miraculous victories; for God might in the course of nature have swept away the people of Canaan either with wasting wars or plagues and emptied the land of almost all its inhabitants; or when they came to fight with a numerous host of the most powerful nations combined against them, he might either have set them a-contending together or have struck their minds with fear or have rais'd such a violent tempest of wind and hail to beat in their faces at the first of the battle as to bear them away before the armies of Israel.

Or instead of these and many other natural causes, he might have accomplished it all by this one easy course of his providence (easy I mean for us to conceive): the royal family of Egypt being without a male heir, he might have made both Pharaoh's daughter and the other Egyptians so fond of the wise and excellent Moses her adopted son as to raise him to the throne upon the King's decease; and then Moses might send a powerful army to make way for the tribes of Israel, to bear down all opposition before them, and put them into the possession of Canaan.

And now if the sovereign God in the midst of their sore oppression, anguish, and despair, had appear'd to some of their elders and said:

I have heard the groaning of the children of Israel whom the Egyptians keep in bondage and I will soon deliver and bring them into the land of Canaan. I will set the nations there to fight against and destroy each other and I will send wasting plagues among the survivors till they are almost consumed. And then I will raise such an aversion in the Egyptians to you as they will even drive you out of their country. And the nations remaining in Canaan shall thro' enmity among themselves be indisposed and unable to combine against you; and those that agree shall be struck with terror when they come to the battle. But I will give you courage and in their last and most united effort I will raise up a furious storm of wind and hail that shall beat in their faces as they begin the fight and make them fly before you; and you shall destroy them and take their land for your own inheritance. Or that little infant Moses, which now lies crying in the flags of Nilus and is doom'd by the King to die, shall be quickly found by his own daughter, adopted by her, brought up with her, raised to the throne of Egypt; and he shall send a mighty army with you that shall conduct you with triumph to Canaan, destroy and expel the nations there, and put you into the possession of the land.

And if these things were soon to come to pass accordingly, wou'd not they all appear to be the operations of God, tho' they were brought about agreeable to the course of nature? Wou'd not their deliverance out of Egypt and their entrance into Canaan be as truly the works of the Lord and as happy to Israel as if they were accomplished in a way beside the usual way of his acting? Or wou'd not these works of God have been exactly the same in themselves and as happy in the end to the people tho' he had never declared his designs beforehand, as if he had given a previous discovery of them?

And these beneficent acts of God being the same, wrought by the same wisdom, power, and goodness in this particular way of his acting in the course of nature as well as in the other beside it, having the same benevolent design and the same happy influence in their operation—they very nearly, if not equally, oblige his people to adore him and be grateful to him, to love and fear him, to obey and honor him, and to keep in mind the

---

ᵏ On Saturday June 12, 1630, arrived in Salem River the *Arbella* with Governor Winthrop and some of his Assistants, bringing the Charter of the Massachusetts Colony and therewith the government transferred hither; the other ten ships of the fleet with Deputy-Governor Dudley and the other Assistants arriv'd in Salem and Charles rivers before July 11. In the same month the Governor, Deputy-Governor, and Assistants came with their goods to Charlestown and the first Court of Assistants was held there on August 23, the same year.

lively memory both of his remarkable works of providence and their continued obligations to him for them.

And as a confirmation of all this: tho' the holy prophet hints at the extraordinary and miraculous works of God for Israel in the verse immediately following our text, yet in the rest of his sermon he only mentions the righteous acts of the Lord towards them according to the ordinary course of nature—as his suffering their enemies to prevail against and oppress them for their heinous sins, and his working out their deliverance and safety upon their penitent and earnest supplications; and from these ordinary acts of God the prophet reasons with the people they immediately concerned.

Having said thus much to clear our observations, it is needless to endeavor further to enlighten them. We therefore now go on to the III. and last general head, which is to apply the words and those observations to this particular people in our own land.

And here I cannot forbear observing that there never was any people on earth so parallel in their general history to that of the ancient Israelites as this of New England. To no other country of people cou'd there ever be so directly applied a multitude of Scripture passages in the literal sense as to this particular country; that excepting miracles and changing names, one wou'd be ready to think the greater part of the Old Testament were written about us, or that we, tho' in a lower degree, were the particular antitypes of that primitive people.[3]

However, I'm sure that upon the present occasion I may justly turn the text into a like address, in the name of God, to this great and general assembly, comprehensive both of rulers and people of every order, and say: "It is the Lord that advanced your primitive civil and ecclesiastical leaders, and that brought up your fathers out of the land of their affliction. Now therefore stand still, that I may reason with you before the Lord of all the righteous acts of the Lord, which he did to you and to your fathers!"

And how extremely proper is it upon the close of the first century of our settlement in this chief part of the land, which will now within a few weeks expire,[k] to look back to the beginning of this remarkable transaction, and first commemorate the righteous and signal works of God towards us both in our own days and in the days of our fathers, and then

[3] For *antitype,* see p. 94n above.

199

consider the great and special obligations they have laid upon us, with the nature of our carriage towards him for the time past, and our interest and wisdom for the future.

Give ear therefore O my people to my law; incline your ear to the words of my mouth. I will utter things of old: Which we have heard and known, and our fathers have told us. We will not hide them from their children, showing to the generation and century coming on the praises of the Lord, and his strength, and his wonderful works that he has done. For he established a testimony in Jacob, and appointed a law, a law of gratitude in Israel, which he commanded our fathers, that they should make known the works of God to their children: That the generation to come might know them, even the children which should be born; who should arise and declare them to their children: That they might also set their hope in God, and not forget his works, but keep his commandments [Psal. 78. 1–7].

And here we must own that very many have been the wondrous works which the Lord our God has wrought for us. They cannot be reckoned up in order before him; if I would declare and speak of them they are more than can be numbered. We may now therefore only touch on some of the most material—those of the most important, public, and comprehensive nature.

And first let us consider who the fathers of these plantations were and what were their distinguishing characters, that we may give to God the glory of the excellent honor he was pleas'd to put upon them and see our own obligations to him for deriving us from such eminent ancestors.

For the generality of them, they were the near descendants of the first reformers in England. They were born of pious parents who brought them up in a course of strict religion and under the ministry of the most awakening preachers of those days. Like so many Timothies, they were from their childhood taught to know the holy Scriptures, to reverence them as the inspirations of God, as the only rule of faith and piety, and to aim at both a pure scriptural way of worship and at the vital power and practice of godliness; and they continued in the things they had learned and had been assured of, as knowing of whom they had learned them.

Under such means as these they became inspired with a spirit of piety and with a growing zeal to reform the worship of God to the most beautiful and perfect model of his own institutions.

In points of doctrine they entirely held with the Church of England, their judgment of orthodoxy being the very same; but they apprehended it to be the sole prerogative of God himself, and a glory that he would not give to another, to appoint the orders of his own house and the acceptable ways of his own worship; that religion is a free obedience to the known laws of God and it is neither in the power of men or angels to make that religion which he has not made so himself; that his own institutions ought not to be set on a level, mixed or debased with the low devices of men; and that it is a plain, full, and decisive rule of his own injunction—to the law and to the testimony; if they speak not according to this Word, it is because there is no light in them.

This is the pure religion which our fathers admir'd and aim'd at, and at nothing in religion but what was inspir'd of God. This and nothing else they earnestly breath'd and labored after; but for laboring after it, tho' some of the most pious on earth, they were censured, pursued, seized, imprisoned, fined, and suffered a world of hardship not now to be named.

Their native country, which ever since the Glorious Revolution has been an happy land of ease and liberty, was in those former times as the land of Egypt to those pious men; and their lives were made exceeding bitter with religious bondage.

However, thro' the infinite mercy and wisdom of God, it was well for our fathers, and for us in the end, that they were thus afflicted. For had there been then a succession of such indulgent princes and bishops in England as there have since the Prince of Orange ascended the throne, there never had been such a country as this for religion, good order, liberty, learning, and flourishing towns and churches, which have given us a distinguishing name in the world and have reflected a singular honor to the persons and principles of its original settlers for this hundred years. But having a rougher surface, a barrener soil, a more inclement air than the southern countries, it wou'd in all human prospect have been at this day as the wastes of New Scotland or the wilder deserts between us, but abundantly fuller of barbarous natives; or at most in no better condition than the bordering plantations.

But the omniscient and sovereign God had espied and chosen this land for our fathers, for a refuge and heritage for them and their children, that here they might set up his worship and churches according to the inspired pattern, behold the beauty of the divine appointments in their scriptural purity, and leave these inestimable privileges which they justly preferred above all things else in the world as a blessed inheritance to their posterity, as we see at this day.

And now let us look back and behold in what a remarkable manner the God of our fathers was pleased to bring them out of the land of their sorrows to this far distant and quiet recess of the earth and put it into their hands.

First, he sends a smaller company into a neighboring state,[1] that there they might form themselves into a regular ecclesiastical body till this hidden part of the earth shou'd appear to the light, and yet come under such a discouraging character that none but men inspir'd with a zeal for religion would go on to settle it. He disappoints the successive endeavors of others who came hither only out of secular views, till the country comes to be given up and abandoned as not worthy the looking after by any trading nation. And then he sends both wasting diseases among the native inhabitants and fierce contentions among the survivors that greatly diminished their numbers and made room for his people.[4]

But O how horrid and dismal do these new-found regions appear! On the shores and rivers, nothing but sights of wretched, naked, and barbarous nations, adorers of devils—the earth covered with hideous thickets that require infinite toils to subdue—a rigorous winter for a third part of the year—not a house to live in—not a Christian to see—none but heathen of a strange and hard language to speak with—not a friend within three thousand miles to help in any emergency—and a vast and dangerous ocean to pass over to this!

But the Almighty inspires with a zeal and courage that nothing can daunt, with a faith and patience that nothing can break. He raises up men of superior piety, resolution, and wisdom to lead and animate in the great design.[m] And on they come, all alone, a small and feeble number, thro' contrary storms and boisterous seas they were never us'd to, tho' twice driven back, a terrible winter approaching, their wives and poor piteous children with them, and like Abraham of old they know not whither. But the Lord is their guide; he divides the seas before them; he leads them thro' in safety; he brings them with joy to the border of his designed sanctuary, to this mountainous country which his right hand had purchased. And having cast out multitudes of heathens before their arrival, he gives them favor in the sight of the rest; he divides his people an inheritance

[1] Viz., into Holland in 1610.
[m] Such as Mr. Carver, Mr. Bradford, and Mr. Winslow, successive Governors of Plymouth Colony, who came together in the first ship which set sail the last time from Plymouth in England on Sept. 6, and arrived in Cape Cod harbor on November 11th, 1620.

by line and makes them to dwell in peace in the midst of many powerful nations that cou'd have swallow'd them up in a moment, for above fifty years together.

But a greater colony is now coming on to strengthen the other and to fill up the land from sea to sea and from the river to the ends of the earth. And here, behold and wonder how this is also accomplished.

Great numbers of eminent persons and others of the same pious and pure dispositions in the main with the former yet continued in the churches of England and in communion with them as long as the higher powers indulg'd them, with earnest desires, labors, and hopes of a farther reformation of worship. But a spirit of severe imposition is now let loose upon these. The book of sports on the holy sabbath of God must be read by the ministers in the public assemblies, and their assent to unscriptural ways of worship must be subscribed as a necessary term of their preaching, even tho' they were solemnly ordain'd in the church to the office, requir'd by Christ himself to discharge it, and had a woe laid on them if they desisted to do it. And for preserving their consciences pure, they are driven out of their churches, they are forced from their flocks that lov'd them as the light of their eyes, and are more harassed and worried than the vilest of men.

And now at once, to the surprise of the nation, in almost every corner they are moved of God to look to this part of the wilderness he had been preparing for them. Many persons of shining figures are raised up to espouse their cause and venture with them. Their Prince is prevail'd on to grant them a charter of distinguishing privileges. They hear, they rise, they flow together; their flocks in great numbers attend and follow them. They all relinquish their delightful seats and their dearest friends, they put off their fair estates, they cast themselves and their children on the tumultuous ocean, and nothing can move them, so they may come into a wilderness rude and hideous to hear the voice of their teachers, become a covenant people of God, observe his laws, set up his tabernacle, behold his glory, and leave these things to their offspring forever.

And the Lord preserves them; he makes the depths of the sea a way for the ransomed to pass over; he brings them in thousands to these peaceful shores, and here, they that knew not each other before salute and embrace

---

⁴ Prince draws here upon the manuscript of William Bradford's *History of Plymouth Plantation* which came to him from Cotton Mather's library and was as yet unpublished.

with joy; he unites them in the most lovely agreement to profess and serve him; they publicly and solemnly enter into covenant with him, to love and obey him, to make his doctrines the only rule of faith and his institutions the only rule of worship; and with united joy they sing to the Lord:

Thou in thy mercy hast led forth the people which thou hast redeemed: thou hast guided them in thy strength to thy holy habitation. Thou hast bro't them in, and planted them in the mountain of thine inheritance, in the place, O Lord, which thou hast made for thee to dwell in, in the sanctuary which thy hands have established. And the Lord shall reign for ever and ever [Exod. 5. 13, 17, 18].

At first indeed they met with very grievous trials and endur'd a world of hardship and affliction; for tho' the Lord had thus redeem'd and gather'd them out of other lands and bro't them hither, yet here they had only solitary ways and thickets to wander thro' and no towns or houses to receive or cover them. Those who before had liv'd in the midst of plenty and delights now greatly suffer for want of lodging, bread, and defense from weather. Hungry and thirsty, their souls fainted in them. They are wet with the showers of the mountains and embrace the rocks for shelter. They quickly sink their worldly substance; they are forc'd to give their pleasant things for meat to relieve the soul; and many of their wives and children expire about them. But they endure with patience and cry to God and he sends relief. He satisfies their longing souls and filleth them with goodness. He builds them houses and towns for habitation; he prepares them fields for planting and he turns the desert into a fruitful land. He increas'd their cattle and he blessed their persons, so that they multiplied greatly, and he made them families and churches round about.

And now the wilderness and the solitary place is glad for them; the desert rejoices and blossoms as a rose; it blossoms abundantly with peace and righteousness; it rejoices with joy and singing. The glory of Lebanon is given to it, the excellency of Carmel and Sharon; they see the glory of the Lord and the excellency of our God. The waters of the divine influence break out in the wilderness and the streams in the desert; the parched ground becomes a pool and the thirsty land, springs of water; in the habitations of dragons where they lay there grows up the grass, and an high

[n] Twelve or 13 in Plymouth Colony, 47 in the Massachusetts, 19 in Connecticut, 3 in Long Island, and 1 at Martha's Vineyard.

way now is there which is call'd the way of holiness over which the unclean do not pass and the wayfaring men do not err therein.

And to the great glory of God be it spoken—there never was perhaps before seen such a body of pious people together on the face of the earth. For those who came over at first came hither for the sake of religion and for that pure religion which was entirely hated by the loose and profane of the world. Their civil and ecclesiastical leaders were exemplary patterns of piety; they encouraged only the virtuous to come with and follow them; they were so strict on the vicious both in the church and state that the incorrigible could not endure to live in the country and went back again. Profane swearers and drunkards are not known in the land. And it quickly grew so famous for religion abroad that scarce any other but those who lik'd it came over for many years after. And indeed such vast numbers were coming that the crown was obliged to stop them, or a great part of the nation had soon emptied itself into these American regions.[5]

And for those who were here, the Spirit from on high is poured * upon them and the wilderness becomes a fruitful field; judgment and righteousness continue in it and the effect of righteousness is peace. While a cruel war rages in the kingdom they left, lays it waste, and drowns it in blood, the people here dwell in peaceable habitations, in sure dwellings, in quiet resting places. And the Lord enlarges the bounds of their tents; he stretches forth the curtains of their habitations; he makes them to break forth on the right hand and on the left; he makes their seed to inherit the lands of the Gentiles, the desolate places to be inhabited. And in fifty-four years from the first plantation there appear above fourscore English churches,[n] composed only of known, pious, and faithful professors, dispersed thro' the wilderness.

But now comes on a cloud which covers our glory! This excellent generation passes away and there arises another which provokes the holy One of Israel to anger.

The Lord set up our neighboring enemies against us; he united them

[5] Daniel Neal quotes from the Proclamation of April 30, 1637, "to restrain the disorderly transporting of his Majesty's subjects to the plantations in America"; reports the detention of eight ships in the Thames about to embark for America—one of which carried Oliver Cromwell; and quotes from a subsequent order "that no clergyman should be suffered to go over without approbation of the Lords Archbishop of Canterbury and Bishop of London" (*The History of New England*, London, 1720, I, 151).

together who never could unite till now, the western Indians before and the eastern behind; they devour'd our Israel with open mouth.

The western nations first came up ° like the waters of a flood, strong and many; they came up over all our banks, they passed thro' our country, they overflowed and came over, they reached to the neck and filled the breadth of our land! They lay our country desolate; they burn our towns round about with fire; they devour our land in our presence! They draw near and threaten even the chief and central town itself; and there are those now living who remember that every man therein was ready to shut up his house and go out for the preservation of the remnant of the people! There was the noise of a multitude in the mountains, like as of a great people; a tumultuous noise of the kingdoms and nations gathered together; the Lord of hosts mustered the host of the battle! All hands grew faint and every heart melted; we were afraid; pangs and sorrows took hold of us; we were in pain as a woman that travaileth; we were amazed at one another, for the day of the Lord came, cruel both with wrath and fierce anger, to lay the land desolate!

But when the Lord had brought us to the brink of destruction, then he heard our earnest cries and arose for our rescue. At the lifting up of himself, the nations were scattered—he rebuk'd and set them against one another; he made them to flee afar off; he chas'd them as the chaff of the mountains before the wind and like a rolling thing before the whirlwind. As smoke is driven away, so he drove them away; as wax melteth before the fire, so they perish'd at the presence of God.[6]

And then, how often has he made ᵖ the eastern Indians the rod of his anger and the staff of his indignation with us! He has sent them against us and given them the charge to take the spoil and tread us down as the mire of the street. They came with open mouth upon us; they thrust thro' everyone they found abroad; they ensnared and slew our mighty men who went forth for our defense; they spoil'd our fields and pastures; they burnt up our houses; they destroy'd our towns and garrisons; they murdered our wives; they carried our young men and virgins into captivity; they had no pity on the fruit of the womb; their eyes spared not our children, they dash'd them in pieces.

But when the Lord had perform'd his work, his righteous work upon

° In 1675 and 1676. [King Philip's War.]
ᵖ In four several terrible wars, especially the three former, from 1675 to the conclusion of the last peace in 1726.

us, he punished the stoutness of their hearts and the glory of their looks. For they said, "By the strength of our hands we have done it, and by our wisdom; for we are prudent: and have remov'd the bounds of the people, and have robb'd their treasures, and have put down the inhabitants like a valiant man" [Isa. 10. 13]. Therefore the Lord of hosts has sent among their fat ones leanness and under their glory kindled a burning like the burning of fire; and it consumed the glory of their forest and they were as when a standard-bearer fainteth; and the rest of the trees of their forest are now grown so few that a child may write them.[7]

I might go on to mention a great variety of other righteous acts of the Lord our God to this covenant people, both corrective and merciful—as distressing droughts and scarcities; contagious and wasting sicknesses; impoverishing disappointments, fires, and losses of a public nature and influence; vexations from those that have envied and hated us; the cruel taking away of our most dear bought privileges (the most grievous affliction of all others) and their wonderful restoration; the insupportable power of strange oppressors and the surprising appearance of God for our rescue when no other arm could save us and our hope was almost perished from before him—but the time would fail me.

I shall therefore only mention one remarkable work of God which appears to me to be full of wonder and a visible and constant monument of his special favor and appearance for us—and that is this: on the account of our pure religion we have been all along a people misrepresented, envied, and maligned above any other on earth. We have had continually for this hundred years many powerful and active enemies and but few and feeble friends to stand up for us and plead our cause. How comes it then to pass that we have greater civil and religious privileges than almost any others? The most high God has been our mighty Friend. To him have our dear forefathers and we consign'd our greatest interests and he has stood up for us; he has removed kings and set up kings; he has carried the devices of the crafty headlong, that those who mourn'd might be rais'd to safety; and when our case has been so helpless that we cou'd only pray, we have then stood still and seen the salvation of

---

[6] "He rebuk'd and set . . . whirlwind." See Isa. 17. 13. "As smoke is . . . God." See Psal. 68. 2.

[7] "But when the Lord . . . looks." See Isa. 10. 12. "Therefore the Lord . . . write them." See Isa. 10. 16, 18, 19.

God. It is all a continued work of his; it can be ascrib'd to nothing else; let it be ever marvelous in our eyes; and let him have all the glory.

And so let him have the glory likewise of all his other works both of judgment and of mercy to us. Let us frequently call them to mind, peruse the published histories of them, and teach them to our children after us.

But I must now come on "to reason with you before the Lord, of all these righteous acts of his, which he has done to you and to your fathers."

And here in the first place then, we see what a surpassing favor and honor the most High has shown to this particular people in our first formation, and so down to this day. He form'd us of a pious people devoted to him and he brought them and their offspring into a special, open, express, and solemn covenant with him. They began with this and this has been successively laid in the foundation of every church and explicitly own'd at the administration of every sacrament and at the admission of every member.

Now the substance of this covenant is that he will deal with us and we will carry to him according to his inspired Word. The sacred Scriptures, the promises and threatenings exhibited in them, are the declared rule of his dispensations to us; and the same divine writings, the doctrines and injunctions represented in them, are the professed rule of our carriage to him. This is the rule and the only rule for the people, churches, and religion of New England. We hold to nothing but what we apprehend to be revealed, taught, and required in them; and we leave everyone to search and judge for themselves.

By our sacred covenant we are therefore under the most solemn obligations to preserve an entire and strict adherence to this divine standard, both in belief and practice, both in life and worship; and woe unto us if we depart therefrom! For if we do, we break our covenant with the holy God and become expos'd to all the fearful and signal judgments denounc'd in Scripture upon the violators of it; and he is a true and jealous God and will signally avenge the quarrel of his broken covenant. But if we faithfully

ꝗ Purity in churches is oppos'd to human mixtures, and the freer they are from these the purer they are; which is the great and profess'd design of ours who in religious matters make the revelations of God their only rule and admit of nothing but what they apprehend these revelations require, both in discipline and worship as well as doctrine and manners. And freedom in churches is a liberty to judge of the meaning of these revelations, and of professing and acting according to our judgment of the meaning of them; and in particular the free choice of our own pastors and ways of discipline and worship, and our consciences in these things not subjected to any power on earth.

keep to this holy engagement, then we are entitled to all the distinguishing promises which God has made to his covenant people; and he is a gracious and a faithful God and will surely fulfill them for us.

We are also to look on all his past dealings, both afflictive and merciful, both with us and our fathers, as his righteous and faithful acts according to his wise and well-ordered covenant; they are nothing else but his just and faithful performance of it, and by the tenor of this sacred indenture we are to expect his treatment of us for the future.

But then, O the extraordinary obligations we are under, both from the covenant of the Lord our God and from all his signal works both of judgment and of favor to us!

Have any of the other plantations suffered so much as we by cruel wars, depredations and bloodshed, impoverishing disappointments, fires and losses, both by sea and land, contagious sicknesses and other evils, which have mark'd us out for the censure and condemnation of the world?

And yet, what people on earth have had more distinguishing advantages than we? Deriv'd of pious ancestors; possess'd of a good and large land with commodious harbors and fruitful seas; living in a clear and healthy air and in the enjoyment of great privileges civil and sacred; having wise and religious laws, pious and learned magistrates and ministers, sober and virtuous educations, grammar schools in every town of an hundred families free for the poorest without expense, well-ordered colleges to perfect the accomplishments of our growing youth for the public service—in fine, free and pure churches,[q] divine institutions, sacred sabbaths for the preservation of religion in its power and practice—and as the effect of this, in general, a sober, civil, charitable, quiet, loyal people; who earnestly wish'd and pray'd for and now greatly rejoice in the happy advancement and succession of the illustrious House of Hanover to the British throne in which alone under God, we trust to preserve our constitution, laws, and liberties, and desire nothing but the continuance of all these things—and where can they be found in so great a measure as in this happy land?

And here give me leave to observe that tho' the principal seaport towns of the province are exceedingly exposed and deprav'd by the pouring in of trade and strangers, yet we may by no means judge by these of the rest of the country. For to tell you my own experience, tho' for the acquirement of grammar learning I liv'd when young in four considerable country towns, yet I never heard a profane oath or curse till I was fifteen years of age, when I came down and heard them first from a profane youth of our metropolis.[8]

And are not all these distinguishing advantages the plain consequence under God of the pious principles and characters of the first settlers of these plantations? Don't they reflect a singular and everlasting honor on them? And are they not the strongest obligations on us to maintain the same happy principles and characters, that we may transmit the same advantages to our posterity?

But then as all these advantages have been bestowed upon us by the Lord our God and on these accounts we may with humble admiration say he has scarce dealt so graciously with any other people under heaven, how distinguishingly great and multiplied are our obligations to remember, love, and praise him, to persevere in our ancient choice and profession of him, to preserve his pure worship without imposing on any, to obey his laws, to fear him and trust in him for the time to come; and how ungrateful, how sinful, how provoking, how dangerous to forget him and his signal works which both our fathers and we admir'd and were greatly affected with in the days wherein he wrought them for us—and much more so, to forsake him and rebel against him.

But O! Alas! Our great and dangerous declensions! To what an awful measure are they gone already, how transcendently guilty do they make us, how threatening do they grow! What a melancholy prospect wou'd lie before us were we to draw the parallel between the first and present generation! In comparison with this they made a heaven upon earth; but as when their heads were laid in the grave there arose another generation after them which did not so much know the Lord nor the works he had done for Israel, so the following generation has still declined further; and now we are risen up in our fathers' stead, an increase of sinful men, to augment the fierce anger of the Lord against his people.

And is not this the word of the Lord this day—go and cry in their ears and say:

Thus saith the Lord; I remember thee, the kindness of thy youth, and the love of thine espousals, when thou wentest after me into the wilderness,

---

[r] See the excellent election sermons of Mr. Higginson, Mitchel, Stoughton, Danforth, Shepard, Oakes, Torrey, etc., which might be of public service, were they reprinted and dispersed. [The dates of these sermons are, respectively, 1663, 1667, 1668, 1670, 1672, 1673, 1674. Danforth's (1670) is reprinted above.]

into a land that was not sown. This land was holiness then to the Lord, and the firstfruits of his increase: all that devour'd thee offended me; and I brought evil upon them. And now thus saith the Lord, What iniquity have you or your fathers found in me, that you are gone far from me, have followed after vanity, and are become so vain a people? Nor do you say, Where is the Lord that brought us up out of a distant land, that led us thro' the wilderness, thro' a land of deserts and pits, a land of drought, and of the shadow of death? And he brought you into a plentiful country, to eat the fruit thereof and the goodness thereof; but now ye have entered, ye have defiled my land, and made my heritage an abomination. Wherefore I will yet plead with you, saith the Lord, and with your children's children. Hath a nation changed their gods? but my people have changed their glory for that which profiteth not. Be astonished, O ye heavens, at this. For my people have committed two evils; they have forsaken me the fountain of living waters, and hewed them out cisterns, broken cisterns, that can hold no water [Jer. 2. 2, 3, 5–7, 9, 11–13].

Now we are guilty of these provoking evils when we turn from the predominant love of God and of his holy ways, neglect his interest, and seek the pleasures, wealth, or honors of the present world with a greater ardor as a more desirable source of good and happiness. And tho' 'tis true we still maintain in general the same religious principles and professions with our pious fathers, yet how greatly is the spirit of piety declin'd among us, how sadly is religion turning more and more into a mere "form of godliness," as the apostle speaks [II Tim. 3. 5.], without the power, and how dreadfully is the love of the world prevailing more and more upon this professing people! And this notwithstanding all the zealous testimonies which have from time to time for above this threescore years been borne against these growing evils.

Like as to Israel of old, so the Lord has sent us from the early days of our apostasy his faithful ministers to testify against it and to warn us of the fatal consequence. With what wonderful life and earnestness have they upon all occasions, and especially on such as these, delivered their anxious souls and mourned over us, as their printed sermons show; [r] and how solemn, plain, and faithful in their public admonitions of our sin and danger! But like that ancient people also, we have not hearkened to the voice of God but hardened our necks against him and have done worse and worse in every generation. And what will be the consequence of this—unless a reformation save us—but severer chastisements than

[8] For the beginning of this oathless anecdote, see p. 95 above.

others suffer, a growing separation between our God and us, the with-drawment of his Holy Spirit from us, the loss of piety, the increase of all corruption both in worship and in manners (as they usually go together), and a terrible entail of vice and ruin to our dear posterity!

And have we not sufficient cause to apprehend that we are already come to such an awful pass, to such a stupid, careless, and incorrigible frame as they when the Lord directed such a word as this to be delivered to them:

Since the day that your fathers came forth out of the land of Egypt unto this day I have sent unto you all my servants the prophets, daily rising up early and sending them. Yet they hearkened not unto me, nor inclined their ear, but hardened their neck: they did worse than their fathers. Therefore thou shalt speak all these words unto them; but they will not hearken unto thee: thou shalt also call unto them; but they will not answer thee. But thou shalt say unto them, This is a nation that obeyeth not the voice of the Lord their God, nor receiveth correction (Jer. 7. 25–28).

The following verse I dread to read and hope it does not yet belong to this backsliding people. But I must needs confess that considering the inclinations in the children of pious ancestors to degenerate, and the usual course of providence among them, with our own past behaviors and present state and prospects, I can't but fear that this declining people will grow worse and worse in every age, if the world continues, till they come to be as much remark'd for sinfulness and miseries as they have been here-tofore for piety and great advantages.

Now then let the affecting view of all these things, both present, past, and future, excite us all in our several places to do our utmost that we may not share in the dreadful guilt of this declension, nor have our part in drawing on the lamentable consequences of it. But let us lay it to heart and mourn before the Lord, first our own apostasies and sins and then the apostasies and sins prevailing among this people. Let us cry earnestly for the spirit of grace to be poured forth on us and them, that the hearts of the children may be returned to the God of their fathers and may continue steadfast in his sacred covenant. And being revived ourselves, let us labor to revive religion in our several families, and then rise up for God in this evil day, bear our open witness also against the public degeneracy and do what in us lies for the revival of the power of piety among all about us.

And to direct and quicken us here, let us improve the shining patterns which our ancient fathers have set before us.

Let our honorable rulers of every kind and order, from the highest to the lowest, remember those admirable civil leaders of this people that have gone before us and imitate their great example.

They were mostly men of good estates and families, of liberal educations, and of large experience; but they chiefly excell'd in piety to God, in zeal for the purity of his worship, the reverence of his glorious and fearful name, the strict observance of his holy sabbaths, the respect and maintenance of an unblemish'd ministry; the spread of knowledge, learning, good order, quiet, thro' the land, a reign of righteousness, and the welfare of this people. In short, the making and executing wholesome laws for all these blessed ends, and in wisdom, courage, patience, meekness, self-denial for the public good, and steadfast perseverance in their endeavors after it.

They laid the wise foundations of our succeeding and present happiness; they united with their pastors in consultations and endeavors for the advancement and preservation of religion and the privileges, peace, and order of the churches; by their grave and prudent carriage they happily preserv'd a veneration for their persons and authority among the people and yet carefully protected them in the full enjoyment of their precious liberties.

Mr. Mitchel, speaking of them in his election sermon in 1667, observes that "that was the thirty-seventh year current with the Massachusetts Colony (I may add—the forty-seventh then with Plymouth) that God had given them godly magistrates," and that "the sun did not shine upon an happier people than they were, in regard of this mercy." [9] And Mr. Oakes in his election sermon in 1673:

Many and wonderful are the favors and privileges which the Lord your God hath conferred upon you. As to your civil government, you have had Moses, men I mean of the same spirit, to lead and go before you; the Lord hath not given children to be your leaders . . . but pious, faithful, prudent magistrates, men in wisdom and understanding . . . men of Nehemiah's spirit that sought not themselves but sincerely design'd the good and consulted the welfare and prosperity of these plantations . . . men that did not rigorously exact the bread of the governor but cheer-

---

[9] Jonathan Mitchel, *Nehemiah on the Wall* . . . (Cambridge, 1671), 23–24. Prince has misquoted; Mitchel was quoting from Richard Mather's election sermon of 1660.

fully receded from their own right, sympathizing with and compassionately considering the low estate and condition of this people. . . . Good magistrates, good laws and the vigorous execution of them, hath been the privilege and glory of New England wherein you have been advanced above most of the nations of the earth.[10]

In fine, they faithfully serv'd their generation according to the will of God; they were greatly concern'd for the religion and welfare of their posterity; they now enjoy the glorious fruits of all their services and have left their excellent examples for those to follow who should rise up in their places, as you are this day.

We the ministers and people account it happy that we see so many in place of public power descending from the ancient founders of these towns and churches, and others, in such a measure like them, in exalted stations. We also esteem it a joyful smile of heaven that our most gracious King has given us principal rulers out of ourselves, men of known virtue and well acquainted with our constitution, genius, circumstance, and chief concern and interest. And the late surprising turn of providence in favor to this distressed people fills us with humble adorations of the sovereign power and government of God, and gives us such raised apprehensions of the gracious dispositions of our King and Queen to favor us as both inspires us with universal joy and gratitude, and also assures us that your honors will best please their Majesties by pursuing your own inclinations to render us an easy and happy people.[11]

And how is it imaginable that this can be better done than by following the distinguishing examples of the ancient fathers of this country by whose auspicious conduct this plantation grew and flourished under many disadvantages, without any expense or help from the crown, and soon outstripp'd all others in virtue, learning, power, and figure, tho' not in riches.

Let our ministers likewise call to mind and imitate the burning and shining lights that were first set up in this dismal wilderness.

Instead of my drawing their exalted character, I would rather give it in the more authentic terms of those who personally knew them. They are

---

[s] Mr. William Hubbard of Ipswich.

[t] I say others, because it has been a fundamental principle with us that as churches are composed both of ministers and brethren, and ecclesiastical councils or synods are proper representatives of churches, that therefore there should sit in all such assemblies not only ministers but also others chosen by the churches to represent them; that they may not be merely clerical, or synods of the clergy, but ecclesiastical, or synods of the churches. And such have been all our New England synods and councils from the first—agreeable to that famous precedent in Acts XV.

the joint and expiring testimony of the venerable and aged Mr. Higginson and Hubbard[8] in the year 1701:

Above seventy years (say they) have passed away since one of us, and above sixty since the other of us, came into New England. . . . We are therefore capable to make some comparison between the condition of the churches when they were first erected in this country and the condition into which they are now fallen and more falling every day. . . . We that saw the persons who from four famous colonies assembled in the synod that agreed on our platform of church discipline[12] cannot forget their excellent character. They were men of great renown in the nation from whence the Laudean persecution exiled them. Their learning, their holiness, their gravity struck all men that knew them with admiration. They were Timothies in their houses, Chrysostomes in their pulpits, Augustines in their disputations. The prayers, the studies, the humble enquiries with which they sought after the mind of God were as likely to prosper as any men's upon earth. And the sufferings wherein they were confessors for the name and truth of the Lord Jesus Christ add unto the arguments which would persuade us that our gracious Lord would reward and honor them with communicating much of his truth unto them. The famous Brightman had foretold, *clariorem lucem adhuc solitudo dabit*: "God would yet reveal more of the true church state to some of his faithful servants whom he would send into a wilderness that he might there have communion with them." And it was eminently accomplished in what was done for and by the men of God that first erected churches for him in this American wilderness.[13]

Thus those two ancient witnesses who brought up the rear of the first generation that came from England.

Indeed the inspired Scripture, as was observ'd before, is our only authoritative rule of faith and worship; and our *Platform* is no other than the declared judgment of the sense of Scripture in matters of church order, discipline, and worship which our ancient ministers and others,[t] with

---

[10] Urian Oakes, *New England Pleaded With . . .* (Cambridge, 1673), 17–19. Prince has slightly misquoted; he does not follow Oakes' italics and he has changed the punctuation.

[11] Prince undoubtedly refers here to the appointment of Jonathan Belcher, Harvard graduate (1699), Boston merchant, Councilman, and recent representative of the General Assembly in England, as the new Governor of Massachusetts following the death of Governor Burnet. Belcher was commissioned in January 1730 and arrived the following August.

[12] The synod of 1647–48.

[13] John Higginson and William Hubbard, *A Testimony to the Order of the Gospel . . .* (Boston, 1701), 3, 4–5. The *Testimony* was also bound in with Jonathan Wise's *A Vindication of the Government of New England Churches . . .* (Boston, 1717).

abundant prayers and humble, free, and diligent enquiries and conferences, almost unanimously came into. But then, as no other people in these later ages have been favored with such advantages as the founders of these churches to search into, discover, and put in practice the Christian way of church order, discipline, and worship described in the Word of God—they being entirely men of piety, knowledge, judgment, the most about the middle age of life, who had made the Bible their familiar study, many of them persons of superior learning, and all free from any influence of human powers and constitutions in religious matters—they wholly relinquish'd all devised schemes of men and set themselves to consult the sacred Scriptures only, that they might happily see what these directed, and submit thereto; and having renounced all prospects of worldly riches, powers, and dignities for this very end, they were on these accounts most likely to find out the truth in those affairs. And tho' our faith is not to be subjected to their judgment, but we should also humbly, sincerely, and carefully search the Scriptures and try these things by them and see whether they are conformable to those oracles of God or no, as the noble Bereans did when even the apostles taught them;[14] yet the result of their united, pious, anxious, and laborious enquiries under such advantages demands a very extraordinary veneration from all impartial men and especially from us their dear posterity.

And can we do anything better, both for the advantage of our ministry, the satisfaction of our people, and the quiet of our churches, than to go on upon the scriptural foundations these excellent men have already laid? Not to set aside, or build anew, but to go on further as the light of Scripture leads us for our common peace and edification? And I know of nothing of greater moment than to advise to methods about calling councils in a fairer, more peaceable, equal, and harmonious manner than we are now unhappily liable to, that so this sacred ordinance may not be so subject to be frustrated by the dark intrigues of crafty men nor anti-councils rais'd to support contending parties, to the great dishonor of Christ, the grief of all good men, and the inflammation and continuance of hatred and divisions.

And how happy for these churches and for all this country both to

---

[14] Then a preacher of the Gospel in Dorchester, but three years after chosen a Magistrate of the Massachusetts Colony, and afterwards made by King William and Queen Mary of ever glorious memory, Lieutenant-Governor and Commander-in-Chief of this province.

this and future generations, as I would with submission hope, if with the countenance and invitation of our civil fathers we might have a synod in due time convened; not to make the least injunctions upon any, which is contrary to our known principles, but only to advise and propose those methods which may conduce to the promoting piety, peace, and good order in our own churches—but left to everyone to receive or not, as they think best. Two such happy synods we had in the reign of King Charles I and two more in the reign of King Charles II, without offense, invited by the civil rulers who also sat among them as chosen representatives of our churches and as grave advisers with the rest, but all without the least coercive power.[15] Even the Protestants in France were often allowed by their kings to meet in synods and benevolences given them out of the royal treasury. Nor can we think his Majesty can be displeased with us if he were to know that our New England synods are not like those of other countries, to make decrees or canons, but for counsel only, for the peace and order of the churches who send their pastors and other delegates to consult together and give their free advices; and that as no authority is or ever was put forth by our civil rulers by deriving any power to such a synod or in inviting the churches to them—the churches being always left at liberty whether to send or no, to comply or no—there can be no invasion on any power in such a free invitation, it being impossible, as I humbly apprehend, there should be any power invaded where there is none assumed.

In fine, let the people in general both now and frequently look back to their excellent forefathers and labor after that spirit of grace and prayer, of purity and charity, of zeal for God and love to men, which dwelt so eminently in them.

And that we may know something more concerning them, let us hear that great and immortal honor of his country, Mr. William Stoughton, in his election sermon in 1668,[14] who liv'd among them:

As for extraction and descent—if we be considered as a posterity, O what parents and predecessors may we the most of us look back unto, thro' whose loins the Lord hath stretched forth the line of his covenant, measuring of us out and taking us in to be a peculiar portion to himself! . . . And then . . . As to New England's first ways, what glorious things might here be spoken unto the praise of free grace and to justify

---

[14] See Acts 17. 10–13.

[15] For the synods of 1637, 1647–48, and 1662, see p. 67n above; for the synod of 1679, see p. 97n above.

the Lord's expectations upon this ground! . . . O what were the open professions of the Lord's people that first enter'd this wilderness? How did our fathers entertain the Gospel and all the pure institutions thereof and those liberties which they brought over? What was their communion and fellowship in the administrations of the kingdom of Jesus Christ? What was the pitch of their brotherly love, of their zeal for God and his ways and against ways destructive of truth and holiness? What was their humility, their mortification, their exemplariness? How much of holiness to the Lord was written upon all their ways and transactions? God sifted a whole nation that he might send choice grain over into this wilderness. (Again), Those that have gone before us in the cause of God here, who and what were they? Certainly choice and pick'd ones whom he eminently prepared and trained up and qualified for this service; they were worthies, men of singular accomplishments and of long and great experience. Yet did they walk with fear and trembling before the Lord, in the sense of their own nothingness and insufficiency for the work here to be done. (And again), Consider and remember always that the books that shall be opened at the last day will contain genealogies in them. There shall then be brought forth a register of the genealogies of New England's sons and daughters. How shall we many of us hold up our faces then when there shall be a solemn rehearsal of our descent as well as of our degeneracies! To have it published whose child thou art will be cutting to thy soul, as well as to have the crimes reckoned up that thou art guilty of![16]

These were the distinguish'd settlers of New England! And as we are now rejoicing in the happy fruits of their excelling piety, wisdom, magnanimity, hardships, pains, and labors, does it not become us to remember and mention them with the most grateful esteem and honor, to treat their names with veneration as the worthy fathers of this country, to rise up and call them blessed, to follow their bright examples, to observe their living exhortations and their dying charges, and constantly adhere to the great and noble ends of all their arduous undertakings, sufferings, cares, prayers, and labors for us?

But in a steady adherence to these great ends, let us continue also to exceed all others in our extensive charity. To account their churches to be true churches and their ministers to be true ministers, as we have always done, whether they will ours or no; to own and treat them as our Christian brethren tho' they shou'd refuse to own us in the same relation; to assume into our worship nothing but reveal'd religion or what we apprehend of scriptural example or appointment; that so the doors of our communion may be as wide as Christ allows, there may be nothing on our part to hinder it, and we may still have the glory, safety, and satisfaction to be of the most generous and charitable of churches, as being one of the brightest marks as well as ornaments of true religion and of pure Christianity.

And now blessed be the Lord our God, even the God that form'd this people for himself to show forth his praises; who redeemed them out of distant lands, who brought them thro' the depths of the seas and showed them his great salvations; who took them into his covenant and gave them the land of the heathen that they might observe his statutes and keep his laws. They have seen thy goings O God in the sanctuary! Bless ye the Lord in the congregations; even the Lord, ye descendants from the fountain of our Israel! Thy God hath commanded thy strength; strengthen O God that which thou hast wrought for us! Let thy work appear to thy servants and thy glory to their children! Let the beauty of the Lord our God be on us and establish thou the work of our hands to future generations.

May our princes always rule us in righteousness and mercy; may our governors be tender fathers to us as they have been of old; may our country never want of her own sons bro't up in her to take her by the hand and guide her; may those that lead us never cause us to err nor destroy the way of our path, but rule in judgment and the fear of God! May those be always wise and pure both in heart and life that bear the vessels of the sanctuary, and may the Lord our God create upon all our churches, as it were, a cloud and smoke by day and the shining of a flaming fire by night, and on all the glory create a defense. May this seminary of learning,[17] so fair and pleasant in our eyes, which our wise and pious fathers set up so early to enlighten and rejoice our land, yet still produce such illustrious persons as Stoughton, Dudley, Saltonstal, and Belcher, and send forth such great and burning lights as it has already into our churches, and may they flow forever! May the Lord of hosts reign among us and be for a crown of glory to us, and our salvation in times of trouble; may he forever plead the cause of this his people, defend this country to save it for his own name's sake, contend with them that contend with us and save our children; may no weapon form'd against us ever prosper and every tongue that shall rise against us in judg-

[16] William Stoughton, *New England's True Interest* . . . (Cambridge, 1670); "As for extraction . . . into this wilderness," 17–19; "Those that have gone . . . to be done," 30; "Consider and . . . guilty of!" 33.
[17] Harvard College, where this sermon was given.

ment be condemned! May we be the blessed of the Lord and our offspring with and after us; may they spring up as the grass, as willows by the watercourses; may they be taught of God and their peace be great; may they take root and blossom and fill the face of the land with fruit; and may the kindness of the Lord never depart from us or them, nor his covenant of peace be removed from them! May we be Emmanuel's land, the people of the holy One of Israel; and may the Lord make us an eternal excellency, a joy of many generations. May our righteousness go forth as brightness and our salvation as a lamp that burneth; may the nations see our righteousness and all kings our glory,[18] and may the Lord delight in us and rejoice over us, and make us a praise in the earth.

And to conclude with that most public, solemn, and final charge of another illustrious prophet to all the princes of the tribes and others assembled then before him, in I Chronicles 28. 8: "Now therefore in the sight of all Israel the congregation of the Lord, and in the audience of our God, keep and seek for all the commandments of the Lord your God: that ye may continue to possess this good land which the Lord hath given you, and may leave it for an inheritance to your children after you forever."

FINIS.[19]

---

[18] "May the Lord of hosts . . . our glory" contains several excerpts from Isa. 33. 2; 54. 17; 44. 3, 4; 62. 1, 2.

[19] An "Appendix" of three unnumbered pages follows, "to fill up these vacant pages"; it quotes passages from William Stoughton's election sermon of 1668, *New England's True Interest.*

VI JOHN BARNARD'S SERMON OF 1734

AN INTRODUCTION

ALTHOUGH John Barnard's *The Throne Established by Righteousness* was preached only four years after Prince's *The People of New England,* they seem a century apart. The difference between the ideas and styles of these two sermons dramatizes the gradual shift that was taking place as the old Puritanism lost its monopoly on the New England mind.[1] There would continue to be references to the errand and the apostasy, but not again after 1730 would an election sermon in Massachusetts devote itself so passionately and exclusively to the motif; Prince's sermon is the errand's swan song; Barnard's is the harbinger of the age of reason.

A brief review of Barnard's main points will suggest the shift to the reasoned discussion of practical government which one associates with Locke, Montesquieu, and the eighteenth century. Though government is ordained of God, the specific form is left to man to choose depending on his immediate needs. A governor's authority comes not directly from God, but indirectly through the commission of the people ruled. The end

---

[1] For discussions of the gradual breakdown of the covenant idea, new emphasis on "doing good," and changes within the church from a Calvinistic view of fallen man's little residue of reason to an increasing appreciation of both man's capacity for reason and the idea that the voice of reason is the voice of God, see Herbert M. Morais, "Rise of Deism in Colonial America (1713–1763)," *Deism in Eighteenth Century America* (New York, 1934), 54–84; Perry Miller, *The New England Mind: From Colony to Province* (Cambridge, 1953), 395–485; Claude M. Newlin, "The Dawn of the Enlightenment in New England," *Philosophy and Religion in Colonial America* (New York, 1962), 23–71.

of government is the good of the people. There must be harmony among the groups in a government; there must be mutual respect by those governed for their governors, and by those in power for those whom they govern. A government must be secure, well established, so as not to crumble under slight disturbances, whether from within or without. The executive power in government must act righteously and justly. All aspects of government, executive and popular, must abide by a constitution; it is both a source and a check of their power. Government does not consist of capricious action; it must be guided by written law. There must be a balance of power, a scheme of checks and balances so that no one branch of government can assume undue advantage over another. Laws must be enforced. Distribution of the awards of government must be made equitably, according to merit. The people governed must clearly understand both the justice of taxes and the amount required of them to support their government; executive officers should receive a fair stipend, thus avoiding the necessity of such offices being taken up only by the rich. Magistrates must defend the country against aggressors and maintain strong defenses for war in times of peace so as to convince foreign powers of the foolishness of invasion. Good governors will promote industry and manufactures and see to it that the country maintains an equal balance of payments. Magistrates should leave their people free to worship as their consciences dictate, but they should create laws to punish atheists, especially when they militantly attack the church and advertise themselves. Those who are ruled must respect their magistrates, pay their taxes, and defend their country when called upon.

There were earlier sermons dealing with many of Barnard's topics here.[2] He differs from his predecessors, however, in his quiet, careful

[2] Although the selections to this point have all been errand sermons, I have said that there was another equally large strain in the Massachusetts election sermons, one concerned with the nature of government and the good ruler. Readers interested in tracing this strain up to 1734 should look at the following: Jonathan Mitchel, *Nehemiah on the Wall* . . . (Cambridge, 1671); William Hubbard, *The Happiness of a People* . . . (Boston, 1676); Increase Mather, *The Great Blessing of Primitive Counsellors* . . . (Boston, 1693); Samuel Willard, *The Character of a Good Ruler* . . . (Boston, 1694); Joseph Belcher, *The Singular Happiness* . . . (Boston, 1701); Ebenezer Pemberton, *The Divine Original and Dignity of Government Asserted* . . . (Boston, 1710); Benjamin Wadsworth, *Rulers Feeding and Guiding Their People* . . . (Boston, 1716); John Hancock, *Rulers Should Be Benefactors* . . . (Boston, 1722); Joseph Sewall, *Rulers Must Be Just* . . . (Boston, 1724); Peter Thacher, *Wise and Good Civil Rulers* . . . (Boston, 1726); Jeremiah Wise, *Rulers the Ministers of God for the Good of Their People* . . . (Boston, 1729). Professor Miller has written: "Under the new charter the form [of the jeremiad] was cultivated with

precision, and in the far-reaching scope of his survey. He carries these features of Pemberton's sermon of 1710 even further. There are copious Biblical quotations and references in his sermon, but there is no emphasis on God's providence until page 52 of the sixty-page text as originally printed. The Bible is a source book of examples of laws. The sermon is noteworthy for what it doesn't say. Barnard does not emphasize a God of wrath or jealousy, but man's own abilities. Jonathan Swift says through his model king in Brobdingnag (*Gulliver's Travels* was published eight years before this sermon was preached) that government need not be mysterious and highly specialized, but amenable to "common sense and reason, to justice and lenity." [3] Such a premise underlies Barnard's sermon. His approach to government is rational rather than providential. Instead of man being dependent on God's Word and on searching his providence for messages, man can know God's will through "the inward sentiments of [his] own mind" and "understanding."

One would be ready to think it hardly possible for any who are not destitute of the understanding of men and lost to all true reverence to the Deity to entertain such a monstrous conception that God Almighty, the wisest and the best of beings, should make whole nations of men and bring them together in societies for no other end but the promoting the honor . . . of any single person or any particular set of men.

God acts through the political constitutions of reasonable men. In the errand sermons there is a continual harangue to the people to pray for God's return, to win back his grace, to reconstitute the conditions of the first settlers, as if good government were contingent on the return of God, wooed back through prayer, penance, and reform. Barnard as much as says that if man will sit down at a table and create a sensible law, all will be well. The sermon underscores Harrington's adage that good government comes not from good men but from good laws. [4]

Barnard replies to another of the errand sermon's basic tenets with a

new vigor, and persisted well into the eighteenth century, although from time to time an election preacher might lay it aside and devote himself to discussing the principles of political science. Except for a few such deviations, election sermons continued to be cast in the form of the jeremiad . . ." ("Declension in a Bible Commonwealth," *Proceedings of the American Antiquarian Society*, LI, Worcester, 1942, 67). It is misleading to suggest that sermons on "the principles of political science" were "few" and "deviations" in the election sermon tradition, even during the heyday of Professor Miller's jeremiads, 1665–1700. See my introductions to the sermons of Danforth (1670), Willard (1682), and Danforth (1714) above.

[3] *Gulliver's Travels*, ed. John F. Ross (New York, 1948), 125.
[4] See n. 11 to the text, below.

quite different view. Prince's sermon carries a distrust of the present; it wishes to recapture a better past. Barnard, however, looks at man not as once he was and should try to be again, but as he is and may yet become. Barnard is not concerned with the good old days but with the present and future.

The more one studies this sermon and others in a similar vein after it, the more one realizes that it was neither miracle nor accident that at the end of the century Americans were able to create a workable constitution. Sermons like Barnard's surely played a role, especially in their pamphlet form, in making New Englanders politically alert and critical. When the need came to make a constitution and have it ratified, there existed already in the Puritan colonies the tradition of close scrutiny of the nature of government.[5]

One further point deserves mention. Barnard is a product of Massachusetts. He was born in Boston in 1681 and graduated from Harvard in 1700. His thesis was proposed by Increase Mather, then Harvard's President, and he was so close to the Mathers that after graduation he was spoken of as their "tool."

Later he broke with the Mathers, becoming much more liberal, as this sermon shows. Perry Miller calls him "one of the finest examples of the eighteenth-century New England parson." He was "a scholar, linguist, mathematician, an expert on ships and shipbuilding, an amateur musician, an upholder of inoculation."[6] His range of interests reminds one of Ben-

---

[5] This is only to reiterate what others have said: John Wingate Thornton, "Introduction," *The Pulpit of the American Revolution* (Boston, 1860), xxvii; C. H. Van Tyne, "Influence of the Clergy, and of Religious and Sectarian Forces, on the American Revolution," *American Historical Review*, XIX (1913–14), 48–49, 54–55; Alice M. Baldwin, *The New England Clergy and the American Revolution* (Durham, 1928; New York, 1958), 6 and *passim*; Perry Miller, "From the Covenant to the Revival," *The Shaping of American Religion*, ed. James W. Smith and A. Leland Jamison (Princeton, 1961), 334–344.

[6] *The Puritans*, ed. Perry Miller and Thomas H. Johnson (New York, 1938), 270. Moses Coit Tyler also describes Barnard as "one of the clerical titans of our later colonial period" (*A History of American Literature*, Ithaca, 1949, 412). Barnard had a strong influence on the economy of Marblehead, where he was preacher from 1716 until his death in 1770. He instructed the townspeople in the art of shipbuilding, encouraging them to engage in foreign trade instead of allowing the merchants of Boston, Salem, and Europe to market and distribute the town's chief commodity, dried fish. By 1766, Barnard could be proud to see over thirty Marblehead "square-riggers" plying the seas. There is no book-length study of Barnard; it is to be hoped that one will be undertaken soon. For biographical sketches of Barnard, see John Langdon Sibley and Clifford K. Shipton, *Biographical Sketches of Those Who Attended Harvard College*, 13 vols. (Cambridge and Boston, 1873–1965), IV, 501–512;

jamin Franklin (Barnard also wrote a fine *Autobiography* [7]). When he gave this sermon the Boston centennial was four years past, but the Harvard centennial was still three years away. As nations go, his homeland was hardly out of its swaddling clothes. Yet this sermon is an impressive document in the early history of American political thought. Barnard is a tribute to the maturity of his culture.

DAB, I, 625–626; William B. Sprague, *Annals of the American Pulpit* . . . , 9 vols. (New York, 1857–69), I, 252–255.

[7] "Autobiography of the Rev. John Barnard," *Collections of the Massachusetts Historical Society*, 3rd ser., V (Boston, 1836), 177–243.

A

S E R M O N

Preach'd

Before his EXCELLENCY

Jonathan Belcher, Efq;

His Majefty's Council,

AND THE

Reprefentatives of the Province

OF THE

Maffachufetts-Bay in *New-England*,

May 29. 1 7 3 4.

Being the Day for the Electing His
Majefty's Council there.

By *John Barnard*, A. M.

Paftor of a Church in *Marblehead.*

Ifai. i. 27. *Zion fhall be redeemed with Judgment, and her
Converts with Righteoufnefs.*

B O S T O N : Printed MDCCXXXIV.

An Election Sermon.

"THE throne is established by righteousness" (Prov. 16. 12).

That the supreme Ruler of the world is to be acknowledged in all our ways and more especially in all the grand and important concerns, whether of public societies or of private persons, is a principle that stands in the strongest light to the natural reason and conscience of every man who is not sunk into the lowest stupidity and the vilest atheism. It was the prevailing force of this truth upon the minds of our renowned forefathers, impressed with a firm belief of a God and his governing providence, that led them into the religious solemnities of this day. They saw how necessary the concurring influence of the great God and a steady observation of his wise and good laws were to the establishment of their government, both in the choice of proper persons to be as strong rods for a scepter to rule over them, to lead them into the best concerted laws, and afford the desired success unto all their mature debates and wise administrations; and therefore they looked upon it as their incumbent duty to improve some part of this day of the gladness of their hearts, because of their valuable and distinguishing privileges, in acts of religious worship, humbly and earnestly to ask the divine direction and blessing and meekly to receive counsel from the sacred Oracles, as in the particular elections before them, so in all the affairs of the government thro'out the ensuing year—that they and their posterity might be a people highly favored of the Lord, and the good land they had taken possession of might be as a garden which the Lord hath watered.

Thro' the tender mercy of the most High to us (whatever revolutions have been brought upon the form of the government since the first founding the British Empire in this distant part of the world), we are yet in the full possession not only of all the privileges which belong to Englishmen as the happy subjects of Great Britain, but over and above, of such peculiarly valuable ones (and it may be of all that our circumstances would bear of the former) confirmed to us by a royal Charter from the ever memorable King William, as sufficiently demands it of us to go on in imitating the laudable example of our pious ancestors in our thus assembling to worship the Lord our God.

And since it has pleased God, by the mouth of your Excellency and his Majesty's honorable Council, to call me (the very least of the ministers of the Lord) to stand and wait this day at his holy altar and present your offerings to the divine Majesty and set the counsel of God before you, as collected from the dictates of right reason and revelation, I trust you will overlook my weakness and bear with my liberty and freedom of speech—wherein I hope I shall not go out of my own line, nor, while I keep within the bounds of my duty and office, offer anything that shall be just matter of offense. I am very sensible the times we are fallen into are attended with such peculiar circumstances as render it very difficult to speak out some necessary truths with any certainty and plainness, without being liable to the severe censure of such as may possibly think themselves too nearly concerned in them, or the more feeble exceptions of little witlings who will attempt to criticize upon what they scarce understand. However, I trust I shall not be so unfaithful to your Excellency and the honorable Board and much less so to my great Master to whom I must be accountable, as to forbear expressing myself upon the subject before me as becomes my relation and the place I stand in at this critical juncture, according to the best light I shall receive from the fountain of truth—at which I am sure no one ought to be offended.

The words I have read for the foundation of my present discourse are enrolled among the Proverbs of Solomon, the great and the wise King of

[a] "A great sagacity and piercing judgment to discern dubious and difficult cases." Mr. *Pool* in L. [Matthew Poole (1624–79), *Annotations upon the Holy Bible* . . . 3rd edn. (London, 1696), I, Proverbs XVI.]

Israel. And because we have here the sentiments of one so renowned for wisdom beyond all that went before him or have come after him, we may reasonably expect to find in these few words the true *arcana imperii,* the deepest mysteries, and the best policies by which a government stands firm and unshaken as a rock against the roaring of the sea and the dashing of its waves.

"The throne is established by righteousness." Tho' we are not to expect much of connection and dependence among adages, yet we may observe some considerable relation between several verses in my context in which the royal teacher lays down his aphorisms about kings and the thrones which they sit on, wherein he rather gives direction than recites an history, and more truly informs them what they ought to be than what they always are; and so places the most beautiful picture in full view before them to excite a laudable ambition in their best endeavors to copy it.

"A divine sentence," says he, "is in the lips of the king: his mouth transgresseth not in judgment" (ver. 10). The Hebrew is, "Divination in the lips," etc. That is, he speaks oracles;[a] his determinations in judgment should be as tho' we had enquired of the oracles of God for the clear discovery of the truth and the certain direction in all weighty matters, that there may be no error or mistake in his administrations; as one under the influence and inspiration of God, "with whom is the just weight and balance" (as he adds in the next verse), that is, the power to discern clearly and determine justly. Such, in some good measure, was the admirable foresight and clear discernment of Solomon himself, which struck his admiring subjects with the deepest veneration, rendered his name famous in distant lands, and brought the Queen of the South [1] from her far country to hear and applaud his wisdom.

He goes on (in the verse where my text is) to observe that "It is an abomination to kings to commit wickedness." To be sure, it ever ought to be the constant practice of the rulers of a people to manifest their utmost hatred of all wickedness or of everything that is unrighteous and oppressive to their people. It should be the fixed temper of God's vicegerents on earth to have all perverting of right in the greatest abhorrence and detestation. It should be an abomination to kings to commit or do wickedness either themselves or by their ministers and under-officers. For what is done by every officer under the supreme, with his allowance and

---

[1] The Queen of Sheba. See I Kings 10.

231

connivance, is said to be done by him whose authority they bear; and as the glory of their wise and regular conduct in the faithful discharge of their office reflects honor upon their principal, so the odium and discredit of their mean and base and unrighteous management of the trust reposed in them will forever finally center in him from whom they derive their authority. And therefore as kings and rulers should have all wickedness in such detestation as never to allow themselves in any, so should they be very careful whom they derive their authority to, and not suffer others under them to prey upon their people by any acts of injustice and oppression.

And we may observe a very strong and cogent reason given for this in the words of my text: "For the throne is established by righteousness."

"The throne": The ensigns of royalty are here put for royalty itself; and the badge of the highest power is substituted for the whole power of dominion, rule, and government, because all flows from the throne as its fountain. So that the "throne" does not mean only the royal seat, but the royal power; and that in all the branches of it wheresoever or in what channel soever it flows. It denotes the government among a people, be it of what form it will, and includes in it every person that has a hand in the administration, whether in making laws or in the execution of them— all lesser power being included in and derived from the supreme.

The throne "is established": The word[b] here used is in the passive voice and the future tense, as grammarians speak. The throne "will" or "shall be established," be made strong and sure, abide firm and unmoved. 'Tis probable that from this word is derived our English word "cone," which also is the same in the Greek and Latin with their proper terminations. As a cone seems to be the best contrived figure for stability and is least liable to be shaken with the blasts of wind and tempest or overturned by any accident, being broad at bottom and still lessening inwards as it ascends, and the center of its gravity every way equally distant from the circumference, which renders its position firm and steady—so the throne or government is established, rendered safe and secure, calm and unmoved, and is very much put out of the power of any accidents ordinarily to overthrow or hurt it.

"By righteousness": As its wide and every way extended base which upholds and supports and keeps all in their proper place and in a due

---

[b] The printer asks the learned author's pardon, and his reader's excuse, for the want of Hebrew types.

poise, tending to the center of unity; and admits of no excrescences of oppression, fraud, and violence in a misuse of power, betraying of trust, sacrificing the public to a private interest, or other instances of wickedness, as a mighty dead weight projecting aloft to a constant tottering and final overthrow of the whole fabric. Critics observe that the word here used is of a more extensive signification than mere justice in dealing, and rather comprehends in it all moral duty to our fellow creatures. The Hebrews have another word which is more strictly confined to justice and equity, and by this in the text they understand the whole moral rectitude of our actions and words: of our actions that they be just and right, fit and convenient, necessary and becoming, suitable and expedient; of our words that they be true and bear a perfect agreement with what they are intended for, that they be faithful and constant, and we abide by our promise and engagement. So that as it is here used, we may suppose it to mean the equity and justice, the truth and fidelity of the government—not only of kings who have the throne appropriated to them, but of all that are raised to any seat of eminency and honor and service in the government.

And well may the throne or government be said to be established by righteousness when this is such a basis as stands every blast and endures the shock of ages and bears the nearest resemblance to the throne of the most high God himself, whose visible images earthly rulers are; and therefore the inspired psalmist says: "Righteousness and judgment are the habitation of his throne" (Psal. 97. 2). The dominion and government of God inhabits or dwells as in an impregnable palace, being secure in the perfect rectitude of his nature and administrations; and were it possible any unrighteousness should be found in him, it would soon undermine the very foundations of his empire and lay the most beautiful pile in amazing ruins.

Thus you see what lies before me, namely the consideration of the throne or government, the establishment of it, and the means leading to it.

"The throne is established by righteousness."

And therefore I shall reduce what I have further to say upon these words into this plain method:

I. I shall offer some things concerning the nature of government which I here understand by the throne.

II. I shall consider what it is for the throne or government to be "established."

III. I shall take a view of that "righteousness" by which the throne or government is established.

IV. Lay before you some evidence that the throne or government "is" and "will be" established by righteousness.

I begin with the first of these, viz.:

I. To offer some things concerning the nature of government which is here intended by the throne. And there are these things considerable with respect thereto, namely the original, the form, the personal right, and the ends of government.

1. The first thing I would observe here is the original of government and whence it takes its rise. And I doubt not to say that it is from God who is the "God of order and not of confusion."[2] That is to say, that upon supposition that mankind dwell together in societies, which the human nature cannot well avoid, it is not a matter of liberty and freedom and left to the option and choice of the will of man whether there shall be government or no, or whether there shall be any rules for the regulating of that society; but it has the stamp of the divine authority upon it and comes to us with a "thus saith the Lord."

This the voice of nature plainly declares to us. Forasmuch as the divine sovereignty and unerring wisdom has formed and fitted the human nature for rule and government and necessitated it to it, this may be justly looked upon as the voice of God to mankind, because the Almighty's adapting his creatures to a particular end is one way of making known his mind and will concerning them; and every true dictate of right reason is no other than God speaking to his rational creatures by the inward sentiments of their own mind. Thus 'tis that they who are destitute of the written law "are a law unto themselves," as the apostle expresses it (Rom. 2. 14)—the law or will of God being written upon their hearts and legible in some measure by the candle of the Lord, which he hath lighted up within them.

'Tis very evident the nature of man is formed for government and necessitated to it, from that power of reason and understanding that is in him, his fixed bent to society, and the many weaknesses and imperfections that attend him.

Thro' the distinguishing favor of the Almighty, he has by his inspiration given us understanding and made us wiser than the beasts of the field or the fowls of the air;[3] and thus he hath formed us capable of acting by rule, which sufficiently intimates his will to us, that we are not left to live and range at large, but that we keep ourselves within due bounds and walk by rule; and this necessarily supposes some certain rule for us to regulate ourselves by.

And because society is the natural result of reason in a dependent being (and he must have all in himself and be master of an unbounded understanding and unlimited power, or be void of all true reason and knowledge, that can subsist by himself without having any regards to another), therefore it is necessary that this rational agent, who yet falls short of perfection, should be under subjection not only to such laws as more especially relate to his conduct, to his Maker, but such also as have a more particular reference to his fellow creature to whom he stands related, on whom he has some dependence for the necessaries and conveniencies of the present life, and all adapted to the nature of that society of which he is a part; and this clearly infers the superiority of some to give law for the well-ordering of the society and the subjection of all to those laws, according as they have a special reference to them. And what is this but government?

Thus I doubt not but government would have been necessary to man even in a state of innocency, because society would then have been as agreeable to his rational nature and more delightful to his pure mind and as necessary to him upon many accounts as now; and in the midst of all his purity he would still have remained but a fallible creature—all of which would have required a rule suited to direct his actions in the several relations he would sustain and businesses he would have been employed in; and this infers government, tho' probably very different in its kind from what is to be found in the world in our day.[4] In short, the fifth commandment as well as others of the moral law would have been in force and obligatory upon the innocent creature.

Yea doubtless there is government among the holy angels; and the account which the sacred Scripture gives us of "thrones, dominions,

---

[2] See I Cor. 14. 33.

[3] See Job 35. 11.

[4] Whether civil government would have been natural before the fall of man or whether it was introduced only upon his apostasy is, as Samuel Willard points out in his election sermon of 1694, "a question about which all are not agreed" (*The Character of a Good Ruler . . .* , Boston, 1694, 1). Still, Willard takes the position of most of the election sermon preachers that even in Eden government would have been necessary and natural. See for example Ebenezer Pemberton's election sermon, *The Divine Original . . .* (Boston, 1710), 15: "There would doubtless have been order and civil subordination among men had they still walked in the blissful shades of Paradise in their native light, purity, and glory."

principalities, powers, angels, archangels" [Col. 1. 16] and the like in the invisible world is well understood by learned men as intending not the different species but the different orders among them.

However, since sin has broke in upon the world and vitiated the human nature, there is but so much the more reason and necessity for government among creatures that are become so very weak and depraved—to restrain their unruly lusts and keep within due bounds the rampant passions of men, which else would soon throw human society into the last disorder and confusion. For if all men were left to live and act as they please, 'tis undoubted the different views and interests, humors and passions of mankind, and these often excited by false principles and strongly moved by a corrupt bias upon the mind, would unavoidably produce a continual jar and strife, a constant endeavor in everyone to promote his own and gratify self, and so a perpetual preying of the stronger upon the weaker; and no man would be able to call anything his own, nor be secure of his life and limbs from the rapine and violence of his fellow creature; and by how much the views, interest, and passions of men are more numerous, appropriated, and strong, by so much would they become fiercer upon one another than the beasts of prey. And does not this necessitate laws to tame this fierce creature, to bound his appetites and bridle his passions, that he may not be injurious to his neighbor? Who is the man that would be willing that all the injury of ungoverned lust and passion should fall upon himself? And what is the result of all this but that there be a legislative power to enact such laws and an executive one to put the laws in force and compel to obedience to them, lodged somewhere, as shall be best adapted to the order and preservation of the society? And this is government. Thus the light of nature shows us the reason and necessity of government; and this voice of nature is the voice of God. Thus 'tis that *vox populi est vox Dei*.[5]

But besides this, God Almighty has sufficiently manifested his will to mankind by his Word; and therein plainly declared to all that are advantaged with the divine Oracles that it is his sovereign pleasure that there be government among men. Hither look all those passages in Holy Writ which more directly speak of civil rule, authority, and power, as derived from God. Thus, "By me kings reign, and princes decree justice.

---

[5] Hence is that of Hesiod: Ἐκ δὲ διὸς βασιλῆες; and thus Homer: τιμὴ δ' ἐκ διός ἐστι. ["Hesiod: The rulers are from Zeus . . ." *Theogony*, ed. M. L. West (Oxford, 1966), 115; "Homer: Honor comes from Zeus . . ." *Iliad*, II, l. 197.]

By me princes rule, and nobles, even all the judges of the earth" (Prov. 8. 15, 16). "By me," that is, by my authority and appointment it is that there are any kings, princes, nobles, and judges of the earth; that is, that there is rule and government among men. Thus the apostle tells us: "The powers that be are ordained of God: there is no power but of God" (Rom. 13. 1). That is, the power, the authority, the rule itself, as well as the subject invested with it, is of God who has ordained it, appointed it as his sovereign Will, that there should be such. And hence, tho' God himself was in a peculiar manner King in Jeshurun, yet he appointed a visible head over them and sent Moses his servant "to be a ruler and deliverer to them" (Acts 7. 35*); and he directed them "to make judges and officers in all their gates" (Deut. 16. 18).

Hither also look all those places in the sacred Scripture that direct civil rulers to the faithful discharge of their office—as in my text and context: "A divine sentence is in the lips of the king: his mouth transgresseth not in judgment. It is an abomination to kings to commit wickedness: the throne is established in righteousness." And all such as direct mankind in their carriage towards them, as that "Thou shalt not revile the gods, nor curse the ruler of thy people" (Exod. 22.* 28); and that command "every soul to be subject to the higher powers" (Rom. 13. 1); that require us "to submit ourselves to every ordinance of man for the Lord's sake: whether unto the king, as supreme; Or unto governors, as unto them that are sent by him" (I Pet. 2. 13, 14); that assure us, "he that resisteth the power, resisteth the ordinance of God"; and let us know the penalty of unreasonable resistance, that "they that resist shall receive to themselves damnation" (Rom. 13. 2).

So that we see the original of government is from God who has taught it to mankind by the light of natural reason[c] and plainly required it in his Holy Word. And that there are any who walk in the shape of men that do not diligently attend to the voice of reason, nor enquire after understanding, but sit down contented in the most abject stupidity, scarce distinguishing themselves from the brute by any true acts of reason, is no more an

---

[c] "The voice of the people is the voice of God"—apparently already an adage by the time Alcuin uses it in a letter to Charlemagne. Although John Bartlett attributes the phrase to Alcuin (*Familiar Quotations*, 13th edn., New York, 1955, 74), Alcuin actually said: "*Nec audiendi qui solent dicere: 'Vox populi, vox Dei,' cum tumultuositas vulgi semper insanie proxima sit* [Nor should you listen to those who are wont to say: 'The voice of the people is the voice of God,' since the noise of the rabble is always one step away from madness]" ("Epistolae Karolini Aevi," *Monumenta Germaniae Historica, Epistolae, IV*, Bk. 2, ed. E. Dümmler, Berlin, 1895, 199).

objection to government's being a true dictate of nature than one man's shutting his eyes would be against the sun's being risen, when all who have their eyes open walk in the full light of it.

2. The second thing I proposed to offer something upon, under the head of government, was the form of it. And here the enquiry is, what form of government is chiefly to be regarded by a people? Since government originates from God and is of divine appointment, is there any particular form of divine ordination? Or if not, what form shall a people put themselves under as most eligible?

To the first of these enquiries, I think there is no great difficulty in answering that I know of no particular form of civil government that God himself has directly and immediately appointed by any clear revelation of his mind and will to any people whatever.[6] The Scripture speaks of civil rulers under the several denominations that were in use at that day; but it nowhere directs to and enjoins any one scheme of civil government, even upon God's own peculiar, favorite people; but we find when they became a settled nation in the land which God had promised to their fathers, it was the people's own choice to come under a monarchical form of government, and they said, "Nay; but we will have a king over us; That we also may be like all the nations; and that our king may judge us, and go out before us, and fight our battles" (I Sam. 8. 19, 20). And tho' there was some manifestation of the divine displeasure against them for their asking a king, yet this was not for their assuming that particular form of civil government but for their throwing off the theocracy they and their fathers had so long experienced the benefit of.

So that it is evident God Almighty has left it to the natural reason of mankind in every nation and country to set up that form which upon a thorough consideration of the nature, temper, inclinations, customs, manners, business, and other circumstances of a people, may be thought best for them. And hence it is that some nations have tho't it best for them to keep the power of government in the hands of the body of the people, while others have thought fit to lodge it in the hands of their chief families and nobles; others again have devolved the weight of the government upon a single person, leaving it wholly with him to assign what part to what persons he pleases; and another people have looked upon it most advisable for them to take a middle way between these extremes, and have laid up the honors of government in a single person as their supreme head, to flow from him down to all the members, and then have divided

238

the weight and burden of it between this single person, a body of nobles of his creating, and a select assembly of their own choosing—by which means sovereignty is so happily tempered with righteousness and mercy, and will and pleasure directed and limited by liberty and property, as to guard against tyranny on the one hand and anarchy on the other. Tho' neither of these schemes nor any other that may be tho't of are immediately and directly of divine appointment, yet so far as any or all of them are the result of right reason, so far it may be said of them that they are of God. Thus the "powers that be," be they what they will, meaning government, "are ordained of God" [Rom. 13. 1]. And as every people are left to their liberty to constitute what form of civil government, all things considered, may appear best to them as to anything to the contrary from the law of God, so doubtless it remains with any civil society to alter and change the form of their government when they see just reason for it and all parties are consenting to it.[7]

But if there be no particular form of civil government appointed by God and every nation and people are left to their own prudence to establish what form they please, which form and scheme is best? If this enquiry means, what form is best, considered absolutely and by itself, I answer, that form which is best accommodated to all the ends of government. What that is may be tho't an hard question and it is not my business to determine it. Tho' I would observe that possibly it may be a just answer to the enquiry to say that it is an improper question, because there can be no government without a people or subject of it, and the good or ill qualities of it can fall under no consideration but as government stands related to its subject; so that the circumstances of a particular people must come into consideration, to determine what is best. If the question mean, what form is relatively best, I answer, that which will suit the people best, which requires a thorough knowledge of them, their situation,* produce, genius, and the like, to resolve. If still it be insisted on, what form is best

---

[6] That God has not decreed a particular form of government for man is a frequently expressed maxim in the election sermons. See for example Samuel Willard in 1694: "Civil government is seated in no particular persons or families by a natural right, neither hath the light of nature nor the Word of God determined in particular what form of government shall be established among men, whether monarchical, aristocratical, or democratical . . ." (*The Character of a Good Ruler,* 20).

[7] That a people may remove a king or magistrate when he clearly no longer rules for their good was a dearly held Puritan political principle, announced before in Massachusetts election sermons; but that a society has a right to change the *form* of its government is an important extension of the idea of democratic prerogative.

for ourselves, to this I answer, were we absolutely free to choose for ourselves, it must be left to the wisest heads, the greatest politicians among us, and those best acquainted with the people and country to advise upon it; but as we are not at liberty now to choose, I can readily answer, that form of civil government is best for us which we are under—I mean the British Constitution. And this I can say not only because we are a dependent government but because were I at full liberty, I should choose to be (as, blessed be God, we are) of the number of the happy subjects of Great Britain whom God hath blessed above all people upon the face of the earth, in the felicity of their Constitution; and I look upon myself happy that I know not of a single true New England man in the whole Province but what readily subscribes to these sentiments and hopes we shall continue to be the genuine members of that glorious Constitution thro'out all ages.

3. Another thing I am to offer something upon is the person or persons invested with the authority of the government. And here it may be enquired, who among the children of Adam has a right to take the reins into his hands? Where shall we find the right, certain and indisputable? And whence does this personal right and claim arise? Or who gave this person and not another the authority to preside over and give law to his brethren and enforce obedience? I scruple not to answer. This right is found in whomsoever the government constitutes and appoints to be their ruler or rulers. There, and there only, is the certain claim, full right, and lawful authority; and thence does it derive. And this, upon a due consideration of things, will appear to hold good, let the form of civil government be of what kind it will.

For if we consult strength and force and trace them to their utmost extent, we shall find that (however unlikely they may be thought, upon a cursory view, to agree with this principle, yet) upon a more thorough examination they resolve themselves at last into compact and agreement. For (upon supposition of what is called government founded in conquest) it is very evident that there must be a conquest to found the right in it; and a conquest necessarily supposes one of these two things, either that there is an entire destruction of the contending party or else that they come to terms of submission. If the conquest consist in an entire destruction of the enemy, there is an end of all civil government over them, for "the dead hear not the voice of the oppressor," and "there the servant is free from his master" [Job 3. 18, 19]; but if they come to terms of submission (the very hardest of which supposes a right to life and the necessaries of it and such further accommodations as the conqueror in his clemency shall allow, which is a submitting to mercy and surrendering upon discretion), 'tis apparent the right to rule over them is founded in compact; tho' the strength of the arm has made the terms harder for those who are forced to submit than possibly they would have been otherwise. Mere natural force and power gives no person a right to rule over another, and all pretensions to rule, founded in this only, without consent, will forever leave the government to be bandied about by the perpetual cuffs of contending rivals and endless revolutions from every bold usurper that has got the longest sword and the strongest arm; and he that is forced to resign today may recover strength eno' tomorrow; or where strength fails, stratagem and craft may succeed and carry the game. And who sees not that while the royal ball is thus tossed about, and catch who can, the state will become giddy with a continual whirl and all things run into such confusion as oversets the foundations of government. "He beareth the sword," not the sword him.[8]

He therefore that sits upon the throne of empire must have a moral right and lawful authority to rule; and this moral right must be either natural to him and what he was born with (I mean now, antecedent to an act of the government's conveying such a birthright to any man), or it must arise from an immediate divine appointment, or lastly, flow from the election or consent of the community.

Some have been so vain as to attempt to find out a natural right to dominion, belonging unalienably and indefeasibly as they call it to such or such a particular person, to support which they carry us up to the "patriarchal scheme" as it is termed, or rather "Adamitical," and imagine that because the first father of mankind had a natural right (as they say) to rule his descendants, that therefore kings have a natural right to rule over their subjects. But what if the first man had a natural right to dominion over those that descend from him? Would not this necessarily infer these two things, namely, that this right be continued in the next male heir in a lineal descent to the world's end; and that this male heir in a lineal descent be an absolute monarch over all nations, states, and kingdoms in the earth—the first of which has been impossible to be put

---

[8] See Rom. 13. 4. This paragraph may also be influenced by Locke's chapter "On Conquest" in *Of Civil Government: Second Essay*, Intro. Russell Kirk (Chicago, 1955), 129–144.

in practice this many hundreds, yea thousands of years; the other as impossible to consist with the tempers and interests of all nations—which shows the absurdity of the scheme upon their own principles. But I very much doubt the validity of the principle that the first man, were he living, would have a natural right to rule all his descendants. That he would have a natural right to rule his own family, whether descendants or not, is very readily acknowledged, and so has every man now; but then it is to be remembered that there is a very wide difference between a man's ruling his own immediate family and his ruling over another man's family. For the immediate children of the first man, upon their becoming heads of families, would have the same natural right to govern their own as Adam to govern his—by which means the grandchildren are unavoidably freed from all subjection to a sovereign dominion over them in their grandfather that is inconsistent with the natural sovereignty of their father; and the great-grandchildren would be yet at a greater distance from submission to the will and pleasure, the rule and authority, of the great-grandfather—from whence it appears that the power of the first man lessens so much every descent by a new sovereign coming upon the stage of equal natural right with himself, that by the fourth generation he could have no government over them; tho' the latest generations while he lived would be under obligations to the profoundest veneration, respect, and honor to him as their progenitor. If therefore he ever become the sovereign lord over all his descendants, it must be by the consent of the several heads of families making choice of him as the properest person to bear rule over them and giving up so much of their own power over their families to him, as is necessary for the general benefit of the public society they are now formed into. And this I think entirely overthrows the patriarchal scheme and the whole set of fine thoughts built upon it.[9]

Others have endeavored to find out such a divine right for civil rulers as is wholly exclusive of all election or consent of the community; and have fancied that they derive their power immediately from God by a particular and immediate designation of them personally to their high office—from whence they conclude their power unalienable and their authority absolute and unlimited as well as their persons unaccountable. But these also have greatly failed in their attempt.

[a] *Causa efficiens reip. principalis est consensus mutuus, et obligatio.* Alst. ["The principal directing force in a republic is the general consensus." Possibly Johann Heinrich Alsted (1588–1638).]

For besides what I have already observed, that it hath pleased God to leave the particular form of civil government to human prudence (which infers the designation of the person to his office is from man also), so far are we from having any proof of such a divine right in our day as that when the Lord of hosts himself gave some particular directions to his peculiar people about the king that should reign over them, and solemnly consecrated with the holy anointing oil both Saul and David successively to the throne of Israel, they were first presented to the choice of the people, and their right to take the power into their hands and administer in the affairs of government was by no means thought good until they had obtained the suffrages of their brethren—as is very clear from the sacred History. (Compare I Sam. 9, 15 with I Sam. 10, 17 and 11, 15; and compare I Sam. 16, 13 with II Sam. 2, 4 and ver. 2, 3.) And hence the apostle Peter calls the civil government an "ordinance of man" (I Pet. 2, 13), because both the form of it and the particular persons invested with the power are purely human and result from the reason and prudence of nations and societies of men.

So that after all that is said, the right to rule takes its rise from the [d] consent and agreement, that is the choice and election, of the community, state, or kingdom. And whether they reserve the power to themselves to elect anew, successively, as in some kingdoms, or fix the succession unreservedly in such a line to perpetuity; or whether they establish the line of succession with certain limitations and salvos and reserve to themselves the power, upon fitting emergencies, to make what alterations may be thought needful—it amounts to the same thing; and he, and he only, has the right to rule, to whom the government commits the power and authority. And he whom the government so sets up as their ruler, head, and king so far has a divine right as God in his holy and wise providence mediately by the voice, consent, agreement, and constitution of that particular nation and people over whom he reigns has raised him to such or such a place of dignity and power; and consequently and in like manner, all that by virtue of the constitution derive their authority from the supreme ruler. And so far "the powers that be," as denoting the particular person in whom the authority is lodged as well as the power itself or

[9] In several of his works, James Harrington (1611–95) points out the fallacy of the patriarchal scheme in an argument similar to Barnard's. See for example "The Grounds and Reasons of Monarchy," *The Oceana . . . and His Other Works . . .* (London, 1700), 3–32, especially 5–12.

government, "are ordained of God." This I think is sufficient to establish the divine right of kings and fix the claim in opposition to such turbulent spirits as are uneasy at the disappointment of their secret views in another; and gives all to civil rulers that is due to them as visible images of the Deity in their royal authority, tho' not so in their original right to empire. Thus "the most High rules in the kingdom of men, and giveth it to whomsoever he will" (Dan. 4, 17) and "pulleth down one, and setteth up another" at his pleasure (Psal. 75. 7).

4. I am now to consider what are the great ends of government. And here I must observe that the ultimate and supreme end of government is the same with the last end of all creatures and all their actions: "that God in all things may be glorified" [I Pet. 4. 11]. But then the subordinate end and that which is the main as it respects man, is the common good of the society, state, or kingdom.

It is beneath the dignity of a rational agent to act for no end; and it is contrary to reason and religion to propound any but a good one; and the good aimed at cannot be appropriated to this or that set or party of men in the state without having a suitable regard to others; but must necessarily extend to the whole body, otherwise it would soon be subversive of itself. For let us consider the ends of government as having respect either to the ruler or ruled, separately taken.

If on the one hand we could suppose the good, benefit, and advantage of the throne or ruler were the sole ends of government, this would introduce tyranny, oppression, injustice, and by degrees prove the overthrow of the state. For while civil rulers either thro' mistake of their end or want of rectitude to act up to it appropriate all unto themselves and seek only their own grandeur, the making of their families, and the gratifying of their own appetites and passions; while their constant cry is "give, give" and they cannot content themselves without their subject's vineyard, and snatch his ewe lamb from his bosom and exert their authority to suppress all that they think stands in their way—whether by placing them in the front of the battle to fall by a foreign hand, or proceeding against them with an apparent solemn form but real prostitution of justice, or dispatching them with a bowstring—it is evident that they will be no better than "roaring lions and ranging bears" [Prov. 28. 15] which gradually devour up their subjects and their substance till there is no more to give or none to give it; or else the continual oppressions "which make wise men mad" [Eccles. 7. 7] will produce such ferments and tumults among the people as in time to shake off the yoke and free themselves from the tyrant.

Possibly there have been some so giddy with power as to imagine that the whole body of their people were made for no other end but their use and service, as if Issachar's fate in the most literal and full meaning of it belonged to them, to be as "a strong ass couching down between two burdens: and bowing their shoulders to bear" (Gen. 49, 14, 15); and they have not wanted of mean and despicable sycophants who have gaped after some scraps of their power, to flatter them into such a fond opinion of themselves that they were absolute, unaccountable, uncontrollable, and that their subjects' lives and fortunes were at their entire disposal and their own will was the only law to them. But the world has often had full experience that such false ends of government have issued in the destruction of it; and those who have been most forward to offer their necks to the feet of princes have given conviction how little able they were to resist the force of nature in them when they themselves have begun* to feel what they meant for others.

One would be ready to think it hardly possible for any who are not destitute of the understanding of men and lost to all true reverence to the Deity to entertain such a monstrous conception that God Almighty, the wisest and the best of beings, should make whole nations of men and bring them together in societies for no other end but the promoting the honor, the increasing the riches, and nourishing the lusts of any single person or any particular set of men.

On the other hand, if the good of the subject, considered as distinct from that of the ruler, were the end of government, what would the consequence of this be but anarchy, wild disorder, and universal confusion?—which would be as destructive to government as the hottest tyranny could be. For the civil rulers of a people have not only their interests in many respects twisted together with the subjects', but some things which belong to them in a peculiar manner as rulers, which are very essential to the support of government—I mean their distinguishing honor, their authority and power, their more special security, and the like—and if these interests which are appropriated to them should not be duly consulted in the administration, their glory would soon become dim, their authority be trampled on, and their persons liable to the insult of everyone that had more sense than understanding and more of passion than either. And anyone may easily see where this would end.

So that it is the good of the whole community, both rulers and ruled in conjunction, that is the great and main end of government; and therefore we find Dr. Tillotson thus expressing himself: "The great end of government is to preserve men in their rights, against the encroachments of fraud and violence." [e] To preserve "men," not this or that person or this set of men only, but the whole body of mankind and every individual member of the body politic. Hence I suppose arose that maxim, *"Salus populi est suprema lex,"* [10] the safety and welfare of the whole (not the subjects only, as some are ready enough to understand it), is to give law to the government, and to be preferred to the separate interest of any particular person whatever. As the rights, liberties, defense, protection, and prosperity of the subjects are to be consulted, so the honor, majesty, and authority of the ruler are to be considered as unitedly the ends of government; and tho' possibly the first may be tho't the primary and the latter the secondary ends, yet cannot they well be separated without the destruction of the government. And this I think is sufficiently taught us in the holy Scriptures, as when the civil ruler is styled "the breath of our nostrils" (Lam. 4. 20), which speaks his dignity and authority and the eminency of his station and how necessary he is to the very existence of a political body—that were he to die officially as well as personally, the body politic would as assuredly die with him as the natural body does at the ceasing of the breath of our nostrils—from whence doubtless is that maxim in our English law: "The king never dies," that is, the regal authority never dies. Thus also he is styled "the light of Israel" (II Sam. 21, 17) and "the light of the morning" (II Sam. 23, 4), to notify to us how essential he is to the well-being of a people; that when this light is quenched, such a people would walk in darkness and stumble and fall, not knowing whither they went. Thus he is said to "come down like rain upon the mown grass: and as showers that water the earth" (Psal. 72. 6) —which further expresses the dependence of the prosperity and flourishing of a people upon their civil rulers, as the springing of the grass and the fruits of the earth have their dependence upon the showers of heaven. Hence also our Savior has styled them "benefactors" (Luke 22. 25) and the apostle of our Lord assures us in plain terms: "He is a minister of

[e] Vol. I. page 39. [John Tillotson (1630–94), "Sermon III: The Advantages of Religion to Societies," *The Works . . . Containing Fifty-Four Sermons and Discourses . . .* 8th edn. (London, 1720), 43.]

God to thee for good" (Rom. 13. 4); and as if all were too low, the Almighty says of them, "I have said, Ye are gods" (Psal. 82. 6).

Having thus offered some things upon the nature of government, I now proceed to the second thing proposed, which was:

II. To show what it is for the throne or government to be "established." And I need not to enlarge upon this head, nor would the time allow it; it shall suffice therefore only to hint at things. It does not mean that the throne only or him that sits upon the throne, or the supreme ruler of a people, shall be established; that is, that the chief seat of government be so fixed as to admit of no unreasonable alterations and sad changes and revolutions. For tho' this is to be considered as a very essential part of the establishment of the throne, yet this alone is not all that is intended. As the throne includes the whole government, so the establishment of the throne means the establishment of the whole, so far as is necessary to the well-being of the community. Thus the establishment of the throne carries in it the firmness and stability of the state—that it be fixed upon solid foundations and that all the parts of it be well cemented and put together. Hence the psalmist says: "Jerusalem is builded as a city that is compact together: there are set the thrones of judgment, the thrones of the house of David" (Psal. 122. 3, 5). "Jerusalem," there, means the whole body of that people, state, or kingdom, and their throne was established by their being as a city compact together—that is, firmly united in all their parts. So when the several branches of the authority closely adhere to the supreme head and return all to it as their original, as the rivers fed by the sea return thither; when the rulers are most firmly united to the people in their most tender affection and jealous concernment for their good, as the common fathers of their country; and when the people are as closely united to their rulers in their profound honor and respect to their persons and dutiful obedience to their lawful authority—then is the throne said to be established.

The stability of the throne further includes in it the success of the administrations, both for the preservation of the regalia and the security of the rights of the subject and the promoting of the good order and virtue, the humanity and moral honesty, the peace, harmony, and unity of the state, and the flourishing of the whole in wealth, honor, and renown. Thus the throne or government becomes established at home and fears no

[10] "The welfare of the people is its supreme law." This adage is quoted by Locke in *Of Civil Government: Second Essay,* 116.

revolutions to its disadvantage; but amidst all the vicissitudes and changes which human affairs are subject to, it remains fixed upon its strong and steady foundations; and tho' the wisdom of the state may see reason to make some alterations in some particulars, yet they will only be for the greater beauty, proportion, and durableness of the whole.

And while the government is thus established at home, it is capable of enduring the shock of accidents from abroad, and fears not to be insulted or devoured by any foreign adversary, but its renown goeth forth into distant lands and their terror falls upon all that think evil against them. Thus, "In righteousness shalt thou be established: thou shalt be far from oppression; for thou shalt not fear: and from terror; for it shall not come nigh thee" (Isa. 54. 14). So when in the admired reign of Solomon Israel enjoyed peace among themselves and rested from their enemies round about and was made greatly to prosper, it is said: "Because thy God loved Israel, to establish them forever, therefore made he thee king over them, to do judgment and justice" (II Chron. 9. 8). And this leads me into the third thing proposed, viz.:

III. To take a view of that "righteousness" by which the throne or government is established. I have already observed that righteousness is to be understood as comprehensive of the social virtues; and it is to be remembered that I am now to consider it as it relates to the throne or government and not to private persons; that is, I am to consider the public righteousness of a nation and people. And here it will be fitting that I should distinctly view it in its several aspects upon the ruler and upon the ruled and both together—in all of which I hope I shall approve myself a minister of Jesus Christ preaching righteousness.

1. I am to consider righteousness as it relates to the ruler or governing part of the state, by whom I mean both the legislative and executive powers in their several stations and branches. "The God of Israel said, the Rock of Israel spake, He that ruleth over men must be just, ruling in the fear of God" (II Sam. 23. 3). And there are several things to be considered as peculiar to rulers, which are so many parts of that righteousness which has a happy tendency to establish the throne. As:

1. An acting upon and preserving the constitution in all the main branches of it. Whatever be the constitution or form of government among a people, it is what they have chosen for themselves. For all government, as we have seen, is finally resolved into choice and consent. And however the descendants of the first founders may groan under the burden of those

inconveniencies which their fathers either did not foresee or could not prevent, yet it is certain (with a proper salvo to the natural rights of mankind, which it is the end of all government to preserve) none can have any right to act contrary to the fundamental laws of that state till all parties concerned agree upon such alterations as are thought needful; and then those alterations become wrought into the constitution and are a certain rule for all the parts of the government to go by, in their future administrations. For where (as in mixed government especially) there are peculiar rights and powers belonging to the throne, and some peculiar rights and privileges belonging to the people; and where again the rights and powers of the throne are branched out and divided among the several partners in rule, to each their proper portion, nothing is more plain than that righteousness requires that no one invade the right that peculiarly belongs to another. For this is the very notion of injustice between man and man; and it makes no alteration in the nature of right and wrong, justice and injustice, to carry this up from private persons to those of a public character. So that it is the first point of righteousness in a state to act upon the constitution, because every part of the government (whether we consider kings as supreme or governors set over a people by him or such branches of the legislative or executive power as are necessarily included in the constitution, as well as the body of the people) have as full and just right, title, and claim in and to that part of power or to those privileges which are assigned and made over to them in the very foundation of the government, as any man has or can have to what he calls his own; and consequently it is the demand of righteousness that these powers and privileges be preserved in their proper channels, without the use of any secret craft or open violence to dam up the current or divert its course another way. That is to say that rulers are to govern according to law. Hence when the kingdom was founded in Israel, Samuel wrote the manner of the kingdom in a book and laid it up before the Lord (I Sam. 10. 25), that it might be their Magna Charta, the fundamental constitution of the kingdom and the standing rule of their government for the future. Thus where there are peculiar regalia belonging to the throne itself as a sacred inclosure around it which serves to set majesty aloft in full view and yet at an awful distance, that by too near access and familiarity it may not grow contemptible, righteousness requires that every part of the government pay a profound reverence and come not near to touch the royal prerogative—in which sense may well be applied the words of our Savior: "Render unto Caesar the things that are Caesar's" (Matt. 22. 21); they belong to Caesar and therefore can't be taken from him without the highest injustice—as to Caesar himself in divesting him of his appropriated royalty—so to the state in bringing majesty into contempt, which unavoidably weakens the government.[f]

Thus where the constitution provides what may be called a balance of power by distributing the several branches of power to such particular parts of the government as may have a happy tendency to prevent the encroachments of sovereignty and the insults of the populace, there righteousness requires rulers to act up to the powers committed to them without assuming more than belongs to them in their particular station; and all things are carefully to be avoided which tend to weaken any particular branch of power and render those who are rightfully possessed of it uncapable of exerting themselves according to their original trust, because this would be a depriving one part of the government of its due; and however craftily the design may be carried on, will in the end issue in such a sway of power one way as will overset the government. Thus it will be found upon examination an equal departure from the rule of righteousness to wrest the sword out of the hand of him to whom the constitution has committed it, as to snatch the purse from those that have the keeping of it. And whether these things be considered as in an independent state or in a dependent government, and their several powers as arising from their original incorporation or subsequent royal grants, I fear they will be found a taking from another and appropriating to themselves what does not belong to them; and I very much doubt whether any political views and fetches of wit will be sufficient to justify such an apparent falsehood in trust and injuriousness to their neighbor; to be sure, such would be far from the character of David, of whom 'tis said: "He fed them according to the integrity of his heart; and guided them by the skilfulness of his hands" (Psal. 78. 72).

Thus righteousness in rulers requires them to adjust all the parts of their administration to the true rights, liberties, and privileges of the subject. These are various in their kind and more or less in number and degree according to the nature of the constitution, and are inwrought into it;

---

[f] Hence is that political axiom, *Amissam authoritatem magistratus, sequitur amissio et mutatio imperiorum.* ["The loss and change of empires follow the lost authority of the magistrate."]

[g] Mr. *Burkit* in Loc. [William Burkitt, "The Acts. Chap. 23," *Expository Notes, with Practical Observations, on the New Testament* . . . 5th edn. (London, 1712).]

and every subject has a just claim to the benefit of them as his proper inheritance, contracted for by his forefathers, and, it may be, dearly bought and paid for and left to him in a long descent as a pledge of their paternal wisdom and affection. There is nothing a people are more tender of than these; they look upon the security of their persons and interest and the comfort of their lives as dependent upon them; and therefore will not be persuaded easily to part with them, but say to such as attempt to invade them, as Naboth to Ahab: "The Lord forbid it me, that I should give the inheritance of my fathers unto thee" (I Kings 21. 3). How jealous were the old Romans, that brave people, of their privileges? At what a price did they hold them? And how greatly could they glory in them? Thus Lysias says, "With a great sum obtained I this freedom"; and Paul boasts, "But I was free born" (Acts 22. 28 *); and this made the chief captain so much afraid of his usage of Paul, when he knew he was a Roman, and so careful to preserve him afterward, because it was death by the Roman law for any in authority to violate the Roman privilege.[g] No sum would be tho't too much to be given for the peculiar privileges of some people, nor can they be defended at too dear a rate; and therefore these ought to be preserved inviolate and not easily given up to the ambitious humor of such as imagine it can never be well with themselves till they have full liberty to prey upon their brethren. Hence it is the highest point of righteousness in the rulers of a people (the primary design of whose institution was to secure the community in their rights) to be very careful to maintain entire and untouched those natural and civil liberties and privileges which are the property of every member of the society; and to guard against the dark designs of those who are secretly endeavoring to undermine or more openly attempt to destroy them; or thro' the rashness of their counsels and stubbornness of their spirit will rather choose to hazard the sacrificing of them than lay aside their own will and humor. It is no new thing for persons of a boundless ambition and close designs to foment a popular clamor about liberty and property, as if all was in danger, under the best of administrations, by which they delude an unthinking people and wind themselves into their high opinion of them as the only patriots of their country, while they mean nothing less than what they make the greatest noise about, and only make use of this politic fetch to get uppermost and rule with the more uncontrolled sway. Thus Absalom could caress the meanest of the people and say to every man: "See, thy matters are right; but there is none deputed of the king to hear thee. Oh that I were made judge in the land, that every man which hath any suit or cause might come unto me, and I would do him justice!" (II Sam. 15. 2, 3, 4). Do him justice! 'Tis likely indeed he should do him justice who could be guilty of so great a wickedness as to accuse and drive from his throne his own father as well as royal master; but this was the governing view, whatever was the pretense, that "every man might come to me"; so all might but bow down to him, he cared not for father, king, or country. And, it may be, nowhere had the rulers of a people more need to place a strong guard than against such dark-laid designs which are founded in the affections and jealousies of the people and in which they are most easily deceived. Nor is it exceeding difficult to discover the cheat by their readiness to give up all rather than not have their humor gratified; so Solomon discovered the true mother of the living child from the pretended one (I Kings 3. 25).

Only while rulers put on righteousness as a robe and justice as a diadem in the preservation and defense of this part of the constitution, it seems necessary that these two rules be observed, namely, that what they so vigorously defend be a real privilege worth contending for, and that they truly have a right to it.

2. Another branch of righteousness in rulers, requisite to establish the throne, is the providing righteous, good, and wholesome laws. The first notion of government is a right to enact and then to execute certain laws for the regulating the society;[11] and wherever this legislative power is lodged, it is of the highest consequence that the laws themselves be just and righteous, because since the government is to proceed by them, if the rule itself be not straight, whatever is measured by it must needs be crooked. "If the foundations be out of course, what can even the righteous man himself do?" [Psal. 11. 3]. Rulers must therefore be very careful that all their laws be righteous ones, lest * the subsequent acts founded upon them be oppressive and injurious, and they involve themselves in all the guilt of putting them in execution. David's command to Joab to place Uriah in the front of the hottest of the battle and retire from him that he may be smitten and die, possibly may sufficiently excuse Joab while he was ignorant for what crime his master had ordered this as a

^ʰ Body of Div. p. 707. [*A Compleat Body of Divinity* . . . (Boston, 1726). Barnard has misquoted slightly.]

^ⁱ Are God's work, made by his direction and appointment, so as no man can corrupt or alter them without violating God's right and incurring his displeasure. *Pool. in Loc.* [This appears to be Poole's commentary on Lev. 19. 19; *Annotations* . . . (London, 1696).]

punishment, but the murder is charged home upon David: "Thou hast killed Uriah the Hittite with the sword, and slain him with the sword of the children of Ammon" (II Sam. 12. 9).

Thus one of the first things the law is to provide for seems to be the establishment and ascertaining of the value of the medium among a people, that they may have a sure rule to go by in all their commerce and business. And here I cannot but think it worthwhile to transcribe a passage or two from that great casuist, the Reverend Mr. Samuel Willard:

There ought (says he) to be one standard to regulate the prices of things by, if men would observe righteousness in the way of commerce. . . . Tho' the prices of things may rise and fall, still . . . everything is to be valued by one standard; otherwise it is impossible that honesty should be maintained. . . . The wise man tells us "that money answereth all things" [Eccles. 10. 19]. . . . It will not only procure any other thing, but it is the standard for the settlement of the value of everything else, as to its currency among men.[h]

Thus he. And how necessary is it that this standard be fixed and certain, nay it is not a standard without it be so; and I presume this can be done only by law or the civil authority putting a certain value upon that which is money, properly so called, that all other things may be reduced to it as to a certain and straight rule. It was the positive law of God (yet in itself a moral precept): "Ye shall do no unrighteousness in judgment, in meteyard, in weight, in measure. Just balances, just weights, and a just ephah, and a just hin, shall ye have" (Lev. 19. 35, 36).[12] And so my context says—the "just weight and balance are the Lord's" [Prov. 16. 11]. They are what God strictly requires.[i] They are his weight and measure and not to be altered by man at pleasure. And if the weight and measure by which men deal out to their neighbors must be just, certain, and invariable, much more ought that to be so which is the standard of all others and the only sure rule by which to proportion the value of everything— which it cannot be while it is left to every man's discretion, justice, or probity to lengthen or shorten, to widen or contract, to add to or take from it, as may best suit with his particular occasions. Till a government

[11] Cf. James Harrington: " 'Give us good men, and they will make us good laws,' is the maxim of a demagogue. . . . But 'give us good orders, and they will make us good men,' is the maxim of a legislator, and the most infallible in the politics" ("The Commonwealth of Oceana," *The Oceana*, 75–76).

[12] *Ephah*: a Hebrew dry measure identical in capacity with the "bath," or between 4½ and 9 gallons (*NED*, III, 235). *Hin*: a Hebrew liquid measure of slightly more than a gallon (*NED*, V, 290).

have made the balance even and the weight, meteyard, ephah, and hin of such a certain size that every man may know what certain rule to go by in dealing with his neighbor, it will be left to each person to act as he pleases; and when every man is left at such a lawless liberty, it will not be to be wondered at if some that can't help it are forced to accept of the one-half of the weight and measure that others can demand; or if what was but an ounce a while ago be grown up to a pound anon, and the nail stretches itself to a yard; I mean the variations of all measure will be without bounds because the medium that proves them is itself variable; and there will as certainly be a progression in the variation on the diminishing hand, let the quantity of the medium be more or less, as that there are men that buy and sell and hope to get gain. What the consequence * of this must be to a people needs no great foresight to determine. And where the fault of all the confusion brought upon such a people will at last be found to lie (tho' it might have taken its rise from human frailty and mistake, but becomes greatly aggravated by the continuance of the error after the discovery of it), everyone may plainly see.

However, this seems pretty certain, that where a standard and fixed measure of all commerce is provided by the state, it will not be in the power of any mercantile craftiness to alter it—which I think is apparent in all kingdoms and governments where there is a fixed standard; or if some might possibly find their interest in little variations from the standard, yet the government has done its duty and so far acted righteously as to provide a known, certain, and unvariable rule to go by. In short, all I plead for is righteousness—that a people ought to have a stated measure, a fixed medium, and there can be none but what the law makes so.[13]

Having thus provided a public standard in their medium, the next thing seems to be the Legislature's reducing all things which the members of the community may be concerned about in the way of barter and exchange—to number, weight, and measure—that there may be no door left open for persons of no principle or conscience or honor (and such there will be in every state) to impose upon their neighbors in the quantity, as perhaps they may after all imaginable care to prevent it, in the quality, of their goods. This is that righteousness which the divine Oracle * calls for when it assures us "that divers weights are an abomination to the Lord; and a false balance is not good" (Prov. 20. 23); and lays its injunctions upon us: "Thou shalt not have divers weights, a great and a small; nor divers measures, a great and a small. But thou shalt have a perfect and just weight, and a perfect and just measure shalt thou have" (Deut. 25. 13–15).

Thus the righteousness of rulers is seen in the laws being calculated to encourage all that is virtuous and laudable and to banish whatever is any ways injurious to the state or to the person, name, and interest of any particular member of it, that they may "be a terror to evildoers, and a praise to them that do well" [I Pet. 2. 14]. Their righteousness is displayed in so tempering the laws that they may equally take hold on the great and small and not be traps to one and open doors to another; that one may not be burdened and another eased, but that all parts of the body may proportionably bear the weight and render it light; and in adjusting all their acts and laws to the temper and genius, to the condition and circumstances of the people—to which end a very great regard is to be paid to the divine laws, not only moral but judicial, as far as the condition of a people will admit, as the result of the highest wisdom and rectitude.

And as righteousness must enter into the nature of the laws, so into the sanctions of them also, that they may be duly confirmed and enforced, and that the penalty be proportioned to the nature of the crime considered in itself and in its circumstances, as they more or less affect the preservation of the peace and welfare of human society and every member of it.

[18] By 1734, problems of currency in Massachusetts were well on their way to the Land Bank crisis of 1740. Three kinds of difficulty had now converged in the debtor economy: (1) There had been a steady depreciation in the value of paper currency for twenty years, "from 8s.6d. an ounce [of silver] in 1713 to 27s.6d. an ounce in 1735" (Robert E. Brown, *Middle-Class Democracy and the Revolution in Massachusetts, 1691–1780*, Ithaca, 1955, 84). (2) Governor Belcher wished to uphold the new instructions to him from England not to emit new issues of currency beyond £30,000 to fall due in 1741; a conflict emerged between him and the House of Representatives, many of whom wished to push the burden of interest farther into the future (Thomas Hutchinson, *The History of the Colony and Province of Massachusetts-Bay*, ed. Lawrence Shaw Mayo, 3 vols., Cambridge, 1936, II, 287). (3) The competition from Rhode Island currency so distressed Boston merchants that a group formed a corporation for trade which refused to accept a new issue of Rhode Island bills and issued £110,000 of its own notes "redeemable in 10 years, in silver at 19s. per oz." (Barnard's "mercantile craftiness" may refer to this group.) Hutchinson continues: "All these emissions made a flood of money, silver rose from 19s. to 27s. the oz. and exchange with all other countries consequently rose also, and every creditor was defrauded of about one third of his just dues" (*ibid.*, 289). For a detailed account of the problem up through 1734 and the issue of "new Tenor" money in 1737, see Andrew McFarland Davis, *Currency and Banking in the Province of the Massachusetts-Bay* (New York, 1901), I, 84–127.

3. A third instance of the righteousness in rulers by which the throne is established is the due execution of the law and dispensing the rewards of the government; for all of this is but distributive justice.

Thus there is righteousness required in the due execution of the laws. A state or kingdom has a right to see all their just laws obeyed, and therefore is the sword put into such and such hands jointly or separately, that obedience may be enforced and they may be governed according to law; and perhaps it may be as great a wrong to the government not to put the laws in execution as to make none. The willful neglect therefore of executing the law, by those to whom it belongs, will be looked upon as the betraying an important trust and dissolving of the government. For should the laws be ever so good, if they are suspended or the executive power acts contrary to them, 'tis evident the design of the ruler's office is perverted. The sword therefore must not be sheathed, but drawn and made use of to punish the bold—tho' there may be room for mercy to the unwilling offender—that vice and disorder may be suppressed and virtue and good manners may be encouraged. Hence the apostle says of the civil ruler: "He beareth not the sword in vain: he is the minister of God, a revenger to execute wrath upon him that doeth evil" (Rom. 13. 4).

And then righteousness goes into the administration in the strict observation of law and justice[j] in all matters of judgment, whether civil or criminal. Hence is that:[14] "Judges shalt thou make thee: and they shall judge the people with just judgment. Thou shalt not wrest judgment; thou shalt not respect persons, neither take a gift: for a gift doth blind the eyes of the wise, and pervert the words of the righteous. That which is altogether just shalt thou follow" (Deut. 16. 18–20). The law must be impartially executed without favor to the wealthy and great or a false pity to the poor and unhappy; no particular affections or distaste or aim at private interest should be allowed to sway in judgment, lest the righteous should be condemned and the guilty cleared, and so "judgment be turned into gall, and the fruits of righteousness into hemlock" [Amos 6. 12].

Thus righteousness requires a due distribution of the rewards of the government in the promotion of persons to places of honor, trust, and

[j] *Magistratus enim debet esse jus animatum, et lex loquens.* Alst. ["For the magistrate must be justice come to life, and law given voice."]

[k] The Emperor Severus strictly forbade the sale of places, saying, "*Necesse est ut qui emit, vendat.*" ["He who buys must of necessity sell."]

[l] *Honor civilis debetur soli actioni virtutis.* ["The performance alone of virtue merits civil honor."]

service. Here therefore the advice of Jethro to Moses is to be observed: "Provide out of all the people able men, such as fear God, men of truth, hating covetousness; and place them over them" (Exod. 18. 21). The favors of the government are not to be distributed promiscuously, much less to any for their unwearied hunting after them, and least of all to them that have the impudence to offer at the purchasing of them—[k] because this will bring on the sacrificing of merit and the prostitution of justice—but the distribution should be made to able men, men suitably qualified, furnished with wisdom and knowledge, sagacity and penetration, fortitude and resolution, vigor and diligence, chastity and purity of manners, proportioned to the duties of their station and equal, if it may be, to the weight that is laid upon them.[l]

How unrighteous would it be in those who have the power of dispensing such favors to call to the council board such as have not so much as a general knowledge of the nature of government and are strangers to the constitution, the state, and interests of their country? Or to place upon the bench in the seat of judgment such as know nothing of the law, nor how to apply it, but must be wholly directed by those who are too ready to think it their business to bend the law to their interest? How odious would it be to see a man of no principles and dissolute manners set to watch over others, to preserve them within the bounds of religion and morality? This would not only be very impolitic but unrighteous and an unfaithful dealing out of the stock to unmeet persons from whom little or no real service could be reasonably expected.

Besides, there is some regard to be had to the outward circumstances of men, that they be able men—able to support the visible honor and dignity of their station. For there is something considerable in external pomp and grandeur; and a figure answerable to a man's station goes further than everyone is aware of to uphold government itself. If therefore (in places purely honorary and much more of great trust and service) promotions are made from the lowest of the people to serve a turn, whose straight circumstances, low education, and mean employment, as

[14] Barnard introduces some quotations by the phrase "hence is that," meaning "consider for example" or "hence we see the meaning of the words . . ."; in some cases he uses only the word "that" as a demonstrative adjective whose noun is missing, as if he were saying "that adage of . . ." or "those words of . . ." Sometimes "that" reads smoothly in his context as a conjunction linking his text and the quotation; at other times (such as here), there appears to be a jar or grammatical error.

well as personal incapacity, cannot comport with the dignity and majesty, the grandeur and state of the post they sustain, this would be so far from distributive justice that it would be a doing the government one of the greatest injuries. For a state or kingdom ever designs their rewards to the most worthy and have a just right to the service of the ablest heads and best hands; and it must therefore come vastly short of righteousness for secret ends to prefer such as are incapable to men of known ability and experience, courage and fidelity; and would be no greater kindness to the persons themselves than the hanging out of Solomon's fool as an object of derision. "Honor is not seemly for a fool" (Prov. 26. 1); and "Delight is not seemly for a fool; much less for a servant to have rule over princes" (Prov. 19. 10). The stupid thing would make but an unseemly figure encircled with the gay trappings of a private life; but what a despicable one would he then appear in, surrounded with the majestic ornaments of public honors ill-placed? And what a shock would it give to a thoughtful mind to see such a servant, one of a servile spirit and born to be under command, taking upon him to rule over princes, men of a more noble, enlarged, and superior mind?

Such a distribution of the rewards of a government would unavoidably bring it into contempt at home and abroad. For the common people (who have scarce anything else to keep them at a distance and procure their respect and veneration but the impressions which outward grandeur makes upon their minds) would be very apt to grow too familiar and despise the men whom they find upon a level with themselves, in their capacity and circumstances. And men of real worth and distinction will hardly brook it to be ranked with those who are upon all accounts so much below them; nor can they easily bear to have their brighter understanding overruled in matters of importance by a perfect silence or the numerous hands of such as scarce understand their actions. When it comes to this, that "the wicked rise, men hide themselves," as Solomon speaks (Prov. 28. 28), ashamed to be seen in their company and afraid of the wild effects of their rise. Nor will a man of wisdom and probity (much less others) who would readily lay himself out to preserve the dignity of government, always be able with his utmost care to distinguish the feather from the head that wears it. This was what Solomon complains of in his day: "There is an evil which I have seen under the sun, as an error which proceedeth from the ruler: Folly is set in great dignity, and the rich (in mind as well as purse) sit in low places. I have seen servants upon horses, and princes walking as servants upon the earth" (Eccles. 10. 5–7).

4. Another branch of righteousness in rulers by which the throne is established is that of commutative justice, which indeed is no other than a part of that positive justice by which we render to every man his dues, and is therefore the payment of a debt and not an act of grace and favor. Tho' there is much of righteousness in the gratuitous rewards conferred upon those that faithfully serve the state in the senate or in the field, yet this of the payment of due debts is pure righteousness and what is most strongly enforced by the light of nature and revelation. For all the laws of God which demand this righteousness between private persons equally concern the public which has its debts.

And here may be considered the debts of the government which necessarily arise from the nature of things and become due by virtue of special services done by those that are called to devote themselves to the public, tho' there should be nothing in particular covenanted for. For all government necessarily includes in the foundation of it the support of itself and consequently of its chief officers who are taken off from attending upon their own private concerns to wait upon the public. For "Who goeth a warfare at his own charge?" as the apostle argues in a like case (I Cor. 9. 7). Nor can it be supposed that those who devote their thought and time to direct and rule, to protect and defend the state, and secure the interest of others, should have no just right to a support equal to the station they are in and the figure they ought to make. Tho' doubtless it belongs to the generous prudence of the government to judge of the *quantum*,[15] yet not so whether a support is due; and where there has been any hope given of any particular sum by those who have a right to give it, this will in reason and conscience be looked upon to amount to the nature of a promise from which I cannot see how they can recede. With respect to this debt founded in the very nature of government, the Word of God gives us some direction. Thus our blessed Savior himself directs us about the paying of tribute (Matt. 17. 24, 25) and commands us "to render unto Caesar the things that are Caesar's" (Matt. 22. 21); and the apostle of our Lord says: "For this cause pay you tribute: for they are God's ministers, attending continually upon this very thing" (Rom. 13. 6)—which shows us the obligation arising from conscience and honor, from religion and gratitude,

15 "Amount."

to afford a proper support unto them. And Nehemiah tells us "that he had not required the bread of the governor, because the bondage was heavy upon this people" (Neh. 5. 18)—which plainly speaks his right to the bread of the governor tho' he saw cause in his fatherly compassion not to exact it under their present difficulties. From all which it may very reasonably be concluded that the ruler of a people has a right to his bread or a maintenance equal to his character. And hence, as it cannot be according to righteousness to withhold it from him to whom it is due, nor from his heirs after his demise—who have a right to what was due to him during his life—so neither can it be righteous for the bread of the governor to be left at such uncertainties as to have a precarious dependence upon the will or humor of any men whatever; and therefore we find justice and equity leading all governments to ascertain the dues and establish the fees of their officers.[16] And how it can be thought agreeable to the rule of righteousness to have the lesser branches of the government certainly provided for with what is thought a proper stipend for their service, and those who have it in their power to fix the wages making their own secure, while some of the greater and more significant branches are left precarious and dependent, I confess is beyond me to see. Doubtless, while the bread of the governor is more secure and Caesar knows what is the tribute he is to receive, that he may not exact more, or others think themselves at liberty to pay less, there will be room left for any state to confer more ample rewards for his greater honor and encouragement.

Here also are considerable the public debts that arise from contract and promise, whether to private persons for any labor and service done, or to persons of a public character who have their established fees. As each of these have some way or other their demands upon the government, so the rule of righteousness by which the public as well as private persons are to proceed is that: "Withhold not good from them to whom it is due, when it is in the power of thine hand to do it. Say not to thy neighbor, Go, and come again, and tomorrow I will give thee, when thou hast it by thee" (Prov. 3, 27, 28). And as there should be no needless delay in the payment, so have they a just right to the fees or stipend settled upon them *usque ad valorem,* to the full value of the establishment; and no change of the specie * into another of much less value tho' of the same denomination can by any rule of righteousness be looked upon as just, because so much less in value as that other specie is, so much do they come short of receiving their due debt in full weight. And however some may not be able to help it, yet will it be esteemed nevertheless oppressive to them. The rule of righteousness here is that: "I will pay thee all" (Matt. 18. 26), and that: "Our money in full weight" (Gen. 43. 21).

Here also may be considered the debts of a state that are due upon bond. And (besides what may be borrowed by a state of their neighbors upon plain bond, which no one will question their obligation to refund), I suppose of this nature are the notes issued out by any state upon emergent occasions, which if well-founded and suitably guarded may perhaps be of great advantage to the government. These receive their whole value from the act of that particular state by which they are emitted, by which act that state becomes bound to the receiver to exchange them for money by such a certain time; and because the time of redemption is one of the main things that gives any real value to them and without which their worth would be but imaginary (as is evident in that no man of thought would have anything to do with such notes as carry in them no time for payment), therefore no one can suppose it agreeable to the rule of righteousness to postpone the fixed time, because by the same rule it may be postponed one year, it may forever—which would amount to a *lex expurgatoria* [17] and be a canceling the bond at one dash, without payment.

5. A fifth branch of righteousness in rulers by which the throne is established is the defense of the state, the preservation of its peace, and promoting of its prosperity. The safety, peace, and flourishing of a state or kingdom are some of the main ends of government; and hence it is but righteousness in rulers in these regards to be true to their trust and use their best endeavors that they may be promoted. Thus "kings should reign in righteousness, and princes rule in judgment," that they may be

[16] The Governor's salary was determined yearly by the House of Representatives in spite of repeated instructions from England to secure it at a fixed figure. "Governors dependent on the people for salaries could not serve the Crown . . . but would always be tempted to make a bad bargain for the king" was the argument of an English judge, Colonel Quary, in a report to the Lords of Trade in 1703 (Brown, *Middle-Class Democracy*, 122). "Governor William Shirley . . . reported to the Lords of Trade that the people generally had a strong aversion to a fixed salary, an aversion which made the issue so unpopular among the representatives that even those who favored it dared not support it because they were elected annually and were extremely dependent on their constituents" (*ibid.*, 55). By 1734 there had been a three-year controversy between Governor Belcher and the House which had recently "neglected to vote his salary" (John A. Schutz, *William Shirley, King's Governor of Massachusetts*, Chapel Hill, 1961, 11).

[17] Literally, "a law of complete washing away." Barnard here upholds the "prerogative men" who supported Governor Belcher in his desire to follow the royal instructions forbidding an issue of currency whose due date would fall beyond 1741. See n. 13 above.

"as a hiding place from the wind, and a covert from the tempest; as rivers of water in a dry place, and the shadow of a great rock in a weary land," as the prophet speaks (Isa. 32. 1, 2).

Thus they are obliged in righteousness to take care of the defense of their people from foreign enemies; and that by all proper endeavors to prevent the mischiefs of a war by guarding against giving any just occasion to a neighbor state to take up arms against them; by cultivating a good understanding with them and bearing, as far as is consistent with the end of government, with the lesser and more common disputes and contests which often happen between subjects of bordering dominions; and by suppressing that ambition and thirst of empire which would embroil their subjects in war and blood. To this end also should they be careful, according to the condition and ability of their people, to provide for war in a time of peace, as by proper magazines of armament and stores of war, that it may not be said, "There is neither spear nor sword found among them" [I Sam. 13. 22]; so, by securing their exposed coasts and borders with such bulwarks as may render them the more formidable and make it more difficult and hazardous for any enemy to make a descent upon them. For it will be looked upon not only as an act of imprudence but of unrighteousness for those who are entrusted with the care of their defense to leave their subjects open and unguarded, and by this means invite an ambitious neighbor to make his inroads and insult over them thro' their supine neglect. Thus Asa took care to "provide fenced cities, with walls, and towers, gates, and bars, while the Lord had rest" (II Chron. 14. 6, 7).

Thus also righteousness obliges to a prudent tho'tfulness how to preserve the state in peace at home, and that not only by good and wholesome laws, but by a particular care not to lay any unreasonable and grievous burdens upon the people, or by a timely removal of them if any such should happen—agreeable to the advice of the old men to Rehoboam (I Kings 12. 7). And it will be incumbent upon the several rulers of a people to do their part to promote the peace in their several towns and districts and not allow themselves to stir up emulations and strife and foment contentions and factions and form parties with a view to the promoting of themselves to greater honor; and when such uncomfortable things happen, it lies with them timely to suppress them, either by showing the people the unreasonableness of their actions and the falseness of the principles they go upon, and by prudent keeping from any share in the government such turbulent spirits as cannot be easy except they have all; or finally, if all other means fail, by exerting their authority to subdue them.

Thus righteousness obliges them to seek the wealth and prosperity of their people. For therefore are they set over them, that they may "lead them in a right way" [Psal. 107. 7], and be "as the clear shining of the sun after rain" [II Sam. 23. 4]. Hence 'tis recorded of Mordecai after his advancement in the Persian Court that "he was accepted of the multitude of his brethren, seeking the wealth of his people" (Esther 10. 3). And Nehemiah could appeal to God in those terms: "Think upon me, O God, for good, according to all that I have done for this people" (Neh. 5. 19). The flourishing and prosperity of a people will ever lie near the heart of a true father of his country and is to be promoted by rendering the government easy and supportable, by preserving the just rights of the subjects, by a free course of law and justice, by due encouragement of labor and industry, by proper premiums for serviceable manufactures, by suppressing all that tends to promote idleness and prodigal wasting and consuming of estates, by a due testimony against all fraud and deceit and unrighteousness in dealings, by cultivating frugality and good husbandry, and using due care, as far as lies in their power, that their export be at least equal to their import.[18] These and the like will have a very great tendency to the prosperity of a people, which therefore very much lie upon the rulers, in justice to them, to take care of.

6. A further instance of righteousness in rulers is a strict observation of leagues and treaties with neighbor nations. States and kingdoms generally have some relation to and dependence upon one another, as well as private persons; and as society cannot be maintained among private persons without government or their covenanting to submit themselves to such or such regulations, so neither can states and kingdoms uphold a profitable correspondence with one another without treaties, leagues, contracts, and terms of agreement—which are to those nations the laws by which they are to govern themselves in their conduct to each other. Sometimes these leagues and treaties are entered into for the sake of carrying on a trade which may be advantageous to both parties in the consumption of the surplus manufacture of the one and the supply of the

---

[18] "In the debtor economy of Massachusetts, money was always scarce because an excess of imports over exports drew hard coin to Britain in payment of balances" (Schutz, *William Shirley*, 29).

wants of the other. Such was the league between Solomon and Hiram (I Kings 5. 12). Sometimes such contracts are made to strengthen themselves by alliances against such nations and people as they may have just cause to be apprehensive of—as the league between Ahab and Benhadad (I Kings 20. 34). Or, whatever be the motives of neighbor nations entering into treaties and contracts with one another, this is certain, that it is a plain moral duty carefully to observe all the articles of agreement and preserve the treaty inviolable. For this is no other than truth to their word and promise, which gathers strength the nearer it approaches the throne; for "where the word of a king is, there is power" to make it good [Eccles. 8. 4]; and as Solomon says in the verse following my text: "Righteous lips are the delight of kings; and they love him that speaketh right." It is therefore articled against Antiochus Epiphanes, for which he is stigmatized with the brand of a "vile person," that "after the league made with him he shall work deceitfully" (Dan. 11. [21], 23). The king's mouth should not transgress in judgment by making use of leagues and treaties to ensnare their neighbor kingdoms with a punic faith and the more easily overrun them, as has been the manner of some of infamous memory.

7. But I must add that righteousness in rulers is to be manifested in the preservation of the religious rights of a people—that every man may be left free and undisturbed in the profession of his religion, that is not inconsistent with the welfare of the state. For surely men have a natural right to worship God in that way which their own conscience stimulates them to, as most pleasing and acceptable to him. And tho' proper pains are to be taken with the erroneous to convince their reason and understanding, yet civil rulers are not to assume a power to decide articles of faith and appoint particular modes of worship and compel any man by external force to the belief of the one or practice of the other; but they are to imitate the laudable example of Gallio, the deputy of Achaia, in whose commendation it is recorded that in a religious controversy he determined with himself: "I will be no judge of such matters" (Acts 18. 15).

Civil rulers are to be nursing fathers to the church, by their own bright

---

[m] Plato could say, "*Praecipua pars magistratus religio est.*" ["Religion is the most excellent part of a magistrate."]

[n] Vol. I. *pag.* 40. ["Sermon III: The Advantages of Religion to Societies," *The Works* . . . (London, 1720), 44.]

example of undissembled religion, by taking care that religion be upheld and that God is worshipped, and by suppressing all that tends to root out religion from among them; for when that goes, the strength and beauty of government goes with it. Religion is calculated for the benefit of states and kingdoms as well as particularly persons; and the influence of it is so great to the public welfare (as is seen in the one instance of righteousness I am speaking of) that it greatly concerns rulers to be religious themselves and to use their best endeavors that their subjects may be so too.[m] Tho' I do not think our holy religion will be a loser by searching it to the bottom and making all the objections that can in reason be brought against it, but it will shine the clearer and be established the stronger when it is seen that it can endure the trial and overcome all opposition; yet I doubt the running upon the Christian religion with banter and ridicule, with flout and jeer, with railing and scurrility, which so unhappily chimes in with the depraved inclinations of mankind and gives such a titillation to the wild imagination which is easily hurried away with the laugh, will go far in banishing all religion out of the world—which seems to be the last and strongest effort of diabolical policy in the satanic agents of the present age, if God in infinite compassion to mankind do not prevent it. Here therefore the rulers of a people are to exert themselves and prevent such insults upon our holy religion.

The heathen (said Dr. Tillotson) would never suffer their gods to be reviled, which yet were no gods; and shall it among the professors of the true religion be allowed to any man to make a mock of him that made heaven and earth and to breathe out blasphemies against him who gives us life and breath and all things?[n]

Surely rulers in a Christian state owe it unto that incarnate Word and wisdom of God from whom they receive their authority, to assert his holy religion and defend it from contempt; and they owe it unto their people who are to be protected from insult in their religious as well as civil rights—so should they be shields of the church.

Thus the civil ruler should preserve the rights of the Christian church not only by countenancing their assembling to worship, their choice of their officers, and their church administrations, but by encouraging their associating in councils and synodical assemblies for the mutual benefit of all the parts of the church of Christ and the communion of churches, which is so necessary to their well-being. Thus they should speak comfortably to the ministers of the Lord, as it is recorded of Hezekiah: "He spake comfortably to all the Levites that taught the good knowledge of the Lord" (II Chron. 30. 22). And since those that teach the good knowledge of the Lord are greatly instrumental to preserve the peace of the state and promote the honor and obedience which the people pay to their rulers, by preaching the laws of Christ which strongly enjoin these duties, it is but just in the civil ruler to show a decent respect to the minister of Christ and remember the honor that belongs to him in his place and encourage him to his work; and not as some little minds are too apt to do, who as soon as they are raised to a small figure in the state, think they must rule in the church also and therefore enter a contest with their minister and excite such as now have some dependence on them to a disrelish of his person, gifts, or performances, that if possible they may subdue him to their humor and by that means bring the people where they dwell to what terms they please.

Thus the civil ruler should secure the rights of the church by taking care of the support of its officers who have a right to their maintenance by the light of nature and the law of the Gospel, if there were no promise from their people. Thus Hezekiah "commanded the people to give the portion to the priests and Levites, that they might be encouraged in the law of the Lord" (II Chron. 31. 4). And where the difficulties of that order of men are peculiarly great, and the one-half the value of what they might expect and has been promised to them is not paid them thro' a defect in an uncertain medium, and they have no ways to help themselves (but the very asking of justice of their people is the certain road to a quarrel, which puts an end to their opportunities for service), while all others can alleviate the difficulty by advance upon their labor and wares and even their interest, it seems a point of justice due to so great and, I trust I may say, valuable a branch of the community (and the obligation thereto is the stronger where the government has, tho' not designedly, brought the difficulty upon them) to secure them from oppression by particular provision in the law for them, proportioning their stipend to some certain standard, that the quarrels about it may cease and they and their offspring may not be made contemptible by their poverty, nor the offerings of the Lord be despised because of the mean and low circumstances of them that present them. This I thought fitting to observe not for my own sake, who thro' the favor of God and kindness of my people need is not, but in compassion to my poor brethren thro' the country who suffer for want of such particular provision for them.[19] I pass—

2. To consider righteousness as it relates to the ruled or governed part of the state. And what is needful here may be reduced to these heads: of honor, obedience, maintenance, defense, and prayer, which are so plain that I need not to enlarge upon them.

1. The first branch of righteousness in the subject is the paying all due honor to the ruler. For the peculiar characters of the Deity upon them, beyond what is to be found upon other men, in their authority and dominion over rational agents and the special relation they stand in to the subjects as fathers to their country, shows that it is an act of righteousness to give the highest civil honors to them proportionable to their rank and station. This honor is to be paid to them in the inward love and affection we are to bear them, the high opinion and esteem we are to entertain of them, and the very great veneration and awe of the mind to them. Hence is that: "My son, fear thou the Lord and the king" (Prov. 24. 21). This honor is to be manifested in our outward behavior by our speaking honorably of them, treating them with the greatest deference, with all the customary marks of respect, and observing our due distance. Hence says the apostle: "Fear God. Honor the king" (I Pet. 2. 17 *). This honor is to be paid to them for the sake of their office and should be greatly encreased from their personal worth and the superiority of their powers and their filling and honoring their station with a wise and prudent, righteous and just, generous and paternal management.

2. Another instance of righteousness in subjects is obedience to their rulers. If it be righteous in the ruler to make good and wholesome laws, it is equally righteous in the subject to obey them. Hence says the apostle: "Put them in mind to be subject to principalities and powers, and obey magistrates" (Titus 3. 1). Obey them in the execution of their office and in their laws, even all of them that do not interfere with the prior obligations every man lies under to obey God rather than man. For it cannot be supposed that any man should, nor indeed can he, give up this right because it is not at his own disposal; nor may any man rightfully assume

[19] According to Professor Robert E. Brown, rural ministers' salaries in 1764 varied from Northampton's £266.13.4 to settle, £100 a year, and £6.13.4 for firewood, to Pittsfield's yearly £80 plus forty cords of firewood. The governor, in contrast, received "£1,000 sterling or £1,333 lawful money a year" (*Middle-Class Democracy*, 35–36). Those who lived on a small, fixed income, such as ministers and widows, suffered most from depreciation of the currency.

what belongs to another, much less what belongs to God. But all the judicial laws of a state (as well as plainly moral ones) that are calculated to promote their peace and flourishing, the support and defense of the government, and the like, wherein the rights of the great Lord of conscience are not specially concern'd, are readily to be obeyed. For thus the Word of God teaches us: "Let every soul be subject to the higher powers" (Rom. 13. 1); and "Ye must needs be subject, not only for wrath, but for conscience' sake" (Rom. 13. * 5). Yea tho' the law should prove injurious, as possibly it may, to a particular person when it designs the good of all, yet it is to be submitted to; and if all fair and lawful means cannot bring an innocent person off from the penalty he has unhappily fallen under, it must be endured without any resistance, because every man has so far resigned up his own private thoughts of right and wrong in civil matters to the public judgment of the ruler in a legal process as to be determined by it.

3. A further instance of righteousness in the subject is the honorable maintenance and support of the throne or ruler. I considered this under another head as the act of those who have the legal power of conferring the rewards and payment of the debts of the government; but now it is to be considered as the duty of every individual subject upon whom the tax is levied for the supplying the treasury. This the body of a people owe to their rulers who lay out their time and strength, their ability and opportunities in their service, to bear the burden of their support without thinking much of the small pittance that falls to every man's share. This God and nature requires: "Render unto all their dues: tribute to whom tribute is due" (Rom. 13. 7). And as the taxes which are raised for the support of the rulers and other charges of the government are to be proportioned in righteousness upon the subjects by those who have the power of the assessment, so should every man look upon himself bound in justice, with cheerfulness, to do his part towards the honorable support of their rulers, without murmuring and complaint or necessitating a distraint.

4. A readiness to defend the person and authority of the ruler is justly due from the subject. For as the civil ruler in the very nature and design of his office is set for the defense of the subject's person and rights, natural, civil, and religious, against any foreign adversary or intestine foe, so it is but just that the subject should be ready upon all proper occasions to protect the person and secure the authority of their rulers against all unjust

attempts that may be made upon them. This they should do by carefully avoiding factions, seditions, conspiracies, and reasonably discovering such as they may know of. This is the advice of Solomon: "My son, meddle not with them that are given to change" (Prov. 24. 21). And when it shall happen that their rulers are exposed in the midst of riots at home or from an open enemy attempting to strip them of their authority, their subjects should readily take up their lives in their hands and expose them to the greatest hazards in defense of their persons and government, saying as the men of Israel to David: "Thou art worth ten thousand of us" (II Sam. 18. 3). And well may they be reproached with their valor and fidelity and be looked upon as worthy to die who will not expose themselves to any hardships and dangers "to keep their master, the Lord's anointed" (I Sam. 26. 15, 16).

5. The last instance I shall mention of righteousness in subjects to their rulers is their earnest prayer to God for them. That wisdom and skill which are profitable to direct; that courage, resolution, and vigor which are necessary to prosecute the affairs of government, come down from the Father of lights; the care and burden, the labor and toil, the fatigue and perplexities of government are undertaken and borne with for the benefit of the subject; the whole community reaps the advantage of the wise and just administrations of their rulers, all of which loudly calls upon the subjects, as a righteous debt, to be importunate in their daily supplications to heaven on the behalf of them that have the rule over them, that the supreme Ruler of the world, in whose hands are the hearts of kings, princes, and nobles, would cause the spirit of government to rest upon them, furnish them with wisdom and largeness of heart, to know how to go in and out before his people, choose out a right way for them, and crown their administrations with desired success, for the preservation of the peace and advancement of the prosperity of their people, for the suppressing of disorder and the encouragement of virtue and pure and undefiled religion—that they may sit down under their shadow with delight and be greatly refreshed with their benign influences and there may be none to make them afraid. Thus prays the psalmist: "Give the king thy judgments, O God, and thy righteousness unto the king's son" (Psal. 72. 1). And thus the apostle of our Lord hath taught us: "I exhort . . . that prayers be made . . . for kings, and for all that are in authority; that we may lead a peaceable and quiet life in all godliness and honesty" (I Tim. 2. 1).

3. The third and last thing under this head is to consider the righteousness which promiscuously belongs both to rulers and subjects. And here it may suffice only to hint at two things, viz.:

1. First, righteousness in dealings one with another. That is, that no man go beyond or defraud his brother in any matter, either by unfaithfulness in the trust committed to him respecting any business or disposition of any interest, or by falsifying his word and promise; by unreasonable detaining the hire of the laborer or wasting another's time that should have been spent in his service; by overreaching another in bargains and contracts and sales, imposing upon their ignorance or preying upon their necessity; by palming false wares, defective merchandise, and unperfected manufactures, for good and perfect; by overcharges and false accounts and deceitful reckonings; by unjust and litigious and expensive lawsuits; or by any other way in which one man may be a sufferer from another. And here the rule by which every man is to proceed in his dealings is that "All things whatsoever ye would that men should do unto you, do ye even so unto them" (Matt. 7. 12).

2. A public spirit—which is every man's seeking the good of the whole. This was one of the master virtues of the old Romans and possibly more than any one thing contributed to their greatness. And it is but a piece of justice in every member of a community to be fired with a generous resolution of soul to devote himself and his interest to the public and look upon his all as a part of, and belonging to, the whole; and not by a disordered and sordid temper appropriate the nourishment so to himself as to bring on a stagnation in any part of the political body which will endanger the whole. The apostle's rule is that: "Let no man seek his own, but every man another's wealth" (I Cor. 10. 24). No man was born for himself, but for mankind. A contracted, narrow, selfish, spirit will unavoidably be guilty of injustice; for while such an one can see nothing but self-interest, he is blind to his neighbors. And he that withholds from the public its due, what right has he to the benefits of the community? A public-spirited man will ever be a just man; and his generous soul will expand itself in great and noble actions for the service of his country, especially in those extensive services of founding and endowing of schools and colleges where the rising generation are in a peculiar manner trained up and fitted for public usefulness. Thus they return into the public a part at least of what they have amassed under the advantages of it; and leave behind them lasting monuments of the largeness of their hearts. How

famous will the name of Hollis, that man of a truly undisguised and generous soul, be to all succeeding generations! [20] May his noble example provoke others and such among ourselves in particular as have equal capacity and stronger obligations, to a noble imitation. This is that righteousness which establishes the throne on which the security and happiness of a people has a great dependence. But I must pass to the last head, viz.:

IV. To lay before you some evidence that the throne "is" and "will be" established by righteousness. And I need only to sum up the evidence under these heads.

1. That this will render the throne or government firm and stable within itself. For when their constitution is acted upon, all due honors are paid to the rulers of a people, and their rights, liberties, and privileges are securely enjoyed, their persons are free from insult, and their property from encroachments by fraud or violence; while none but good and wholesome laws are enacted and these duly executed, to the suppressing of all disorder and immorality, which forever is more or less detrimental to the state; while men of an excellent spirit are preferred and merit is suitably rewarded and every man reaps the benefit of the services he does for the public; while the administrations are calculated to promote the peace and flourishing of the government and every man is in the possession of his truly valuable religious liberties; while every man is careful to treat his neighbor by the laws of justice and a public spirit runs thro' the whole community—what would the necessary result of all this be but the stability of the throne and government at home? For what could there be among such a people to render them uneasy? The prince would smile under the weight of the crown and the burden of empire because they sit easy upon him. The people would salute their rulers with their joyful acclamations, "Let the king live forever," because of their safe possessions and quiet habitations. There would be nothing to stir up mutiny and sedition or provoke them to conspiracies or to make them so much as entertain a secret wish for a change in the person of their rulers or in their constitution. If a malignant spirit should happen to start up in some by-nook or corner of the land, he would not find materials to work upon

[20] Thomas Hollis (1659–1731) was a London merchant and Baptist who began gifts of books and money to Harvard in 1719 that were continued by his family, "to whom Harvard owes more than to any other benefactors outside her own alumni" (Samuel Eliot Morison, *Three Centuries of Harvard 1636–1936,* Cambridge, 1936, 66).

because every man would sensibly perceive himself safe under the shadow of his own vine and fig-tree and that he eats the fruits thereof with joy and gladness of heart.

So that from the very mention of these things it is apparent that the throne is established, the government is safe, and the persons of their rulers secure. Then, as the prophet speaks:

Judgment shall dwell in the wilderness, and righteousness remain in the fruitful land. And the work of righteousness shall be peace; and the effect of righteousness quietness and assurance forever. And my people shall dwell in a peaceable habitation, and in sure dwellings, and in quiet resting places (Isa. 32. 16–18).

When "righteousness shall be the girdle of his loins, and faithfulness the girdle of his reins," then "the wolf shall dwell with the lamb, and the leopard shall lie down with the kid; and the calf and the young lion and the fatling together; and a little child shall lead them. And they shall not hurt nor destroy in all my holy mountain" (Isa. * 11. 5, 6, 9). Whereas the reverse of this righteousness will unavoidably sooner or later bring on rapine and violence, tyranny and oppression, murmuring and discontent, contempt of authority and trampling upon laws, tumults, seditions, conspiracies, which will shake the foundations of the throne and if not timely prevented, prove the overthrow of the government.

2. This righteousness will procure them admiration, reverence, and fear from abroad, and this will establish the throne. For the distant prospect of the continual fresh and untarnished glories of the rulers, and the happy liberty, riches, flourishing, and unity of the subjects will naturally raise the admiration of surrounding nations as rare and great things do, and extort from them the transport of the southern Queen upon the view of Solomon's glory: "Happy are thy men, and happy are these thy servants . . . because the Lord loved Israel, therefore made he thee king over them, to do judgment and justice" (I Kings 10. 8, 9). And who could contemplate the steadiness of their counsels, the evenness of their conduct, and the regularity of their behavior, without an inward reverence, saying: "Surely this great nation is a wise and understanding people. For what nation is there so great, that hath statutes and judgments so righteous?" (Deut. 4. 6, 8). As this would tend to draw foreigners to them and enlarge their trade and promote their prosperity (for who would not choose to dwell with such a righteous and happy people?), so the perfect harmony and agreement among themselves, their regular and

prudent provision for their own defense, and the generous concern for the public running thro' all their actions, would render them formidable to all that behold their comely order, united force, and displayed banners. And while there is nothing among themselves to move any to call in a foreign power, and alliances, treaties, and leagues of friendship and commerce are inviolably maintained, the seeds of war (the lust of empire and revenge of injuries) are rooted up and they will have but little cause to be apprehensive of a foreign adversary.

Whereas, on the contrary, unrighteousness in tyranny and oppression, in seditions and tumults and the like, invite a foreign enemy; and a perfidious breach of articles provokes them to revenge their own cause. Thus Solomon observes, "Righteousness exalteth a nation: but sin is a reproach to any people" (Prov. 14. 34). Righteousness renders them loved, honored, and feared both at home and abroad, and so exalts them, establishes their throne, and very much sets them out of the reach of danger; while the want of it renders them despicable and obnoxious, makes their throne totter and their government unstable, and they become an easy prey to their own feuds and an adjacent adversary.

3. This righteousness will be the most direct way to the divine protection and blessing. If there were no natural influence in this rectitude and purity of the manners of a people to establish the throne, yet such a blessing might rationally be expected from the conduct of divine providence. For thus God Almighty has been wont to favor a righteous nation and encompass them with his protection as with a shield; and his overruling providence has been a pillar of fire to them to enlighten them in a time of darkness, of a cloud to defend them in times of danger. And many are the promises of God in his Holy Word to this purpose. Thus in my text: "The throne shall be established by righteousness"; thus: "Take away the wicked from before the king, and his throne shall be established in righteousness" (Prov. 25. 5); so, "The king by judgment establisheth the land. The king that is faithful judgeth the poor, his throne shall be established forever" (Prov. 29. 4, [14]). This was God's covenant to his people of old:

If thou will hearken diligently unto the voice of the Lord thy God, to observe and do all his commandments, the Lord thy God will set thee on high above all nations of the earth . . . The Lord shall establish thee an holy people unto himself; and all the people of the earth shall be afraid of thee (Deut. 28. 1, 9, [10]).

Thus we read:

I will lay thy stones with fair colors, and thy foundations with sapphire. I will make thy windows of agate, and thy gate of carbuncles, and all thy borders of precious stones. And all thy children shall be taught of the Lord; and great shall be the peace of thy children. In righteousness shalt thou be established: thou shalt be far from oppression; for thou shall not fear: and from terror; for it shall not come near thee (Isa. 54. 11–14).

The Lord is exalted; for he dwelleth on high: he hath filled Zion with judgment and righteousness. And wisdom and knowledge shall be the stability of thy time, and strength of salvation. He that walketh righteously, and speaketh uprightly; he that despiseth the gain of oppressions, that shaketh his hands from holding of bribes, and stoppeth his ears from hearing of blood, and shutteth his eyes from seeing evil; He shall dwell on high: his place of defence shall be the munition of rocks: bread shall be given him; and his waters shall be sure (Isa. 33. 5, 6 and 15, 16).

And let me add that in Psalm * 72 *init.*,[21] which contains the description of a righteous nation and the blessing of God upon it:

Give the king thy judgments, O God, and thy righteousness unto the king's son. He shall judge the people with righteousness, and the poor with judgment. The mountains shall bring forth peace, and the little hills, by righteousness. He shall save the children of the needy, and break in pieces the oppressor. . . . He shall come down like rain upon the mown grass: as showers that water the earth. In his days shall the righteous flourish; and there shall be abundance of peace so long as the moon endureth. . . . They that dwell in the wilderness shall bow before him; and his enemies shall lick the dust.

And what greater assurance can we have of the establishment of the throne?

Thus God dealt not only with his own people, but when pagan Rome was renowned for righteousness in their administrations and a public spirit influenced them in their actions, how happy were they within themselves and glorious in the eye of the world? Till luxury and covetousness, pride and ambition brought on unrighteousness in their several orders and then "they sunk in minutes, who in ages rose."

And how can it be expected otherwise? "Shall the thrones of iniquity

° *Quicquid a vobis minor extimescit / Major hoc vobis dominus minatur: / Omne sub regno graviore regnum est.* Sen. ["Whatever a lesser ruler fears from you, a greater one threatens you with." Seneca, *Thyestes*, ll. 610–612.]

ᵖ Dr. *Colman's* Elec. Serm. 1718. pag. 48. [Benjamin Colman, *The Religious Regards We Owe to Our Country* . . . (Boston, 1718), 47–48. Colman quotes a letter from "Belcher" to "his son in London when a black cloud was gathering over have fellowship with thee, which frameth mischief by a law?" [Psal. 94. 20]. Will such a nation as this be the darling heaven? And shall their throne be established? Who can reasonably look for such a thing? When "wickedness gets into the place of judgment, and iniquity into the place of righteousness" [Eccles. 3. 16], it may well be feared that the most High will take such a people into his own hands and make such distraints upon them as shall cost them dear for every act of unrighteousness; for "tho' hand join in hand, yet shall not the wicked go unpunished" [Prov. 11. 21]; and that he will not give over punishing them (if they refuse to be re-formed) till by giving them up to their own counsels and leaving them to the ways of their own heart (grievous oppressions and civil discords, a mad zeal and a perverse spirit), the foundations of their throne be torn up and they become a ruinous heap—of which the Jewish nation are a standing monument.

Having thus gone thro' the several heads I proposed to speak to, I shall leave the more particular application to be made by those who are more especially concerned; and only say:

And now, O Israel, "what doth the Lord thy God require of thee, but to do justice?" [Mic. 6. 8]. Righteousness is the great comprehensive duty considered in our public relation; and we have seen what it is and the vast influence of it to our establishment. Give me leave then, much honored, to press this important duty upon the government and especially upon those who are concerned in the elections of this day.

My fathers, great is the trust that is reposed in you; great are the expectations of God and his people from you; and great the[o] account you have to give how this opportunity is improved.

I look upon it as an unspeakable privilege we enjoy by virtue of the royal Charter, above the inhabitants of Great Britain itself, that the representative body of this people in conjunction with his Majesty's Council in being have the power and liberty to choose the succeeding councilors; and if it were only for this, our Charter may well be esteemed as an hedge about us and much too valuable to be parted with, whatever may be the secret views of some that would bring us into a light opinion of it. So thought that great and just man who sat so long the prime minister of our state, when, apprehensive of the danger we were in of losing our Charter, he gave that generous order to his son then in England, which sixteen years ago we were publicly informed of upon this occasion.[p] God

---

[21] "At the beginning."

has honored that his son in making him instrumental to preserve our liberties, and now has further honored him before all the people in placing him at the head of the government among us. And when we consider your Excellency not only as one of the sons of our people but the son of such a father, and under his dying charge, we may doubtless with safety repose our confidence under your shadow and have nothing to fear from your administrations that will be detrimental to the true interests of your native country, the place of your father's sepulcher. The distinguishing grace of our royal Master in filling the reserved posts of honor in the government with our own sons, as well as his most favorable answers to us in cases that have excited some uneasiness in our superiors, may fully convince us that our real liberties are in no danger, unless we make them so, under a reign of so much righteousness and clemency, the happy fruits of the match of the Prince of Orange with a daughter of England—and may the late intermarriage of the same illustrious house with a daughter of Great Britain have its happy influences to the confirming the throne in righteousness and us in the privileges we derive from the glorious King William.[22] It lies therefore with the great and General Assembly of this Province, under God, to render us safe and happy by the rectitude and justice of their proceedings—the first step to which is in the choice of proper persons to fill the Council Board.

The nobles of Great Britain, after all the stir that sometimes has been made by the Commons about liberty and property, have generally if not always been the strongest bulwark to the subjects' liberties and have made the best stand when encroachments upon them have been attempted; and I doubt not but his Majesty's honorable Council of this Province, who are a medium between the sovereign and the people, are generally as vigorous defenders of the subjects' just liberties, as strenuous assertors of his Majesty's royal prerogative.

May we * always have the Council filled with the ablest and best men in the country, men of probity and undissembled religion which only will

us which threaten'd our Charter," urging him to "improve all the interest [he] can possibly make to secure our Charter privileges." This was the Boston merchant Andrew Belcher who died in 1717 and was the father of Jonathan Belcher, the recipient of the letter and the present Governor since 1730. Andrew Belcher was a member of the Council from 1702 until his death.]

[q] Mr. *Pemberton's* Serm. pag. 196. [Ebenezer Pemberton, *Sermons and Discourses on Several Occasions* (London, 1727). Barnard (or the printer) has raised the case of initial letters of nouns, changed the punctuation, and altered the italics of the London edition.]

keep a man steadily just under all temptations; men of the best knowledge and understanding in the state and interests of their country; men of a plain and open integrity that despise craft and hate insincerity and abhor an unjust action; men of courage and resolution that will dare to appear on the behalf of righteousness; men of the best interests who, however ready they are to serve the public with them, cannot easily be persuaded to sacrifice them to the humors of such as may be set over us, or to entail such difficulties upon their posterity as they dread themselves. Not only is this honorable Council necessary as the ablest heads to the framing our laws, but without them 'tis not in the power of any that may be over us to constitute judges, justices, or sheriffs, nor to make any disposition of our money; so that neither can our treasures be improved, our persons seized, our causes civil or criminal tried, but in such a way and by such persons as they shall approve of. Happy privileges! And whose fault will it be if we have such councilors as either are not able to advise or cannot be trusted? If such are chosen to that honorable Board as may and ought to be, we may safely confide in them and have nothing to fear from their abuse of power or ill disposition of our treasures; but if such as are destitute of all personal qualifications, and of low and mean fortunes should be chosen to that important trust, we have all to fear that is the natural result of weakness and dependence.

Suffer me upon this occasion to mind you of the words of that great man whose masterly hand delineated the earthly ruler in the bright characters of gods.

Elections (said he) must not be made by personal favor. None must be chosen nor overlook'd barely because they are not friends to these or enemies to those. Be not led in your choice by secret suggestions in a corner, where one man may be canonized and a better reprobated; but be governed by the known characters of men that are generally approved of. This was the ancient rule: "Take men known among your tribes" [Deut. 1. 13].[q] The rule of elections many times is not merit, capacity, and integrity, but some other considerations that rather argue persons unfit than qualified for service. Such as have too much the command of the public voice will have this man preferred because he is of the right party . . . tho' wholly destitute of wisdom, probity, and a true genius for government. On the other side, this and that man must be laid aside as unqualified only because . . . he has not just the same set of thoughts with

[20] William III married Mary, daughter of the Duke of York and niece of King Charles II, on November 4, 1677. Anne, daughter of King George II, married William, Prince of Orange, on March 14, 1734, in London.

some others who would fain set up for the first ministers of state and masters of policy; these despair to carry on their own private, dark designs by them; they can't make them their tools, speak thro' them, and act by them. And by this means it comes to pass the most worthy are rejected and not empowered,* while the unworthy, the weak, the halt and blind are exalted.[r]

Thus he.

And may I add, if ever such an unhappy thing should happen as that those who are entrusted with so great an interest and in which the welfare of this country is so much concerned should suffer themselves to be so much imposed upon as, instead of choosing the best and ablest men, to attempt to weaken his Majesty's Council by calling to that honorable Board men utterly unqualified for so high a station—that they may be the more easily managed, be kept under the influence, and improved to promote the secret designs of those that advanced them—farewell the glory of New England. For it would be next to impossible that such should be able either to choose out a right way for us or prevent the designs of those that would lead us wrong; but either their weakness and narrow, contracted view of things or their mean and low and criminal regards to them that set them up and can pull them down, would expose us to such rash and hasty measures which intriguing men may have on foot, as would render us obnoxious to the just resentments of those we have our dependence on, and greatly entangle and embarrass all our affairs. And besides the indignity and affront to majesty, to make mean men its companions and children its advisers, would it not be an act of the greatest unrighteousness to the country and have the most direct tendency to unsettle the government, so to betray such an important trust? Yea what more severe threatening has God himself denounced against a people than that "I will give children to be their princes, and babes to rule over them" (Isa. 3. 4)?

That there has been a struggle in the country for several years is too evident to be denied. But I fear it would puzzle the ablest head to give a good account of it and say for what we have spent so much treasure, lost so much time, gained the displeasure of our superiors, and kindled divisions among ourselves. What have we got or what are we in pursuit of that is equal to all this? Have any of our essential privileges as Britons or New England men been struck at? Blessed be God and thanks to our gracious Sovereign, these remain yet firm and unshaken.

[r] Ibid. *pag.* 188. [–189.]

My fathers, we beseech you, suffer not a party cause to influence you this day, but dare to be true to your God, to your King, and to your country in choosing such for his Majesty's Council as both can and will support their character, answer to their station, and approve themselves loyal to their Sovereign and faithful to the best interests of their country— that are men of too big souls and too strongly fortified with the steady principles of righteousness to be overawed by the chair of state or meanly modeled by the most leading among the tribunes of the people. Ever be jealous of those that are obstinate in trifles. And look upon such as the most unfit to influence you in your choice who can bid such open defiance to heaven as when they have in a solemn manner called upon the ministers of the Lord to enquire of God on their behalf, to turn their backs upon the religious solemnities and retire to their secret chambers to form a party to accomplish their designs. "Is it not because there is not a God in Israel, that they go to enquire of the god of Ekron?" [II Kings 1. 3, 6, 16].

How many solemn warnings have once and again both formerly and lately been given by the faithful ministers of the Lord against those things that have the most melancholy aspect upon us and greatly threaten the desolation of our country? And give me leave to address you in the words of Jehoshaphat: "Hear me, O Judah, and ye inhabitants of Jerusalem; believe in the Lord your God, so shall ye be established; believe his prophets, so shall ye prosper" (II Chron. 20. 20).

Forgive me if I observe to you that my greatest fears arise from the threatening aspect the want of righteousness has upon our land.

As for that unrighteousness which is to be observed in the private life, there seems to be a necessity of further provision in the law to prevent it. And particularly, what we fear will be the consequence of the public notes being called in at their appointed time before particular persons have discharged their obligations arising upon them, seems to require timely provision to guard against the oppression and injustice which probably will ensue. But this has been set in so good a light and spoken to with such cogency by the very reverend Dr. Colman in his late discourse, "Preparatory to a Fast," that I shall say nothing further concerning it.[23]

[23] Benjamin Colman, *The Fast Which God Hath Chosen . . . Preached at the Lecture in Boston March 21, 1734, Preparatory to an Appointed Day of Public Fasting . . .* (Boston, 1734), 17–18. Colman warns that the current bond interest rate of 10 percent at a time of depreciating paper currency will cause suffering for rich as well as poor.

As to public righteousness, the righteousness by which the throne is established, this has been set before this honorable Assembly; and it will now lie with those more especially concerned to view over the instances that have been named and see whether there is nothing that wants to be amended, and to enter upon the business of the year with this first act of righteousness, an unbias'd choice of his Majesty's honorable Council, that it may be a happy token of the rectitude of the administrations thro'out the whole of it.

O remember the awful commination of God to his people of old:

How is the faithful city become an harlot! it was full of judgment; righteousness lodged in it; but now . . . Therefore saith the Lord, the Lord of hosts, the mighty One of Israel, Ah, I will ease me of mine adversaries, and avenge me of mine enemies (Isa. 1. 21, 24).

But surely

his salvation is nigh unto them that fear him; that glory may dwell in our land. Mercy and truth are met together; righteousness and peace have embraced each other. Truth shall spring out of the earth; and righteousness shall look down from heaven. Yea, the Lord shall give that which is good; and our land shall yield its increase. Righteousness shall go before him; and place our feet in his way (Psal. 85. 9–[13]).

Then shall thy light break forth as the morning, and thy health shall spring forth speedily: and thy righteousness shall go before thee: and the glory of the Lord shall be thy rearward (Isa. 58. 8). And for brass I will bring gold, and for iron I will bring silver: I will also make thy officers peace, and thy exactors righteousness. Violence shall no more be heard in thy land, wasting nor destruction within thy borders; but thou shalt call thy walls Salvation, and thy gates Praise (Isa. 60. 17, 18).

Then shall they use this speech in thy land and in the cities thereof (with which Benediction I conclude): "The Lord bless thee, O habitation of justice, and mountain of holiness" (Jer. 31. 23).

FINIS.

VII JONATHAN MAYHEW'S SERMON OF 1754

AN INTRODUCTION

I

UNTIL 1734 there is a fairly even balance between the number of election sermons preached on the errand motif and political sermons on the nature of government and the good ruler. Between 1734 and 1754, however, the political type perfected by Pemberton and Barnard predominates. Although Edward Holyoke brushes aside the errand motif in 1736 when he says he will depart from those who have chosen "to discourse of the apostasy of this people of God and drop their tears over their immoralities,"[1] Israel Loring of Sudbury comes back the following May with the only complete errand sermon of these years. His is followed by a series of political sermons which can be characterized by their titles: *The Government of Christ Considered* . . . (1738); *The Great Blessing of Good Rulers* . . . (1742); *Magistracy: An Institution of Christ upon the Throne* . . . (1744); *Civil Magistrates Must Be Just* . . . (1747); *The Dignity and Duty of the Civil Magistrate* (1751).

There are some differences between these political sermons and their earlier counterparts. There is more discussion of immediate issues, especially the problem of depreciation of currency (and its effects on ministers' salaries) which plagued the administrations of Governors Belcher and Shirley until its resolution in 1750. The extensive use of Biblical quota-

[1] *Integrity and Religion* . . . (Boston, 1736), 6.

tions (as in Barnard's sermon, for instance) begins to decrease. The ministers reflect the changes that are taking place around them, in the new, anti-Calvinistic views of man's reason, Deism, and the Great Awakening. Because the election sermon is so stylized and the occasion so ceremonious, however, ministers who might otherwise develop their views more fully on such matters usually restrain themselves to a few, sometimes sharp, comments.

For example, Nathaniel Appleton says in 1742 that the Judaic laws of the Old Testament are not binding on modern governors just because God gave them to the Jews, but because "they are founded upon the nature and relation of things, and are of universal and perpetual obligation."[2]

> Remember, Man, 'the Universal Cause
> Acts not by partial, but by gen'ral laws' . . .[3]

Nathaniel Eells, on the other hand, challenges the new emphasis on reason as another voice of God.

God never designed human reason to be the rule of his religion, but his own Word and law; and that man that hath no other rule for his religion than his own natural reason and understanding, is no better of it than the heathen. . . . Human reason is good in its place, and when under proper regulation useful in religion, but it can never contrive a religion that will lead a man to heaven.[4]

In 1744, James Allen refutes a tenet of Deism: "To suppose that when [God] had made the world he . . . left it to shift for itself" is absurd; for one must conclude either that he "made it for no wise design, or through some mistake in its formation it did not answer his original purpose."[5] There is an attempt in many of these sermons to maintain the Puritan views of fallen man and God's providence.

Except for Eells in 1743, the Great Awakening makes little impact on the election sermons. John Webb in 1738 hopes that Jonathan Edwards' *Faithful Narrative* is evidence of God's renewed interest in New England,[6] but Nathaniel Appleton in 1742 advises the Representatives to beware of voting for a so-called religious man if he is one of "enthusiasm," "rap-

---

[2] *The Great Blessing of Good Rulers* . . . (Boston, 1742), 12.
[3] Alexander Pope, "An Essay on Man," *Complete Poems*, ed. John Butt (London, 1963), 537.
[4] *Religion Is the Life of God's People* . . . (Boston, 1743), 16.
[5] *Magistracy an Institution of Christ upon the Throne* . . . (Boston, 1744), 6.
[6] *The Government of Christ Considered and Applied* . . . (Boston, 1738), 26.

tures, ecstasies, and immediate impulses of the spirit, without any use of regular judgment." He then becomes more specific: "I pray God that . . . the great awakenings that have been of late, and are still among people, may issue in such a sober, humble, obedient, regular carriage, as may give us more and more occasions for thanksgivings to God upon this account."[7] Nathaniel Eells in 1743 draws up in three pages the pros and cons of whether the Awakening is "a time of great reformation" or "a time of great delusion and giddiness and little reformation"; he concludes safely by saying that there are some places where the new awakenings are undoubtedly genuine and others where they are surely counterfeit.[8]

II

When Governor William Shirley returned to Boston in August 1753, after four years in London and Paris, he came back to trouble.[9] Frontier defenses were inadequate and further conflict with the French, who now contained the English colonies along a thousand miles of frontier, was inevitable. His first efforts to persuade the assembly to increase defense appropriations met with a rebuff, and his plans for cooperation with other colonies received the answer from a committee of the House that Massachusetts would look out for itself and the others must do likewise. Also, House committees voted the Governor only £50 more than his annual salary for his time abroad working on New England's behalf; this was an insult. His power over the House diminished, Shirley filled the vacancies which had come up in his absence and prepared for the elections in May. Two events in the spring made the forthcoming session all the more important: the Board of Trade in London called for a meeting in Albany to discuss Indian relations and measures for cooperative defense, and there were reports of French troop movements in Maine. The legislature voted funds for an expedition to Maine, promised to send delegates to Albany, and asked to be dissolved.

The minister invited by the Representatives to preach at the opening of the new session in May was already famous.[10] Jonathan Mayhew's first

[7] *The Great Blessing of Good Rulers*, 36, 58.

[8] *Religion Is the Life of God's People*, 17–21.

[9] The information here is drawn from John A. Schutz' fine study, *William Shirley, King's Governor of Massachusetts* (Chapel Hill, 1961), 168–177.

[10] Since Mayhew, like Cotton Mather, is better known than the other preachers included in this volume, there is less need for a brief sketch here. The most recent study of Mayhew is Charles W. Akers, *Called unto Liberty: A Life of Jonathan May-*

call after receiving his Harvard degree was to West Church, Boston's newest and wealthiest, whose preacher had just scandalized the local clergy by turning Anglican and moving to King's Chapel. Mayhew's liberal views prevented some of the Boston clergy from supporting his ordination. By the time of his *Seven Sermons* (1749), "Arminian he already was, and the path his ideas would take . . . toward the gentle, creedless faith of Unitarianism was even then clear." [11] Those who saw Mayhew as too liberal had their view confirmed when in January 1750 he preached his famous sermon attacking the martyrdom of Charles I, later published as *A Discourse Concerning Unlimited Submission* . . . one of the classic statements by a clergyman (along with Wise's *Vindication* of 1717) on individualism and freedom in eighteenth-century America. Newspaper controversies which lasted for over two months following the sermon made him the most talked-about minister in Boston; "he stood out thereafter as a preeminent spokesman in the colonies for everything that was new, bold, and radically nonconformist in matters of church and state." [12] Four years later on election day, May 29, 1754, he was again in the spotlight.

The first part of the sermon is a concentrated review of the basic ideas of the source and ends of government, which includes ideas that go back to the seventeenth century. His main thesis, that the end of government is the public good, is an old Puritan one, but "good" has now come to mean, after filtering through such writers as Harrington, Hoadley, and Locke, the people's right to democratic procedures. Mayhew need only mention his ideas on the authority of kings and governors and the limited submission of subjects, for *A Discourse,* where he deals with them fully, was by now in its third printing.

When he moves into the application (and notice how the formal division headings of the earlier sermons are gone), he challenges the apostasy theme of the errand sermons: "Nor can I think we are so far degenerated from the laudable spirit of our ancestors . . ." There follows an application that must have made those Representatives who welcomed a wider separation between church and state start in amazement; this man should have been a politician! Under the persona of an apologetic minister who

hew 1720–1766 (Cambridge, 1964). For a bibliographical note on other studies of Mayhew, see *Pamphlets of the American Revolution,* ed. Bernard Bailyn (Cambridge, 1965), I, 695.

[11] *Pamphlets,* ed. Bailyn, I, 205.
[12] *Ibid.,* 210.

doesn't wish to overstep the traditional bounds of his place on such occasions, he takes up one by one the pressing needs of his Colony: removal of non-toleration laws; an act to settle frontier land disputes; the need for more research in agriculture and measures to increase trade; the need for more Protestant immigrants in imitation of Pennsylvania; the necessity of increased missionary work to secure Iroquois allegiance to the colonies; the threat of French attack and the pressing need for more supplies and improved forts; the necessity of naming delegates to the Albany congress and giving them a strong directive to press for a plan of union for inter-colonial defense; an equitable distribution of the costs of such defenses and of the inevitable war with France. If some of the Representatives had suggested that Mayhew preach the election sermon as a political move to annoy the Governor (Mayhew's strictures on Anglicans were by now well known and it was bruited that the butt of his attack in *A Discourse* was the assistant minister of King's Chapel, the Governor's church), they were disappointed. Mayhew raps the supporters of the Divine Right of Kings theory, but he supports the Governor's proposals for defense, the importance of the Albany congress, and the need for a plan of union. In his reference to Crown Point, he even implicitly reminds the House that if it had executed Shirley's plans in the last war to attack the fort, there might not be as great a threat facing them as there now was. History has proven that Mayhew's support for these ideas was astute and his vision prophetic.

Mayhew's ideas may be liberal for his day and his use of the application unprecedented in its political immediacy, but his flamboyant style is in the tradition of Increase and Cotton Mather. In contrast to Barnard's quiet exposition, Mayhew uses rhetorical questions ("Shall our gold and silver lie cankering in our coffers?"), long catalogs, heavily loaded, emotional language, satirical humor, the persona of the meek man who would restrain himself from an impropriety (making his proposals all the more sensational), and the dramatic vision of a Catholic Boston—all to sway his audience to his purpose. This latter highlight of the sermon is reminiscent of Cotton Mather's vision in his sermon of 1689 of the first settlers rising from their graves. The *Discourse* of 1750 is a more important document in the history of American ideas on liberty; but in the history of American oratory, this election sermon is surely its equal.

A

S E R M O N

Preach'd in the Audience of His Excellency

*WILLIAM SHIRLEY,*Esq;

Captain General, Governour and Commander in Chief,

.The HONOURABLE HIS MAJESTY's

C O U N C I L,

And the HONOURABLE Houſe of

REPRESENTATIVES,

Of the Province of the

MASSACHUSETTS-BAY,

IN

𝔑𝔢𝔴-𝔈𝔫𝔤𝔩𝔞𝔫𝔡.

May 29*th* 1754.

Being the Anniverſary for the ELECTION of His
MAJESTY's COUNCIL for the Province.

N. B. *The Parts of ſome Paragraphs, paſſed over in the* Preaching *of this*
Diſcourſe, are now inſerted in the Publication.

By JONATHAN MAYHEW,*D.D.*

Paſtor of the Weſt Church in *Boſton.*

B O S T O N : N. E.
Printed by SAMUEL KNEELAND, Printer to the Honourable
Houſe of Repreſentatives. 1754.

An Election Sermon.

"His Lord said unto him, Well done, thou good and faithful servant: thou hast been faithful . . ." (Matt. 25. 21).

This is part of our Savior's well-known parable of the talents, the moral of which is in general this, that whatever powers and advantages of any kind men severally enjoy are committed to them in trust by the great Lord and Proprietor of all, to whom they are accountable for the use they make of them; and from whom they shall, in the close of this present scene, receive either a glorious recompense of their fidelity or the punishment due to their sloth and wickedness. The subject then is very general and equally interesting. All men of whatever rank or character are concerned in it. It leads our thoughts from what we possess up to the great source thereof; from what we are at present, to what we shall be hereafter. It connects this world with another, and comprehends both our probationary and final state under the righteous administration of God.

But tho' the subject is very general and of the last importance to all, yet civil power being one of the principal of those talents which heaven commits to men, and the present occasion requiring a more particular consideration of it, the ensuing discourse will be confined thereto. Nor would I injure our honored rulers by the least suspicion that they can possibly take it amiss to be reminded of their duty to God and man upon this occasion, with all the plainness and simplicity becoming a minister of the Gospel, and consistent with decency, the rules of which, it is hoped, will not be violated.[1]

Indeed were one to discourse upon this subject before rulers in an arbitrary government, or before unfaithful rulers even where the constitution is free, there would be almost a necessity of disguising and suppressing the truth on one hand, or of giving umbrage on the other. A miserable dilemma! But surely there can be no necessity of the former, nor any danger of the latter, under such a government as the British, and before such rulers as I have the honor to speak to.

It is customary for those who are called to speak upon such public occasions to apologize for their want of proper qualifications for the task. But how much reason soever they may often have for this, I think it is usually their unhappiness not to be tho't very sincere in doing it. I shall therefore wholly omit this common ceremony because I would fain be thought quite in earnest in everything I say before so grave and venerable an auditory, and upon so important an occasion.

It may not be improper, in the first place, to speak of the source and origin of civil power, and then of the great end of government, which two particulars will be dispatched in a few words. In the third place, it will be useful to recollect some of those arguments by which those who are vested with authority should be induced to exercise it with fidelity, suitable to the design of it. And so the subject will be closed with some reflections chiefly relative to this anniversary, and to the present state of the Province.

As to the source and origin of civil power, the parable on which my discourse is grounded suggests that it is ultimately derived from God, whose "kingdom ruleth over all" [Psal. 103. 9], this being as truly a talent committed by him to the fidelity of men as anything else can be. In this light it is considered in the holy Scriptures. It is not only agreeable to the original scheme and plan of God's universal government that civil rule should take place among men, in subordination to his own, but his providence is actually concerned in raising those persons to power and dominion who are possessed of it. In the language of the prophet, "Wisdom and might are his: he removeth kings, and setteth up kings. The most High ruleth in the kingdom of men, and giveth it to whomsoever he will" [Dan. 2. 20, 21; 4. 17, 25, 32]. The language of the apostles is not less emphatical. They tell us that "there is no power but of God"; that "the powers that be are ordained of God"; and that "they are God's ministers" [Rom. 13. 1, 2, 4].

But then it is to be remembered that this power is derived from God not immediately, but mediately, as other talents and blessings are. The notions of any particular form of government explicitly instituted by God, as designed for a universal model—of the divine right of monarchy in contradistinction from all other modes; of the hereditary, unalienable right of succession; of the despotic, unlimited power of kings by the immediate grant of heaven; and the like—these notions are not drawn from the holy Scriptures but from a far less pure and sacred fountain. They are only the devices of lawned[2] parasites or other graceless politicians to serve the purposes of ambition and tyranny. And tho' they are of late date, yet being traced up to their true original they will be found to come by uninterrupted succession from him who was a politician from the beginning.

God did indeed formerly take one nation under his more immediate care and patronage, establishing therein a kind of civil polity. But with this the other nations of the world had no concern; nor were they required to imitate it. It might be added that even this commonwealth of Israel was not molded and modeled wholly by the immediate dictates of heaven. Moses, who sometimes consulted God in the mount, at other times consulted his father-in-law Jethro in Midian, the prince and priest of that

[1] Mayhew begins by observing (perhaps with tongue in cheek) the proprieties and conventions of the election sermon. Many eighteenth-century election sermons begin with a statement in which the minister charts his path carefully between assuming on the one hand that he has the practical answers for the Colony's secular problems, and on the other, that a sermon based on Scripture and theoretical in content has little value for the immediate politics of the election and the forthcoming legislation for the year. Ebenezer Pemberton's in 1710 is perhaps the most detailed and delightful of any:

"I hope there are none so vain as to imagine that I appear this day in this awful desk only to beat the air and play the orator in an artful address to our rulers, either by way of unmannerly satyr or fulsome panegyric. This would not well become the solemnity of this place nor the gravity of my audience, and much less would it suit my own character. Nor may it be supposed that I am called forth to read a lecture in politics before our venerable senators, for thus I should go beyond my own line and boast of a false gift. I desire to keep in mind what place I stand in, in whose name I speak, what critical inspection I am under, and what an awful account I must give in of my present performance to our common Lord and Judge; and under the commanding awe of these thoughts I shall endeavor to speak, and must intreat my audience, under the same awe, to hear" (*The Divine Original and Dignity of Government Asserted* . . . Boston, 1710, 4–5).

[2] *Lawned*: dressed in lawn, a kind of fine linen; lawn was used for the sleeves of a bishop's robe—hence the dignity or office of a bishop (*NED*, VI, 119–120).

country, by whose advice, tho' a mere pagan, it was that the great Hebrew lawgiver partly framed his government. And it is to be observed that this government did not put on the regal form at all till after a long time, and then, in express contradiction to the counsel of the prophet, God declaring that this people rejected him in requesting a king. To say the least, monarchical government has no better foundation in the Oracles of God than any other. And after the establishment of it amongst the Hebrews, the crown, instead of descending uniformly to the elder branch of the male line, was often bestowed on a younger; sometimes transferred to another family; and sometimes even into another tribe—and this not without the divine approbation.

All the different constitutions of government now in the world are immediately the creatures of man's making, not of God's. And indeed the vestiges of human imperfection are so manifest in them that it would be a reproach to the all-wise God to attribute them directly to him. And as they are the creatures of man's making, so from man, from common consent it is that lawful rulers immediately receive their power. This is the channel in which it flows from God, the original source of it. Nor are any possessed of a greater portion of it than what is conveyed to them in this way. Or at least, if they have any more, they have it only as the thief or the robber has the spoil which fraud or violence has put into his hands. Agreeably to what is here said concerning the medium or channel thro' which power is derived from God, government is spoken of in Scripture as being both the ordinance of God and the ordinance of man—of God, in reference to his original plan and universal providence; and of man, as it is more immediately the result of human prudence, wisdom, and concert.

In the second place, we are just to mention the great end of government. And after the glory of God, which we usually consider as the end of all things in general, that can be no other than the good of man, the common benefit of society. This is equally evident whether we consider it as a divine or an human institution.

As it is God's ordinance, it is designed for a blessing to the world. It is instituted for the preservation of men's persons, properties, and various rights, against fraud and lawless violence; and that by means of it, we may both procure and quietly enjoy those numerous blessings and advantages which are unattainable out of society, and being unconnected by the bonds of it. It is not conceivable that the all-wise and good God should ordain government amongst men but with a view to its being subservient to their happiness and well-being in the world; to be sure, not that it might be subservient to a contrary one, their misery. We cannot imagine it possible that he who is good unto all and whose tender mercies are over all his works should exalt a few persons to power over the rest, to be their oppressors; or merely for their own sakes, that they may amass riches, that they may live in ease and splendor, that they may riot on the produce of others' toil and receive the homage of millions without doing them any good. It were blasphemous to think that God has instituted government for such a partial, unworthy end.

So far as God interposed in founding the commonwealth of Israel, it was in favor to his chosen people that he did it—not that they might be oppressed and enslaved by their own rulers, but that they might be delivered from oppression and slavery and their taskmasters in Egypt; and that, being brought out of the house of bondage, they might be conducted into a good land, flowing with milk and honey; that they might there possess property, enjoy the blessing of equal laws, and be happy. Nor is the general design of government and magistracy now, throughout the world, different from what it was among the Israelites, viz., the happiness of men. Accordingly the apostle tells us that the civil magistrate "is the minister of God to us for good" [Rom. 13. 4]; and from hence argues the reasonableness of submitting to his authority. And all the instructions and admonitions which God has given to rulers in his Word exactly correspond to this declared end of their institution. The end of government then, as it is a divine ordinance, must be human felicity.

And if we consider it as it is more immediately the ordinance of man, the end must evidently be the same. It being founded in, and supported by, common consent, it is impossible the design of it should be any other, since we cannot suppose that men would voluntarily enter into society and set up and maintain a common authority upon any other principles than those of mutual security and common good. Nor is there any medium betwixt such common consent as is here intended, and plain lawless force and violence, for which Christians surely ought not to be advocates. Some states may have owed their beginning, and more, their progress and enlargement, to the latter of these causes. But these are not to be drawn into example or to have any regard paid to them when we are speaking of the end of government. We ought not to take our estimate of the design hereof from the views of banditti and robbers, associated to plunder and oppress others (tho' even they have a common interest which they profess to regard, and which keeps them together). But we are to form our idea of this end by what reason suggests must be the motive with reasonable and honest men to unite together in the bonds of society. And if we judge by this rule, the end of government must be the common good of all, and of every individual, so far as is consistent therewith.

We are therefore brought exactly to the same point at last, whether we consider government as it is originally an appointment of heaven, or, more immediately, the voluntary choice of men. The security and happiness of all the members composing the political body must be the design and end thereof, considered in both these lights. God is too good to ordain it for any other purposes; and men at least love themselves too well to choose it from any other principles—unless perhaps we may suppose that a farther design of political union is the defense and patronage of other persons out of the society; and the doing of good to all as opportunity is, in providence, afforded for it. But if this is really any end at all, yet it being only a secondary and remote one, it might have been passed over in silence.

But tho' the grand end of government under all its different forms is one—the good of the political body—this general end admits of various subdivisions and is prosecuted in a variety of ways, to speak of which is quite beyond the design of this discourse; and indeed that would be to deliver a system of politics rather than a sermon. I shall therefore only add under this head that as the happiness of men in society depends greatly upon the goodness of their morals, and as morals have a close connection with religion, the latter as well as the former ought doubtless to be encouraged by the civil magistrate; not only by his own pious life and good example, but also by his laws, as far as is consistent with the natural, unalienable rights of every man's conscience. Protection is, in justice, due to all persons indifferently, whose religion does not manifestly

[a] "Not only Germany but all the Christian states bled at the wounds . . . received in . . . religious wars; a rage which is peculiar to Christians, who are ignorant of idolatry, and is the unhappy consequence of that dogmatical spirit which has so long been introduced into all parties. There are few points of controversy which have not been the occasion of a civil war; and foreign nations (perhaps our own posterity) will one day be unable to comprehend how it was possible that our forefathers could kill one another for so many years together, and yet at the same time be preaching patience." Volt. Age of L. XIV. [Cf. London, 1753, I, 10.]

[b] *Harrington.* [James Harrington, *The Prerogative of Popular Government* . . . (London, 1658), 133. Mayhew has misquoted slightly.]

and very directly tend to the subversion of the government. And a general toleration, with this single exception, is so far from being pernicious to society that it greatly promotes the good of it in many respects. Persecution and intolerance are not only unjust and criminal in the sight of God, but they also cramp, enfeeble, and diminish the state. And many states in other respects politic enough, have hereby greatly prejudiced themselves and strengthened their rival neighbors. For what else is it, to butcher multitudes of their own people on religious accounts as they have done; and to oblige others of them to betake themselves to flight with their effects and arts into foreign countries, where they may live securely? So that setting aside the great impiety and unrighteousness of this practice, the impolicy of it is a sufficient argument against it. Nor indeed can it be doubted but that the interest of true religion has been greatly prejudiced by that notion which has so generally prevailed in Christendom from the days of Constantine—I mean, that kings could not be nursing fathers nor queens nursing mothers to the church, unless they suckled her with human blood and fed her with the flesh of those whom angry ecclesiastics are pleased to stigmatize with the names of heretic, schismatic, and infidel.[a]

Thirdly: It is now time to mention some of those arguments by which rulers should be induced to exercise their power with fidelity, suitable to the great end and design of it. It is asserted by a great man of the last age "that the pretended depth and difficulty in matters of state is a mere cheat." And "from the beginning of the world," says he, "to this day, you never found a commonwealth where the leaders, having honesty enough, wanted skill enough to lead her to her true interest both at home and abroad."[b] It belongs not to my function to determine how far this assertion will hold true. But I may venture to say that if honesty and public spirit are all that are wanting, there are not wanting arguments enough, founded in reason and religion, to engage rulers to act from those principles.

To a generous mind, the public good, as it is the end of government, so it is also such a noble and excellent one that the prospect of attaining it will animate the pursuit, and being attained, it will reward the pains. The very name of patriotism is indeed become a jest with some men, which would be much stranger than it is had not so many others made a jest of the thing, serving their own base and wicked ends, under the pretext and color of it. But there will be hypocrites in politics as well as in religion.

Nor ought so sacred a name to fall into contempt, however it may have been prostituted and profaned, to varnish over crimes. And those times are "perilous" indeed wherein "men shall be" only "lovers of their own selves" [II Tim. 3. 2], having no concern for the good of the public. Shall we go to the pagans to learn this godlike virtue? Even they can teach it. And is there a Christian who is required to love all men and to do good to all, as he may have opportunity for it; is there a Christian who does not love even his brethren, the members of the same body with himself? Is there a Christian who is void of all generous solicitude for his country's welfare? Is there, who has no desire to see it in a prosperous and flourishing condition, who has no pleasure in actually seeing it so? Is there, who has no grief in beholding its calamities, no disposition to serve it? Such a person, tho' he were of a private character, would be a reproach not only to his religion, a religion of charity and beneficence, but even to our common nature, as corrupt and depraved as it is. But how much more infamous were this in persons of a public character, in those on whom the welfare of their country, under providence, immediately depends?

But it is not to be thought merely an office of generosity and charity for rulers to exert themselves in the service of the public. This is an indispensable duty of justice which they owe to it by virtue of their station. They have taken the care and guardianship thereof upon themselves; yea they are commonly laid under the solemn obligation of an oath, to study and pursue its interest. And why are they honored, why rewarded by the public, but that the public may receive benefit from them? Here then are ties if possible more strong and sacred than those of charity; ties, which being violated, leave the violators of them guilty of manifest injustice and great impiety.

Another argument of some weight is that people are not usually either so blind and insensible as not to know when they are well governed, or so ungrateful as not to acknowledge it and to requite their benefactors suitably to their merits. Some men will indeed be captious and find fault without reason. But it is a mere calumny to represent them of this turn and temper in general. All history scarce affords an example of a people ruled with prudence, justice, and due clemency, but what lov'd and honor'd their rulers, but what loudly proclaimed their virtues, but what, in all proper ways, requited their paternal care and goodness while living, and reverenced their memory when dead. And how much more desirable is this than for them to have their ears filled with cries, complaints, and murmurings? How much more eligible is it to live esteemed and to have their names transmitted with honor to posterity, than to be the objects of public hatred, as being rather taskmasters than fathers; and to leave no remembrance behind them but of their selfishness and injustice, their unfaithfulness and oppressions?

It were moreover to be wished that rulers (especially legislators, whom I have all along chiefly in view) would seriously consider how much their own beloved posterity may be affected by their counsels and conduct. The effect of public counsels and resolutions, whether good or bad, is not so transient as they are themselves. Even remote generations often feel the consequence of them. By wise and good laws and a proper conduct in other respects, the governors of a people lay a foundation, by God's blessing, not only for the welfare of the generation present, but also for the prosperity of those who may come after them. In doing which they in effect leave the most valuable legacy to their own offspring, whereas by a contrary conduct they entail on them only misery and ruin. This consideration will be of great weight not only with persons of a truly patriotic and public spirit, but even with all such as are not "without natural affection" [Rom. 1. 31]; with all who would not have their memory cursed after they are gone, even by those who should "rise up, and call them blessed" [Prov. 31. 28].

A farther argument may be drawn from this consideration, that rulers derive their power from God and are ordained to be his "ministers for good." They are not only entrusted by man with the care of the public, but by God himself, the supreme Lawgiver, that they may be the instruments of his goodness and munificence. This doctrine that rulers are God's ministers and clothed with authority delegated from him, has far too often been made use of as a topic of compliment and adulation in order to soothe them and puff them up with vain imaginations. And so successful have the servile adorers of princes sometimes been in the management of it, as to make them conceit themselves almost literally gods, and to think their subjects scarce better than brutes made only for their service. That the title intended, denotes, their dignity and the honor which they may justly expect, no one can question. But the grand inference they themselves ought to draw from hence is that they should imitate the justice and unwearied goodness of that God whose ministers they are, and exercise the power with which his providence has clothed them to that gracious end for which it is given. When they prosecute the true interests of the public and diffuse happiness around them, then and only then they act up to their honorable character. They then answer the noble purposes for which heaven exalted them, and are seconding the benevolent designs of providence, being "workers together with God" [II Cor. 6. 1]. And what can more animate a considerate man to fidelity in his trust than this reflection, that while he is thus serving his generation, he is doing it "according to the will of God" [I Pet. 4. 19], that he therein concurs with the designs of the greatest and best of beings, the Creator and Lord of all, who is good unto all? It is an honest joy, a pleasure truly divine, that must result from such conscious integrity.

Christian rulers should moreover always have in view the example of our blessed Lord and Redeemer, to whom "all power in heaven and in earth is given" [Matt. 28. 18]. All his laws are calculated for the good of his subjects; and he governs them in order to render them happy. He was the King foretold who was to "reign in righteousness" [Isa. 32. 1]. After him should all the princes and rulers of the earth copy. And if they did so, the great object and end of their government would be to bless mankind.

But the argument suggested in my text is of the greatest weight and solemnity of any that can be tho't of, viz., the account which all men are to give of their conduct hereafter to the Judge of quick and dead.[3] That same Lord who has given to one of his servants five talents, to another two, and to another one,[4] will come at the appointed time to reckon with them and to render to every man according to his deeds. Nor are there any persons who have more reason to aim at approving themselves to him than civil rulers, who have so great a charge. It is an established maxim of God's equal government that "unto whomsoever much is given, of him shall much be required" [Luke 12. 48]. Nor does he at whose tribunal they are to appear regard the persons of princes any more than of their slaves. They are all equally his servants. Happy! thrice happy! those who shall then be found faithful, for then shall they "enter into the joy of their lord" [Matt. 25. 21, 23]. Not so the slothful and wicked servant who has either neglected or willfully misapplied the talents committed to him! Innumerable, alas! innumerable are the miseries and calamities which have accrued and are daily accruing to mankind, from the abuse of that very power which was designed to prevent them and to be instrumental of good to all that are under it. Heaven beholds these things; and shall not heaven at length visit for them! "Shall not the Judge of all the earth do right?" [Gen. 18. 25].

Rulers surely, even the most dignified and powerful of them, should not be so elevated with the thoughts of their power as to forget from whom it comes, for what purposes it is delegated to them, whose impartial eye it is that surveys all their counsels, designs, and actions, and who it is that will one day exact an account of their stewardship. If only the "hand upon the wall" [Dan. 5. 5] caused the haughty Babylonian's knees to smite one against another, what amazement will seize the proud oppressors of the earth when they shall behold the "Son of man coming in the clouds of heaven, with all the holy angels with him [Matt. 24. 30, 31; Mark 13. 26, 27; Dan. 7. 13]! The Apocalypse of St. John informs us how different sentiments "the kings of the earth, and the great men, and the chief captains, and the mighty men" [Rev. 6. 15], shall then entertain of themselves, from those which they are too apt to entertain at present. You will then see many of those who made the world tremble and stoop before them, in vain attempting to "hide themselves in the dens and in the rocks of the mountains" [*ibid.*]!

But it now remains to make some reflections upon this subject and to apply it to the present occasion.

And we are reminded by the preceding discourse how great a blessing good government is, and what gratitude becomes those whom God in his providence favors with it. Inconsiderate men are too apt to think government rather a burden than a blessing; rather as what some persons have invented for their own particular advantage than what God has instituted for the good of all. This is, under him, the great guard and security of men's property, peace, religion, lives; of everything here for which it is worthwhile to live. And this is a blessing which British subjects enjoy in as high a degree, perhaps, as any other people. It is their felicity to be governed by such men, and by such laws, as themselves approve; without which their boasted liberty wou'd indeed be but an empty name. The form of our government is justly the envy of most other nations, especially of those which have either no parliaments at all, or such as may be banished at the word and pleasure of a tyrant, which comes much to the same thing. We have also for several late reigns been blessed with princes too just and good to encroach upon the rights of their subjects, and too wise to think that Britons can endure a chain. Happy had it been for some

³ See Acts 10. 42.
⁴ See Matt. 25. 15.

former princes, as well as for their people, had they been endowed with the same moderation, justice, and wisdom!

Persons of a private character are, moreover, admonished of the reverence and submission which they owe to government, as it is God's ordinance and as rulers derive their power from him. Were this no more than an human institution, yet it would in the nature of the thing demand great respect, that being necessary even to the preservation of it in the world, and so to peoples reaping those numerous advantages which accrue from it. But when we reflect that this is an appointment of heaven, it suggests that we should be subject even "for conscience' sake" [Rom. 13. 5; I Cor. 10. 25, 27, 28], and that we cannot behave undutifully towards our rulers without also rebelling against God. Nor is it easy to mention any duty which the Gospel inculcates upon the consciences of men with greater solemnity than that of paying due honor to kings and all that are in authority. However, it is not to be forgotten that as in all free constitutions of government, law, and not will, is the measure of the executive magistrate's power, so it is the measure of the subject's obedience and submission. The consequence of which I shall at present leave others to draw, only observing that it is very strange we should be told at this time of day that loyalty and slavery mean the same thing—tho' this is plainly the amount of that doctrine which some, even now, have the forehead to ventilate, in order to bring a reproach upon the Revolution, upon the present happy settlement of the crown, and to prepare us for the dutiful reception of an hereditary tyrant.[5]

It is moreover suggested by what has been said upon this subject, how much care and integrity should be exercis'd in the choice of those who are to have a share in government, that they may not be unworthy of it. If it ever happens in countries of liberty that the conduct of public affairs falls into the hands of weak or dishonest men, the people will scarce be the less miserable because they had the choice of these men themselves; tho' they will be the less to be pitied. People have in some countries been so regardless of their own welfare as to give too much encouragement to designing men who would practice upon them, yea, as to make an infamous merchandise of their hands and voices to the highest bidder, without any consideration of merit, of capacity, or inclination to serve the public. It is not easy to determine who are the most criminal—they who would make their way to places of power and trust by indirect means, or they who have so little concern for the welfare of their country as to hearken to them and to become the tools of their ambition and covetousness. And how faithfully they are likely to serve their country who set out with corrupting it, they who aspire to a part in the government by bribing the avaricious, by flattering the foolish, and making fine promises to the credulous, is not hard to conjecture.

Sir Thomas More tells us in his model of a commonwealth that the wise and virtuous Utopians "take an oath, before they proceed to an election, that they will choose him whom they think meetest for the office"; and that "if a man aspires to an office, he is sure never to compass it." [6] Some will perhaps think it a pity that it is only an Utopia, an imaginary region, where such maxims are said to prevail. People being under no undue influence would doubtless make a better choice than they often do in those places where importunity supplies the want of wisdom in the candidate, and the spirit of corruption, the spirit of patriotism. As to men of real worth, it is a pity they should be put upon violating their natural modesty by proclaiming their own superior qualifications for serving the public, and by soliciting an acknowledgment hereof. It is still harder that those who are most capable of serving their country should be obliged to reward others for the liberty of doing it. Such men should surely be made choice of, freely and voluntarily, without being forced, as it were, either to beg or to buy a confession of their great merit; especially because, in this case, some people of a jealous temper may be apt to suspect that they have something else more at heart than the good of their country. Indeed the experience of all ages has proved that men of the greatest merit do the most disdain those arts and practices of which others serve themselves with the unwary; and that those who are the most addicted to them are commonly the least fit to be trusted, either in respect of capacity or integrity, or both.

God forbid that ever such things should become fashionable and reputable amongst us, or that any son of New England should prove such a profane Esau as to sell his birthright! Our ancestors, tho' not perfect and infallible in all respects, were a religious, brave, and virtuous set of men,

---

[5] For Mayhew's early reading and continuing interest in literature of the divine right theory, see *Pamphlets*, ed. Bailyn, I, 205–206. Mayhew's allusion here is probably to the arguments supporting divine right which emerged in the newspaper controversy over his *Discourse Concerning Unlimited Submission*, especially in Thomas Fleet's *Boston Evening Post*. See Carl Bridenbaugh, *Mitre and Sceptre* (New York, 1962), 101–102.

[6] *Utopia* . . . trans. Gilbert Burnet (London, 1684), 76, 148. Mayhew has misquoted slightly.

whose love of liberty, civil and religious, brought them from their native land into the American deserts. By their generous care it is, under the smiles of a gracious providence, that we have now here a goodly heritage; and see these once desert and solitary places rejoicing and blossoming as the rose, the glory of Lebanon being given unto them, the excellency of Carmel and of Sharon. By the wisdom and piety of our forefathers it is, under that God who hath determined the bounds of all men's habitation, that we here enjoy many invaluable privileges, of which this day, amongst other things, is a proof and monument. Tho' we are not an independent state, yet, heaven be thanked! we are a free people. However, all know that it is not from our privileges and liberties, simply considered, but from the use we make of them, that our felicity is to be expected. And they are so great and ample that the right improvement of them cannot but make us happy, provided we have the virtue and honor to make such a one of them. Nor can I think we are so far degenerated from the laudable spirit of our ancestors as to despise and abuse what they procured for us at so dear a rate. I am not willing to believe we are running so fast into the evil practices and customs of other places, or so fond of imitating the fashionable follies and vices of any, even of those whom decency may perhaps require us to call "our betters," as some would insinuate that we are, and from hence prognosticate our destruction. No, I will not believe but that we fear God, reverence the memory of our forefathers, love our country and ourselves, more than to do thus; and that God will still give us to see the good of his chosen.

But long custom requires that upon this occasion I apply myself more particularly to our honored rulers; or, at least, custom will screen me from the imputation of presumption in doing it. To you, therefore, the legislators and political fathers of the country, I would now, with all proper humility and deference, direct my discourse.

I would not, much honored fathers, willingly go beyond my line in any respect. But surely I should forget the proper duty of my station if I did not embrace the opportunity which this day affords me to beseech you— as you fear God, whose ministers you are; as you love the country whose welfare depends upon you; as you regard that good name which is as "precious ointment" [Eccles. 7. 1], and "rather to be chosen than great riches" [Prov. 22. 1]; as you have any concern for posterity, even your own; as you would enjoy the blessed peace of a good conscience, in life and death; and, in fine, as you would be found of our common Judge in peace in the day of his appearing—if I did not beseech and exhort you by all these motives, to be faithful in the discharge of that trust which is devolved upon you by God and man; to let no unworthy views influence your conduct, but in all things to consult and prosecute the public good. You are very sensible, my fathers, that this is your indispensable duty. Your God, your King, your country, all expect this of you. Nor could you answer it to either of them—no, not even to yourselves—should you neglect it. It is, I trust, from a sense of duty to God in whose name I am now called to speak, and from an affectionate concern for the welfare of my dear, native country, not from a vain affectation of putting on the monitor towards my superiors, that I use this freedom of speech and such importunity. And if it serves in any measure by the blessing of God to awaken your zeal for his honor and for the prosperity of this people, the intent of it is answered.

There is but little probability that those who fear not God will much regard man, or that they who have not an habitual sense of his authority over themselves will exercise that which he has given them over others, as they ought to do. Be pleased, therefore, always to bear in mind that glorious Being who is ever with you; who spake all worlds into existence; whose power sustains and governs all things; in whose presence no seraph is unveiled; at whose frown, apostate spirits tremble; before whom all "the inhabitants of the earth are reputed as nothing" [Dan. 4. 35]; whose "eyes ever view, and whose eyelids try, the children of men; that righteous Lord who loveth righteousness" [Psal. 11. 4, 7]; and under whose administration all men shall at last find their account in an upright conduct, and in that alone. While you have a just sense of these things upon your minds, you will pursue no unworthy ends; you will have the interest of the public at heart; you will be inquisitive about the best measures of promoting it, and "attend continually upon this very thing" [Rom. 13. 6].

It is an important branch of the Legislature for the ensuing year that is this day to be chosen; a branch of great honor, weight, and influence in the government. Besides the known part which the gentlemen of that honorable board will have to act in a legislative capacity, they will have another which demands at least equal wisdom, equal uprightness, equal fortitude—that of "freely giving advice at all times to the Governor, for the good management of the public affairs of the government," according to the form of their oath. The world does not abound with persons in whom all those qualities concur which render them fit for advisers and counselors, even in matters of far less moment. But superior wisdom and discretion; a good knowledge of the nature of government in general, of the British in particular, of our charter rights, and this provincial constitution; a thorough acquaintance with the circumstances of the province, and with its true interests; a generous and public spirit; great honesty and intrepidity, such as will not waver with every gale of popular breath, or any other breath—these surely are the qualities which are naturally expected to be found in all who have a seat at that respectable board. Should there be ever seen hereafter (a supposition which I do not make without great reluctance)—but should there ever be seen hereafter at the council board a person of a low capacity, of little knowledge and discretion; one almost ignorant of the laws, government, and circumstances even of his own country; one of a narrow, selfish, avaricious turn; one of little integrity and little fortitude; one afraid to disclose his mind when advice is to be given "freely for the good management of the public affairs"—should such a one be ever seen hereafter at that board, this surely would not seem very agreeable to its known style and character of "honorable." And all who are concerned in the approaching election will regard those qualities which tend to support and justify that title, exercising a care proportionate to the importance and dignity of such a trust—I mean they will do so, provided they are actuated in this affair by such principles as become men and Christians: the principles of fidelity to God and love to the country. Taking it for granted therefore that these are the principles which will govern in the ensuing choice, in opposition to those of party, personal friendships, and personal enmities, and to all private interest—taking this for granted, I say—I would now beg leave, honored fathers, to mention some other things that may possibly deserve consideration, tho' with great submission and deference, knowing that to prescribe is not my province.

It may be worth considering whether we have not some laws in force hardly reconcilable with that religious liberty which we profess and which the royal Charter expressly requires should be preserved inviolate. A neighboring colony, we know, has lately been reprimanded on account of some laws of a persecuting aspect.[7] And whether some of our own are of a genius and complexion sufficiently abhorrent from the same spirit is not, perhaps, unworthy the consideration of the Legislature.

The state of our college can neither be forgotten nor enough lamented by those who wish to see learning duly honored and in a flourishing condition. Indeed if literature and the muses chiefly haunted where poverty resides—but this is * a threadbare topic. Long live the names of our venerable forefathers who did so much for the promotion of liberal science in the infant state of the country! Long, the names of all the generous benefactors to this seminary of learning! Long, the names of Harvard, Stoughton, Hollis, Berkeley! [8]

The want of some act effectually to settle claims and quiet possessions, especially in the frontiers of the Province, is much complained of by many; not merely as what renders private property too precarious, but also as what is prejudicial to the public, in more respects than one.

There is such a spirit in some respects now appearing and growing amongst us, as being duly encouraged by the Legislature cannot, with the ordinary blessing of providence, but be of happy consequence. We are grown pretty sensible of the importance of improving our lands, better than formerly, that so we may not be beholden for our daily bread unless it is to him to whom we pray for it. It is not improbable, from the late experiments of some public-spirited gentlemen, that we might have a valuable staple by means of that fruit which delights so much in our soil, as well as greatly lessen the importation of foreign liquors. Something considerable has of late been done towards the establishing of useful manufactures among us, none of which, it is to be hoped, will fall thro' and miscarry for want of proper encouragement from the government. The fishery now of late projected and carried on from this capital, cannot fail to be of great advantage to it in the low and declining state of its

[7] Perhaps Connecticut, criticized by the Committee of English Dissenters in England, to whom the Baptists in Connecticut frequently appealed. See M. Louise Greene, *The Development of Religious Liberty in Connecticut* (Boston, 1905), 275–280.

[8] John Harvard (1607–38) came to Charlestown from England in the spring of 1637 and died in September the following year, leaving the newly formed college in Cambridge his library, half his estate, and, unknown to him, his name. William Stoughton (1631–1701) was a Harvard graduate (1650), preacher, judge, and unrelenting condemner of witches; his benefactions to Harvard of land in Dorchester and funds to build Stoughton Hall, 1699—the first building given by an individual donor—"exceeded those of any other person during the century" (John Langdon Sibley and Clifford K. Shipton, *Biographical Sketches of Those Who Attended Harvard College*, 13 vols., Cambridge and Boston, 1873–1965, I, 203). For Thomas Hollis see p. 271n above; Rev. George Berkeley, Bishop of Cloyne (1685–1753), philosopher, friend of Swift and Pope, university projector, and sometime resident of Newport, Rhode Island, gave the Harvard Library a set of Greek and Roman classics, "most of them the best editions" (Josiah Quincy, *The History of Harvard University*, 2 vols., Boston, 1860, II, 481); he is unique in Mayhew's list only in that he gave a larger gift to Yale.

commerce, and indeed to the whole province—at least as long as the mortifying religion of lent is upheld in foreign countries.

To these things which have a favorable aspect may be added the zeal shown by many for the introduction of foreign Protestants. It is large importations of this sort, not of other European commodities, that has made one of our British provinces rich and populous in the course of a few years; so that, of an inconsiderable settlement, it now vies with the greatest and most opulent.[c] And that which may perhaps render it the more expedient thus to increase our numbers, is the probability that we shall before long have other employment than agriculture and the blessed arts of peace for many of our own people—I mean in curbing and chastising the insolence of our neighbors on the continent, neighbors whose perfidy renders them a more formidable enemy even in peace than either their number or bravery in war.

It is not a little surprising to many persons abroad that this government has been at no greater expense, and taken no more pains, to civilize the natives of the country, and to propagate amongst them the glorious Gospel of our Redeemer—especially considering one professed design of our forefathers in coming hither, our own high pretensions to religion, and our own interest.[9] Indeed there is some reason to fear that even the donations of persons abroad, and entrusted with others here in America for carrying on so pious and good a design, have not always been applied with that care, impartiality, and faithfulness, which might have been justly expected. But this not being a matter wherein the government is immediately concerned, I shall say no more of it; and some will perhaps think that even this is too much.

It is to be hoped that you, our honored rulers, will not neglect any

[c] Tho' the province alluded to has in fact been made both populous and rich by the introduction of foreigners, yet it is apprehended that some inconveniencies may arise hereafter, if they have not arisen already, for want of due precaution in the distribution of them, etc. Which inconveniencies will doubtless be guarded against by any others of our British colonies and plantations which shall bring in great numbers of such settlers—this not being impracticable, tho' there may be some difficulty attending it. And altho' it should be tho't that the Germans in Pennsylvania—however they had been dispos'd of and whatever precautions had been taken with regard to them—are too numerous in proportion to the other inhabitants, yet the Province of the Massachusetts is already so populous with English that there seems not to be the least or most remote danger here of too large importations of this nature.

[d] Query: Whether, if the Society for Propagating the Gospel in Foreign Parts was well acquainted with the state of religion in these parts of America, gentlemen of so great piety, charity, and loyalty, would not rather send missionaries among the

means that are proper to be used by the government, to humanize and Christianize these poor savages. Charity requires this, and requires it the more because they will otherwise be in great danger of apostatizing from their natural paganism and barbarity into that which is worse, the religion of Rome—a religion calculated rather to make men wicked than to keep them from being so, or to reform them after they are become so. We know the great pains and various artifices that are used by the Romish missionaries to convert them to this wicked religion. Nor can one well help calling to mind here the words of our blessed Savior: "Woe unto you! for ye compass sea and land to make one proselyte; and when he is made, ye make him twofold more the child of hell," etc. [Matt. 23. 15].

But, as was intimated before, were compassion to the souls of these miserable pagans wholly out of the case, even policy requires us to bring them if possible to embrace the Protestant faith. This would be one great means, amongst others not so proper to be mentioned in this place, of attaching them to the British interest—whereas they will, otherwise, probably be our enemies. And what sort of enemies we are to expect in them is no hard matter to conjecture, since the great duties which the missionaries of Rome inculcate upon their savage converts are those of butchering and scalping Protestants—generous enemies, doubtless, when their native ferocity is whetted and improved by a religion that naturally delights in blood and murder!

That which seems at present chiefly to engage the attention of the public is the British settlements on the continent being now, in a manner, encompassed by the French. And this is a matter of much more serious importance than it would be, were it not for the numerous tribes of warlike natives on our back, who, it is to be feared, are more generally disposed to fall in with that interest than with ours. The principal reason of which is, doubtless, this—that our politic neighbors take much more pains to gain them over than our colonies have hitherto done. Nor can it be thought a thing of less importance for us, by all means that are lawful and practicable, to secure the friendship of the one, than it is to put a stop to the encroachments of the other. Indeed, whoever has the friendship of most, or all, of these natives, may probably in time become masters of this part of the continent. Whether we, or they who are now making such a resolute push for it, heaven knows! [d]

⁹ Mayhew's father and grandfather were successful missionaries on Martha's Vineyard, where Jonathan grew up. See Akers, *Called unto Liberty*, 5–17.

The warlike preparations that are made and making in our southern colonies, prove that they are not unapprehensive of what may be the consequence of those quick advances and gigantic strides which the French are making towards us, the consequence of the strict alliances they are forming with those Indians who are already our enemies, of their endeavors to secure such as are yet neuters, and of their practices and many artifices to corrupt those who are in amity with us.[10] We, surely, who have always distinguished ourselves by a jealousy of our rights, by our loyalty, and our zeal for the common interest of his Majesty's dominions on the continent—we, surely, shall not be inattentive to these commotions, nor inactive when the general good, yea the very being, of all these colonies is threatened. Shall not be inattentive and inactive did I say? We are not, we cannot be. We see from the late conduct of our neighbors, from their recent encroachments and unprovoked hostilities (unless to breathe on our own territories be a provocation to such men)— we see from these things in what manner all controversies about bounds and limits are to be settled—how very amicably![11] Punic faith! unless perhaps Gallic is become sufficiently proverbial. No one that is not an absolute stranger to their ambition, to their policy, to their injustice, to their perfidiousness, can be in any doubt what they aspire at.

And indeed the progress they have made in a short time might seem strange, were it not for their union amongst themselves, and for the nature of their government. The slaves are content to starve at home in order to injure freemen abroad, and to extend their territories by violence and usurpation. Their late conduct may well alarm us, especially considering our disunion, or at least want of a sufficient bond of union amongst ourselves—an inconvenience which, it is to be hoped, we shall not always

savages (by which they might at once both enlarge the kingdom of Christ, and increase the number of his Majesty's friends and subjects), than continue to support missions here, where the people are already Christianized and also well able to maintain their own clergy? Some have suggested that the gentlemen of the worthy and honorable Society mentioned are not unacquainted with these circumstances. But is not this supposition very injurious? For if that is really the case, we must necessarily conclude they wretchedly pervert the design of the charities intrusted with them, and that their great aim in supporting these missions is not the converting of heathens to Christianity, but the converting of Christians of other Protestant denominations to the faith of the Church of England—an imputation so irreconcilable with their known probity, honor, and catholicism, that it can never be believed; and which must certainly bring shame upon the authors of it in the end! [Mayhew's lifelong battle against the Society erupted in his "frontal attack," *Observations on the Charter and Conduct of the Society for the Propagation of the Gospel in Foreign Parts* . . . (Boston, 1763). See Bridenbaugh, *Mitre and Sceptre*, 224–229.]

labor under. And whenever all our scattered rays shall be drawn to a point and proper focus, they can scarce fail to consume and burn up these enemies of our peace, how faintly soever they may strike at present. What union can do, we need only look towards those provinces which are distinguished by the name of the united, to know.[12] But in the meantime each government that considers its own true interest will undoubtedly * concur in such measures as are necessary and practicable for the common safety.

Our present situation, my fathers, calls to mind that of the tribes of Israel, surrounded and harassed by their common enemies, at a time when they were under no common direction. Then it was that "Judah said unto Simeon his brother, Come up with me into my lot, that we may fight against the Canaanites; and I also will go up with thee into thy lot. So Simeon went with him" [Judg. 1. 3]. Tho' peace is very desirable upon just and honorable terms, yet we know very well that God's ancient people were not wont to be frighted out of their possessions, nor patiently to endure the incursions and ravages of their neighbors. And I am sure

[10] In November 1753, Governor Dinwiddie of Virginia sent George Washington with a message of protest to the new forts built by the French in Northwestern Pennsylvania; the French commanders refused to recognize English claim to the territory. Washington's journal report of his mission was circulated to colonial Governors and England by March 1754. Virginia voted £10,000 to defend British settlers in the Ohio valley, and a fort was begun at the forks of the Ohio (now Pittsburgh), a site recommended by Washington. The French seized the fort in April before British troops could arrive, completed it, and named it Fort Duquesne. On May 28, the day before this sermon was preached, George Washington's troops fought the French at Great Meadows near what is today Farmington, Pennsylvania. See Bernhard Knollenberg, *George Washington: The Virginia Period, 1732–1775* (Durham, 1964), 11–20.

[11] The Treaty of Aix-La-Chapelle had left the boundary disputes between England and France to negotiation by special representatives. Counterclaims and legal arguments had dragged on for several years with little hope of amicable settlement, as Shirley well knew, having taken part in them in Paris. Meanwhile France continued to press forward and fortify the frontier. Mayhew's allusion here is to the recent news which shocked Boston to almost panic proportions, that French troops had moved into the upper Kennebec regions of Maine, perhaps preparatory to an invasion of Boston. An expedition was formed which failed to find any French troops. See Schutz, *William Shirley*, 174–179.

[12] In an address of April 2, 1754, Governor Shirley asked the House of Representatives to endorse the need for a plan of union for the colonies because "there is no time to be lost" (*Correspondence of William Shirley . . .* , ed. Charles Henry Lincoln, New York, 1912, II, 40–46). He had already suggested to the Board of Trade that the colonies be unified for purposes of defense (Schutz, *William Shirley*, 171). Benjamin Franklin's cartoon of a snake in eight pieces with the caption JOIN OR DIE, in his *Pennsylvania Gazette* of May 9, was reproduced in the *Boston Gazette* on May 12 and the *Boston News Letter* on May 23, five days before Mayhew's sermon.

there is not a true New England man whose heart is not already engaged in this contest, and whose purse, and his arm also if need be, is not ready to be employed in it; in a cause so just in the sight of God and man, a cause so necessary for our own self-defense, a cause wherein our liberties, our religion, our lives, our bodies, our souls, are all so nearly concerned. We have indeed of late done something to secure ourselves, and are doing more. We have "put our hand to the plough"; and he that "looks back" is so far from being worthy the privileges of a "citizen of heaven" [Luke 9. 62], that he is not worthy to enjoy the rights of an Englishman.

We are morally sure from the steps which our neighbors are taking that there must, sooner or later, be some great turn of affairs upon this continent which will put it out of our power, or out of theirs, to dispute about boundaries. We have heard their threats and insolent menaces; we have seen their more insolent behavior. And what a turn may be given to the affairs of Europe should heaven permit Gallic policy and perfidy to prevail here over English valor, I need not say and even tremble to think! We are peaceably extending our settlements upon our own territories; they are extending theirs beyond their own by force of arms. We must meet at length, which cannot be without a violent concussion, and the time seems not to be far off.[13] In short, their conduct must be very different from what it has all along been, especially of late, before we shall have any reason to think that we can live in peace and good neighborhood with them, how much soever we may desire it. The continent is not wide enough for us both, and they are resolved to have the whole. The Court of Versailles, for extending the French dominions in America, hath ever adopted this maxim: *Divide et Impera*;[14] and in pursuing it, hath stuck at no measures of perfidy,[e] or violence, for rooting out their neighbors.

And what horrid scene is this which restless, roving fancy, or something of an higher nature, presents to me, and so chills my blood! Do I behold these territories of freedom become the prey of arbitrary power? Do I see the motley armies of French and painted savages taking our fortresses, and erecting their own, even in our capital towns and cities!

[e] One flagrant instance of this appears in the murderous manner of Captain Howe's being killed in the year 1750 at Chiegnecto, by a party of Indians in the interest and under the direction of the French, in presence of Monsieur Le Corne, their commandant, when he was received by them under the protection of a flag of truce— for which outrage no other cause can be assigned than that he had distinguish'd himself by his activity in the service of his King and country against the attempts of the French in those parts.

Do I behold them spreading desolation thro' the land! Do I see the slaves of Louis with their Indian allies dispossessing the freeborn subjects of King George of the inheritance received from their forefathers, and purchased by them at the expense of their ease, their treasure, their blood! To aggravate the indignity beyond human toleration, do I see this goodly patrimony ravished from them by those who never knew what property was, except by seizing that of others for an insatiable Lord! Do I see Christianity banished for popery! the Bible, for the mass-book! the oracles of truth, for fabulous legends! Do I see the sacred edifices erected here to the honor of the true God and his Son on the ruins of pagan superstition and idolatry, erected here, where Satan's seat was—do I see these sacred edifices laid in ruins themselves! and others rising in their places, consecrated to the honor of saints and angels! Instead of a train of Christ's faithful, laborious ministers, do I behold an herd of lazy monks, and Jesuits, and exorcists, and inquisitors, and cowled and uncowled impostors! Do I see a Protestant there, stealing a look at his Bible, and, being taken in the fact, punished like a felon! What indignity is yonder offered to the matrons! and here, to the virgins! Is it now a crime to reverence the hoary head! And is he alone happy that taketh the little ones and dasheth them against the stones! Do I see all liberty, property, religion, happiness, changed, or rather transubstantiated, into slavery, poverty, superstition, wretchedness! And, in fine, do I hear the miserable sufferers (those of them that survive) bitterly accusing the negligence of the public guardians! and charging all their calamities less upon the enemies than upon the fathers of their country! O dishonest! profane! execrable sight! O piercing sound! that "entereth into the ears of the Lord of sabaoth" [Jas. 5. 4]! Where! in what region! in what world am I! Is this imagination (its own busy tormentor)? Or is it something more divine? I will not, I cannot believe 'tis prophetic vision, or that God has so far abandoned us!

And how different a scene is now opening upon me with clearer indications of truth and reality! There, insolence and injustice punished! Here, "the meek inheriting the earth" [Matt. 5. 5; Psal. 37. 11]! Liberty victorious! Slavery biting her own chain! Pride brought down! Virtue exalted! Christianity triumphing over imposture! And another Great

---

[13] If George Washington's fight with the French on May 28 is considered the beginning, then the French and Indian War had just begun.

[14] "Divide and conquer," an old Roman adage.

Britain rising in America! But I must not declare the whole—"the Lord God omnipotent reigneth [Rev. 19. 6]! Just and true are all thy ways, O thou King of saints [Rev. 15. 3]. And them that walk in pride thou art able to abase" [Dan. 4. 37]! "What has pride profited! Or what good hath vaunting brought you," ye restless disturbers of our peace! What good, your masses, your relics, your crossings, your Ave Maria's? "And to which of your saints will ye now turn" [Job 5. 1]!

But we are not, my honored fathers, to presume on God's protection, much less on his giving us any signal advantages over them that are ever either planning or executing mischief against us, without using the proper means for obtaining that protection and these advantages. As the apostle said to the mariners after assuring them of deliverance from the impending danger, "Except these abide in the ship, ye cannot be saved" [Acts 27. 31]; so it may be said to our British colonies, "Ye cannot be saved from the storm you are now threatened with, yea which is already begun, except ye are at union amongst yourselves, and exert your strength together for your common interest. Upon this condition you are safe even without a miracle; otherwise, nothing short of one can save you. And can you without the utmost indignation think of becoming a prey to those who are so much inferior to you in all respects, merely for want of unanimity, public spirit, the manly resolution of your forefathers, and a little expense!"

It is not, may it please your Excellency (for to you, Sir, I must now beg leave more particularly to direct my discourse), it is not one of the least felicities of this province to have at the head of it a gentleman so well acquainted with its true interest, so capable of serving it, and so heartily disposed to do it, as we have reason to think your Excellency is.[15] We have had experience of your warm zeal for his Majesty's service and for the welfare of this his most loyal province. In the long war during your administration, had all concerned been, I will not presume to say equally faithful, but equally successful, neither the European nor the American Dunkirk would probably have been a port and fortification at this day; or, which is still better, they might have been in other hands than they are at present. However, we in some measure reap the happy fruits of your subjecting the latter of them to the British crown, in the change of our medium; and are likely, by God's blessing, to reap them in much greater perfection hereafter when time has matur'd them.[16]

The zeal which your Excellency has lately shown with relation to the encroachments and hostilities of our bad neighbors gives us assurance, Sir, that nothing will be wanting on your part towards their meeting with timely and effectual opposition. And the ready concurrence of the other branches of the legislature with what you were * pleased to propose to the last General Assembly, at once shows the confidence that is placed in you, and renders it probable at least that no necessary supplies will be wanting hereafter in order to prosecute designs of this nature—whether of erecting fortresses for our own security, or of demolishing in season those of our injurious and trespassing neighbors.[17] Crown Point, Crown Point, will surely be a lasting monument of the danger of delays in such cases! [18]

It is upon your Excellency, under God and the King, that we chiefly depend for protection and happiness. We are sensible how much you have the union of these colonies at heart. Nor can we, without an implicit taxing of your former administration, which we would be far from doing, doubt but that for the future you will use all your power and influence for the good of this province in particular, and of all his Majesty's dominions on

[15] William Shirley (1694–1771) came to Boston in 1731 and was appointed Governor of Massachusetts in May 1741. He helped build up defenses and was the mastermind of a successful siege of Louisburg, June 17, 1745, during the war with France. Having just returned from a leave in London and Paris, 1749–53, he was preparing both London and Massachusetts for more conflict. George Arthur Wood's biography of Shirley up through 1745, *William Shirley, Governor of Massachusetts, 1741–1756: A History* . . . (New York, 1920), is superseded by Schutz' study.

[16] An expedition of New England soldiers, sloops, and British ships captured Louisburg, "the American Dunkirk," in June 1745. To Massachusetts' chagrin, the fort was returned to the French in the Treaty of Aix-La-Chapelle in 1748. Britain's reimbursement to Massachusetts of £183,649 for the expedition's expenses enabled the Colony to retire its depreciated paper money and substitute a "hard money" currency based on silver reserves. Thomas Prince used the phrase "Dunkirk of North America" in a pamphlet of 1745 (Schutz, *William Shirley*, 79) and it seems to have become a popular phrase, for Thomas Hutchinson also uses it in *The History of the Colony and Province of Massachusetts-Bay,* ed. Lawrence Shaw Mayo, 3 vols. (Cambridge, 1936), II, 311.

[17] In December 1753, the legislature rejected Shirley's proposals for fortifying frontier garrisons like Fort Dummer; with the more recent scare of French invasion of Maine, however (see n. 11 above), and the Board of Trade's announcement of a conference of all colonies at Albany to discuss defense and Indian alliances, the legislature in April 1754 supported Shirley's request for mobilizing militia companies for Maine, reinforcements for garrison posts, and delegates for the Albany Conference. See Schutz, *William Shirley*, 169–176.

[18] Shirley had advocated attacks on the French fort at Crown Point in 1746 and again in 1748. (For the causes of delay see Schutz, *William Shirley*, 115–120, 133–134.) By the time of Shirley's return from England in 1753, Crown Point had become the symbol of French armed strength on the frontier, and was being referred to in Boston newspapers as "the American Carthage."

this continent in general. You will never forget, Sir, whose minister you are; what God, the King, and this people reasonably expect from you considering the paternal relation in which you stand towards us.

In some respects we have peculiar need of a faithful and skillful pilot at this time. By the looks of the clouds we are to expect bad weather, such as will require an experienced and resolute mariner to carry us safely and happily thro' it. But if that which has the appearance of a long and violent storm gathering or rather actually breaking upon us should soon blow over and leave us a clear sky, yet even when the heavens are serene and the gale prosperous, it demands at least an upright heart (such a one as we trust your Excellency is possessed of) to keep the state in the right channel, and steer her to her true felicity.

And as we are confident, Sir, you will in all things do the duty of a good Governor towards us, so it is to be hoped that your public services will never meet with an ungrateful return from us. But I may venture at least to assure your Excellency that none of your good deeds shall be forgotten by our common Master in heaven. He whose providence has put you into this place of honor and trust will surely recompense all the diligence and fidelity which you have shown in it already, or shall show hereafter, "at the resurrection of the just" [Luke 14. 14]. Nor can we wish you, Sir, any greater felicity than that you may in every respect discharge this important trust in such a manner as to have his approbation at the last, and to be accounted a "good and faithful servant" [Matt. 25. 21, 23].

I could not with propriety and in due consistency with the established form of our government apply myself particularly to his Majesty's Council for the present political year, now expiring, unless it were with relation to the new election this afternoon, wherein they are to bear a part. But having nothing to add upon that subject to what has been said already to them in common with others concerned, it is humbly hoped that the omission of a particular address to that honorable board will not be imputed even to forgetfulness, much less to any disrespect.

The honorable House of Representatives, at the command of whose predecessors it is that I appear in this place, will indulge me in a short application to them.

As you, honored gentlemen, are delegated immediately by the good people of the province to represent and act for them, you are, if possible, under a nearer and stricter obligation to regard their welfare than the other branches of the legislature. You are more particularly the guardians of their rights and privileges. It is therefore to be presumed that you will always be zealous to maintain them; and not only so, but in all things, studious of their real and best interest. Private, personal interest, you are very sensible, has nothing to do in the supreme Court of the province. You are not deputed hereto by your constituents, gentlemen, that you may prosecute your particular interests or the interests of others any farther than they coincide with the common good and are involved in it. Nor can you be at any loss what ought to be done to the vile, mercenary tongue that should toil; what to the guilty hand, that "right hand of falsehood" [Psal. 144. 8], which should either be lifted up or kept down to serve the particular ends of any man or party whatever, to the detriment of the public! Such things are indeed almost too infamous and horrid to be supposed possible in a Christian country. But alas! it is a degenerate world, if not a corrupt age of it, that we live in!

However, it were very injurious to suspect, honored gentlemen, but that you are all assembled here from different parts of the land with upright views and an ardent love to your country. And if you mean to serve the public, as doubtless you do, you will always "study the things that make for peace" [Rom. 14. 19], both amongst yourselves and with the other branches of the legislature. For it is by these things only that the commonwealth is edified; not, surely, by party disputes and factions; not by indulged animosities and studied oppositions which greatly dishonor and weaken any government, and have both their origin and end in evil. They who promote and foment them have always something else in view than what they would be tho't to have, the public good. This is indeed always the pretense; but private pique, or private interest, or a general temper and turn to wrangling, is at the bottom. It is, usually at least, the pursuit of separate, distinct interests, and a want of public spirit, that is the source of party and contentions in any state. When all are united heartily in the main end, having nothing so much in view as the good of the public, party names, distinctions, and disputes vanish of course, and that unanimity and harmony take place which give both beauty and strength to government, and without which the public affairs cannot be carried on to advantage. A public spirit is a spirit of union; and union is the source of public happiness; and public happiness is the great end which you should have in view.

As you, honored gentlemen, have a distinct part in the legislature, nothing considerable can be done without you for the public good—and I may add, or contrary to it, tho' I am far from thinking that this is designed by any. God forbid! But the granting of monies, a thing of the utmost importance, lies more immediately with you. And tho' you will always have a tender concern for the interest of your respective constituents, yet you will have a greater for the good of the whole province—to be sure, for the common interest of his Majesty's dominions on this continent. Nor will you be over thrifty, when that calls for liberality. And this will probably be the case before it is long, if it is not actually so already.

I speak now with particular reference to the necessary defense of this, and all these colonies, against those who are making inroads upon us, and who have even within the space of a few weeks had the hardiness to commit such hostilities as are not to be endured, unless we are determined to sit down in inglorious ease and patiently to look on, while our trade with the natives is ravished from us, our fortresses taken, our friends and brethren captivated, butchered, scalped, our fields laid waste, our territories possessed by those that hate us, and the British interest on the continent brought to nothing. Peace is a great blessing; peace is what we would choose; peace is the desire of all who deserve the name of Christians. But shall the trumpet sleep? Shall the sword rust? Shall our gold and silver lie cankering in our coffers? [19] Shall our military garments be motheaten for want of use, when such things are doing! It is impossible, gentlemen, you should be any ways backward or parsimonious in such a cause as this, a cause wherein the glory of God, the honor of your King, and the good of your country, are so deeply concerned—I might perhaps add, a cause whereon the liberties of Europe depend. For of so great consequence is the empire of North America (and that, you are sensible, is the thing now aimed at by our neighbors), that it must turn the scale of power greatly in favor of the only monarch from whom those liberties are in danger, and against that prince who is the grand support and bulwark of them. Consider then, gentlemen, in the name of God, consider what you owe him and to your holy religion; what to the Protestant in-

---

ᶠ A certain part of this community (which surely there is no need of mentioning!) has fallen under such great decays and difficulties of late thro' that same providence which has been smiling upon the other parts of the province, that I verily believe righteous heaven will be justly and greatly provoked unless some pity and relief is afforded to it. Poor Boston! once the glory of British America, what art thou coming to! What, rather, art thou come to already!

terest in general; what to your King and to Great Britain in particular; what to your native country; what to the honor of your ancestors; what to the present generation; what to future ones; what to yourselves; and what to those whom the God of nature has made dearer to you than yourselves, your children. It is even uncertain, gentlemen, how long you will have an house to sit in unless a speedy and vigorous opposition is made to the present encroachments and to the farther designs of our enemies! This, surely, is not a time to be saving, unless in our private expenses.

And while I am speaking of grants for the common good, I cannot but just add that neither the honor of the province can be promoted at present, nor its true interest in the end, by great parsimony towards those who serve the public in a public capacity and receive salaries from it. There is another thing which I would beg leave to hint at here. So far, honored gentlemen, as fixing the proportion which the different parts of the community are respectively to bear in the public expenses lies with you, you will doubtless be far from desiring that any particular part should bear a greater proportion than is just and equal, being regulated by its ability and circumstances relatively considered. You are too religious, just, and impartial to desire this.[f]

In fine, honored gentlemen, I persuade myself that you will in all your debates and consultations, in all you do in your political as well as private capacity, remember you are to give an account of yourselves to the all-knowing, all-just, and impartial Judge of the world. And if you keep this most solemn and awful truth uppermost in your minds, it will be almost impossible for you to do amiss. You will then act in all respects with such a disinterested view to the common good of your country, with such unblemished, irreproachable integrity as will be both acceptable to God your Savior and to those for whom you act; with such prudence and fidelity at least as will afford no handle to persons of captious tempers and licentious tongues, under the pretext of blaming former houses, to couch a real and just sarcasm on the present.

If anything has been said in this discourse not sufficiently conformable to the usual style of the pulpit; if anything that approaches too near to politics; if the discourse has not been enough confined to matters altogether spiritual; if our temporal and worldly concernments have been too long

[19] See Jas. 5. 3.

dwelt upon; in fine, if there has been any greater liberty of speech used; if any greater pathos of expression than becomes an English subject, a lover of his country, and a Protestant minister, upon such an occasion and at such a juncture as the present—if this is the case, as perhaps it is, the great candor of the audience is humbly relied on to make the most favorable apology that the nature of the thing will admit of for him that has thus transgressed. And that will be at least as good a one as any he could make for himself, should he attempt one. But an apology would certainly be necessary in another respect, were this discourse protracted to a much greater length. My reverend fathers and brethren in the ministry will therefore readily excuse me if I do not honor myself by a particular address to them, as is customary upon these occasions—tho' the subject I have been upon is very applicable not only to civil rulers but also to those whom our blessed Lord has "counted faithful, putting them into the ministry" [I Tim. 1. 12].

However, I cannot conclude without just reminding this great assembly that all men have certain talents committed to them for which they are accountable to him that gave them. The least and lowest of us need not live without honoring God in some way or other and being in a degree serviceable to the world. Nor shall anyone that is faithful to his trust lose his reward, tho' he is so far from being in a capacity to do great and extensive good in his generation that he can only "give a cup of cold water to a disciple in the name of a disciple" [Matt. 10. 42]. For "if there be first a willing mind, it is accepted according to that a man hath, and not according to that he hath not" [II Cor. 8. 12].

As we have many members in one body, and all members have not the same office: So we, being many, are one body in Christ, and members one of another. Having then gifts differing according to the grace that is given to us, whether ministry, let us wait on our ministering: Or he that exhorteth, on exhortation; he that giveth, let him do it in simplicity; he that ruleth, with diligence [Rom. 12. 4–8].

And in all of us, "let love be without dissimulation," while we "abhor that which is evil and cleave to that which is good" [Rom. 12. 9]. Thus thro' faith and patience in well-doing shall we at length "inherit the promises" [Heb. 6. 12]; for "he is faithful that has promised" [Heb. 10. 23].

We must unavoidably concern ourselves in some measure about the things of this mortal life so long as it shall please the Father of spirits to continue us in it. But our great interest lies in another region far beyond the sphere and verge of mortality. And whosoever is faithful to the death shall receive a crown of life that fadeth not. There is nothing here, men, brethren, and fathers! there is nothing here that can claim our highest love and affections. "All that cometh is vanity" [Eccles. 11. 8]. Riches take to themselves wings; pleasures pall; "favor is deceitful and beauty is vain" [Prov. 31. 30]. "All things are full of change" [20] and in perpetual rotation. "The fashion of the world passeth away" [I Cor. 7. 31]; and God alone is without "variableness" and "shadow of turning" [Jas. 1. 17]. Even all the kingdoms of the earth, tho' they had their foundations laid in iron and brass and adamant must sooner or later be dissolved and their place be nowhere found. All empire shall be blotted out excepting his, "of whom, and thro' whom, and to whom, are all things" [Rom. 11. 36]. All shall terminate in a monarchy, truly universal. The kingdom of the glorious Mediator shall first break in pieces, consume, and absorb all inferior ones.[21] And when he shall have "put down all rule and all authority and power and subdued all things unto himself, then cometh the end," when, as the Scriptures inform us, even he shall no longer reign, but "deliver up the kingdom to God, even the Father, that put all things under him, that God may be All in All" [I Cor. 15. 24, 27, 28].

THE END. [22]

[20] See Eccles. 1. 8.

[21] See Dan. 2. 44.

[22] The following is printed in the pamphlet at the conclusion of the sermon: "Errors of the Press that have escaped are left to the judgment and candor of the reader to correct."

VIII SAMUEL COOKE'S
SERMON OF 1770

AN INTRODUCTION

THE Boston massacre on March 5, 1770, killed four people. While the citizens awaited the outcome of a trial of the British soldiers who fired on the mob, Thomas Hutchinson learned he was to be the new Governor of Massachusetts and received instructions to move the General Court to Cambridge. As he looked into the future, "he had the prospect of a succession of uncommon difficulties, for a long time to come."[1]

It soon became evident that the Boston Representatives did not want the new assembly to be held in Cambridge at Harvard College. Although on several earlier occasions the Court had been moved to Cambridge, Salem, or Concord, the inhabitants of Boston seized on the present removal as symbolic of far deeper infringements of their liberties and rights with "words more open and express than had been before ventured on," in their *Instructions from the Town of Boston to Their Representatives, May 15, 1770.*[2] Jealous of their election day ceremonies and holiday, "the selectmen and many of the principal inhabitants" of Boston asked Dr. Chauncy "as senior minister of the town" to preach to them at the Old South Church, while "less than common" the number of Representatives met officially at Cambridge.[3]

[1] Thomas Hutchinson, *The History of the Colony and Province of Massachusetts-Bay*, ed. Lawrence Shaw Mayo, 3 vols. (Cambridge, 1936), III, 207.
[2] *Ibid.*, 209. The *Instructions* . . . are printed in "Appendix R" of *ibid.*, 370–377.
[3] *Ibid.*, 209.

Election day began at nine o'clock. The Representatives took their oaths and elected Samuel Adams as Clerk and Thomas Cushing as Speaker. Thomas Hutchinson, still officially Lieutenant-Governor, arrived from Milton at ten o'clock, "escorted by his troop of Guards." An hour later the Lieutenant-Governor, Council, and Representatives, "and some other gentlemen," preceded by Brigadier Brattle's First Cambridge Company of Militia, moved in procession to Cambridge's Second Church where its minister, Samuel Cooke, delivered the annual election sermon.[4]

Cooke's sermon stands with Barnard's in 1734 as one of the finest reviews of enlightened political theory in the history of Massachusetts election sermons. Although his appeal to reduce slavery is new, there is little else that is not either a repetition or a projection of ideas announced in election sermons of the last forty years. Its force lies rather in its comprehensiveness; it says it all for 1770. The election sermon had not traditionally been the place to announce new ideas; its strength had been in its opportunity to absorb, summarize, and catalog. It had been the occasion to popularize the ideas of others, to select and direct the political ideas of the church, which would then flow out into each town in the Colony. With only the election sermons as evidence, it would be difficult to chart the origin of new concepts and shifts in emphasis in political ideas. They accrue and change each year gradually and subtly. And yet to contrast Cooke's sermon with its counterparts on political theory a century earlier is to see how different they are. Cooke's sermon has few Biblical quotations and references; it is more disinterested, more philosophical than the earlier Biblical sermons. It blends a presentation of ideas because they come from God with a presentation of ideas because they are true and reasonable in themselves. Many of the principles on which the Declaration of Independence rests are already here: Civil government is an ordinance of God; only the people have the right to choose who will rule them; government must contain a balance of power with built-in checks (a subject he returns to for special emphasis); people have a "right" to good government; a ruler will not forget that his subjects are

---

[4] The *Boston Evening-Post*, June 4, 1770. Samuel Cooke (1709–83) was born at Hadley and graduated from Harvard in 1735. He became a schoolmaster and tutor, did graduate work, preached at several churches, and in September 1739 was ordained minister of the newly formed First Congregational Church of Menotomy (now Arlington). Cooke was chosen chaplain of the General Court in the spring of 1776. He published several sermons which contributed to the growing unrest with British rule in America.

"by nature equal" to himself; the people will be subjected to no restrictions not founded on reason; laws must be clear and explicit; the constitution of a government must not be supported by a standing army (as with the present King's directives to Massachusetts); freedom of speech is a "right inherent in the people." Although he hopes for a reconciliation of the differences with Britain, his review of colonial history—the first Charter and the revolution against Andros—is clear in intent; America has a right to enjoy and direct her own domain—a right sanctioned not only by God (the chosen people motif takes on new political meaning), but now by almost one hundred and fifty years of history.

Cooke's sermon has its own style. The paragraphs are short, the majority of them containing only one sentence. The prose is jerky; smooth transitions are sacrificed to a note-form style, an unfolding catalog of statements. Bernard Bailyn comments that much of the pamphlet literature of the time is aphoristic and singles out Cooke's sermon, "a mosaic of aphorisms," as an example.[5] Cooke may be modeling his style on this aspect of the journalistic writing of his day, but there is another explanation. There are times when the sermon has the ring of the Bible, especially Ecclesiastes. Cooke is writing in verses. Blending the ideas of Locke with the idiom and structure of Biblical verse, he creates a new kind of psalm, an experiment in a vehicle that will transmit the new ideas with the echoes and cadences of the authoritative Word of God. We must remember that this was written for the ear, not the eye. The form Cooke has developed is less a discussion, in the tradition of the essay, than an announcement of laws, precepts, and rights that have already been discussed or, in the case of his model, the Bible, handed down from God.

[5] *Pamphlets of the American Revolution,* ed. Bernard Bailyn (Cambridge, 1965), I, 12.

A

S E R M O N

PREACHED AT CAMBRIDGE,

IN THE

AUDIENCE OF HIS HONOR

THOMAS HUTCHINSON, Esq;

LIEUTENANT-GOVERNOR AND COMMANDER IN CHIEF ;

THE HONORABLE

HIS MAJESTY's COUNCIL,

AND THE HONORABLE

HOUSE OF REPRESENTATIVES,

OF THE PROVINCE OF THE

Maſſachuſetts-Bay in *New-England,*

MAY 30th, 1770.

BEING THE ANNIVERSARY FOR THE ELECTION OF HIS
MAJESTY's. COUNCIL FOR THE SAID PROVINCE.

BY SAMUEL COOKE, A.M.

Paſtor of the Second Church in CAMBRIDGE.

B O S T O N :

PRINTED BY 'EDES AND GILL, PRINTERS TO THE
HONORABLE HOUSE OF REPRESENTATIVES.

MDCCLXX.

An Election Sermon.

"HE THAT ruleth over men must be just, ruling in the fear of God."

"And he shall be as the light of the morning, when the sun riseth, even a morning without clouds; as the tender grass springing out of the earth by clear shining after rain" (II Sam. 23. 3, 4).

The solemn introduction to the words now read, respectable hearers, is manifestly designed to engage your attention and regard, as given by inspiration from God, and as containing the last, the dying words, of one of the greatest and best of earthly rulers, who by ruling in the fear of God had served his generation according to the divine Will. Transporting reflection! when his flesh and his heart failed, and his glory was consigned to dust.

From this and many other passages in the sacred Oracles, it is evident that the supreme Ruler, tho' he has directed to no particular mode of civil government, yet allows and approves of the establishment of it among men.

The ends of civil government in divine Revelation are clearly pointed out, the character of rulers described, and the duty of subjects asserted and explained. And in this view civil government may be considered as an ordinance of God; and when justly exercised, greatly subservient to

327

the glorious purposes of divine providence and grace. But the particular form is left to the choice and determination of mankind.

In a pure state of nature, government is in a great measure unnecessary; private property in that state is inconsiderable, men need no arbiter to determine their rights; they covet only a bare support; their stock is but the subsistence of a day; the uncultivated deserts are their habitations; and they carry their all with them in their frequent removes; they are each one a law to himself, which in general is of force sufficient for their security in that course of life.

It is far otherwise when mankind are formed into collective bodies or a social state of life; here, their frequent mutual intercourse, in a degree, necessarily leads them to different apprehensions respecting their several rights, even where their intentions are upright. Temptations to injustice and violence increase and the occasions of them multiply in proportion to the increase and opulence of the society.

The laws of nature, though enforced by divine Revelation, which bind the conscience of the upright, prove insufficient to restrain the sons of violence who have not the fear of God before their eyes.

A society cannot long subsist in such a state. Their safety, their social being depends upon the establishment of determinate rules or laws with proper penalties to enforce them, to which individuals shall be subjected. The laws, however wisely adapted, cannot operate to the public security unless they are properly executed. The execution of them, remaining in the hands of the whole community, leaves individuals to determine their own rights, and in effect, in the same circumstances, as in a state of nature.

The remedy in this case is solely in the hands of the community.

A society emerging from a state of nature, in respect to authority are all upon a level; no individual can justly challenge a right to make or execute the laws by which it is to be governed, but only by the choice or general consent of the community. The people, the collective body only, have a right under God to determine who shall exercise this trust for the common interest, and to fix the bounds of their authority.

And consequently, unless we admit the most evident inconsistence, those in authority, in the whole of their public conduct, are accountable to the society which gave them their political existence.

This is evidently the natural origin and state of all civil government, the sole end and design of which is not to ennoble a few and enslave the multitude, but the public benefit, the good of the people, that they may be protected in their persons and secured in the enjoyment of all their rights, and be enabled to lead quiet and peaceable lives in all godliness and honesty.

While this manifest design of civil government, under whatever form, is kept in full view, the reciprocal obligations of rulers and subjects are obvious, and the extent of prerogative and liberty will be indisputable.

In a civil state, that form is the most eligible which is best adapted to promote the ends of government, the benefit of the community; reason and experience teach that a mixed government is most conducive to this end.

In the present imperfect state, the whole power cannot with safety be entrusted with a single person, nor with many acting jointly in the same public capacity.

Various branches of power concentring in the community from which they originally derive their authority, are a mutual check to each other in their several departments and jointly secure the common interest. This may indeed, in some instances, retard the operations of government, but will add dignity to its deliberate counsels and weight to its dictates.

This, after many dangerous conflicts with arbitrary power, is now the happy constitution of our parent state. We rejoice in the gladness of our nation—may no weapon formed against it prosper—may it be preserved inviolate till time shall be no more.

This, under God, has caused Great Britain to exalt her head above the nations—restored the dignity of royal authority—and rendered our kings truly benefactors.

The prince upon the British throne can have no real interest distinct from his subjects; his crown is his inheritance; his kingdom his patrimony, which he must be disposed to improve for his own and his family's interest; his highest glory is to rule over a free people and reign in the hearts of his subjects. The peers who are lords of parliament are his hereditary council. The Commons, elected by the people, are considered as the grand inquest of the kingdom, and while incorrupt, are a check upon the highest offices in the state.

A constitution thus happily formed and supported, as a late writer has observed, cannot easily be subverted but by the prevalence of venality in the representatives of the people.

How far septennial parliaments conduce to this, time may further show. Or whether this is not an infraction upon the national constitution is not for me to determine.

But the best constitution, separately considered, is only as a line which marks out the inclosure, or as a fitly organized body without spirit or animal life.

The advantages of civil government, even under the British form, greatly depend upon the character and conduct of those to whom the administration is committed.

When the righteous are in authority the people rejoice; but when the wicked beareth rule, the people mourn.

The most High, therefore, who is just in all his ways—good to all—and whose commands strike dread, has strictly enjoined faithfulness upon all those who are advanced to any place of public trust.

Rulers of this character cooperate with God in his gracious dispensations of providence and under him are diffusive blessings to the people—and are compared to the light of the morning when the sun riseth, even a morning without clouds.

By the ruler in the text is intended not only the king as supreme, but also everyone in subordinate place of power and trust, whether they act in a legislative or executive capacity or both. In whatever station men act for the public they are included in this general term—and must direct their conduct by the same upright principle.

Justice as here expressed is not to be taken in a limited sense, but as a general term, including every quality necessary to be exercised for the public good by those who accept the charge of it.

Justice must be tempered with wisdom, prudence, and clemency; otherwise it will degenerate into rigor and oppression.

This solemn charge given to rulers is not an arbitrary injunction imposed by God, but is founded in the most obvious laws of nature and reason.

Rulers are appointed for this very end—"to be ministers of God for good" [Rom. 13. 4]. The people have a right to expect this from them and to require it, not as an act of grace but as their unquestionable due. It is the express or implicit condition upon which they were chosen and continued in public office that they attend continually upon this very thing.

Their time—their abilities—their authority, by their acceptance of the public trust, are consecrated to the community and cannot in justice be withheld; they are obliged to seek the welfare of the people and exert all their powers to promote the common interest.

This continual solicitude for the common good, however depressing it may appear, is what rulers of every degree have taken upon themselves; and in justice to the people—in faithfulness to God—they must either sustain it with fidelity or resign their office.

The first attention of the faithful ruler will be to the subjects of government in their specific nature. He will not forget that he ruleth over men—men who are of the same species with himself and by nature equal —men who are the offspring of God, and alike formed after his glorious image—men of like passions and feelings with himself, and as men, in the sight of their common Creator of equal importance—men who have raised him to power and support him in the exercise of it—men who are reasonable beings and can be subjected to no human restrictions which are not founded in reason, and of the fitness of which they may be convinced—men who are moral agents and under the absolute control of the high Possessor of heaven and earth and cannot, without the greatest impropriety and disloyalty to the King of kings, yield unlimited subjection to any inferior power—men whom the Son of God hath condescended to ransom and dignified their nature by becoming the son of man.

Men who have the most evident right in every decent way to represent to rulers their grievances and seek redress.

The people forfeit the rank they hold in God's creation when they silently yield this important point and sordidly, like Issachar, couch under every burden wantonly laid upon them.

And rulers greatly tarnish their dignity when they attempt to treat their subjects otherwise than as their fellowmen—men who have reposed the highest confidence in their fidelity and to whom they are accountable for their public conduct. And in a word, men among whom they must without distinction stand before the dread tribunal of heaven.

Just rulers therefore in making and executing the laws of society will consider who they are to oblige, and accommodate them to the state and condition of men.

Fidelity to the public requires that the laws be as plain and explicit as possible, that the less knowing may understand and not be ensnared by them—while the artful evade their force.

Mysteries of law and government may be made a cloak of unrighteousness.

The benefits of the constitution and of the laws must extend to every branch and each individual in society, of whatever degree, that every man may enjoy his property and pursue his honest course of life with security.

The just ruler, sensible he is in trust for the public, with an impartial hand will supply the various offices in society; his eye will be upon the faithful—merit only in the candidate will attract his attention.

He will not without sufficient reason multiply lucrative offices in the community, which naturally tends to introduce idleness and oppression.

Justice requires that the emoluments of every office constituted for the common interest be proportioned to their dignity and the service performed for the public. Parsimony in this case enervates the force of government and frustrates the most patriotic measures. A people therefore for their own security must be supposed willing to pay tribute to whom it is due, and freely support the dignity of those under whose protection they confide.

On the other hand, the people may apprehend they have just reason to complain of oppression and wrong and to be jealous of their liberties, when subordinate public offices are made the surest step to wealth and ease.

This not only encreases the expenses of government but is naturally productive of dissipation and luxury, of the severest animosities among candidates for public posts, and of venality and corruption—the most fatal to a free state.

Rulers are appointed guardians of the constitution in their respective stations and must confine themselves within the limits by which their authority is circumscribed.

A free state will no longer continue so than while the constitution is maintained entire in all its branches and connections. If the several members of the legislative power become entirely independent of each other, it produceth a schism in the body politic; and the effect is the same when the executive is in no degree under the control of the legislative power—the balance is destroyed and the execution of the laws left to arbitrary will.

The several branches of civil power, as joint pillars each bearing its due proportion, are the support and the only proper support of a political structure regularly formed.

A constitution which cannot support its own weight must fall. It must be supposed essentially defective in its form or administration.

Military aid has ever been deemed dangerous to a free civil state and often has been used as an effectual engine to subvert it.

Those who in the camp and in the field of battle are our glory and defense, from the experience of other nations will be thought in time of peace a very improper safeguard to a constitution which has liberty—British liberty—for its basis.

When a people are in subjection to those who are detached from their fellow citizens—under distinct laws and rules—supported in idleness and luxury—armed with the terrors of death—under the most absolute command—ready and obliged to execute the most daring orders—what must! what has been the consequence! *Inter arma silent leges.*[1]

Justice also requires of rulers in their legislative capacity that they attend to the operation of their own acts and repeal whatever laws, upon an impartial review, they find to be inconsistent with the laws of God, the rights of men, and the general benefit of society.

This the community hath a right to expect. And they must have mistaken apprehensions of true dignity who imagine they can acquire or support it by persisting in wrong measures and thereby counteracting the sole end of government.

It belongs to the all-seeing God alone absolutely to be of one mind. It is the glory of man, in whatever station, to perceive and correct his mistakes.

Arrogant pretenses to infallibility in matters of state or religion represent human nature in the most contemptible light.

We have a view of our nature in its most abject state when we read the senseless laws of the Medes and Persians or hear the impotent thunders of the Vatican.

Stability in promoting the public good, which justice demands, leads to a change of measures when the interest of the community requires it, which must often be the case in this mutable, imperfect state.

The just ruler will not fear to have his public conduct critically inspected, but will choose to recommend himself to the approbation of every man. As he expects to be obeyed for conscience' sake, he will require nothing inconsistent with its dictates and be desirous that the most scrupulous mind may acquiesce in the justice of his rule.

As in his whole administration, so in this, he will be ambitious to imitate the supreme Ruler—who appeals to his people, "Are not my ways equal?"

Knowing therefore that his conduct will bear the light and his public character be established by being fully known, he will rather encourage

[1] "In the presence of arms, the laws are silent" (Cicero, *Pro T. Annio Milone* . . . ed. Albert C. Clark, Oxford, 1895, 10).

than discountenance a decent freedom of speech, not only in public assemblies but among the people.

This liberty is essential to a free constitution, and the ruler's surest guide.

As in nature we best judge of causes by their effects, so rulers hereby will receive the surest information of the fitness of their laws and the exactness of their execution—the success of their measures—and whether they are chargeable with any mistakes, from partial evidence or human frailty—and whether all acting under them, in any subordinate place, express the fidelity becoming their office.

This decent liberty the just ruler will consider not as his grant but a right inherent in the people, without which their obedience is rendered merely passive.

And tho' possibly under a just administration it may degenerate into licentiousness, which in its extreme is subversive of all government, yet the history of past ages and of our nation shows that the greatest dangers have arisen from lawless power.

The body of a people are disposed to lead quiet and peaceable lives and it is their highest interest to support the government under which their quietness is ensured. They retain a reverence for their superiors and seldom foresee or suspect danger till they feel their burdens.

Rulers of every degree are in a measure above the fear of man, but are equally with others under the restraints of the divine Law.

The Almighty has not divested himself of his own absolute authority by permitting subordinate government among men. He allows none to rule otherwise than under him and in his fear. And without a true fear of God, justice will be found to be but an empty name.

Though reason may in some degree investigate the relation and fitness of things, yet I think it evident that moral obligations are founded wholly in a belief of God and his superintending providence.

This belief deeply impressed on the mind brings the most convincing evidence that men are moral agents, obliged to act according to the natural and evident relation of things—and the rank they bear in God's creation —that the divine Will, however made known to them, is the law by which all their actions must be regulated and their state finally determined.

Rulers may in a degree be influenced to act for the public good from education—from a desire of applause—from the natural benevolence of their temper. But these motives are feeble and inconstant without the superior aids of religion. They are men of like passions with others, and the true fear of God only, is sufficient to control the lusts of men and especially the lust of dominion—to suppress pride—the bane of every desirable quality in the human soul—the never-failing source of wanton and capricious power.

"So did not I," said the renowned governor of Judah, "because of the fear of God" [Neh. 5. 15].

He had nothing to fear from the people. His commission he received from the luxurious Persian court where the voice of distress was not heard—where no sad countenance might appear. But he feared his God. This moved him to hear the cries of his people and without delay redress their wrongs. He knew this was pleasing to his God, and while he acted in his fear, trusted he would think upon him for good.

This fear doth not intend simply a dread of the Almighty as the supreme Ruler and Judge of men—but especially a filial reverence, founded in esteem and superlative love implanted in the heart. This will naturally produce a conformity to God in his moral perfections—an inclination to do his Will—and a delight in those acts of beneficence which the Maker of all things displays throughout his extended creation.

This fear of God is the beginning and also the perfection of human wisdom.

And tho' dominion is not absolutely founded in grace, yet a true principle of religion must be considered as a necessary qualification in a ruler.

The religion of Jesus teacheth the true fear of God and marvelously discloseth the plan of divine government.

In his Gospel, as thro' a glass, we see heaven opened—the mysteries of providence and grace unveiled—Jesus sitting on the right hand of God, to whom all power is committed, and coming to judge the world in righteousness.

Here is discovered, to the admiration of angels, the joy of saints, and the terror of the wicked, the government of the man Christ Jesus, founded in justice and mercy, which in his glorious administration meet together in perfect harmony.

The scepter of his kingdom is a right scepter. He loveth righteousness and hateth wickedness.

And tho' his throne is on high—prepared in the heavens—yet he makes known to the sons of men his mighty acts, and the glorious majesty of his kingdom. By him kings reign, and princes decree justice, even all the

335

nobles and judges of the earth. His eyes are upon the ways of men. His voice which is full of majesty[2] to earthly potentates is, "Be wise now, O ye kings: be instructed, ye judges of the earth. Serve the Lord with fear, and rejoice in your exalted stations with submissive awe. Embrace the Son, lest he be angry, and ye perish from the way" [Psal. 2. 10–12].

The Christian temper wro't in the heart by the divine Spirit restores the human mind to its primitive rectitude—animates every faculty of the soul—directs every action to its proper end—extends its views beyond the narrow limits of time, and raises its desires to immortal glory.

This makes the face of every saint to shine, but renders the ruler in his elevated station gloriously resplendent.

This commands reverence to his person—attention to his counsels—respect to the laws—and authority to all his directions. And renders an obedient people easy and happy under his rule.

Which leads to the consideration of the last thing suggested in the text, viz., the glorious effects of a just administration of government.

"And he shall be as the light of the morning, when the sun riseth, even a morning without clouds; as the tender grass springing out of the earth by clear shining after rain."

This includes both the distinguishing honor and respect acquired by rulers of this character and the unspeakable felicity of a people thus favored of the Lord.

Justice and judgment are the habitation of the throne of the most High and he delighteth to honor those who rule over men in his fear. He has dignified them with a title of divinity—and called them in a peculiar sense the children of the highest.

And we are not to wonder that in the darker ages of the world, from worshipping the host of heaven, the ignorant multitude were led to pay divine honors to their beneficent rulers—whom they esteemed as demigods.

The light of divine Revelation has dispelled these mists of superstition and impiety and opened to the pious ruler's view the sure prospect of unfading glory in the life to come. And in the present state he is not without a reward.

To find that his conduct meets with public approbation, that he is acceptable to the multitude of his brethren, greatly corroborates his internal evidence of his own integrity and impartiality, and especially of his ability for public action. And, which is the height of his ambition in this state of probation, enlarges his opportunity of doing good.

The shouts of applause, not from sordid parasites, but the grateful, the artless multitude, the pious ruler receives as the voice of nature—the voice of God. This is his support under the weight of government and fixes his dependence upon the aid of the Almighty, in whose fear he rules.

How excellent in the sight of God and man are rulers of this character!

Truly the light is good and a pleasant thing it is to behold the sun. Thus desirable, thus benign, are wise and faithful rulers to a people. The beautiful allusion in the text naturally illustrates this.

The sun as the center of the solar system connects the planetary worlds and retains them in their respective orbits. They all yield to the greater force of his attractive power and thus with the greatest regularity observe the laws impressed upon the material creation.

The ruler of the day, as on a throne, shining in his strength, nearly preserves his station, and under the prime agent directs all their motions— imparting light and heat to his several attendants and the various beings which the Creator has placed upon them. His refulgent rays dispel the gloomy shades and cause the cheerful light to arise out of thick darkness and all nature to rejoice.

The planets with their lesser attendants, in conformity to their common head, mutually reflect with feebler beams their borrowed light, for the common benefit; and all, in proportion to their distance and gravity, bear their part to support the balance of the grand machine.

By this apposite metaphor the divine Spirit has represented the character and extensive beneficence of the faithful ruler—who with a godlike ardor employs his authority and influence to advance the common interest.

The righteous Lord whose countenance beholdeth the upright will support and succeed rulers of this character. And it is an evidence of his favor to a people when such are appointed to rule over them.

The natural effect of this is quietness and peace, as showers upon the tender grass and clear shining after rain.[3]

In this case a loyal people must be happy and fully sensible that they are so—while they find their persons in safety—their liberties preserved— their property defended—and their confidence in their rulers entire.

[2] "The scepter of . . . full of majesty"; see Psal. 29. 4; 45. 6, 7; 145. 12; Prov. 8. 15, 16; Ezra 5. 5.

[3] Cf. Psal. 72. 6.

The necessary expenses of government will be borne by the community with pleasure, while justice holds the balance and righteousness flows down their streets.

Such a civil state, according to the natural course of things, must flourish in peace at home and be respectable abroad—private virtues will be encouraged and vice driven into darkness—industry in the most effectual manner promoted—arts and sciences patronized—the true fear of God cultivated and his worship maintained.

This—this is their only invaluable treasure. This is the glory, safety, and best interest of rulers—the sure protection and durable felicity of a people. This, thro' the Redeemer, renders the Almighty propitious and nigh unto a people in all they call upon him for.

Happy must the people be that is in such a case. Yea, happy is the people whose God is the Lord.

But the affairs of this important day demand our more immediate attention.

With sincere gratitude to our almighty Preserver, we see the return of this anniversary and the leaders of this people assembled (tho' not according to the general desire in the city of our solemnities)—to ask counsel of God and, as we trust, in the integrity of their hearts and by the skillfulness of their hands, to lead us in ways of righteousness and peace.[4]

The season indeed is dark; but God is our sun and shield.

When we consider the days of old and the years of ancient time—the scene brightens—our hopes revive.

Our fathers trusted in God—he was their help and their shield.

These ever memorable worthies, nearly a century and a half since, by the prevalence of spiritual and civil tyranny were driven from their delightful native land to seek a quiet retreat in these uncultivated ends of the earth.

And however doubtful it might appear to them or others whether the lands they were going to possess were properly under the English jurisdiction, yet our ancestors were desirous of retaining a relation to their native country and to be considered as subjects of the same prince.

They left their native land with the strongest assurances that they and their posterity should enjoy the privileges of free, natural-born English subjects, which they supposed fully comprehended in their Charter. The powers of government therein confirmed to them they considered as including English liberty in its full extent.[5]

338

And however defective their Charter might be in form, a thing common in that day, yet the spirit and evident intention of it appears to be then understood.

The reserve therein made of passing no laws contrary to those of the parent state was then considered as a conclusive evidence of their full power, under that restriction only, to enact whatever laws they should judge conducive to their benefit.

Our fathers supposed their purchase of the aboriginals gave them a just title to the lands—that the produce of them by their labor was their property, which they had an exclusive right to dispose of—that a legislative power respecting their internal polity was ratified to them—and that nothing short of this, considering their local circumstances, could entitle them or their posterity to the rights and liberties of free, natural-born English subjects.

And it does not appear but that this was the general sentiment of the nation and parliament.

They did not, then, view their American adventurers in the light ancient Rome did her distant colonies, as tributaries, unjustly subjected to arbitrary rule by the dread or force of her victorious arms—but as sons, arrived to mature age—entitled to distinct property—yet connected by mutual ties of affection and interest and united under the common supreme head.

The New England Charter was not considered as an act of grace, but a compact between the Sovereign and the first patentees.

Our fathers pled their right to the privilege of it in their address to King Charles the Second—wherein they say:

It was granted to them, their heirs, assigns, and associates forever; not only the absolute use and propriety of the tract of land therein mentioned; but also full and absolute power of governing all the people of this place, by men chosen from among themselves, and according to such laws as

---

[4] Hutchinson received orders from the British Secretary of State early in 1770 to move both the winter and spring sessions of the General Assembly from Boston to Cambridge. The legality of such a move became the most controversial issue of the new session, beginning with *Instructions from the Town of Boston to Their Representatives, May 15, 1770,* and including several exchanges between Hutchinson and the assembly during the session. See Hutchinson, *History,* III, 207–223, 370–383.

[5] This paragraph begins with quotation marks in the pamphlet but there is no indication of where the quotation—if it is one—ends. Since there is no change in style and since the paragraph concerns a cherished point of history echoed in many sermons, addresses (such as in n. 6 below), and histories, it has not been set off as a quotation nor has any attempt been made to identify it.

they shall from time to time see meet to make and establish, not being repugnant to the laws of England—they paying only the fifth part of the ore of gold and silver that shall be found here—for and in respect of all duties, demands, exactions, and services whatsoever.[6]

And from an apprehension that the powers given by the crown to the four commissioners sent here were in effect subversive of their rights and government—they add:

We are carefully studious of all due subjection to your Majesty, and that not only for wrath, but for conscience' sake. . . . But it is a great unhappiness to be reduced to so hard a case as to have no other testimony of our subjection and loyalty offered us but this, viz., to destroy our own being which nature teacheth us to preserve; or to yield up our liberties which are far dearer to us than our lives, and which, had we any fears of being deprived of, we had never wandered from our fathers' houses into these ends of the earth, nor laid out our labors and estates therein.[7]

But all their humble addresses were to no purpose.

As an honorable historian observes: "At this time Great Britain, and Scotland, especially, was suffering under a prince inimical to civil liberty. And New England, without a miraculous interposition, must expect to share the same judgments."[8] And indeed, of this bitter cup the dregs were reserved for this people in that and the succeeding, happily short but inglorious, reign.

Our Charter was dissolved and despotic power took place.

Sir Edmund Andros—a name never to be forgotten—in imitation of his royal master, in wanton triumph, trampled upon all our laws and rights. And his government was only tolerable as it was a deliverance from the shocking terrors of the more infamous Kirke.[9]

Sir Edmund at first made high professions of regard to the public good. But it has been observed "that Nero concealed his tyrannical disposition more years than Sir Edmund and his creatures did months."[10]

But the triumphing of the wicked is often short.

The Glorious Revolution under the Prince of Orange displayed a brighter scene to Great Britain and her colonies. And tho' no part of its extended empire did bear a greater part in the joy of that memorable event than this province, yet it was then apprehended we were not the greatest sharers in the happy effects of it.

I trust we are not insensible of the blessings we then received, nor unthankful for our deliverance from the depths of woe.

340

We submitted to the form of government established under our present Charter [11]—trusting, under God, in the wisdom and paternal tenderness of our gracious Sovereign, that in all appointments reserved to the crown a sacred regard would be maintained to the rights of British subjects, and that the royal ear would always be open to every reasonable request and complaint.

It is far from my intention to determine whether there has been just reason for uneasiness or complaint on this account. But with all submission, I presume the present occasion will permit me to say that the importance of his Majesty's Council to this people appears in a more conspicuous light since the endeavors which have been used to render this invaluable branch of our constitution wholly dependent upon the chair. [12]

Should this ever be the case, which God forbid—liberty here will cease. This day of the gladness of our hearts will be turned into the deepest sorrow.

The authority and influence of his Majesty's Council, in various respects, while happily free from restraints, is momentous; our well-being greatly depends upon their wisdom and integrity.

The concern of electing to this important trust wise and faithful men belongeth to our honored fathers now in General Assembly convened.

[6] "Copy of the Address of the Massachusetts Colony to King Charles the 2d, in 1664," Hutchinson, *History*, I, 445.

[7] *Ibid.*, 448–449.

[8] *Ibid.*, 274.

[9] Colonel Percy Kirke was appointed the first royal Governor after the Charter was nullified in October 1684. He did not leave England and his commission was given in May 1686 to Joseph Dudley, who was replaced in December by Sir Edmund Andros.

[10] Thomas Hutchinson, *The History of the Colony of Massachusets-Bay* (Boston, 1764), 354–355 (the edition Cooke used). Oddly enough, Charles Chauncy quoted the passage in his "election sermon" in Boston the same day Cooke preached in Cambridge; "made high professions . . . public good" is borrowed directly from Hutchinson, *ibid.*, 353.

[11] Of 1691.

[12] The privilege of electing the Governor's Council was canceled along with the first Charter in 1684; Governor Andros' Council was appointed. Election of Councilmen returned with the Charter of 1691, but Townshend's policy of colonial restriction, and fear of reprisals for mob violence in the Hancock customs affair and the "massacre," made the Colony sensitive to what new, harsher restrictions might be imposed. *Instructions from the Town of Boston to Their Representatives, May 15, 1770*, begins: ". . . A series of occurrences, many recent events, and especially the late journals of the House of Lords, afford good reason to believe that a deep-laid and desperate plan of imperial despotism has been laid and partly executed, for the extinction of all civil liberty" (Hutchinson, *History*, III, 370).

Men of this character we trust are to be found, and upon such, and only such, we presume will the eye of the electors be this day.

It is with pleasure that we see this choice in the hands of a very respectable part of the community and nearly interested in the effects of it.

But our reliance, fathers, under God, is upon your acting in his fear.

God standeth in the assembly of the mighty [13] and perfectly discerns the motives by which you act. May his fear rule in your hearts and unerring counsel be your guide.

You have received a sure token of respect by your being raised to this high trust; but true honor is acquired only by acting in character.

Honor yourselves, gentlemen—honor the Council-Board—your country—your King—and your God—by the choice you this day make.

You will attentively consider the true design of all civil government, and without partiality give your voice for those you judge most capable and disposed to promote the public interest. Then you will have the satisfaction of having faithfully discharged your trust—and be sure of the approbation of the most High.

The chief command in this province is now devolved upon one of distinguished abilities, who knows our state and naturally must care for us—one who in early life has received from his country the highest tokens of honor and trust in its power to bestow.[14] And we have a right to expect that the higher degrees of them conferred by our gracious Sovereign will operate thro' the course of his administration, to the welfare of this people.

His Honor is not insensible that as his power is independent of the people, their safety must depend, under providence, upon his wisdom, justice, and paternal tenderness in the exercise of it.

It is our ardent wish and prayer that his administration may procure ease and quietness to himself and the province. And having served his generation according to the divine Will, he may rise to superior honors in the kingdom of God.

When the elections of this important day are determined, what farther remains to be undertaken for the securing our liberties—promoting peace and good order—and above all, the advancement of religion—the true fear of God thro' the land—will demand the highest attention of the General Assembly.

We trust the fountain of light who giveth wisdom freely will not scatter darkness in your paths—and that the day is far distant when there shall be cause justly to complain—the foundations are destroyed; what can the righteous do? [15]

Our present distresses, civil fathers, loudly call upon us all, and you in special, to stir up ourselves in the fear of God. Arise, this matter belongeth unto you; we also will be with you; be of good courage and do it. [16]

Whether any other laws are necessary for this purpose or whether there is a failure in the execution of the laws in being, I presume not to say. But with all due respect, I may be permitted to affirm that no human authority can enforce the practice of religion with equal success to your example.

Your example, fathers, not only in your public administrations but also in private life, will be the most forcible law—the most effectual means to teach us the fear of the Lord and to depart from evil.

Then, and not till then, shall we be free indeed—being delivered from the dominion of sin, we become the true sons of God.

The extent of the secular power in matters of religion is undetermined; but all agree that the example of those in authority has the greatest influence upon the manners of the people.

We are far from pleading for any established mode of worship—but an operative fear of God—the honor of the Redeemer, the everlasting King—according to his Gospel.

We whose peculiar charge it is to instruct the people preach to little purpose while those in an advanced state by their practice say the fear of God is not before their eyes. Yet will we not cease to seek the Lord till he come and rain down righteousness upon us.

I trust on this occasion I may without offense plead the cause of our African slaves, and humbly propose the pursuit of some effectual measures at least to prevent the future importation of them.

Difficulties insuperable, I apprehend, prevent an adequate remedy for what is past.

Let the time past more than suffice wherein we, the patrons of liberty,

[13] See Psal. 82. 1.

[14] Thomas Hutchinson acted as Governor from August 1769, when Bernard sailed for England, until he was officially commissioned in 1771. Born and raised in Boston, Hutchinson had both a B.A. and an M.A. from Harvard, and had been a selectman of Boston, member of the Council, Speaker of the House, Lieutenant-Governor, and Chief Justice.

[15] See Psal. 11. 3.

[16] Cf. Ezra 10. 4.

have dishonored the Christian name and degraded human nature nearly to a level with the beasts that perish.

Ethiopia has long stretched out her hands to us. Let not sordid gain acquired by the merchandise of slaves and the souls of men harden our hearts against her piteous moans. When God ariseth, and when he visiteth, what shall we answer!

May it be the glory of this province—of this respectable General Assembly—and we could wish, of this session—to lead in the cause of the oppressed. This will avert the impending vengeance of heaven—procure you the blessing of multiudes of your fellowmen ready to perish—be highly approved by our common Father, who is no respecter of persons— and we trust, an example which would excite the highest attention of our sister colonies.

May we all, both rulers and people, in this day of doubtful expectation, know and practice the things of our peace—and serve the Lord our God without disquiet, in the inheritance which he granted unto our fathers.

These adventurous worthies, animated by sublimer prospects, dearly purchased this land with their treasure. They and their posterity have defended it with unknown cost[a]—in continual jeopardy of their lives— and with their blood.

Thro' the good hand of our God upon us, we have for a few years past been delivered from the merciless sword of the wilderness, and enjoyed peace in our borders—and there is in the close of our short summer the appearance of plenty in our dwellings; but from the length of our winters our plenty is consumed, and the one-half of our necessary labor is spent in dispersing to our flocks and herds the ingatherings of the foregoing season. And it is known to every person of common observation that few —very few, except in the mercantile way—from one generation to another, acquire more than a necessary subsistence and sufficient to dis-

[a] "Be it far from me, O Lord," said the ancient hero, "that I should do this: is not this the blood of the men that went in jeopardy of their lives?" [II Sam. 23. 17]. Therefore he would not drink it. Will not the like sentiments rise in a generous mind, thrust into our possessions?

[b] Their losses and private expenses in watches, guards, and garrisons for their defense and from continual alarms—in all their former wars—have greatly exceeded the public charges.

[c] It is apprehended a greater sacrifice of private interest to the public good, both of Great Britain and the colonies, hath at no time been made than that of the patriotic merchants of this and all the considerable colonies, by their non-importation agreement. And whatever the effects may be, their names will be remembered with gratitude to the latest generations by all true friends to Britain and her colonies.

charge the expenses of government and the support of the Gospel—yet are * content and disposed to lead peaceable lives.

From misinformations only, we would conclude, recent disquiets have arisen—they need not be mentioned—they are too well known—their voice is gone out thro' all the earth—and their sound to the end of the world. The enemies of Great Britain hold us in derision—while her cities and colonies are thus perplexed.

America now pleads her right to her possessions—which she cannot resign while she apprehends she has truth and justice on her side.

Americans esteem it their greatest infelicity that thro' necessity they are thus led to plead with their parent state—the land of their forefathers' nativity, whose interest has always been dear to them b—and whose wealth they have increased by their removal much more than their own.

They have assisted in fighting her battles and greatly enlarged her empire—and God helping, will yet extend it thro' the boundless desert until it reach from sea to sea.

They glory in the British Constitution and are abhorrent, to a man, of the most distant thought of withdrawing their allegiance from their gracious Sovereign and becoming an independent state.

And tho' with unwearied toil the colonists can now subsist upon the labors of their own hands—which they must be driven to when deprived of the means of purchase [17]—yet they are fully sensible of the mutual benefits of an equitable commerce with the parent country, and cheerfully submit to regulations of trade productive of the common interest.

These their claims the Americans consider not as novel or wantonly made, but founded in nature—in compact—in their right as men—and British subjects—the same which their forefathers the first occupants made and asserted as the terms of their removal with their effects into this wilderness c—and with which the glory and interest of their King and all his dominions are connected.

May these alarming disputes be brought to a just and speedy issue—and peace and harmony be restored.

[17] After the imposition of the Townshend Acts in 1767, colonial leaders and merchants encouraged domestic manufacture and organized inter-colonial movements for non-importation of taxed goods so successfully that in April 1770 the Acts were repealed except for the tax on tea. See A. M. Schlesinger, *Colonial Merchants and the American Revolution* (New York, 1918), 91–239, and John Braeman, *The Road to Independence* (New York, 1963), 129–171. For decisions in Boston in April and May to continue the non-importation agreements, see Lawrence Henry Gipson, *The Coming of the Revolution 1763–1775* (New York, 1954), 203–204.

But while in imitation of our pious forefathers we are aiming at the security of our liberties, we should all be concerned to express, by our conduct, their piety and virtue. And in a day of darkness and general distress carefully avoid everything offensive to God or injurious to men.

It belongs not only to rulers but subjects also to set the Lord always before their face and act in his fear.

While under government we claim a right to be treated as men, we must act in character by yielding that subjection which becometh us as men.

Let every attempt to secure our liberties be conducted with a manly fortitude, but with that respectful decency which reason approves and which alone gives weight to the most salutary measures.

Let nothing divert us from the paths of truth and peace which are the ways of God—and then we may be sure that he will be with us as he was with our fathers—and never leave nor forsake us.

Our fathers, where are they? They looked for another and better country, that is an heavenly. They were but as sojourners here, and have long since resigned these their transitory abodes and are securely seated in mansions of glory. They hear not the voice of the oppressor.[18]

We also are all strangers on earth and must soon, without distinction, lie down in the dust and rise not till these heavens and earth are no more.

May we all realize the appearance of the Son of God to judge the world in righteousness, and improve the various talents committed to our trust, that we may then lift up our heads with joy—and thro' grace, receive an inheritance which cannot be taken away—even life everlasting.

AMEN.

[18] See Job 3. 18.

IX SAMUEL LANGDON'S SERMON OF 1775

AN INTRODUCTION

I

BETWEEN June 1770 and May 1775 the citizens of Boston lived through one crisis after another. The tensions which built up previous to the beginning of the Revolution—committees of correspondence, the Tea Party, the Coercive Acts and the closing of the port of Boston, the newspaper and pamphlet debates, the military occupation under Governor Gage, the First Continental Congress, the forming of the Provincial Congress, the training of minutemen and secret buildup of arms, Paul Revere and the call to fight—all have been described many times; there is no need to review the story here.

If one could know nothing about these events except what he heard in the election sermons at Cambridge and in the Old South Church, he would guess there was trouble afoot but he would be starved for details. He would have heard in 1772 that "the day is become gloomy and dark,"[1] in 1773 that "the people of this land" are "firmly and generally persuaded that their most important rights are infringed,"[2] and in 1774 that "the present scenes of calamity and perplexity" are ones in which "the contest in regard to the rights of the colonists rises high"; there are "common sufferings" and an "American cause."[3] The preacher of 1774, Gad

[1] Moses Parsons, *A Sermon* . . . (Boston, 1772), 17.
[2] Charles Turner, *A Sermon* . . . (Boston, 1773), 21.
[3] Gad Hitchcock, *A Sermon* . . . (Boston, 1774), 45.

Hitchcock, becomes more specific: "Our danger is not visionary, but real—our contention is not about trifles, but about liberty and property. . . . If I am mistaken in supposing plans are formed and executing, subversive of our natural and charter rights and privileges and incompatible with every idea of liberty, all America is mistaken with me."[4] Still, with the exception of the closing pages of Hitchcock's sermon in 1774, the election sermons of 1771–74 are generally polite, cautious, their tone conciliatory. The ministers of these years see their role as custodians of basic principles of the source, end, and general nature of government. They will not presume to say whether Britain has gone too far in restraining American liberty—as in this euphemism:

How far any persons may have been charged, injuriously, with an inclination to promote the measures which are grievous to this province and country, we do not pretend to determine. But if the gentlemen on either side of the Atlantic who may be justly said to be engaged in pursuit of such measures confidently judge that they are acting the part which becomes men appointed of God to consult the public happiness, and find their inward tranquillity in no degree disturbed by suspicions that they are infringing the rights of this people, may it not be excusable, nevertheless, in a proper and respectful manner, to recommend to them a consideration of their liableness to be mistaken?[5]

In these years there is no mention of the possibility of a revolution or a separation from Britain; to the contrary, the British Constitution is the finest in the world; present misunderstandings stem from misrepresentation on both sides, a situation which it is to be hoped will soon be cleared up. In addition, these sermons return to the apostasy theme. New England is suffering not because of her mistreatment by England, but because she is sinful. There had been a ceremonious ploy about the election sermon from the beginning, and it continues now. The Governor is praised (even Gage, in 1774, just before Hitchcock turns to the Representatives and says they must listen to "the united voice of America" which speaks "with the solemnity of thunder and with accents piercing as the lightning"[6]) and the Representatives are urged to be exemplary Christians.

And yet within the ploy, at their most ceremonious, uttering the oldest adages, these ministers are very much in the revolutionary ferment, and

[4] *Ibid.*, 46–47.
[5] Turner, *A Sermon*, 20–21.
[6] *A Sermon*, 46.

in their quiet ways as much in the ranks of American patriots as the minutemen darting from tree to tree along the roads from Lexington to Concord and back to Boston. If before 1775 we find no sermon with the passionate oratory of Otis or Paine, there is nonetheless a steady focus on the basic principles of liberty within government. It is not enough to say that Tucker (1771), Parsons (1772), Turner (1773), and Hitchcock (1774) are patriots—which they are. A tradition of one hundred and forty years and the immediate needs of the moment combine to offer them a special role; they realize it, and almost as if their strategy was planned together, they carry it off. Each sermon reiterates the old ideas that if a ruler does not rule for the good of the people they may remove him, and that the source of a ruler's right to govern lies in the people. But in addition, they address the special conditions of 1771–74 by a combined attack on the fallacy of unlimited submission. For many Americans in these days, the question was not whether or not there were legitimate grievances—all but the most Tory could see that there were. The question was what to do about them. If one does not receive redress for complaints, he can continue diplomatic appeals, withdraw, or fight. After Governor Gage arrived with his troops, withdrawal meant fighting. It is one thing to fight a foreign enemy; it's quite another to fight one's King and his God. Thomas Paine's dramatic pamphlets were important to the Revolution because they helped change the picture of George III and England from that of a misinformed old father who should still be revered to that of an unscrupulous and jealous tyrant whom any sane person would instinctively oppose in the name of virtue and justice. The election sermons of 1771–74 do the same thing in a quieter way and at a more theoretical level. They insist that blind submission to a ruler who has seriously restrained liberty is sinful. Christ came to make people free (1770, 7). It is God's declared will in his Word as well as in man's reason, which "may be said to be the voice of God" (1771, 12), that no one has an unlimited right to rule over others. The doctrines of passive obedience and nonresistance are by now "absurd and exploded" (1771, 19).

Upon the whole therefore, proper submission in a free state is a medium between slavish subjection to arbitrary claims of rulers on the one hand, and a lawless license on the other. It is obedience in subjects to all orders of government which are consistent with their constitutional rights and privileges . . . there is a liberty . . . respecting civil government we have a claim to and which should have influence on our conduct, i.e., a liberty to withhold, as well as to yield submission.[7]

So long therefore and so far as civil powers act agreeably to the design of their ordination and do good in their stations, the people are obligated to subjection, and resistance will be blameable; but if these powers forsake their proper sphere, thwart God's design in ordaining them, disserve the people, and take measures which tend to ruin them, the apostle's ground of the people's subjection ceases, and indeed submission becomes a fault and resistance a virtue. . . . To suppose it belongs to the apostle's meaning that it is a damnable sin to resist civil powers because ordained of God, though they act entirely out of character and thwart every kind purpose God had in ordaining them, is in the class of most palpable, grating absurdities. A pretense to ground such ideas as those of indefeasible right, passive obedience, and nonresistance, on the Bible, is criminal—an high, abusive scandal to the Christian religion and its divinely inspired promulgators.[8]

If it be true that no rulers can be safe where the doctrine of resistance is taught, it must be true that no nation can be safe where the contrary is taught. If it be true that this disposeth men of turbulent spirits to oppose the best rulers, it is as true that the other disposeth princes of evil minds to enslave and ruin the best and most submissive subjects. If it be true that this encourageth all public disturbance and all revolutions whatsoever, it is as true that the other encourageth all tyranny and all the most intolerable persecutions and oppressions imaginable.[9]

II

Illegal assemblies were spreading in the fall of 1774. In September, fifty-six delegates from twelve colonies met in Philadelphia in the First Continental Congress. Although the Coercive (or Intolerable) Acts had suspended election of the Council in Massachusetts effective August 1, and resentment of this restriction was running high, early in September Governor Gage called for a meeting of the General Court to be held at Salem on October 5. Three weeks later he canceled it. The Representatives met anyway and organized themselves into a Provincial Congress. They met again in February. It was to their third meeting at Watertown that President Samuel Langdon of Harvard was invited to preach.[10] By

[7] John Tucker, *A Sermon* . . . (Boston, 1771), 32, 37.
[8] Turner, *A Sermon*, 32–33.
[9] Hitchcock, *A Sermon*, 23.
[10] Samuel Langdon (1723–97) was born in Boston and received his B.A. from Harvard in 1740 in the class of Samuel Adams. He was a schoolmaster and occasional preacher until February 4, 1747, when he was ordained at First Church, Portsmouth,

the end of May local circumstances were unique and the future uncertain, as they had been for Mather's sermon in 1689. The Representatives were not meeting in the familiar place; Boston was a city of occupation surrounded by American troops; there was no Governor in the chair; the assembly was illegal; armed hostility had already broken out and the sounds of battle could be heard not far away.[11] Everyone awaited directions from the Congress in Philadelphia; in the meantime, there were immediate decisions to be made pertaining to command, military strategy, and troop support. Langdon matches the circumstances with a sermon very different from those of his predecessors in the last few years.

First, the sermon is partly narrative. Langdon chooses the occasion to review for those who have come long distances the main recent events. The most important anniversary in Massachusetts' political calendar is traditionally the time to take stock of God's providence, but there is a documentary, journalistic realism to Langdon's review. After several election sermons in which specific events had been played down in favor of principles and theory, Langdon, like Paine eight months later, lets the facts (as he sees them) argue their own case.[12]

Langdon's rhetoric also anticipates Paine. In contrast to the polite and restrained sermons of the last few years, he returns to the fiery emo-

N.H. He helped form the New Hampshire Association of Ministers and through it worked actively to establish Dartmouth College. Langdon was interested in astronomy and traced and charted the paths of comets seen from New Hampshire. He became President of Harvard in October 1774 and chaplain to the Continental Army in July 1775. He offered a prayer for the success of the capture of Bunker's Hill to the troops gathered on Cambridge Common on the evening of June 16, the night before the battle, and he read the Declaration of Independence to the troops in Cambridge on July 15, 1775. He resigned the presidency of Harvard in 1780 and became the minister at Hampton Falls, New Hampshire. As the town's delegate to the convention to consider ratification of the Federal Constitution in 1788, he argued for its adoption. For biographical sketches, see John Langdon Sibley and Clifford K. Shipton, *Biographical Sketches of Those Who Attended Harvard College*, 13 vols. (Cambridge and Boston, 1873–1965), X, 508–528; William B. Sprague, *Annals of the American Pulpit* . . . , 9 vols. (New York, 1857–69), I, 455–457; *DAB*, X, 588–589.

[11] As he traveled from Billerica to Concord on his way to the Congress at Watertown, Tuesday morning, May 30, Samuel Cooper heard "a great discharge of guns from towards Boston for more than an hour" which "alarm'd the country." Later in the day he learned that the firing was "only a mock fight of the Regulars at Boston." The following day he heard Langdon's sermon "before the Congress" and thought it "well adapted" ("Diary of Samuel Cooper, 1775–1776," *American Historical Review*, VI, 1900–1901, 309).

[12] *Common Sense* appeared January 10, 1766, in Philadelphia.

tionalism of Mather and Mayhew. The language and imagery are heavily loaded. Gage's troops have "murderously kill'd"; in retreating to Boston from Concord they acted like "robbers and savages." The English ministry shows "despotic power," the machinations of "wicked men," and a "lust" for power. Death scenes focus on the innocent—old men, and babies in their mothers' arms.

Seen from the vantage point of the long tradition of election sermons in Massachusetts, Langdon's performance at this crucial time is a blend of the two strains. At several points he works in the now firmly established principles of the popular base of government and limited submission. But the sermon is also a new version of the errand sermon. It sounds the themes of Danforth's *Errand into the Wilderness*. It is time for England and America to *restore* good government and cut clean to "prime" virtues and principles. America has tasted the corruption of European courts; she can now cleanse herself as did the first settlers in coming to her shores. The sermon closes by reminding the Representatives of the providential, strange destructions God can visit on the enemy of his chosen people. The sermon blends Jeremiah and Locke.

Perry Miller has argued that sermons like Langdon's played a special role in the revolutionary ferment. He maintains that the apostasy theme in these latter-day "jeremiads" imparted "a sense of crisis by revivifying Old Testament condemnations of a degenerate people" without which the "natural-rights philosophy . . . propounded exclusively in the language of political rationalism" would not otherwise have been as forceful or acceptable in New England. These jeremiads of the 1770's did not produce humility and restraint: "the wonderful fusion of political doctrine with the traditional rite of self-abasement . . . had become not what it might seem on the surface, a failure of will, but a dynamo for generating action." [13]

Compared to the sermons of Danforth (1670), Shepard (1672), and Oakes (1673), however, Langdon's charge of apostasy is feeble. In proportion to his sermon as a whole, his discussion of New England's sinfulness seems a passing remark, an overture to a stereotyped pattern. Structurally, the apostasy theme in an errand sermon should dominate the application or second half of the sermon. In Langdon's it is a small, middle section; his heart isn't in it.

[13] "From the Covenant to the Revival," *The Shaping of American Religion*, ed. James W. Smith and A. Leland Jamison (Princeton, 1961), 337, 339, 340.

Langdon surely knew what he was doing and what he wanted. In the tradition of the election sermon, the apostasy theme is intimately tied to the errand theme; one enters into the former only after gazing back to the good old days of the garden enclosed by a wall of godly ministers and magistrates—the goal of the first settlers and the polity they briefly achieved. The jeremiad catalog of sins would have been intolerable year after year without the positive vision of the garden utopia which once, so the story goes, briefly existed. Langdon wants the emotional impact of the errand motif and the appeal of a return to basic, pristine virtues— but he doesn't want a return, literally, to the days of Boston, c. 1650, the way Danforth did in 1670 and perhaps even Prince in 1730. He wants the myth but not the fact, the spirit but not the politics of it. (The republican principles he advocates would have made Cotton and Winthrop shudder.) Most of all, he wants a return to a just government to lie in the future—not the past. Although he reviews the glorious past, he ends his sermon by asking the Representatives to make the new Congress permanent and secure. The old government is dead and the exact forms and pressures of the good old times are no longer viable; but the spirit of the errand is still alive, and still a quest.

Government corrupted by Vice, and recovered by Righteousneſs.

A

S E R M O N

P R E A C H E D

BEFORE THE HONORABLE

C O N G R E S S

Of the Colony

Of the *Maſſachuſetts-Bay*

IN N E W-E N G L A N D,

Aſſembled at *WATERTOWN,*

On Wedneſday the 31ſt Day of *May,* 1775.

Being the Anniverſary fixed by CHARTER

For the Election of COUNSELLORS.

By SAMUEL LANGDON, D. D.

Preſident of Harvard College in CAMBRIDGE.

As a roaring Lion and a ranging Bear, ſo is a
wicked Ruler over the poor People. *Prov:* 28. 15.

W A T E R T O W N:

Printed and Sold by BENJAMIN EDES,
MDCCLXXV.

A Sermon.

"And I will restore thy judges as at the first, and thy counselors as at the beginning: afterward thou shalt be called, the city of righteousness, the faithful city" (Isa. 1. 26).

Shall we rejoice, my fathers and brethren, or shall we weep together, on the return of this anniversary, which from the first settlement of this Colony has been sacred to liberty, to perpetuate that invaluable privilege of choosing from among ourselves, wise men, fearing God and hating covetousness, to be honorable counselors, to constitute one essential branch of that happy government which was established on the faith of royal charters?

On this day the people have from year to year assembled from all our towns, in a vast congregation, with gladness and festivity, with every ensign of joy displayed in our metropolis, which now, alas! is made a garrison of mercenary troops, the stronghold of despotism.[1] But how shall I now address you from this desk, remote from the capital, and

---

[1] For the military buildup of both Royalist soldiers in Boston under General Gage and the patriot force surrounding Boston, between the skirmish at Concord, April 19, and the Battle of Bunker Hill, June 17, see Christopher Ward, "The Siege of Boston," *The War of the Revolution*, ed. John Richard Alden (New York, 1952), 52–62. When Langdon gave this sermon, the naming of Washington as American General by the Continental Congress in Philadelphia and the Battle of Bunker Hill were still fifteen and seventeen days away, respectively. By the end of May Boston was

remind you of the important business which distinguished this day in our calendar, without spreading a gloom over this assembly by exhibiting the melancholy change made in the face of our public affairs?

We have lived to see the time when British liberty is just ready to expire; when that constitution of government which has so long been the glory and strength of the English nation is deeply undermined and ready to tumble into ruins; when America is threatened with cruel oppression, and the arm of power is stretched out against New England, and especially against this Colony, to compel us to submit to the arbitrary acts of legislators who are not our representatives, and who will not themselves bear the least part of the burdens which, without mercy, they are laying upon us. The most formal and solemn grants of kings to our ancestors are deemed by our oppressors as of little value; and they have mutilated the Charter of this Colony in the most essential parts, upon false representations and new-invented maxims of policy, without the least regard to any legal process. We are no longer permitted to fix our eyes on the faithful of the land and trust in the wisdom of their counsels and the equity of their judgment; but men in whom we can have no confidence—whose principles are subversive of our liberties—whose aim is to exercise lordship over us and share among themselves the public wealth—men who are ready to serve any master and execute the most unrighteous decrees for high wages—whose faces we never saw before and whose interests and connections may be far divided from us by the wide Atlantic—are to be set over us as counselors and judges, at the pleasure of those who have the riches and power of the nation in their hands, and whose noblest plan is to subjugate the colonies first and then the whole nation to their will.[2]

That we might not have it in our power to refuse the most absolute submission to their unlimited claims of authority, they have not only endeavored to terrify us with fleets and armies sent to our capital, and distressed and put an end to our trade, particularly that important branch of it, the fishery; but at length attempted by a sudden march of a body of troops in the night, to seize and destroy one of our magazines formed by the people merely for their own security if, after such formidable military preparations on the other side, matters should be pushed to an extremity.[3] By this, as might well be expected, a skirmish was brought on; and it is most evident from a variety of concurring circumstances, as well as numerous depositions both of the prisoners taken by us at that time and our own men then on the spot only as spectators, that the fire began first on the side of the King's troops. At least five or six of our inhabitants were murderously kill'd by the regulars at Lexington before any man attempted to return the fire and when they were actually complying with the command to disperse; and two more of our brethren were likewise kill'd at Concord Bridge by a fire from the King's soldiers before the engagement began on our side. But whatever credit falsehoods transmitted to Great Britain from the other side may gain, the matter may be rested entirely on this—that he that arms himself to commit a robbery, and demands the traveler's purse by the terror of instant death, is the first aggressor, though the other should take the advantage of discharging his pistol first and killing the robber.

The alarm was sudden but in a very short time spread far and wide; the nearest neighbors in haste ran together to assist their brethren and save their country. Not more than three or four hundred met in season and bravely attacked and repulsed the enemies of liberty, who retreated with great precipitation. But by the help of a strong reinforcement, notwithstanding a close pursuit and continual loss on their side, they acted

cut off from the rest of the Colony; patriots were allowed to leave and loyalists to enter with personal effects, food, and medicines only. Generals Howe, Clinton, and Burgoyne had arrived in Boston from England to assist Gage on May 25.

[2] The Massachusetts Government Act of May 20, 1774, one of the "Coercive Acts," rescinded the popular election of Councilors granted under the Charter of 1691 and substituted direct appointment by the King. Councilors would hold office "for and during the pleasure of his Majesty." Assembly for any purpose other than the annual town meetings to elect "selectmen, constables, and other officers" had to have the written consent of the Governor. Extracts from the act are in *Sources and Documents Illustrating the American Revolution* . . . , ed. Samuel Eliot Morison, 2nd ed. (Oxford, 1929), 100–102.

[3] By the end of May, there were in the Boston harbor four large ships of sixty guns or more plus several frigates and sloops. General Gage's army in Boston at the beginning of 1775 has been estimated at about four thousand. In addition to the Coercive Acts of 1774 which closed the Port of Boston to trade after the "tea party," Langdon refers here to the new Fisheries Act which restricted the rest of the New England colonies to trade with Britain and the British West Indies only, and excluded colonial fishermen from the Grand Banks under penalty of forfeiture of vessels—a cruel blow to the fishing industries of centers like Boston and Marblehead. This act, passed in the British Commons on March 20, was still fresh news in Massachusetts on May 31. See Ward, *The War of the Revolution*, 24, and Dan Lacy, *The Meaning of the American Revolution* (New York, 1964), 130–131. For excerpts from firsthand accounts of the skirmishes at Lexington and Concord on April 19, 1775, by both British and American participants—including Paul Revere's account of his famous ride—see *The Spirit of 'Seventy-Six*, ed. Henry Steele Commager and Richard B. Morris (New York, 1958), I, 66–97, and Hugh F. Rankin, "Rebellion in Massachusetts," *The American Revolution* (New York, 1964), 19–32. Ward's "Lexington" and "Concord" chapters in *The War of the Revolution* are excellent, detailed accounts.

the part of robbers and savages by burning, plundering, and damaging almost every house in their way, to the utmost of their power, murdering the unarmed and helpless and not regarding the weaknesses of the tender sex, until they had secured themselves beyond the reach of our terrifying arms.[a]

That ever memorable day, the nineteenth of April, is the date of an unhappy war openly begun by the ministers of the King of Great Britain against his good subjects in this Colony, and implicitly against all the colonies. But for what? Because they have made a noble stand for their natural and constitutional rights, in opposition to the machinations of wicked men who are betraying their royal Master, establishing popery in the British Dominions, and aiming to enslave and ruin the whole nation that they may enrich themselves and their vile dependents with the public treasures and the spoils of America.

We have used our utmost endeavors, by repeated humble petitions and remonstrances—by a series of unanswerable reasonings published from the press in which the dispute has been fairly stated, and the justice of our opposition clearly demonstrated—and by the mediation of some of the noblest and most faithful friends of the British Constitution, who have powerfully pled our cause in Parliament—to prevent such measures as may soon reduce the body politic to a miserable, dismembered, dying trunk, though lately the terror of all Europe.[4] But our King, as if impelled by some strange fatality, is resolved to reason with us only by the roar of his cannon and the pointed arguments of muskets and bayonets. Because we refuse submission to the despotic power of a ministerial parliament, our own Sovereign, to whom we have been always ready to swear true allegiance—whose authority we never meant to cast off—who might have continued happy in the cheerful obedience of as faithful subjects as any in his dominions—has given us up to the rage of his ministers, to be seized at sea by the rapacious commanders of every little sloop of war and piratical cutter, and to be plundered and massacred by land by mer-

[a] Near the meetinghouse in Menotomy two aged helpless men who had not been out in the action, and were found unarmed in a house where the regulars enter'd, were murdered without mercy. In another house in that neighborhood a woman in bed with a newborn infant, about a week old, was forced by the threats of the soldiery to escape, almost naked, to an open outhouse; her house was then set on fire, but soon extinguished by one of the children which had laid concealed till the enemy was gone. In Cambridge a man of weak mental powers, who went out to gaze at the regular army as they pass'd, without arms or thought of danger, was wantonly shot at and kill'd by those inhuman butchers as he sat on a fence.

cenary troops who know no distinction betwixt an enemy and a brother, between right and wrong; but only, like brutal pursuers, to hunt and seize the prey pointed out by their masters.

We must keep our eyes fixed on the supreme government of the eternal King, as directing all events, setting up or pulling down the kings of the earth at his pleasure, suffering the best forms of human government to degenerate and go to ruin by corruption; or restoring the decayed constitutions of kingdoms and states by reviving public virtue and religion, and granting the favorable interpositions of his providence. To this our text leads us; and though I hope to be excused on this occasion from a formal discourse on the words in a doctrinal way, yet I must not wholly pass over the religious instruction contained in them.

Let us consider: that for the sins of a people God may suffer the best government to be corrupted or entirely dissolved; and that nothing but a general reformation can give good ground to hope that the public happiness will be restored by the recovery of the strength and perfection of the state, and that divine providence will interpose to fill every department with wise and good men.

Isaiah prophesied about the time of the captivity of the ten tribes of Israel and about a century before the captivity of Judah. The kingdom of Israel was brought to destruction because its iniquities were full; its counselors and judges were wholly taken away because there remained no hope of reformation. But the scepter did not entirely depart from Judah, nor a lawgiver from between his feet, till the Messiah came; yet greater and greater changes took place in their political affairs; their government

⁴ The "reasonings . . . from the press" in both newspapers and pamphlets were too voluminous by 1775 to document here. A good example of the kind of reasoning Langdon probably has in mind is the series of articles by John Adams published under the pen name Novanglus in the Boston *Gazette* between January and April 1775. The seventh Novanglus paper is in *Sources and Documents*, ed. Morison, 125–136. See also the selections from newspapers and pamphlets in *The Spirit of 'Seventy-Six*, I, and the list of pamphlets to be published in forthcoming volumes of *Pamphlets of the American Revolution*, ed. Bernard Bailyn (Cambridge, 1965), I, 749–752. The "friends . . . who have powerfully pled our cause" are those members who came to America's defense in the parliamentary debates over the effect of the Coercive Acts and the handling of American unrest, in January and February 1775—most conspicuously, Lord Chatham, whose bill for settling America's grievances was rejected, and Edmund Burke, who gave his famous address on March 22. On March 20, Benjamin Franklin, America's ardent representative at Whitehall, who had been in close contact with Camden and his Whig supporters friendly to America, and seen their efforts in Parliament fail, sailed for Philadelphia, "disappointed, disgusted, bored too long," and angry. See Carl Van Doren, *Benjamin Franklin* (New York, 1938), 508–523.

degenerated in proportion as their vices increased, till few faithful men were left in any public offices; and at length, when they were delivered up for seventy years into the hands of the King of Babylon, scarce any remains of their original excellent civil polity appeared among them.

The Jewish government, according to the original constitution which was divinely established, if considered merely in a civil view, was a perfect republic. The heads of their tribes and elders of their cities were their counselors and judges. They called the people together in more general or particular assemblies, took their opinions, gave advice, and managed the public affairs according to the general voice. Counselors and judges comprehend all the powers of that government; for there was no such thing as legislative authority belonging to it, their complete code of laws being given immediately from God by the hand of Moses. And let them who cry up "the divine right of kings" consider that the only form of government which had a proper claim to a divine establishment was so far from including the idea of a king that it was a high crime for Israel to ask to be in this respect like other nations; and when they were gratified, it was rather as a just punishment of their folly, that they might feel the burdens of court pageantry of which they were warned by a very striking description, than as a divine recommendation of kingly authority.

Every nation, when able and agreed, has a right to set up over themselves any form of government which to them may appear most conducive to their common welfare. The civil polity of Israel is doubtless an excellent general model, allowing for some peculiarities; at least some principal laws and orders of it may be copied to great advantage in more modern establishments.

When a government is in its prime, the public good engages the attention of the whole; the strictest regard is paid to the qualifications of those who hold the offices of the state; virtue prevails; everything is managed with justice, prudence, and frugality; the laws are founded on principles of equity rather than mere policy; and all the people are happy. But vice will increase with the riches and glory of an empire; and this gradually tends to corrupt the constitution, and in time bring on its dissolution. This may be considered not only as the natural effect of vice, but a righteous judgment of heaven, especially upon a nation which has been favor'd with the blessings of religion and liberty, and is guilty of undervaluing them and eagerly going into the gratification of every lust.

In this chapter the prophet describes the very corrupt state of Judah in his day both as to religion and common morality, and looks forward to that increase of wickedness which would bring on their desolation and captivity. They were "a sinful nation, a people laden with iniquity, a seed of evildoers, children that were corrupters: who had forsaken the Lord, and provoked the Holy One of Israel to anger" [Isa. 1. 4]. The whole body of the nation, from head to foot, was full of moral and political disorders without any remaining soundness. Their religion was all mere ceremony and hypocrisy; and even the laws of common justice and humanity were disregarded in their public courts. They had counselors and judges, but very different from those at the beginning of the commonwealth. Their princes were rebellious against God and the constitution of their country, and companions of thieves, giving countenance to every artifice for seizing the property of the subjects into their own hands and robbing the public treasury. Everyone loved gifts and followed after rewards; they regarded the perquisites more than the duties of their office; the general aim was at profitable places and pensions; they were influenced in everything by bribery; and their avarice and luxury were never satisfied, but hurried them on to all kinds of oppression and violence so that they even justified and encouraged the murder of innocent persons to support their lawless power and increase their wealth. And God in righteous judgment left them to run into all this excess of vice to their own destruction because they had forsaken him, and were guilty of willful inattention to the most essential parts of that religion which had been given them by a well-attested revelation from heaven.

The Jewish nation could not but see and feel the unhappy consequences of so great corruption of the state. Doubtless they complained much of men in power, and very heartily and liberally reproached them for their notorious misconduct. The public greatly suffered and the people groaned and wished for better rulers and better management. But in vain they hoped for a change of men and measures and better times, when the spirit of religion was gone and the infection of vice was become universal. The whole body being so corrupted, there could be no rational prospect of any great reformation in the state, but rather of its ruin, which accordingly came on in Jeremiah's time. Yet if a general reformation of religion and morals had taken place and they had turned to God from all their sins; if they had again recovered the true spirit of their religion; God, by the gracious interpositions of his providence, would soon have found out methods to restore the former virtue of the state, and again have given them men of wisdom and integrity, according to their utmost wish, to be counselors and judges. This was verified in fact after the nation had been purged by a long captivity, and returned to their own land humbled and filled with zeal for God and his law.

By all this we may be led to consider the true cause of the present remarkable troubles which are come upon Great Britain and these colonies; and the only effectual remedy.

We have rebelled against God. We have lost the true spirit of Christianity, tho' we retain the outward profession and form of it. We have neglected and set light by the glorious Gospel of our Lord Jesus Christ and his holy commands and institutions. The worship of many is but mere compliment to the Deity, while their hearts are far from him. By many the Gospel is corrupted into a superficial system of moral philosophy, little better than ancient Platonism. And after all the pretended refinements of moderns in the theory of Christianity, very little of the pure practice of it is to be found among those who once stood foremost in the profession of the Gospel. In a general view of the present moral state of Great Britain it may be said: "There is no truth, nor mercy, nor knowledge of God in the land. By swearing, and lying, and killing, and stealing, and committing adultery" [Hos. 4. 1, 2], their wickedness breaks out; and one murder after another is committed under the connivance and encouragement even of that authority by which such crimes ought to be punished, that the purposes of oppression and despotism may be answered. As they have increased, so have they sinned; therefore God is changing their glory into shame. The general prevalence of vice has changed the whole face of things in the British government.

The excellency of the Constitution has been the boast of Great Britain and the envy of neighboring nations. In former times the great departments of the state and the various places of trust and authority were filled with men of wisdom, honesty, and religion, who employed all their powers and were ready to risk their fortunes and their lives for the public good. They were faithful counselors to kings; directed their authority and majesty to the happiness of the nation; and opposed every step by which despotism endeavored to advance. They were fathers of the people and sought the welfare and prosperity of the whole body. They did not exhaust the national wealth by luxury and bribery, or convert it to their own private benefit or the maintenance of idle useless officers and dependents; but improved it faithfully for the proper purposes, for the necessary

support of government and defense of the kingdom. Their laws were *
dictated by wisdom and equity, and justice was administered with impartiality. Religion discover'd its general influence among all ranks and
kept out great corruptions from places of power.

But in what does the British nation now glory? In a mere shadow of
its ancient political system? In titles of dignity without virtue? In vast
public treasures continually lavished in corruption, till every fund is ex-
hausted, notwithstanding the mighty streams perpetually flowing in? In
the many artifices to stretch the prerogatives of the crown beyond all constitutional bounds and make the king an absolute monarch, while the
people are deluded with a mere phantom of liberty? What idea must we
entertain of that government, if such an one can be found, which pretends
to have made an exact counterbalance of power between the sovereign,
the nobles, and the commons, so that the three branches shall be an effectual check upon each other, and the united wisdom of the whole shall
conspire to promote the national felicity; but which in reality is reduced
to such a situation that it may be managed at the sole will of one court
favorite? What difference is there betwixt one man's choosing, at his own
pleasure, by his single vote, the majority of those who are to represent
the people; and his purchasing in such a majority, according to his own
nomination, with money out of the public treasury or other effectual
methods of influencing elections? And what shall we say if in the same
manner, by places, pensions, and other bribes, a minister of state can at
any time gain over a nobler majority likewise to be entirely subservient
to his purposes; and moreover persuade his royal master to resign himself
up wholly to the direction of his counsels? If this should be the case of any
nation from one seven years' end to another, the bargain and sale being
made sure for such a period, would they still have reason to boast of
their excellent constitution? Ought they not rather to think it high time
to restore the corrupted dying state to its original perfection? I will apply
this to the Roman senate under Julius Caesar, which retained all its ancient formalities but voted always only as Caesar dictated. If the decrees
of such a senate were urged on the Romans as fraught with all the blessings
of Roman liberty, we must suppose them strangely deluded if they were
persuaded to believe it.

The pretense for taxing America has been that the nation contracted
an immense debt for the defense of the American colonies; and that as
they are now able to contribute some proportion towards the discharge

of this debt, and must be considered as part of the nation, it is reasonable they should be taxed, and the parliament has a right to tax and govern them in all cases whatever by its own supreme authority. Enough has been already published on this grand controversy, which now threatens a final separation of the colonies from Great Britain.[5] But can the amazing national debt be paid by a little trifling sum squeezed from year to year out of America, which is continually drained of all its cash by a restricted trade with the parent country, and which in this way is taxed to the government of Britain in a very large proportion? Would it not be much superior wisdom and sounder policy for a distressed kingdom to retrench the vast unnecessary expenses continually incurred by its enormous vices—to stop the prodigious sums paid in pensions and to numberless officers without the least advantage to the public—to reduce the number of devouring servants in the Great Family—to turn their minds from the pursuit of pleasure and the boundless luxuries of life to the important interests of their country and the salvation of the commonwealth? Would not a reverend regard to the authority of divine revelation, an hearty belief of the Gospel of the grace of God, and a general reformation of all those vices which bring misery and ruin upon individuals, families, and kingdoms, and which have provoked heaven to bring the nation into such perplexed and dangerous circumstances, be the surest way to recover the sinking state, and make it again rich and flourishing? Millions might annually be saved if the kingdom were generally and thoroughly reformed; and the public debt, great as it is, might in a few years be canceled by a growing revenue, which now amounts to full ten millions per annum, without laying additional burdens on any of the subjects. But the demands of corruption are constantly increasing and will forever exceed all the resources of wealth which the wit of man can invent or tyranny impose.

Into what fatal policy has the nation been impelled by its public vices! To wage a cruel war with its own children in these colonies, only to gratify the lust of power and the demands of extravagance! May God in his great mercy recover Great Britain from this fatal infatuation, show them their errors, and give them a spirit of reformation, before it is too late to avert impending destruction. May the eyes of the King be opened to see the ruinous tendency of the measures into which he has been led, and his heart inclined to treat his American subjects with justice and clemency, instead of forcing them still farther to the last extremities! God grant some method may be found out to effect a happy reconciliation, so that the colonies may again enjoy the protection of their sovereign with perfect security of all their natural rights and civil and religious liberties.

But, alas! have not the sins of America, and of New England in particular, had a hand in bringing down upon us the righteous judgments of heaven? Wherefore is all this evil come upon us? Is it not because we have forsaken the Lord? Can we say we are innocent of crimes against God? No surely; it becomes us to humble ourselves under his mighty hand, that he may exalt us in due time. However unjustly and cruelly we have been treated by man, we certainly deserve at the hand of God all the calamities in which we are now involved. Have we not lost much of that spirit of genuine Christianity which so remarkably appeared in our ancestors, for which God distinguished them with the signal favors of providence when they fled from tyranny and persecution into this western desert? Have we not departed from their virtues? Tho' I hope and am confident that as much true religion agreeable to the purity and simplicity of the Gospel remains among us as among any people in the world, yet in the midst of the present great apostasy of the nations professing Christianity, have not we likewise been guilty of departing from the living God? Have we not made light of the Gospel of salvation, and too much affected the cold, formal, fashionable religion of countries grown old in vice and overspread with infidelity? Do not our follies and iniquities testify against us? Have we not, especially in our seaports, gone much too far into the pride and luxuries of life? Is it not a fact open to common observation that profaneness, intemperance, unchastity, the love of pleasure, fraud, avarice, and other vices are increasing among us from year to year? And have not even these young governments been in some measure infected with the corruptions of European courts? Has there been no flattery, no bribery, no artifices practiced, to get into places of honor and profit, or carry a vote to serve a particular interest, without regard to right or wrong? Have our statesmen always acted with integrity? And every judge with impartiality, in the fear of God? In short, have all ranks of men showed regard to the divine commands and joined to promote the Redeemer's kingdom and the public welfare? I wish we could more fully justify ourselves in all these respects. If such sins have not been so notorious among us as in older countries, we must nevertheless remember that the sins of

[5] This is the first time that a separation from Great Britain has been mentioned as a distinct possibility, and in any terms other than unthinkable, in a Massachusetts election sermon.

a people who have been remarkable for the profession of godliness are more aggravated by all the advantages and favors they have enjoyed, and will receive more speedy and signal punishment; as God says of Israel: "You only have I known of all the families of the earth: therefore will I punish you for all your iniquities" (Amos 3. 2).

The judgments now come upon us are very heavy and distressing, and have fallen with peculiar weight on our capital, where, notwithstanding the plighted honor of the chief commander of the hostile troops, many of our brethren are still detained as if they were captives; and those that have been released have left the principal part of their substance which is withheld by arbitrary orders, contrary to an express treaty, to be plunder'd by the army.[b]

Let me address you in the words of the prophet: "O Israel, return unto the Lord thy God, for thou hast fallen by thine iniquity" [Hos. 14. 1]. My brethren, let us repent and implore the divine mercy. Let us amend our ways and our doings; reform everything which has been provoking to the most High, and thus endeavor to obtain the gracious interpositions of providence for our deliverance.

If true religion is revived by means of these public calamities and again prevails among us; if it appears in our religious assemblies—in the conduct of our civil affairs—in our armies—in our families—in all our business and conversation—we may hope for the direction and blessing of the most High while we are using our best endeavors to preserve and restore the civil government of this Colony, and defend America from slavery.

Our late happy government is changed into the terrors of military execution. Our firm opposition to the establishment of an arbitrary system is

[b] Soon after the battle at Concord, General Gage stipulated with the selectmen of Boston that if the inhabitants would deliver up their arms, to be deposited in Faneuil Hall and return'd when circumstances would permit, they should have liberty to quit the town and take with them all their effects. They readily complied; but soon found themselves abused. With great difficulty and very slowly, they obtain passes, but are forbidden to carry out anything besides household furniture and wearing apparel. Merchants and shopkeepers are obliged to leave behind all their merchandise, and even their cash is detained. Mechanics are not allowed to bring out the most necessary tools for their work. Not only their family stores of provisions are stopped, but it has been repeatedly and credibly affirmed that poor women and children have had the very smallest articles of this kind taken from them, which were necessary for their refreshment while they traveled a few miles to their friends; and that even from young children in their mothers' arms, the cruel soldiery have taken the morsel of bread given to prevent their crying and thrown it away. How much better for the inhabitants to have resolved at all hazards to defend themselves by their arms against such an enemy, than suffer such shameful abuse!

called "rebellion," and we are to expect no mercy but by yielding property and life at discretion. This we are resolved at all events not to do; and therefore we have taken arms in our own defense, and all the colonies are united in the great cause of liberty.

But how shall we live while civil government is dissolved? What shall we do without counselors and judges? A state of absolute anarchy is dreadful. Submission to the tyranny of hundreds of imperious masters firmly embodied against us and united in the same cruel design of disposing of our substance and lives at their pleasure, and making their own will our law in all cases whatever, is the vilest slavery, and worse than death.

Thanks be to God that he has given us, as men, natural rights independent on all human laws whatever; and that these rights are recognized by the grand Charter of British liberties. By the law of nature any body of people, destitute of order and government, may form themselves into a civil society according to their best prudence and so provide for their common safety and advantage. When one form is found by the majority not to answer the grand purpose in any tolerable degree, they may by common consent put an end to it, and set up another; only as all such great changes are attended with difficulty and danger of confusion, they ought not to be attempted without urgent necessity, which will be determined always by the general voice of the wisest and best members of the community.[6]

If the great servants of the public forget their duty, betray their trust, and sell their country, or make war against the most valuable rights and privileges of the people, reason and justice require that they should be discarded and others appointed in their room, without any regard to formal resignations of their forfeited power.

It must be ascribed to some supernatural influence on the minds of the main body of the people through this extensive continent, that they have so universally adopted the method of managing the important matters necessary to preserve among them a free government, by corresponding committees and congresses, consisting of the wisest and most disinterested patriots in America, chosen by the unbiased suffrages of the people assembled for that purpose in their several towns, counties, and provinces. So general agreement thro' so many provinces of so large a country in one

[6] "By the law . . . members of the community." Cf. John Locke, *Of Civil Government: Second Essay*, Intro. Russell Kirk (Chicago, 1955), 71, 109, 160, 164–165.

mode of self-preservation is unexampled in any history, and the effect
has exceeded our most sanguine expectations. Universal tumults and all
the irregularities and violence of mobish factions naturally arise when
legal authority ceases. But how little of this has appeared in the midst of
the late obstructions of civil government! Nothing more than what has
often happened in Great Britain and Ireland, in the face of the civil powers
in all their strength; nothing more than what is frequently seen in the
midst of the perfect regulations of the great city of London; and, may I
not add, nothing more than has been absolutely necessary to carry into
execution the spirited resolutions of a people too sensible to deliver
themselves up to oppression and slavery. The judgment and advice of the
continental assembly of delegates have been as readily obeyed as if they
were authentic acts of a long-established parliament. And in every colony,
the votes of a congress have had equal effect with the laws of great and
general courts.[7]

It is now ten months since this Colony has been deprived of the benefit
of that government which was so long enjoyed by charter.[8] They have
had no general assembly for matters of legislation and the public revenue.
The courts of justice have been shut up and almost the whole executive
power has ceased to act. Yet order among the people has been remarkably
preserved; few crimes have been committed punishable by the judge; even
former contentions betwixt one neighbor and another have ceased; nor
have fraud and rapine taken advantage of the imbecility of the civil
powers.

The necessary preparations for the defense of our liberties required
not only the collected wisdom and strength of the Colony, but an immediate cheerful application of the wealth of individuals to the public
service, in due proportion; or a taxation which depended on general consent. Where was the authority to vote, collect, or receive the large sums
required, and make provision for the utmost extremities? A congress
succeeded to the honors of a general assembly as soon as the latter was
crush'd by the hand of power. It gained all the confidence of the people.
Wisdom and prudence secur'd all that the laws of the former constitution
could have given. And we now observe with astonishment an army of
many thousands of well-disciplined troops suddenly assembled and abundantly furnished with all necessary supplies in defense of the liberties of
America.

But is it proper or safe for the Colony to continue much longer in such imperfect order? Must it not appear rational and necessary to every man that understands the various movements requisite to good government that the many parts should be properly settled, and every branch of the legislative and executive authority restored to that order and vigor on which the life and health of the body politic depend? To the honorable gentlemen now met in this new congress as the fathers of the people, this weighty matter must be referred. Who knows but in the midst of all the distresses of the present war to defeat the attempts of arbitrary power, God may in mercy restore to us our judges as at the first, and our counselors as at the beginning.

On your wisdom, religion, and public spirit, honored gentlemen, we depend, to determine what may be done as to the important matter of reviving the form of government and settling all necessary affairs relating to it in the present critical state of things, that we may again have law and justice, and avoid the danger of anarchy and confusion. May God be with you, and by the influences of his Spirit direct all your counsels and resolutions for the glory of his name and the safety and happiness of this Colony. We have great reason to acknowledge with thankfulness the evident tokens of the divine Presence with the former congress, that they were led to foresee present exigencies and make such effectual provision for them. It is our earnest prayer to the Father of lights that he would irradiate your minds, make all your way plain, and grant you may be happy instruments of many and great blessings to the people by whom you are constituted, to New England, and all the united colonies.

Let us praise our God for the advantages already given us over the enemies of liberty; particularly, that they have been so dispirited by repeated experience of the efficacy of our arms; and that in the late action

---

[7] On the invitation of the Virginia House of Burgesses, twelve Committees of Correspondence sent delegates to Philadelphia to form the first Continental Congress in September 1774. They passed a Declaration and Resolves (a selection is reprinted in *Sources and Documents*, ed. Morison, 118–122), and set up an association for commercial retaliation for the "Coercive Acts." The Congress reconvened on May 10, 1775, and was in session when this sermon was given. A Provincial Congress was organized in Concord, October 8, 1774, after Governor Gage called a meeting of the General Court and then failed to attend. This Congress, entirely illegal under the law, acted as "the only effective government of the province outside Boston" (Ward, *The War of the Revolution*, 17). They appropriated money for arms, organized the "minutemen" system of militia, and named officers for the Massachusetts forces. Langdon recognizes the effectiveness of this newly formed group and lends his weight to the idea that the new Congress has replaced the old General Court.

[8] The Massachusetts Government Act (see n. 2 above) became effective August 1, 1774.

at Chelsea, when several hundreds of our soldiery, the greater part open to the fire of so many cannon, swivels, and muskets from a battery advantageously situated, from two armed cutters and many barges full of marines, and from ships of the line in the harbor, not one man on our side was killed and but two or three wounded; when, by the best intelligence, a great number were killed and wounded on the other side, and one of their cutters was taken and burnt, the other narrowly escaping with great damage.[c]

If God be for us, who can be against us?[9] The enemy has reproached us for calling on his name and professing our trust in him. They have made a mock of our solemn fasts and every appearance of serious Christianity in the land. On this account, by way of contempt, they call us "saints"; and that they themselves may keep at the greatest distance from this character, their mouths are full of horrid blasphemies, cursing, and bitterness, and vent all the rage of malice and barbarity. And may we not be confident that the most High who regards these things will vindi-

[c] This action was in the night following the 27th current, after our soldiery had been taking off the cattle from some islands in Boston harbor. By the best information we have been able to procure, about 105 of the King's troops were killed, and 160 wounded in the engagement. [Langdon's account suffers from the exaggeration of early rumor. The Americans captured the schooner *Diana* which went aground in the dark and was scuttled, but "there were few casualties in those twelve hours of fighting; four Americans were slightly wounded, two British killed and several wounded" (Ward, *The War of the Revolution*, 58).]

[d] When we consider the late Canada Bill, which implies not merely a toleration of the Roman Catholic religion (which would be just and liberal) but a firm establishment of it through that extensive province, now greatly enlarged to serve political purposes; by which means multitudes of people, subjects of Great Britain, which may hereafter settle that vast country, will be tempted by all the attachments arising from an establishment to profess that religion, or be discouraged from any endeavors to propagate reformed principles; have we not great reason to suspect that all the late measures respecting the colonies have originated from popish schemes of men who would gladly restore the race of Stuart and who look on popery as a religion most favorable to arbitrary power? It is plain fact that despotism has an establishment in that province equally with the Roman Catholic church. The Governor, with a Council very much under his power, has by his commission almost unlimited authority, free from the clog of representatives of the people. However agreeable this may be to the genius of the French, English subjects there will be discouraged from continuing in a country where both they and their posterity will be deprived of the greatest privileges of the British Constitution, and in many respects feel the effects of absolute monarchy.

Lord Littleton in his defense of this detestable statute, frankly concedes that it is an establishment of the Roman Catholic religion, and that part of the policy of it was to provide a check upon the New England colonies. And the writer of an address of the people of Great Britain to the inhabitants of America, just published, expresses himself with great precision when he says that statute "gave toleration to English subjects."

372

cate his own honor, and plead our righteous cause against such enemies to his government as well as our liberties. O, may our camp be free from every accursed thing! May our land be purged from all its sins! May we be truly a holy people, and all our towns, cities of righteousness! Then the Lord will be our refuge and strength, a very present help in trouble;[10] and we shall have no reason to be afraid though thousands of enemies set themselves against us round about—tho' all nature should be thrown into tumults and convulsions. He can command the stars in their courses to fight his battles, and all the elements to wage war with his enemies. He can destroy them with innumerable plagues, or send faintness into their hearts so that the men of might shall not find their hands. In a variety of methods he can work salvation for us, as he did for his people in ancient days, and according to the many remarkable deliverances granted in former times to Great Britain and New England, when popish machinations threatened both countries with civil and ecclesiastical tyranny.[d]

May the Lord hear us in this day of trouble and the name of the God of Jacob defend us; send us help from his sanctuary; and strengthen us out of Zion. We will rejoice in his salvation, and in the name of our God we will set up our banners; let us look to him to fulfill all our petitions.

FINIS.

---

[9] See Rom. 8. 31.   [10] See Psal. 46. 1.

TEXTUAL NOTES AND INDEX

TEXTUAL NOTES

EACH of the following notes consists of the page number in the present edition on which a textual note (*) occurs, the emended reading in the present edition, followed by a slant line, followed by the original pamphlet reading.

Danforth, 1670
p. 65: assembly is whether/ Assembly, Whether
p. 69: (I Kings 1. 1)/ 2 Sam. 1. 1
p. 69: month after month/ moneth after moneth
p. 71: (ver. 19)/ ver. 18

Willard, 1682
p. 89: God is/ God as
p. 91: (Jonah/ Chap.
p. 94: (Psal. 81. 13)/ Psal. 81. 14
p. 96: (Jer./ Chap.
p. 98: God is/ God be
p. 100: searchings/ searching
p. 101: same/ some

Mather, 1689
p. 122: II Corinthians 5. 8/ 2. Cor. 5. 4
p. 123: Nehemiah 4. 15/ Neh. 4. 13
p. 125: II Corinthians 5. 21/ 2 Cor. 5. 25
p. 125: (Neh. 9. 19)/ Neh. 9. 18

p. 127: (I Kings 8. 57)/ I King. 8. 27
p. 131: Luke 24/ Luc. 23
p. 132: Malachi 3/ Mal. 2
p. 134: Doubtless/ Doubt- [end-of-line hyphen, word not completed]
p. 135: resolutions/ Revolutions
p. 136: his/ [the pamphlet is not clear; the terminal letter may be "s" or "t"]

Danforth, 1714
p. 152: (ver. 15, 17)/ v. 15, 18
p. 160: (Luke 1./ v.
p. 169: (Exod. 2/ Exod. 1

Prince, 1730
p. 184: (I Sam. 12/ I Sam. ii
p. 186: Josh. 13/ Josh. xii
p. 190: it has nothing/ it nothing
p. 193: which ran/ which run
p. 193: streams ran/ Streams run
p. 197: situations/ Scituations
p. 205: poured/ powred

Barnard, 1734

p. 237: (Acts 7. 35)/ Acts vii. 37
p. 237: (Exod. 22/ Exod. xii
p. 239: situation/ Scituation
p. 245: begun/ began
p. 251: (Acts 22. 28)/ Acts xxii. lat. End.
p. 252: lest/ least
p. 254: consequence/ Consequents
p. 254: Oracle/ Oracles
p. 260: specie/ Species [occurs twice]
p. 267: (I Pet. 2. 17)/ I Pet. ii. 27
p. 268: (Rom. 13. 5/ ver. 5
p. 272: (Isa. 11/ xi

p. 274: Psalm/ Psalms
p. 278: empowered/ improved [Pemberton's original pamphlet has "impowred"]

Mayhew, 1754

p. 305: this is a/ this a
p. 309: undoubtedly/ undoubtly
p. 313: you were/ you was

Cooke, 1770

p. 345: yet are content/ yet content

Langdon, 1775

p. 365: laws were/ laws was

INDEX

Titles of books in the Bible are not included in this index, but Biblical characters are; those from the Old Testament are indicated by (O.T.), from the New Testament by (N.T.).

Aaron (O.T.), 55, 56, 61, 184–197 *passim*
Abiram (O.T.), 70
Abraham (O.T.), 28, 60, 131, 159, 183, 188, 202
Absalom (O.T.), 251
Adair, Douglass, 9n
Adam (O.T.), 26, 27, 152–153, 240, 241, 242
Adams, John, 4, 9n, 25, 361n
Adams, Samuel, 13, 324, 352n
Aeneas, 24
Aesop, 133n
Africa, 135n
agriculture, 76, 133, 193, 287, 305, 306, 344
Ahab (O.T.), 104, 251, 264
Ainsworth, Henry, 186n
Aix-La-Chapelle, Treaty of, 309n, 313n
Akers, Charles W., 285n
Albany, N.Y., 110
Albany conference (*1754*), 285, 287, 313n
Alcuin, 237n
Alden, John Richard, 357n
Allen, James (*1632–1710*), 22
Allen, James (*1692–1747*), 40, 284
almanacs, 47n, 74n
Alsted, Johann Heinrich, 242n, 256n

American Antiquarian Society, 38n
"American Carthage" (Crown Point), 313n
American Constitution, 226, 353n
American Dream, 25–31, 180
"American Dunkirk" (Louisburg), 312, 313n
American literature, 3, 4, 5–6, 25, 29, 30, 182
American Revolution, 3, 7, 9, 10, 29, 147, 350, 351: beginnings, 345, 349; ferment preceding, 354; war of, 358–360, 366
American West, 50n
Ames, William, 26, 31
Ammon (O.T.), 253
Amram (O.T.), 188
Anabaptists, 92n
anarchy, 2, 20, 245, 334, 369, 371
Andros, Sir Edmund, 5, 22, 110, 175n, 325, 340, 341n
Angier, Mr., 9
Anglicans, 5, 15, 110, 181, 286, 287. See *also* Church of England
Anne, Queen of England (*1702–14*), 174, 175n
Anne, daughter of George II, 276, 277n
Antichrist, 26
Antinomian, 67n

379